"*The Poverty of Nations* shows what not only poor nations but also America itself must do to create jobs, opportunities, and a more rewarding and better future. This is a very good book!"

Pete du Pont, former U.S. Congressman and former Governor of Delaware

"The religious leaders of the world wonder why poor countries remain poor. Key figures from Billy Graham to Pope Francis and the Dalai Lama have often urged the rich of the world to care for the poor—but how to do it? How to organize government and business to 'remember the poor'? Now, theologian Wayne Grudem and economist Barry Asmus bring forward a book to explain how free enterprise and, crucially, biblical teaching combine to illuminate the path to progress for the poor. Every legislator—every voter—needs to read this."

Hugh Hewitt, nationally syndicated radio talk show host; Professor of Law, Chapman University

"This book will become a standard text that we will use to train every mission team we have in 196 countries. It should be required reading in every Christian college and seminary, by every relief and mission organization, and by every local church pastor."

Rick Warren, *New York Times* #1 best-selling author, *The Purpose Driven Life*; Pastor, Saddleback Church

"Many excellent authors over the past dozen years have felt the elephant's trunk, legs, and tail. Wayne Grudem and Barry Asmus are the first to show the whole behemoth. They explain clearly and simply what we must know to love truly those in need. *The Poverty of Nations* should be required reading at every Christian college."

Marvin Olasky, Editor-in-chief, World News Group; author, *The Tragedy of American Compassion*

"The authors have written clearly that the sustainable solution to the poverty of nations is the free-market system—the most moral and successful economic arrangement and the only one capable of enabling people to produce their way out of poverty and to personal well-being."

Jon Kyl, former U.S. Senator from Arizona

"Grudem and Asmus show how the science of economics can be combined with a morality rooted in religious belief to help us understand why some nations are rich and others poor."

John C. Goodman, President and CEO, National Center for Policy Analysis

"The grinding poverty of hundreds of millions of people made in God's image ought to be of deep concern to every believer. Most Christians I know are generous to the poor without really thinking about the causes of poverty. This vital contribution from Wayne Grudem and Barry Asmus will help us think theologically about poverty. May it inform our prayers, giving, and actions."

Andrew Evans, Minister, Christ Church, Liverpool; Tutor, Wales Evangelical School of Theology

"Grudem and Asmus offer a convincing perspective on the moral foundations of a successful economy and society. Continuing in the great tradition of classical economic thinking, *The Poverty of Nations* argues that a free-market economy, based on private sector initiative and a well-defined but limited role for the government, produces superior results in terms of material wealth accumulation and distribution. However, the unique insight of this book is to ground human interaction, and the political and economic systems it defines, in moral and ethical values originating from Scripture. The authors argue that stable societies, property rights, free will, and the pursuit of happiness are not only moral values, but also prerequisites for long-term growth. The authors pursue this insight to its logical conclusion by drawing concrete and detailed political and economic implications. There is vast literature on this topic, but I remain thoroughly convinced that the clarity of thought and the originality of the arguments will make this book a point of reference for future generations."

Ardian Fullani, Governor, Bank of Albania

"Relying upon a thoughtful combination of objective economic history, a clear understanding of human nature, accurate economic analysis, and a moral code based on personal freedom and the pursuit of happiness, the authors delve into means for alleviating the poverty of nations. The writing style is highly approachable and draws the reader into a realm of ideas that envisions hope for the downtrodden if government authority is properly exercised. Like *The Wealth of Nations*, it demands the attention of good-hearted citizens and hardened government officials to appreciate free markets in their moral light."

Stephen Happel, Emeritus Professor of Economics, W. P. Carey School of Business, Arizona State University

"There are not many Christian books on this subject. Even less those that integrate a Christian worldview with economic systems, free markets, freedom, and prosperity, besides poverty. Grudem and Asmus offer a thorough analysis of several economic systems that went wrong and offer a plausible defense of the biblical basis for the free-market solution and how it could change a nation. There may be some question as to whether such a system would work for Latin American countries. But because of the underlying biblical principles, this book should be translated and studied in other parts of the world besides America. It will help Christians engage the social, economic, and political issues of today in a more significant and effective way."

Rev. Augustus Nicodemus Lopes, Professor of New Testament, Mackenzie Presbyterian University, São Paulo, Brazil

"Economics is too important to leave to economists alone. Theology, likewise, is too important to be left to theologians alone. This book, written for non-specialists by an economist and a theologian, must therefore be taken seriously and used to stimulate debate and action that will address the scourge of poverty."

Peter S. Heslam, Director, Entrepreneurial Leadership Initiative, University of Oxford; Senior Member, Trinity College, Cambridge

"Grudem and Asmus provide a comprehensive set of principles for reducing poverty around the world. Seldom does one find such a complete and thoughtful integration of sound economics with good theology. *The Poverty of Nations* is strongly recommended for anyone concerned with world poverty."

P. J. Hill, Professor of Economics Emeritus, Wheaton College; Senior Fellow, Property and Environmental Research Center, Bozeman, Montana

"For the longest time, in Christian circles certainly, the crisis of poverty has deserved a thorough and practical response. Comprehensive in scope and practical in style, this book offers insights that cannot be taken lightly."

Mutava Musimi, MP, Chairman of Budget and Appropriations Committee, Kenya National Assembly; former General Secretary, National Council of Churches of Kenya; former Senior Pastor, Nairobi Baptist Church

"There are many secular books on poverty, and there are many books on the Christian response to poverty. But Wayne Grudem, a theologian, and Barry Asmus, an economist, have done something far less common and far more valuable. They have successfully integrated Christian ethics and theology with sound economics. The result is a comprehensive and deeply satisfying synthesis. If you want to understand and help alleviate poverty, rather than merely supporting feel-good policies that may do more harm than good, you should read this book."

Jay W. Richards, author, *Money, Greed, and God*, and co-author, *Indivisible*; Visiting Scholar, Institute for Faith, Work, and Economics; Senior Fellow, Discovery Institute

"Given the plethora of myths and misconceptions that so many people hold with regard to the importance of a free economy, its moral foundation, and its practical benefits, especially for the poor, *The Poverty of Nations* provides an easy-to-read, sensibly organized, and morally clear argument on behalf of a free society. Merely reading the table of contents will provide clearer thinking than many graduate students get in economics courses."

Fr. Robert A. Sirico, President, Acton Institute; author, *Defending the Free Market*

"All right-thinking Christians are deeply concerned about the seemingly intractable problems of global poverty and inequality. Many view free-market economics as the cause of the problem rather than the solution, and assume with the best of intentions that aid, debt cancellation, wealth redistribution, environmentalism, and trade protectionism are what is needed. Wayne Grudem and Barry Asmus provide a compelling account of how nations can alleviate their poverty by means of development, increasing the production of goods and services, within a free-market model that guarantees the right to property and personal freedoms. This clear and accessible book is grounded in solid economic theory, historical analysis, and, above all, faithful biblical exegesis. The result is not a call for untrammelled capitalism, but for responsible development shaped by core cultural values that lie close to the heart of the Christian faith. Not everyone will agree with their approach, but anyone concerned to help those affected by poverty in our world will have to take their arguments seriously."

Rev. John Stevens, National Director, Fellowship of Independent Evangelical Churches; former Deputy Head of School, Senior Lecturer in Property Law, and Senior Honorary Research Fellow, University of Birmingham, UK

"I became an economist because I fell in love with the idea that a nation's choices could determine whether citizens faced wealth or poverty. Thirty years of research has led me to believe that wealth comes from a choice to support freedom and limited government. I became a Christian because I fell in love with Jesus Christ. The Bible says we were created in God's image and that while we should love our neighbor, we are also meant to be creators ourselves. I never thought these were mutually exclusive beliefs. In fact, I believe biblical truth and free markets go hand in hand. I have searched far and wide for a book that melds these two worldviews. Asmus and Grudem have done it! A top-flight economist and a renowned theologian have put together a bullet-proof antidote to poverty. It's a tour de force. The church and the state will find in this book a recipe for true, loving, and lasting justice."

Brian S. Wesbury, Chief Economist, First Trust Advisors LP; former Chief Economist, Joint Economic Committee of the U.S. Congress

THE POVERTY
OF NATIONS

A SUSTAINABLE SOLUTION

WAYNE GRUDEM AND
BARRY ASMUS

FOREWORD BY
RICK WARREN

∷ CROSSWAY®

WHEATON, ILLINOIS

Trade paperback ISBN: 978-1-4335-3911-4
Mobipocket ISBN: 978-1-4335-3913-8
PDF ISBN: 978-1-4335-3912-1
ePub ISBN: 978-1-4335-3914-5

Library of Congress Cataloging-in-Publication Data

Grudem, Wayne A.
   The poverty of nations: a sustainable solution / Wayne Grudem and Barry Asmus.
     pages cm
   Includes bibliographical references and index.
   ISBN 978-1-4335-3911-4
   1. Church work with the poor—Developing countries.
2. Poverty—Religious aspects—Christianity. 3. Economic development—Religious aspects—Christianity. 4. Developing countries—Economic conditions. 5. Sustainable development—Religious aspects—Christianity. I. Title.
BV639.P6G78   2013
261.8'325—dc23   2013000955

Crossway is a publishing ministry of Good News Publishers.

SH		28	27	26	25	24	23	22	21	20	19	18
17	16	15	14	13	12	11	10	9	8	7	6	5

To Bret Edson and Brad Edson,
who believed in and supported
this project from the beginning

CONTENTS

DETAILED CONTENTS

FOREWORD

By Rick Warren

There are more than two thousand verses about the poor and poverty in the Bible, yet most evangelical pulpits are strangely silent on a subject that God cares about so deeply. I'm both shocked and saddened to admit that although I attended a Christian college and two seminaries, I cannot recall ever hearing a single message about God's plan for the poor, except that we ought to be personally generous with them. Unfortunately, due to this shortage of clear, biblical teaching on economics, many believers have, without thinking, subscribed to the most common *unbiblical* approaches to poverty, economic justice, and wealth.

The results have been devastating. Today, more than half of the people in our world live on less than $2 each per day, and one billion people are mired in extreme poverty, living on less than $1 each per day. In a world that God created with a superabundance of resources, the fact that so many live in poverty is not only inexcusable, it is sinful, and we Christians need to repent. The solution lies with neither Marx nor the market, but in the words of the Master.

Big government is certainly not the solution. In many countries, it has made the problems worse. Unfortunately, so have many well-meaning, but misguided, Christian humanitarian programs. Having traveled the globe for thirty years and trained leaders in 164 countries, I've witnessed firsthand that almost every government and NGO (nonprofit) poverty program is actually harmful to the poor, hurting them in the long run rather than helping them. The typical poverty program creates dependency, robs people of dignity, stifles initiative, and can foster a "What have you done for me lately?" sense of entitlement.

The *biblical* way to help people rise out of poverty is through wealth *creation*, not wealth *redistribution*. For lasting results, we must offer the poor a *hand up*, not merely a *handout*. You spell long-term poverty reduction "j-o-b-s." Training and tools liberate people. Trade, not aid, builds the prosperity of nations.

I've been waiting for a book like this for a long time. Wayne Grudem and Barry Asmus have brilliantly written a work that is at the same time completely biblical, historical, and practical. Every so often, a book is written that you know will become a classic. *The Poverty of Nations* is such a book. It should be required reading in every Christian college and seminary, by every relief and mission organization, and by every local church pastor. At Saddleback Church, and in all churches participating in the P.E.A.C.E. Plan, this book will become a standard text that we will use to train every mission team we have in 196 countries.

Don't just read this book. Study it! Reread it and make notes, then put it into practice and teach it to others. It could change the world.

Rick Warren

Senior Pastor, Saddleback Church, Lake Forest, California

Founder, Global P.E.A.C.E. Plan

PREFACE

"Why is Africa so poor?" asked the woman from Kenya. "Are we under a curse?" She and her husband were successful business owners in Nairobi, but the continuing poverty in their nation troubled them deeply.

I (Wayne Grudem) had no answer. After a stunned silence, I had to say, "I'm sorry, I don't know." But the question continued to trouble me.

Eventually, I talked about it with my friend Barry Asmus, a professional economist. He had some helpful insight, but no complete answer. Then, as we continued to talk, we discovered that the two of us had a combination of academic resources that might enable us to find a much more complete answer and a solution.

One of us (Barry) is an economics professor with decades of experience in bringing economic analysis to national economic problems. The other (Wayne) is a theology professor with decades of experience in demonstrating how a detailed analysis of the teachings of the Bible can apply to modern-day real-life situations.

Our subsequent conversations led to a rewarding several-year project to combine the findings of modern economics with the teachings of the Bible in an attempt to solve the age-old problem of world poverty. We increasingly found that, despite our vastly different academic backgrounds, the conclusions from our two fields of study matched quite closely, giving the overall solution greater clarity and persuasiveness.

At first, we found just a handful of factors that will lead to prosperity or poverty in a nation. After more study, we had a list of thirty-seven factors. Further research and feedback from seminars in Albania and Peru added more factors, and we began to make presentations on "fifty factors within nations that will lead to wealth or poverty." Finally, this book concludes with a composite list of seventy-nine distinct factors within nations that, we believe, will enable any poor nation to overcome poverty (see Appendix, 369–73).

We are not aware of any other book like this, one that addresses poverty not at the personal or community level, but at the whole-nation level, and that proposes a solution based on a combination of conclusions from economics and theological ethics. We hope that readers will find the book both enlightening and persuasive.

Many people have helped us greatly in the production of this book. We appreciate the valuable comments and suggestions on earlier drafts or sections of this work from Scott Allen, Cal Beisner, John Coors, Ardian Fullani, Toni Gogu, Elliot Grudem, Stephen Happel, P. J. Hill, Ben Homan, John Kitchen, David Kotter, Ernst Lutz, Jeff Michler, Darrow Miller, Christopher Morton, Severin Oman, David Payne, Robb Provost, Nancy Roberts, Brad Routh, Rich Shields, Peter Williams, Keith Wright, and another reader who prefers to remain unnamed. We are grateful to Alexander Grudem for introducing us to Jeff Michler, who provided so much valuable advice. We received valuable feedback from participants in our seminars in Tirana, Albania; Lima, Peru; Eger, Hungary; Beijing, China; Cambridge, England; and Phoenix, Arizona, and from scholars at the annual meeting of the Evangelical Theological Society. We also appreciate the valuable suggestions and comments from the adult enrichment class at Scottsdale (Arizona) Bible Church, where we presented this material.

In addition, I (Wayne) wish to express appreciation to Potter-Brock Associates, who long ago supported my initial attempts to research the Bible's teaching on economic issues; to the members of the board of Trinity Evangelical Divinity School, who several years ago approved a sabbatical research project on the Bible and economics; and to the members of the board of Phoenix Seminary, who approved a sabbatical term in the fall of 2003, during which I was able to study economics at Arizona State University under the excellent instruction of professors Stephen Happel and Nancy Roberts.

Teri Armijo, Jenny Miller, and Angela Yang cheerfully and skillfully typed various sections of the manuscript. Jenny Miller also helped with numerous tasks in the editing process, and Angela Yang helped extensively with research. Joshua Brooks, Jeff Phillips, and John Paul

Stepanian also provided excellent research help. Jeff Phillips and John Paul Stepanian helped with proofreading and indexing the manuscript. We appreciate the skillful design help we received on the cover from Josh Dennis, Oliver Grudem, and Christopher Warrington. Greg Bailey at Crossway Books helped the manuscript significantly with his editorial skills.

We have dedicated this book to two friends, Bret and Brad Edson of Marketplace One, who have firmly believed in this project from the beginning and have graciously supplied both office space and financial support to make this project possible. Their lives are a clear demonstration that committed Christians can work in the business world with integrity and create products and services that bring new economic value to an entire region of a country. They are now devoting their lives and resources so that more people in this nation and other nations can also experience the same kind of earned success.

Our deepest appreciation and gratitude goes to our wives, Margaret Grudem and Mandy Asmus, who have patiently supported, encouraged, and prayed for us as we worked month after month to complete this project. We love them greatly and they continue to bring great joy to our lives.

Wayne Grudem and Barry Asmus

March 2013

Blessed is the one who considers the poor!
In the day of trouble the Lᴏʀᴅ delivers him.

PSALM 41:1

INTRODUCTION

The goal of this book is to provide a sustainable solution to poverty in the poor nations of the world, a solution based on both economic history and the teachings of the Bible. We use the word *sustainable* because this solution addresses the long-term causes of poverty in nations. If those are changed to become long-term causes of prosperity, the solution will last.

Our solution does not claim that everyone can be equally well-off. Some people will always be richer than others, and therefore some will be (relatively) poorer. But the solution we propose explains practical steps that any poor nation can take. These steps will lead the nation out of the poverty trap and into a path of ever-increasing prosperity that will often lift *almost everyone* in the nation to a better standard of living. This solution will permanently open opportunities for even the very poor to gain increasing prosperity.

The solution we propose is not new. Many parts of it have already been put into practice in nation after nation over the last 240 years with amazing results. It can still bring remarkable results in every poor nation today.

At the outset, it is important that we state clearly what kind of book this is.

A. National focus

The title of our book is *The Poverty of Nations* because its focus is on the poor nation as a whole. We focus on national laws, national economic policies, and national cultural values and habits because we are convinced that *the primary causes of poverty are factors that affect an entire nation.*

The solution we propose in this book must include changes in these national laws, policies, and cultural values and habits.

We do not discuss how to help individual poor people, businesses, or communities, because we understand our book as supplemental to those efforts. We recognize that charitable organizations, churches, and governments around the world are already helping individuals and communities, often in very effective ways. For example, our own church in Arizona, Scottsdale Bible Church, has carried out multiple programs to dig wells, provide medical and dental clinics, and build schools, in addition to supporting evangelism and Bible teaching in several nations.

We also applaud the success of microfinance projects in helping individuals in many countries, and we are thankful for thousands of other development projects that have brought access to clean water and sanitation systems, improved crop yields, promoted educational advancement, and made progress toward the eradication of diseases in many nations.

But in spite of all these efforts, it seems to us that something is still needed: a focus on the nationwide laws, policies, and cultural values and habits that determine so much of the course of economic development in a nation.

We recognize that other organizations and other writers have lifetimes of experience and far more wisdom than we have for helping individual poor people and communities. We especially appreciate the wisdom of many Christian charities, such as Food for the Hungry (located in the Phoenix area, where we live), which has as its stated mission "To walk with churches, leaders and families in overcoming all forms of human poverty by living in healthy relationships with God and His creation."[1] We also appreciate the whole-person, societal-transformation emphasis in programs such as the P.E.A.C.E. Plan instituted by Pastor Rick Warren, with its emphasis on church-to-church ministry. The acronym stands for: Plant churches that promote reconciliation, Equip servant leaders, Assist the poor, Care for the sick, and Educate the next generation.[2] Many other such worthwhile programs could be mentioned.

---

[1] Food for the Hungry website, accessed September 4, 2012, http://fh.org/about/vision.
[2] See P.E.A.C.E. Plan website, http://thepeaceplan.com.

Other writers have already provided excellent Christian perspectives on helping the poor. We commend especially *When Helping Hurts: How to Alleviate Poverty Without Hurting the Poor and Yourself*, by Steve Corbett and Brian Fikkert,[3] which explains how to help the whole person while humbly learning and respecting local wisdom, and *Discipling Nations: The Power of Truth to Transform Cultures*, by Darrow Miller,[4] which gives an extensive and insightful explanation of a Christian worldview particularly as it affects economic questions.

Our book is different in that it is aimed at the level of the whole nation. It is also different because it is co-authored by a professional economist (Barry Asmus) and a professor of theology (Wayne Grudem). Therefore, this book combines an economic analysis (based on the history of economic development for more than two hundred years) with a theological analysis (based on the teachings of the Bible about economic issues and government policies). From this dual perspective, we address entire national systems—first, types of economic systems (chaps. 3–6); second, government laws and policies (chaps. 7–8); and third, national cultural values and beliefs, including moral and spiritual convictions (chap. 9). We are not aware of any other book that approaches the question of world poverty at a national level from this combined perspective.

B. Steps from within a nation

The various steps we propose must be implemented from within a nation, by its own leaders. They are not steps that can be imposed by anyone outside the poor nation.

There is a great advantage to focusing on changes that must come from within a nation itself. This follows the sound counsel of Corbett and Fikkert in *When Helping Hurts*. They recommend a good rule of thumb that cuts through much of the complexity of alleviating pov-

---

[3] Steve Corbett and Brian Fikkert, *When Helping Hurts: How to Alleviate Poverty Without Hurting the Poor and Yourself* (Chicago: Moody, 2009).

[4] Darrow L. Miller, *Discipling Nations: The Power of Truth to Transform Cultures* (Seattle: YWAM, 1998). Another insightful book, based on experiences in many poor countries, is Udo Middelmann, *Christianity Versus Fatalistic Religions in the War Against Poverty* (Colorado Springs: Paternoster, 2007). Middelmann rightly claims that any long-term solution to poverty must include a cultural transformation to key elements of a Christian worldview, including a positive view of growth in economic productivity and a hopeful perspective on the possibilities for change in one's life situation. After years of experience, he writes, "Most proposals for aid show a tragic ignorance of the basic economics of poverty and wealth as well as an unawareness of the influence of antihuman cultural and religious practices. In fact, the latter factors are often deliberately ignored" (194).

erty: "Avoid Paternalism." That is, do not do things for people that they can do for themselves. They say, "Memorize this, recite it under your breath all day long, and wear it like a garland around your neck . . . it can keep you from doing all sorts of harm."[5]

Because we emphasize steps that a nation can take to help itself overcome poverty, we hope that our book will be a source of hope and encouragement for leaders in poor nations. Instead of telling such leaders, "You need to depend on people in other nations to solve your problem of poverty," we are saying: "We believe that you can solve this problem yourselves, and here are helpful steps that other nations have taken in the past and that are supported by the teachings of the Bible as well. We believe that you can implement these steps in your own nation, and that when you do, they will bring many positive results."

Other recent studies also emphasize that the solution to poverty in poor nations must come from within those nations. William Easterly, economics professor at New York University, who was for many years a senior research economist at the World Bank, explains that Western "Planners" cannot solve the problem of poverty in poor nations. He says: "A Planner believes outsiders know enough to impose solutions. A Searcher believes *only insiders have enough knowledge to find solutions*, and that most solutions must be homegrown."[6]

Similarly, Oxford economics professor Paul Collier, who was formerly director of development research at the World Bank and is one of the world's leading experts on African economies, writes:

> Unfortunately, it is not just about giving these countries our money. . . . *Change in the societies at the very bottom must come predominately from within;* we cannot impose it on them. In all these societies there are struggles between brave people wanting to change and entrenched interests opposing it.[7]

However, Collier also says that the policies of rich nations can make a difference in the ability of poor nations to overcome their

---

[5] Corbett and Fikkert, *When Helping Hurts*, 115.
[6] William Easterly, *The White Man's Burden: Why the West's Efforts to Aid the Rest Have Done So Much Ill and So Little Good* (New York: Penguin, 2006), 6.
[7] Paul Collier, *The Bottom Billion: Why the Poorest Countries Are Failing and What Can Be Done About It* (Oxford: Oxford University Press, 2007), xi, emphasis added.

poverty. He writes, "Change is going to have to come from within the societies of the one billion, but our own policies could make these efforts likely to succeed, and so more likely to be undertaken."[8]

We do not discuss such policy changes at length in this book (but see pages 98–99 and 267–69 on harmful trade policies). We recommend Collier's book, with its insightful analysis of ways in which wealthy countries can do more to help the poorest countries of the world, especially the fifty-eight countries that he calls "the bottom billion" (the people in these countries comprise the poorest one billion people on the earth).

The policies of wealthy nations that Collier proposes to change include: (1) limited, targeted use of foreign aid (99–123); (2) military intervention to maintain peace after conflicts and to protect against coups (124–34); (3) the adoption by the wealthy nations of laws and charters to help catch and prosecute criminals from poor nations who deposit their money in those wealthy nations, including investment protections and insurance (135–56); and (4) trade policies that use strategic decisions to lower trade barriers and give special help to extremely poor nations (157–72). Collier speaks from decades of experience and outlines specific strategies in each of these four categories.

However, whether wealthy countries adopt such changes or not, the seventy-nine steps toward prosperity that we outline in this book still need to be pursued by poorer nations.

C. Not a simple solution

The solution that we propose is not a simple "quick fix," one that says, "Just do this one thing and poverty will go away." Our solution is a complex one made up of seventy-nine specific factors, as explained in the following chapters (see complete list in Appendix, 369–73). These factors affect economic policies, governmental laws, and cultural values (including moral values and spiritual beliefs). Therefore, we are not proposing a simple approach such as "just give more money" (promoted by Jeffrey Sachs), or "just stop the foreign aid" (promoted by Dambisa Moyo). We are not even saying that the solution is "just establish a free-market economy" (though we do recommend a free-market system),

---

[8] Ibid., 12.

because we point out multiple other legal and cultural factors that affect whether a free market actually functions effectively in a nation.

The solution we propose is complex because economic systems are complex. That is because economic systems are the result of millions of human beings making millions of choices every day. Who can ever expect to understand all of this?

In fact, writer Jay Richards explains why economics can be thought of as more complex than any other field of study:

> In biology . . . we enter a higher order of complexity than in physics and chemistry. We are now dealing with organisms, which resist simple mathematical explanations. . . . From biology we move to the human sciences. Here the effects of intelligent agents appear everywhere. So it's no surprise that it's harder to use math to model human behavior than it is to use it to model, say, the movement of a ball rolling down a hill. By the time we reach economics, we are dealing not only with human agents, but with the complexity of the market exchanges of millions or billions of intelligent agents. As we go from physics at one end to economics at the other, we are moving up a "nested hierarchy" of complexity, in which higher orders constrain but cannot be reduced to lower orders.[9]

Therefore, it should not be surprising that the solution to poverty must be complex. This book discusses seventy-nine factors because all of them influence human decision making. Some of those factors are purely economic, but others have to do with laws, cultural values, moral convictions, long-term habits and traditions, and even spiritual values. Everything plays a part, so everything must be considered.

The fact that we have seventy-nine factors for a nation to consider might at first seem overwhelming. But there is another way of viewing this long list of factors. We hope that leaders in poor nations will approach the factors we discuss by asking, "What is our nation already doing well?" With so many factors, every nation will find it is strong in some areas.

---

[9] Jay W. Richards, *Money, Greed, and God: Why Capitalism Is the Solution and Not the Problem* (New York: HarperOne, 2009), 222–23. Richards uses this observation to argue for God's design in the amazing operation of the free market, because, he says, nowhere along the scale of increasing complexity do we find "evidence of order emerging from chaos" (ibid.). Richards's book as a whole is an outstanding overview of a biblical understanding of economics.

This positive approach, starting by listing the areas in which a nation is strong, is consistent with what Corbett and Fikkert call "asset-based community development" (ABCD). They say:

> ABCD puts the emphasis on what materially poor people already have and asks them to consider from the outset, "What is right with you? What gifts has God given you that you can use to improve your life and that of your neighbors? How can the individuals and organizations in your community work together to improve your community?" Instead of looking outside the low-income individual or community for resources and solutions, ABCD starts by asking the materially poor how they can be stewards of their own gifts and resources, seeking to restore individuals and communities to being what God has created them to be from the very start of the relationship. Indeed, the very nature of the question—What gifts do you have?—affirms people's dignity and contributes to the process of overcoming their poverty of being.[10]

D. Written for ordinary readers, not economists

We have written this book for ordinary adult readers. We have not written it for professional economists (though we hope that many of them will read it and agree with it). The book is therefore written mostly with ordinary language instead of technical economic terminology. Where specialized terms are needed, we explain them in the text where they first occur.

E. Written to leaders, especially Christian leaders, but also those who are not Christians

Our primary audience for this book is Christian leaders in poor nations (but also non-Christian leaders—see below). We are writing especially for Christians who believe the Bible and are willing to follow its principles for economic development. And we are writing to leaders, because they are the ones who can bring about the necessary changes in their countries.

By "leaders" we mean government leaders, business leaders, education leaders, non-governmental organization (NGO) leaders, charitable

---

[10] Corbett and Fikkert, *When Helping Hurts*, 126.

organization leaders, and certainly church leaders, especially pastors (because their preaching and teaching can eventually change a culture). We also hope that some who read this book will be inspired to seek to *become* leaders in their nations so that they can begin to implement the changes we outline.

However, we also hope that Christians in more prosperous nations will read this book, because many of them can have influence on poor nations through mission organizations, mission trips, friendships, development organizations, and denominational networks. We hope that some readers in wealthy nations might even be moved to devote their lives to helping poor nations escape from poverty in the ways we outline here. (Also see some practical suggestions at the end of chapter 5, 184–86.)

If you are reading this book and do not consider yourself to be a Christian, or do not think of the Christian Bible as the Word of God, we still invite you to consider what we say here. Many of our facts and arguments are taken from economic history, not from the Bible. As you read the parts that are based on the Bible, we invite you to at least think of the Bible's teachings as ideas that come from a valuable book of ancient wisdom, and consider whether the ideas seem right or not.

Our book also has some application to wealthier nations today. History shows that many wealthy nations have failed to remain prosperous (think of the once-wealthy kingdoms of Egypt, Babylon, Persia, Greece, Spain, and the Ottoman Empire). We hope that readers in wealthy nations will see applications of this book to their own countries, especially those that are in danger of abandoning the policies and values that made them economically prosperous in the first place.

To anyone in a leadership role in a poor country, the message of our book is this: there is a solution to poverty that really works. It has been proven again and again in world history. And it is supported by the moral teachings of the Bible. If this solution is put into place, we are confident it will lift entire nations out of poverty (not just a few individuals). We are asking you to consider this solution for your own nation.

At this point, someone might object that renowned developmental economist Paul Collier has demonstrated that *one billion* of the world's poorest people live in fifty-eight smaller countries that are essentially caught in four different "traps" that make it much more difficult for them to escape from poverty than for *four billion* other people in developing economies. Those traps are: (1) the conflict trap, (2) the natural resource trap, (3) the trap of being landlocked with bad neighbors, and (4) the trap of bad governance in a small country.[11]

We find Collier's book remarkably well informed and insightful. We recognize that the factors he points out make the task of overcoming poverty more difficult in these nations. But even Collier is hopeful about the possibility of progress, for he wrote his book to explain some steps that wealthy nations can take to help the countries where "the bottom billion" live. We believe that, though the task is difficult, the steps we propose in this book will eventually bring even these poorest of nations from poverty toward more and more prosperity

F. Written for students

We hope that many college students, especially those who are Christians, will find this text helpful as they seek to determine their own convictions about appropriate methods of addressing world poverty. We have both spent many years in classroom teaching at the university level, and we hope that this book will prove helpful as an assigned text in college and seminary classes dealing with care for the poor and a Christian approach to economic questions.

G. Why don't economists agree on a solution to poverty?

Someone might raise an objection at this point: "If there is such a clear solution to poverty, why do economists not all agree about it and write books explaining what the solution is?" In response, we would cite several points:

(1) *Some do agree.* Several respected economists have written books that agree in large measure with the solutions we propose in this book. For example, much of what we have written here is indebted to the work of David S. Landes, *The Wealth and Poverty of Nations: Why Some Are So Rich and Some So Poor.*[12] Landes is professor emeritus at

---

[11] See Collier, *The Bottom Billion*, 17–75.
[12] David S. Landes, *The Wealth and Poverty of Nations: Why Some Are So Rich and Some So Poor* (New York: W. W. Norton, 1999).

Harvard University and one of the world's most respected economic historians.

Readers may notice, especially in chapters 7–9, that we cite Landes's book more than any other source. We do this because his massive study (658 pages, including 126 pages of fine-print documentation) is an unparalleled source of historical information about the economic development of all the nations (or regions) of the world in the last five hundred years. The first sentence in his book reads, "My aim in writing this book is to do world history."[13] And world history, on a grand scale, is what he does. John Kenneth Galbraith said this book "will establish David Landes as preeminent in his field and in his time." Nobel laureate Kenneth Arrow says the book is "a picture of enormous sweep and brilliant insight . . . [with] incredible wealth of learning."[14]

In addition, we agree with several other economists and developmental historians in key sections of our book, especially regarding the economic and legal policies that are necessary to overcome poverty. For example, we cite with approval several key sections from the writings of Hernando de Soto; William Easterly; Paul Collier; P. T. Bauer; Lawrence Harrison; Niall Ferguson (a historian); Daron Acemoglu and James A. Robinson (though we also differ with them on the importance of culture; see below); and William Baumol, Robert Litan, and Carl Schramm.[15]

Of course, many economists do not advocate the solution we propose in this book. They propose only partial solutions or even incorrect solutions because of their underlying assumptions.

(2) *Professional donors.* For example, some economists are "profes-

---

[13] Ibid., xi.
[14] Cited in ibid., i.
[15] Hernando de Soto, *The Mystery of Capital: Why Capitalism Triumphs in the West and Fails Everywhere Else* (New York: Basic Books, 2000); William R. Easterly, *The Elusive Quest for Growth: Economists' Adventures and Misadventures in the Tropics* (Cambridge, MA: The MIT Press, 2001); *The White Man's Burden: Why the West's Efforts to Aid the Rest Have Done So Much Ill and So Little Good* (New York: Penguin, 2006); Paul Collier, *The Bottom Billion: Why the Poorest Countries Are Failing and What Can Be Done About It* (Oxford: Oxford University Press, 2007); P. T Bauer, *Equality, the Third World, and Economic Delusion* (Cambridge, MA: Harvard University Press, 1981); Lawrence Harrison, *The Central Liberal Truth* (New York: Oxford University Press, 2006); Niall Ferguson, *Civilization: The West and the Rest* (New York: Penguin, 2011); Daron Acemoglu and James A. Robinson, *Why Nations Fail: The Origins of Power, Prosperity, and Poverty* (New York: Crown Publishers, 2012); William Baumol, Robert Litan, and Carl Schramm, *Good Capitalism, Bad Capitalism and the Economics of Growth and Prosperity* (New Haven: Yale University Press, 2007). See also Milton Friedman, *Capitalism and Freedom: A Leading Economist's View on the Proper Role of Competitive Capitalism* (Chicago: University of Chicago Press, 1962); William J. Bernstein, *The Birth of Plenty: How the Prosperity of the Modern World Was Created* (New York: McGraw-Hill, 2004).

sional donors." They spend much of their time giving away other people's money, and their primary solution to world poverty is to give away more money (even though they admit that giving away money has not solved the problem so far). The most prominent representative of this approach is Jeffrey Sachs in his book *The End of Poverty*.[16]

(3) *Pure economists*. Others are "pure economists" (at least in their solutions). They do not address cultural, moral, or spiritual values at any length, presumably because they think that these topics are outside the realm of legitimate study for economists. One example of this approach is that of Dambisa Moyo in her book *Dead Aid: Why Aid Is Not Working and How There Is a Better Way for Africa*.[17] Moyo offers a perceptive analysis of the harm caused by foreign aid to Africa, but her solution is simply to stop the foreign aid, assuming that after aid is stopped, "good governance . . . will naturally emerge."[18] She mentions cultural values in passing but minimizes them.

(4) *Cultural equalizers*. Other economists are "cultural equalizers." They are convinced that it is misleading or even wrong to say that any one culture is "better" than any other, even "better" at producing economic growth. Therefore, there must be some other reason, or perhaps it is an accident, that some countries have become wealthy and others remain poor. We should not try to explain the disparity by saying that one country's cultural habits and values are better than another's.

For example, more than a dozen scholars, each with outstanding credentials and publications on economic development and foreign aid, contributed to *Making Aid Work*, a 2007 symposium on foreign aid. There was hardly a word in the entire book about the need for cultural transformation within countries.[19]

(5) *Fatalists*. Still another approach has been taken by those we may call "fatalists." They claim that economic prosperity came about simply because some nations had the good fortune of favorable geographic factors, such as moderate weather, abundant natural resources,

---

[16] Jeffrey Sachs, *The End of Poverty* (New York: Penguin, 2005).

[17] Dambisa Moyo, *Dead Aid: Why Aid Is Not Working and How There Is a Better Way for Africa* (New York: Farrar, Straus & Giroux, 2009).

[18] Ibid., 143.

[19] Abhijit Vinayak Banerjee et al., *Making Aid Work* (Cambridge, MA: The MIT Press, 2007). Acemoglu and Robinson also argue that cultural factors are of little value in explaining economic differences among nations; we discuss their view on 309–15.

and useful animals, from the beginning, so it was inevitable that they would become rich while others would remain poor. The primary example of this approach is Jared Diamond in his book *Guns, Germs, and Steel: The Fates of Human Societies*.[20] According to Diamond, geography is more important than everything else, and his analysis gives no room for the impact of differing human choices, cultural values, and moral and spiritual values.

(6) *Socialists and other "planners."* Still other economists are "socialists," of stronger or weaker varieties. In their view, the solution to poverty is more planning—wise government "experts" should plan and direct most everything in an economy. If it is pointed out that government control of factories and businesses has not worked well in the past, their response is that the wrong government experts were in charge. We simply need different experts, better ones, they say. In fact, if asked, they might even humbly suggest that *they themselves* might just be available to serve as these new experts—in a limited capacity, of course—at least initially. Easterly refers to these economists as "Planners," and says they usually do more harm than good.[21]

With these six viewpoints in mind, consider the predicament of leaders in poor nations. They have at least six radically different opinions, all from economic "experts." With all these "experts" telling poor nations how to solve their problems, it is no wonder that their government leaders find it hard to know whom they should trust. Are the professional donors right? The pure economists? The fatalists? The socialists? The messages are contradictory and confusing.

Abhijit Banerjee, professor of economics at the Massachusetts Institute of Technology and a director of the Abdul Latif Jameel Poverty Action Lab there, summarizes the current confusion in academic studies of aid and economic development:

> Instead of a handful of simple and clear-cut laws that tell us what to do and what to expect, we have a hundred competing tendencies and possibilities, of uncertain strength and, quite often, direction, with little guidance as to how to add them up. We can explain every fact

---

[20] Jared Diamond, *Guns, Germs, and Steel: The Fates of Human Societies* (New York: W. W. Norton, 1999).
[21] See Easterly, *The White Man's Burden*, esp. 3–33 ("Planners Versus Searchers") and 37–162 ("Part I: Why Planners Cannot Bring Prosperity."

many times over, with the result that there is very little left that we can both believe strongly and act upon.[22]

Robert H. Bates, professor of government at Harvard, agrees: "In truth, there is no theory of development that is logically compelling and demonstrably valid. One good indicator of this deficiency is the very abundance of theories. . . . The field of development responds less to evidence than to political fashion."[23]

That is why we think this book can play a unique role. It combines economic analysis with biblical teachings. Once we are able to set aside limiting assumptions and look honestly at results (asking, "What has worked in the past?"), it seems to us that the economic analysis points clearly in the direction that we propose.

On the biblical side, we argue in this book that the moral and economic teachings of the Bible can give confidence to leaders in poor nations that our solutions are supported by the very teachings that God himself gave to the human race. This provides a strong reason for leaders, especially Christian leaders, to follow these principles rather than others that have been proposed.

H. Why should we help the poor?

More specifically for purposes of this book, why should Christians want to help the poor? The Bible gives us two kinds of reasons.

First, there are the general commands of Scripture. Jesus says, "You shall love your neighbor as yourself" (Matt. 22:39). If we love someone who is poor, we will want to help that poor person.

Jesus also said, "Let your light shine before others, so that they may see your good works and give glory to your Father who is in heaven" (Matt. 5:16). If we want to let the "light" of our conduct shine before others, we certainly should give help to those in need. In fact, the apostle Paul says that God has called us to live lives that are character-ized by "good works": "For we are his workmanship, created in Christ Jesus *for good works*, which God prepared beforehand, that we should walk in them" (Eph. 2:10). Certainly one of the good works that God wants us to do is helping those who are in need.

---

[22] Banerjee, writing in *Making Aid Work*, 136–37.
[23] Robert H. Bates, writing in ibid., 68.

Second, we should want to help the poor because there are numer-ous specific commands in Scripture that tell us to do so.[24] Here are some of them:

> If among you, one of your brothers should become poor, in any of the towns within your land that the LORD your God is giving you, you shall not harden your heart or shut your hand against your poor brother, but you shall open your hand to him and lend him sufficient for his need, whatever it may be. (Deut. 15:7–8)

> For there will never cease to be poor in the land. Therefore I com-mand you, "You shall open wide your hand to your brother, to the needy and to the poor, in your land." (Deut. 15:11)

> Blessed is the one who considers the poor! In the day of trouble the LORD delivers him. (Ps. 41:1)

> Whoever oppresses a poor man insults his Maker, but he who is gen-erous to the needy honors him. (Prov. 14:31)

> Only, they asked us to remember the poor, the very thing I was eager to do. (Gal. 2:10)

> But if anyone has the world's goods and sees his brother in need, yet closes his heart against him, how does God's love abide in him? (1 John 3:17)

In terms of the focus of this book, we realize that governmental laws and entrenched special interests in a nation can be "structural" forces that make it impossible for individual people to rise out of poverty. The laws and the powerful elites in a country may keep all the power and retain all the wealth for themselves. Somehow these powerful groups must be persuaded to give up some of their power and privilege, and their tight hold on the wealth of the nation.

In such cases, it seems to us that God's words through Isaiah are appropriate:

---

[24] A very helpful discussion of biblical teachings about the need to care for the poor is found in Cor-bett and Fikkert, *When Helping Hurts*, 31–49. See also Craig Blomberg, *Neither Poverty Nor Riches* (Grand Rapids: Eerdmans, 1999).

"Is not this the fast that I choose:
　　to loose the bonds of wickedness,
　　to undo the straps of the yoke,
　to let the oppressed go free,
　　and to break every yoke?" (Isa. 58:6)

Our hope is that this book will provide for poor people in many nations a means by which the "bonds of wickedness" and the "yoke" of oppression will be broken, and in that way the Lord himself will be glorified. If the Bible commands us to love and care for individual poor people that cross our paths, should not our love for others lead us to be even more eager to seek to change laws and policies in an entire nation when we have the opportunity, and thereby to help many thousands and or even millions of poor people all at once?

Third, love for the poor as fellow human beings created in the image of God should pour from our hearts when we realize the tragic situation faced by many in poverty. Corbett and Fikkert point out that, while North Americans tend to think of poverty in terms of "a lack of material things such as food, money, clean water, medicine, housing, etc.," this is not how the poor themselves evaluate their situation:

> While poor people mention having a lack of material things, they tend to describe their condition in far more psychological and social terms than our North American audiences. Poor people typically talk in terms of shame, inferiority, powerlessness, humiliation, fear, hopelessness, depression, social isolation, and voicelessness.[25]

> Low-income people daily face a struggle to survive that creates feelings of helplessness, anxiety, suffocation, and desperation that are simply unparalleled in the lives of the rest of humanity.[26]

When we understand these aspects of poverty, including a "lack of freedom to be able to make meaningful choices—to have an ability to affect one's situation,"[27] our hearts should be genuinely moved to try to seek a solution to these problems.

---

[25] Corbett and Fikkert, *When Helping Hurts*, 52–53.
[26] Ibid., 70.
[27] Ibid., 71, quoting economist Amartya Sen.

I. The responsibility of leaders

Leaders in poor nations have a special responsibility and a special opportunity in this regard. Sometimes one courageous leader, with the help of God, can change the direction of an entire nation.

Moses led the nation of Israel out of slavery in Egypt (Exodus 12–15). Queen Esther's courageous intervention before King Ahasuerus saved the people of Israel from destruction (Esther 5–9). Likewise, at key points of the history of the United States, leaders such as George Washington and Abraham Lincoln preserved the nation. Many other nations have memories of similar heroes whom they honor for doing great good for their countries, often at great personal sacrifice.

If you have a leadership role in any nation on earth, the Bible is very clear about the purpose for which God put you in this position: it is *to do good for your nation*. Paul says this about anyone serving as a governing official in the Roman government: "He is God's servant *for your good*" (Rom. 13:4). In other words, even an unbelieving, secular government official in the Roman Empire had been put in office to do "good" for the people of the nation. The Bible even calls him "God's servant" for that purpose. This is why God put you in your position of responsibility. It was not so that you might enrich yourself. It was not so that you might make yourself famous. It was not so that you might get extra privileges for your family and friends. It was so that you might do "good" for the people of your nation. That is your responsibility, entrusted to you by God.

The Bible also says that God is watching what you do and will hold you accountable: "The eyes of the LORD are in every place, keeping watch on the evil and the good" (Prov. 15:3).

It is a special responsibility of government leaders to care for the poor:

> If a king faithfully judges the poor, his throne will be established forever. (Prov. 29:14)

> Therefore, O king, let my counsel be acceptable to you: break off your sins by practicing righteousness, and your iniquities by showing mercy to the oppressed, that there may perhaps be a lengthening of your prosperity. (Dan. 4:27)

It is crucial that government leaders have an accurate and true understanding of the causes of poverty and prosperity. In economics as well as in every other area of government, "If a ruler listens to falsehood, all his officials will be wicked" (Prov. 29:12).

If you have leadership responsibility in a poor nation (or a developed one), you also have a tremendous opportunity. You have the potential to do great good for your nation. In doing so, it is possible that you will be honored in history as one of the heroes who served his nation well and changed its history for the better.[28]

If you are not a Christian believer, we must emphasize that doing good for your nation will not earn you eternal salvation (that comes only as a gift to those who trust in Jesus Christ for the forgiveness of their sins; see Rom. 3:23; 6:23; John 1:12; 3:16). Therefore, we urge you now to place your trust in Christ, and also to continue to do good.[29]

If you are a genuine believer in Jesus Christ, and if you work to solve the problem of poverty in your nation, even if you do not immediately receive the praise of your people, you will have the far greater joy of knowing that you have done "what is pleasing to the Lord" (Eph. 5:10). He will reward you in the way he thinks best, both in this life (to some degree), and in the life to come (with great abundance). You will be laying up for yourself "treasures in heaven, where neither moth nor rust destroys and where thieves do not break in and steal" (Matt. 6:20). You will have the joy of knowing God's favor on your life because you are doing things that please him.

That is the challenge we put before you in this book.

J. Material prosperity is a secondary issue

Finally, we must make clear at the outset that we are writing this book as committed evangelical Christians, and a Bible-based viewpoint affects our entire approach to the question of poverty. The Bible gives frequent warnings that a person's relationship to God is far more important than material prosperity, and that the pursuit of material

---

[28] Collier, *The Bottom Billion*, has sobering but realistic assessments of the challenges faced by good leaders who seek to transform poor nations where corruption is widespread: see especially chapters 5, 6, 8, and 11.

[29] For a further explanation by one of us about what trusting in Christ means, see the video by Wayne Grudem, "What Is Salvation?" at http://scottsdalebible.com/sermons/the-turning-point.

wealth can, in fact, very easily take first place in one's life rather than a relationship with God.

Jesus was quite blunt: "No servant can serve two masters, for either he will hate the one and love the other, or he will be devoted to the one and despise the other. You cannot serve God and money" (Luke 16:13). He also said, "What does it profit a man if he gains the whole world and loses or forfeits himself?" (Luke 9:25). And he told a parable about a rich man who decided to build bigger barns for all of his wealth, but God said to him: "Fool! This night your soul is required of you, and the things you have prepared, whose will they be?" Then Jesus added, "So is the one who lays up treasure for himself and is not rich toward God" (Luke 12:20–21). He also said in this context, "One's life does not consist in the abundance of his possessions" (Luke 12:15).

Christian writers Corbett and Fikkert wisely warn that the wrong attitude toward material possessions can easily affect Western Christians and harm our efforts to help the poor if we do not include a spiritual component in the ministry that we do. They point out that economically rich Christians in the West often have a "poverty of being," a "god-complex," and a merely "material definition of poverty" that can cause them to do more harm than good when trying to help the poor.[30]

Corbett and Fikkert also warn that in order for us to help the poor most effectively, both we and they need a proper worldview and right relationships with God, with ourselves, with others, and with the rest of creation.[31] They say, "We are very prone to putting our trust in ourselves and in technology to improve our lives, forgetting that it is God who is the Creator and Sustainer of us and of the laws that make the technology work."[32]

This is why the Bible gives a warning that those who obtain some measure of financial prosperity in this life should not set their hearts and hopes on their wealth, but on God:

> As for the rich in this present age, charge them not to be haughty, *nor to set their hopes on the uncertainty of riches, but on God*, who richly provides us with everything to enjoy. They are to do good, to be rich

---

[30] Corbett and Fikkert, *When Helping Hurts*, 65–67.
[31] Ibid., 84–89, discusses these relationships in detail.
[32] Ibid., 95.

in good works, to be generous and ready to share, thus storing up treasure for themselves as a good foundation for the future, so that they may take hold of that which is truly life. (1 Tim. 6:17–19)

As we begin this book, that is our hope for the nations of the world. We hope that every nation will adopt the principles in this book and begin to experience significant growth in material prosperity. But we also hope that such material prosperity does not come at the cost of the loss of interpersonal relationships, the loss of love for family, and alienation from God. We certainly do not want to encourage a society that worships and serves money, and then is destroyed by that greed and idolatry.[33] We hope, rather, that all nations of the world, while they pursue growth in economic prosperity, will continue to value relationships with family and friends more than they value wealth, and that they will be nations that, in general, truly worship and serve God, not money. "You cannot serve God and money" (Luke 16:13).

---

[33] Paul Mills puts a very high priority on the influence of economic policy on relationships: "The ultimate goal of economic policy ought to be enriching the quality of relationships within a society" (*Jubilee Manifesto*, ed. Michael Schluter and John Ashcroft [Leicester, UK: Inter-Varsity, 2005], 217).

1

THE GOAL

Produce More
Goods and Services

In order to solve the problem of poverty in a poor nation, it is important to have the correct goal in mind. To discover this goal, we must
first understand two economic concepts that determine whether a
country is rich or poor: per capita income and gross domestic product.[1] Once those concepts are understood, it becomes evident that if
we want to solve poverty, the correct goal is that a nation continually
produces more goods and services per person each year.

A. What makes a country rich or poor?

1. The standard measure of wealth and poverty: per capita income

The standard measurement of whether a country is rich or poor (in
economic terms) is called "per capita income" ("per capita" means "per
person"). Per capita income is calculated by dividing the total market

---

[1] We are speaking only of economic wealth and poverty here. As we stated at the end of the Introduction, we recognize that relational and spiritual wealth are more valuable than economic prosperity.
And there are other kinds of wealth, such as moral wealth, the wealth of wisdom, and cultural and
artistic wealth, which are not the focus of this book. We believe that a person's relationship with God
takes priority over everything else: "You shall love the Lord your God with all your heart and with all
your soul and with all your mind" (Matt. 22:37).

Still, our material well-being is important to us and also to God, and we understand growth in
material prosperity to be the best and, in fact, the only real solution for world poverty. Our entire
book therefore seeks to help nations increase their economic wealth as one means of obedience to God.

value of everything produced in a nation in a year by the number of people in the nation.

If we sort countries by per capita income, we get an idea of the differences in economic conditions between rich and poor countries.

For example, some "low-income" nations in 2012 were the Democratic Republic of the Congo ($400 per capita income, which is about $1 per day per person), Somalia ($600), Ethiopia ($1,200), Haiti ($1,300), Uganda ($1,400), Nigeria ($2,700), and Pakistan ($2,900).[2] These are *average* income figures, which included a small number of high-income people within each country (whose income numbers pulled the "averages" up). That means that *more than half* of the people in these countries were *below* these average levels of income.

"Low-middle-income" nations included Ghana ($3,300), India ($3,900), Honduras ($4,600), Guatemala ($5,200), Ukraine ($7,600), and El Salvador ($7,700). The next group, "high-middle–income" nations, included Albania ($8,000), China ($9,100), Jamaica ($9,100), Peru ($10,700), Colombia ($10,700), Brazil ($12,000), Mexico ($15,300), Chile ($18,400), and Hungary ($19,800).

Finally, in the "high-income" category were nations such as Poland ($21,000), Israel ($32,200), South Korea ($32,400), Japan ($36,200), the UK ($36,700), Germany ($39,100), Canada ($41,500), Sweden ($41,700), Switzerland ($45,300), the United States ($49,800), and Norway ($55,300). (The world map on the front cover of this book uses a color code to indicate per capita income for every country.)

Per capita income does not tell us everything we need to know about a nation. For instance, it does not measure important things that are not sold in the market, such as leisure time, religious faith, or strong families. But per capita income is the best numerical measure of whether a country is rich or poor in an economic sense.

Per capita income also does not tell us about the *distribution* of income—whether a large number of people share in the wealth of the nation or whether it is concentrated in the hands of a wealthy few. Increasing per capita income is not an adequate solution if only a few wealthy people benefit. Therefore, in the material that follows, we dis-

---

[2] These numbers are based on purchasing power parity (PPP) rather than official currency exchange rates. Data for specific countries were taken from the *CIA World Factbook*, accessed March 7, 2013, https://www.cia.gov/library/publications/the-world-factbook/rankorder/2004rank.html.

cuss several steps that countries must take to prevent a small, wealthy elite from controlling all the wealth and power in a nation, as happens too often in poor countries today. We recommend numerous policies and values that enable a genuinely free market to function and thereby permanently open opportunities for *any* poor person to rise from poverty to an adequate income or even to prosperity (see chapter 4, section D; chapter 5, sections B, F, and G; chapter 6, sections B and C; all of chapters 7 and 8; and chapter 9, values 4, 5, 8, 9, 14, 15, 18, 21–24, and 29).

But increasing per capita income is very important, for as long as it remains low, the country remains poor. And higher per capita income is strongly correlated with some undeniably important factors, such as longer life expectancy, lower incidence of disease, higher literacy, and a healthier environment (for example, clean air and water, and effective sanitation).[3]

If a country wants to move up the scale from "low-income" to "middle-income" to "high-income," what must it do? *It must increase the total amount of goods and services that it produces*, which means there will be more to go around. Remember that per capita income is calculated by dividing the total market value of everything produced in a nation in a year by the number of people in the nation.

To understand what is needed in more detail, it is necessary to understand the concept of gross domestic product (GDP).

2. The standard measure of what a country produces: gross domestic product (GDP)

The standard economic measurement of what a nation's economy produces is called the gross domestic product (GDP). It is "the market value of all final goods and services produced within a country in a given period of time."[4] The period of time ordinarily used is one year.

This definition includes "goods and services." "Goods" include all the shoes, clothing, vegetables, bicycles, books, newspapers, cars, and every other material thing that is produced and then sold in the market. "Services" include things such as classes taught by teachers, examinations given by doctors, or the work of paid housecleaners.

---

[3] See, for example, the strong correlation between per capita income and life expectancy in Stephen Moore, *Who's the Fairest of Them All?* (New York: Encounter Books, 2012), in the graph on 57.

[4] N. Gregory Mankiw, *Principles of Economics* (Orlando, FL: Dryden Press, 1998), 480.

"Market value" means that goods and services counted in GDP are sold legally in markets. A loaf of bread baked and eaten at home is not counted in GDP because it is not sold in a market. But loaves of bread baked in a home and then sold in public are counted, because they have been sold in a market and a monetary value can be attached to them.

The size of a nation's GDP is the main factor that determines its wealth or poverty. This is because per capita income is calculated by dividing the GDP by the total population. If the population does not change much from year to year but the GDP grows, the per capita income goes up.[5]

For example, in 2011, Honduras had a GDP of $36,100,000,000 (about $36 billion)[6] with a population just over 8 million people. If we divide $36 billion by 8 million, we have a per capita income (in round numbers) of about $4,500.

But if Honduras could somehow double its GDP from $36 billion to $72 billion and still have a population of 8 million, its per capita income would double to about $9,000 per person ($72 billion divided by 8 million people). The "average" person in Honduras would be twice as wealthy as before. Increasing a nation's GDP is what moves it along the path from poverty to greater prosperity.

3. What will increase a country's GDP?

The most important question, then, is this: What will increase a country's GDP?

The answer is complex, involving as many as seventy-nine factors, all of them contributing to or hindering the growth of GDP. Answering this question in detail is what the rest of this book is about.

But we can briefly say here that GDP is increased when a nation continually creates more goods and services that have enough value to be sold in the marketplace. Therefore, the focus of efforts to overcome poverty must be on increasing the production of goods and services.

The correct goal for a poor nation, then, is *to become a nation that continually produces more goods and services each year.* If a nation is going

---

[5] More specifically, as long at GDP grows faster than the population, the per capita income will go up.
[6] In this illustration, we continue to use figures based on purchasing power parity (PPP); see note 2 above. The other method of measuring GDP, the "nominal" GDP based on official currency exchange rates, gives a GDP for Honduras of $15,340,000,000. Our example works no matter which basis is used for the calculation.

to succeed in overcoming poverty, it must be willing to examine its official policies, laws, economic structures, and cultural values and traditions to see whether they promote or restrain increases in the goods and services that the nation produces.

B. Other goals that have been suggested

As we have spoken to various audiences about the solution to poverty, we have heard many people propose other goals for eliminating poverty. Each of these will be discussed more fully in a later chapter, but we can mention them briefly here:

(1) *More aid.* Some people argue that wealthy countries need to give massive amounts of additional aid money to jump-start the economies of poor nations. Unfortunately, aid has not proven helpful in increasing GDP in the long run (see the discussion of aid in the next chapter). To focus on aid as the solution is to focus on the wrong goal. The goal must be to increase a nation's GDP.

(2) *More equal distribution of wealth.* Others say that the solution to poverty is using the power of government to redistribute wealth from the rich to the poor. They argue that greater economic equality is a matter of simple justice that governments should enforce. We certainly agree with the goal of helping the poor share in more of the wealth of a nation, and in several sections of the following chapters we discuss ways this can happen through fair, open, market-based solutions.[7] The goal of this entire book is finding truly workable, sustainable ways to overcome poverty. However, some nations have tried to bring about more economic equality in economically harmful ways, not through opening up free markets but through brute use of government power. Making equality a more important goal than overall economic growth is a mistake for a government, because merely distributing the same amount of wealth in different ways does not change the total amount of wealth a nation produces each year, which is the only way that any nation has grown from poverty to prosperity.

---

[7]See, for example, the sections below on making it easy for even poor people to obtain clearly documented property rights (141–54), on overcoming the oppression when a few wealthy families control all the wealth and power (75–77, 297–307), on protecting genuine opportunities and ease of entry in free markets (263–77), on the importance of widespread education and literacy (253–56, 291–92), and many other sections.

Economic freedom and government-forced economic equality are opposing goals, and when government forces economic equality (for example, through heavy taxes on the rich), it can actually diminish economic incentives and harm the GDP. This can be seen in the history of every nation ruled by communism, whether the former Soviet Union, Cuba, North Korea, or China before it implemented many free-market reforms. Milton Friedman rightly said: "A society that puts equality before freedom will get neither. A society that puts freedom before equality will get a high degree of both."[8] A nation must *produce* wealth before it can distribute or enjoy it. The goal must be to increase a nation's GDP.

(3) *Natural resources.* Some believe that poor nations need to discover new natural resources, perhaps oil, precious metals, or rare earths. This solution has some merit, because when minerals are "produced" from the ground, their value directly increases GDP. But this is too narrow a focus, both because some nations have few resources (therefore this solution does not help them) and because some nations with almost no natural resources (Japan, Singapore) have become very wealthy. In addition, long-term prosperity in a nation cannot be preserved by resource wealth alone. As we will see later, many economists consider natural resources a disguised curse, creating immediate income but hurting the conditions for building the institutions that produce long-term growth. The goal must be to increase a nation's GDP.

(4) *Debt forgiveness.* Others say that rich nations need to forgive the impossibly high debts that have been incurred by poor nations, because the costs of repaying these loans are a crippling burden. Unfortunately, this suggestion is similar to the proposal that more aid be given to poor countries, because it simply changes a loan into a gift, which is more aid. Debt forgiveness is at best a means to an end, not the end itself. It helps only if a nation produces more goods and services in the long run. The goal must be to increase a nation's GDP.

(5) *Better terms of trade.* Still others advocate negotiating more favorable prices for international trade between rich and poor nations. This would increase the value of a country's exports (total exports are

---

[8] Milton Friedman, "Created Equal," Part Five in the *Free to Choose* video lecture series, accessed January 9, 2013, www.freetochoose.tv.

added to GDP, since a country produced these things) and decrease the cost of its imports (imports are subtracted from GDP, since a nation did not produce these things but bought them from abroad). Therefore, if some sellers or buyers in a nation can negotiate more favorable terms of trade in dealing with many thousands of buyers and sellers on a world market, we agree that this would bring some benefit.[9]

But no single poor nation is likely on its own to exert much of an effect on world prices of its goods (as we explain below, 92–99).[10] Focusing one's hope and effort on something that one probably cannot change is not a wise strategy. The goal must be to focus on something that a nation can certainly change: producing more goods and services, and so increasing its GDP.

(6) *Restrain multinational corporations.* Others believe that the solution is to break up or somehow restrain the power of large multinational corporations that are unfairly taking advantage of poor nations. But those who focus on multinational corporations seldom evaluate their actual overall impact on a nation's production of goods and services (see next chapter, 99–106). The goal should not be to hurt productive firms or make them less powerful. The goal must be to make every person and every company within the nation more productive, and thus increase a nation's GDP.

(7) *Fair trade coffee.* Others seem to think that the solution is to persuade Starbucks customers to buy "fair-trade" coffee, and then to expand "fair-trade" agreements to other products and other companies. This is a form of the "better terms of trade" approach, and we analyze it below, but we can say here that most economists believe that the fair-trade movement mostly benefits a small number of producers while it harms others (see below, 92–95), and very little of the higher retail price actually reaches the farmers themselves. In any case, we doubt that this movement can succeed in persuading more than a small portion of the overall world market to pay more than the world price of a commodity, which is determined by the continual interplay of supply and demand. The effect is limited in scope, so this practice

---

[9] In addition, we object to most tariffs and quotas imposed on products that poor countries seek to export to richer countries (see below, 98–99).
[10] We also oppose the practice of rich nations providing above-market subsidies for some agricultural goods and then "dumping" them on world markets (see below, 97–98).

does not have a really significant impact on a nation's overall production of goods and services.

As we will explain below, some of these proposals provide some help and others are harmful. But none of them provides an overall, sustainable solution to poverty. That comes only through increasing a nation's GDP.

C. The amazing process of creating value that did not exist before

When we talk about producing more goods and services, we are referring to an amazing process by which human beings are able to better their own economic situation by creating valuable things that did not exist before. When they do this, they add not only to their own wealth but also to the wealth of their nation. They do this not by taking something of value from someone else (which would not increase total GDP), but by *creating* new products or services that no one ever had because they previously did not exist.

1. Examples of the creation of products of value

To take a simple example, think of a woman in a poor country who has a piece of cotton cloth that cost her $3. If she sews it into a shirt that she sells for $13, then she has created a new product of value. She has made a shirt that did not exist in the world before she made it. She has made the piece of cotton cloth to be $10 more valuable than it was when she bought it.

She has also contributed something to the total value of everything that her nation will produce in that year (the GDP). If the total value of everything produced in her nation that year was $2,000,000,000 before she made the shirt, then after she made the shirt the total value of everything produced was $2,000,000,010.[11] She moved her nation $10 along the path toward prosperity.

This amazing process of increasing GDP by creating products of value is at the heart of the means by which nations can grow from poverty to increased prosperity. If this creative process can be expanded

---

[11] After she uses the cloth to make a shirt, the $3 that she paid for the piece of cloth is no longer a "final good" that can be counted in the GDP, so the GDP increases by $13 − 3 = $10.

to thousands of people making thousands of kinds of products, then the total value of everything in the nation increases day after day. If a nation can increase the value of what it produces each year, GDP will grow, and the nation will become more prosperous each year. This is the process that brings nations from poverty to prosperity.

We can also note at this point that the $10 profit this woman earned when she sold the shirt is a measure of the value that she added to the economy. The buyer of the shirt voluntarily decided that the shirt was worth $13 to him. Therefore (in economic terms), it is worth $13. But the cloth cost the woman only $3. Her $10 profit is important because it shows that new value has been created. We discuss profits more fully below (see 179–180), but it is important to note here that her profit is not immoral, but is a measure of *morally positive value* that has been added to the nation.

When a baker uses $3 worth of flour and other ingredients to make a loaf of bread that he sells for $4, he has suddenly added $1 to the GDP. When a shoemaker uses pieces of leather that cost him $5 to make a pair of shoes that he sells for $30, he has added $25 to the GDP.

Another example is a farmer who grows a crop of beans worth $400. When the ground had no crops, it was producing nothing of value. By cultivating the ground, the farmer "creates" (with the help of God, who directs the weather) $400 worth of beans that did not exist in the world before he grew them and harvested them. He increases the prosperity of the nation by $400 (minus the cost of the seed). And if, with better seeds, fertilizer, and irrigation, he grows $800 worth of beans the next year, then he doubles his contribution to the nation's GDP.

More complex processes can turn simple materials into very expensive items. Think of eyeglasses, for instance. The original value of the raw plastic in the lenses might be about 3 cents and the original value of the metal in the frame might be about 5 cents. But a pair of eyeglasses can cost $200 or more in the United States today. How can 8 cents worth of materials end up with a value of $200? It is because skillful human beings create a product of value from the resources of the earth, and so the GDP grows.

It is crucial to keep this creative process in mind in trying to solve the problem of poverty in poor nations. A nation will expand its GDP not by taking products from other nations, but by creating more goods and services within the nation itself. This is the only permanent solution to poverty in poor nations.

2. Transfers of goods from one person to another do not increase GDP

When a man who has two shirts gives a shirt worth $13 to a man who has none, this is a good deed that genuinely helps the poor man (see Luke 3:11). But it does nothing to increase the GDP. No new product was created, so no new $13 of value was added to the nation's GDP. The shirt was just moved from one person to another.

3. Printing money does not increase GDP

Increasing a nation's production of goods and services is also different from simply printing money, because money itself is not a "product of value." People cannot eat money, or wear, ride, drive, or plant it. They cannot put it over their heads to protect them from the sun and the rain. They can use money to buy other things, of course, but this is because money is a medium of exchange. It is not a product of value in itself.[12]

To understand this difference between printing money and creating goods and services, think back to our example of the woman who sewed a $3 piece of cotton cloth into a shirt worth $13. She increased the GDP of the nation by $10, from $2,000,000,000 to $2,000,000,010.

Now imagine that the government of that poor country suddenly prints an additional 3,000,000,000 "dollars" of paper money (in the currency of that nation). Now what is the total value of all the products and services in that country? It is still only $2,000,000,010. There is more paper money in the nation, but there are no more shirts, shoes, beans, or houses, no more products of value that people can sell or buy and use for themselves. Printing money does not increase the GDP or improve the wealth of a nation. That must be done through producing more goods and services.

Here is another example. Imagine that two hundred people from

---

[12] We are oversimplifying here to make the point. In another sense, money is a "product of value" because it gives to the society a commonly recognized medium of exchange (which saves time over bartering), acts as a store of value, and provides a commonly recognized measure of value and unit of accounting.

a sinking ship find themselves stranded on a fertile but uninhabited island and have to support themselves. They organize themselves, and after a few days, some people are building houses, some are catching fish, some are planting vegetables, some are picking cotton to make into cloth to make clothing, and so forth. They are all producing useful goods and services, so they are increasing the total "GDP" of the island, but they are still cut off from the outside world.

Now imagine that someone salvages a copier and a generator from the crippled ship, prints $100,000 worth of "Lost Island Dollars," then gives $500 of that money to each person so that people can buy and sell their goods and services more easily. Does printing that money make the people of the island any more prosperous? No. It does not give anyone more food, clothing, or shelter. It does not produce any more goods and services. It does not increase the island's GDP.

Of course, the money makes commerce easier than just bartering, and that adds value to the society because it saves people's time and enables them to become more productive, but printing money in itself does not make the island more prosperous in terms of the goods and services the people have. Money is a medium of exchange and a measure of value, but (in this over-simplified example) printing money does not increase the value of the things on the island.

4. How can a nation create more goods and services?

If we keep our focus on the goal of continually producing *more* goods and services, then the question becomes, how can a nation *increase* the total value of the products and services that it produces? For example, how can the woman produce more shirts per week? And how can she produce higher-quality shirts that people value more and pay more to purchase? Many factors contribute to such an increase (such as having a sewing machine, having easy access to markets, having expert training, having a microloan to buy more materials and better equipment, having confidence that she can keep and use her profits, and so forth). We will discuss these factors in detail in subsequent chapters. For now, the important point is to maintain our focus on this single goal: nations can move from poverty to prosperity only by continually creating more goods and services.

D. Examples of nations that have become prosperous by producing more goods and services

Throughout history, countries that have moved from poverty to prosperity have learned how to produce more and more goods and services. Soon they found that they were no longer producing products and services for their own nation only, but also valuable products and services that they could export and sell to people in other countries.

History shows that every nation that is prosperous today has doubled and then redoubled its GDP many times over in past years. Although each nation chose a somewhat different path, they all increased GDP through increasing productivity.

1. Britain: cotton manufacturing and the Industrial Revolution

The primary example of the creation of more goods per person is Britain, the birthplace of the Industrial Revolution (about 1770–1870). British inventors gradually discovered how to make machines that would spin raw cotton into thread and other machines that would weave cotton threads into cotton fabric many times faster and more cheaply than could be done by hand workers, either in Britain or in India.[13]

In cotton, the British found a product for which there was seemingly unlimited demand throughout the world. Prior to the easy availability of cotton cloth, people often wore wool undergarments, which were hard to clean and hardly comfortable, or linen, which was expensive, or no undergarments at all, which was not hygienic. Cotton clothing of all kinds was cooler to wear in warm climates, but even in cooler climates people wanted cotton undergarments as soon as they became available.

Economic historian David S. Landes says:

> The principal product of the new technology that we know as the Industrial Revolution was cheap, washable cotton, and along with it mass-produced soap made of vegetable oils. For the first time, the common man could afford underwear, once known as body linen because that was the washable fabric that the well-to-do wore next

---

[13] David S. Landes, *The Wealth and Poverty of Nations: Why Some Are So Rich and Some So Poor* (New York: W. W. Norton, 1999), 154, 190–94. Landes says cotton was "a commodity of such broad and elastic demand that it could drive an industrial revolution" (154).

to their skin. . . . Personal hygiene changed drastically, so that commoners of the late nineteenth and early twentieth century often lived cleaner than the kings and queens of a century earlier.[14]

By producing immense amounts of cotton and then other desirable products (such as high-quality steel and machinery), England became the world's wealthiest nation. Income per person in England doubled between 1780 and 1860, and then between 1860 and 1990 it multiplied another six times![15]

2. Nations that have grown more prosperous today

Most wealthy nations today have also become more prosperous by finding out how they could continually create more goods and services (this is the primary goal that we recommend in this chapter). For example, Japan, which has no significant natural resources (except fish), improved its relatively poor agricultural economy of the early 1900s to the second-largest economy in the world (by total GDP) for several decades in the late twentieth century (it is third today, after the United States and China). Japan became wealthy by creating many products that were exported to the rest of the world: cars (of better quality than those made in the United States), computers, other electronic equipment such as TVs and sound systems, machine tools, steel, ships, chemicals, and other things.

China transformed itself from a very poor nation even in the late 1970s to the world's second-largest economy. It did this by keeping in mind the goal that we advocate in this chapter: continually creating more goods and services. China has become the world's center for the production of millions of kinds of small manufactured consumer products. It is important to note that this growth happened only after China introduced some significant components of free-market reform into an economy that had been entirely communist, with no private ownership allowed.[16]

Some parts of India have increased their prosperity by providing a

---

[14] Ibid., xviii.
[15] Ibid., 194.
[16] However, there are significant concerns that China's "extractive" political system will not be able to sustain its explosive economic growth for long: see Daron Acemoglu and James A. Robinson, *Why Nations Fail: The Origins of Power, Prosperity and Poverty* (New York: Crown Publishers, 2012), 436–37.

service—telephone help for owners of computers and other electronic goods—that is in demand all over the world. The small country of Taiwan (about the size of Maryland) has few natural resources, but it continually produces valuable goods such as electronics, chemicals, machinery, and textiles. South Korea, which was among the poorest countries in the world in the 1950s, today exports large quantities of semiconductors, wireless phones, cars, computers, steel, ships, and petrochemicals, and is the twelfth-wealthiest country in the world in terms of per capita income.[17]

Malaysia has made significant steps from poverty to prosperity by privatizing some of its banking, media, and automobile companies, and by exporting electronic and information-technology products, as well as many agricultural goods. Even though 40 percent of Thailand's population is engaged in agriculture, it has become a thriving manufacturing sector, producing high-technology products such as integrated circuits. Chile became the wealthiest country in Latin America by privatizing its businesses to create incentives, and then mining copper and producing a wide array of agricultural products, such as grapes, apples, pears, onions, wheat, corn, oats, peaches, garlic, asparagus, and beans, much of it for export to the United States, China, and Japan.

Hong Kong is another remarkable example. Economist Milton Friedman wrote:

> [I]n 1960, the earliest date for which I have been able to get [statistics], the average per capita income in Hong Kong was 28 percent of that in Great Britain; by 1996, it had risen to 137 percent of that in Britain. In short, from 1960 to 1996, Hong Kong's per capita income rose from one-quarter of Britain's to more than a third larger than Britain's. It is easy to state these figures. It is more difficult to realize their significance. Compare Britain—the birthplace of the Industrial Revolution, the nineteenth-century economic superpower on whose empire the sun never set—with Hong Kong, a spit of land, overcrowded, with no resources except for a great harbor. Yet within four decades the residents of this spit of over-crowded land had achieved a level of income one-third higher than that enjoyed by the residents of its former mother country.[18]

---

[17] South Korea is twelfth-wealthiest based on purchasing power parity data for per capita income.
[18] Milton Friedman, "The Hong Kong Experiment," *Hoover Digest*, no. 3 (July 30, 1998), accessed January 3, 2013, http://www.hoover.org/publications/hoover-digest/article/7696.

All of these nations have risen from poverty to increased prosperity through the same process: continually creating more goods and services. These goods and services include both products made for consumption within the nation (food and agricultural products, as well as services, are mostly consumed within a nation) and products produced for export (such as many manufactured goods and some agricultural products).

E. Biblical support for creating more goods and services

At this point, we turn from basic economics to the teachings of the Bible. We will do this at various points throughout this book. The Bible contains significant teachings that encourage the creation of goods and services.

One example is the description of an "excellent wife" in Proverbs 31:10–31: "She makes linen garments and sells them; she delivers sashes to the merchant" (v. 24). She makes valuable products and so increases the GDP of Israel. This woman is productive, for "she seeks wool and flax, and works with willing hands" (v. 13). She produces agricultural products from the earth, because "with the fruit of her hands she plants a vineyard" (v. 16). She sells products in the marketplace, because "she perceives that her merchandise is profitable" (v. 18). (The *Holman Christian Standard Bible* translates this as, "She sees that her profits are good"; this is also a legitimate translation because the Hebrew term *sakar* can refer to profit or gain from merchandise.)

The idea of creating profitable and useful products from the earth began with God's command to Adam and Eve: "Be fruitful and multiply and fill the earth and *subdue it*, and have dominion over the fish of the sea and over the birds of the heavens and over every living thing that moves on the earth" (Gen. 1:28). The Hebrew word translated "subdue" is *kabash*, and it implies that Adam and Eve were to make the resources of the earth useful for their own benefit and enjoyment.

This means that God intended Adam and Eve to explore the earth and learn to create products from the abundant resources that he had put in it. It was God's purpose for Adam and Eve, as they followed this command, to discover and develop agricultural products and domesticated animals, then housing and works of craftsmanship and beauty, and eventually buildings, means of transportation, and inventions of various kinds.[19]

This is the process that ultimately resulted in the creation of computers and cell phones, modern houses and office buildings, and automobiles and airplanes. All of this is what God wanted Adam and Eve and their offspring to produce when he told them to "subdue" the earth.

The idea that Adam and Eve would make useful products from the earth is also implied by the verse that says that God "took the man and put him in the garden of Eden to work it and keep it" (Gen. 2:15). As Adam worked in the garden, and Eve alongside him, they would discover and develop useful products from the earth.

Creating such goods and services from the earth is an activity that is unique to the human race. It is not found in the animal kingdom to any significant degree. Birds build the same kinds of nests they have built for a thousand generations, and rabbits live in the same kinds of dens they have always dug. But God created human beings with a desire to invent and create new goods and services, imitating God's own creative activity.

This ability to create is part of what it means that God made us "in his own image" (Gen. 1:27). He created us to be like him and to imitate him in many ways. That is why Paul can say, "Be imitators of God, as beloved children" (Eph. 5:1). God is pleased when he sees us imitating his creativity by creating goods and services from the resources of the earth.

Therefore, God's ideal for us is not that we live in caves and barely survive on a subsistence diet of nuts and berries, but rather that we discover and develop the abundant resources that he has placed in the earth for our benefit and enjoyment. Paul says that God is the one "who richly provides us with everything to enjoy" (1 Tim. 6:17).

Another reason God is pleased when we create goods and services is Jesus's command, "You shall love your neighbor as yourself" (Matt. 22:39). The woman who creates a shirt that someone wears and appreciates, the man who creates a pair of shoes that someone wears and enjoys, and the teacher who genuinely helps her children learn can do all this with an attitude of love for their neighbors—that is, seek-

---

[19] Darrow L. Miller and Stan Guthrie, *Discipling Nations: The Power of Truth to Transform Cultures* (Seattle: YWAM, 1998), 221–37, have an excellent discussion of the wonder of human creativity as a key part of responsible stewardship in obedience to God.

ing to bring benefit to other people. In this way, creating goods and services for others is one way of obeying Jesus's command to love our neighbor as ourselves.

Jesus himself gave us an example of such productivity, for he worked for about fifteen years as a "carpenter" (Mark 6:3). The apostle Paul worked as a tentmaker and supported himself in that way (Acts 18:3; 2 Thess. 3:7–10). Peter and some of the other disciples worked as fisherman (Matt. 4:18); they did not actually "create" fish (only God can do that), but they caught them from the sea and brought them to a market where they were useful new food products for others to eat.

Paul's epistles also told the early Christians that they should work with their hands, implying that he wanted them to continually create goods and services that were of value to other people:

> Let the thief no longer steal, but rather *let him labor, doing honest work with his own hands,* so that he may have something to share with anyone in need. (Eph. 4:28)

> Aspire to live quietly, and to mind your own affairs, *and to work with your hands,* as we instructed you. (1 Thess. 4:11)

> For even when we were with you, we would give you this command: *If anyone is not willing to work, let him not eat.* (2 Thess. 3:10)

In the new heaven and new earth, it seems that the nations of the earth will continue to produce goods and services for others, perhaps products that are unique to each nation. This would follow a well-established historical pattern whereby the kings of various nations would send abundant products as tribute or as gifts to other nations (see 2 Chron. 9:9, 10, 24, 28). It is said of the new Jerusalem: "the kings of the earth will bring their glory into it. . . . They will bring into it the glory and honor of the nations" (Rev. 21:24–26).

F. What goods and services can your country create?

The challenge for every poor nation is this: What goods and services can it create that other people want? And what can you do to increase your nation's creation of such goods and services? These products include both items wanted by other people inside your nation and products produced for export to other nations.

The correct answer to these questions is not "Nothing." It might be discouraging to look at the wealthy nations of the world and see the complex products that they produce. You might think, "We can never produce better automobiles than Germany or better electronics than Japan," and then give up. Doing nothing is a mistake.

There will always be *something* that each country can make that people within the nation and even people in other countries will want to buy. This is true for two reasons, which we will explain in more detail in the next chapters: (1) The principle of comparative advantage in economics says that no person and no country can make everything, so there will always be something that you can produce that will earn a profit. (2) Human beings have limited needs but they have unlimited wants, so they will always be seeking additional products (see further explanation below, 173–74). There are always some goods or services of value that your country can create profitably.

Most countries realize that the many traditional products (such as arts and crafts) that they have produced and sold through the centuries have not been able to sustain their need for economic growth. Even though people in these countries already know how to make these things, if these traditional products were going to bring the country from poverty to prosperity, they probably would have done so already. Apparently there was not a sufficient demand for these products on the world market. Insufficient demand strongly suggests that you must change what you are doing and pursue other opportunities. It is time to find other products for which people in other countries will pay a good price.

The people of Britain had not "traditionally" worked at weaving machines to produce cotton cloth, because such machines had not previously existed. But they eventually shifted from their traditional occupations and learned to use machines to make a product that was in demand all over the world.

The people of Japan had not "traditionally" worked in automobile manufacturing plants producing high-precision products using modern technology. Many of them had been rural farmers. But they abandoned their traditional occupations and learned to work in automobile factories. The nation began to thrive. The same thing happened with electronics manufacturing in Japan, Taiwan, and elsewhere. The question is not what a country has traditionally made, but what valuable product can it make for the local and world market. A nation must produce what others want if it wants to move from poverty to prosperity.

However, we are *not* saying that government planners should try to decide what products a country should produce. They simply need to create the right conditions for innovation and entrepreneurship to happen in a free-market system. Individual entrepreneurs, operating within the free market, will eventually find successful products once the economic and legal structures in the nation allow them to do it and the cultural values encourage it. We will explain this further in our discussion of the free market, where "no one" decides what is produced (see 163–67).

2

WRONG GOALS

Approaches That Will Not
Lead to Prosperity

Many goals have been set forth as solutions to poverty, as we noted earlier. In order to better show that the goal of continually producing more goods and services is the only route from poverty to prosperity, we will now look more closely at some of these alternative goals and demonstrate how they fail.

A. Dependence on donations from other nations

1. The harmful results of dependence on foreign aid

No poor nation in history has grown wealthy by depending on donations from other nations. Massachusetts Institute of Technology economics professor Daron Acemoglu and Harvard University economist and political scientist James A. Robinson wrote recently in their lengthy study *Why Nations Fail*:

> The idea that rich Western countries should provide large amounts of "developmental aid" in order to solve the problem of poverty in sub-Saharan Africa, the Caribbean, Central America, and South Asia is based on an incorrect understanding of what causes poverty. Countries such as Afghanistan are poor because of their extractive institutions—which result in lack of property rights, law and order, or

well-functioning legal systems and the stifling dominance of national and, more often, local elites over political and economic life. The same institutional problems mean that foreign aid will be ineffective, as it will be plundered and is unlikely to be delivered where it is supposed to go. In the worst-case scenario, it will prop up the regimes that are at the very root of the problems in these societies. . . .

[F]oreign aid is not a very effective means of dealing with the failure of nations around the world today. Far from it. Countries need inclusive economic and political institutions to break out of the cycle of poverty. Foreign aid can typically do little in this respect, and certainly not with the way that it is currently organized.[1]

William Easterly, professor of economics at New York University and a senior research economist at the World Bank for sixteen years, writes about the tragic failure of massive foreign-aid programs:

[In January 2005, Gordon Brown, the United Kingdom's chancellor of the exchequer,] gave a compassionate speech about the tragedy of extreme poverty affecting billions of people. . . . He called for a doubling of foreign aid. . . . Brown was silent about the other tragedy of the world's poor. This is the tragedy in which the West spent $2.3 trillion on foreign aid over the last five decades and still had not managed to get twelve-cent medicines to children to prevent half of all malaria deaths. The West spent $2.3 trillion and still had not managed to get four-dollar bed nets to poor families. The West spent $2.3 trillion and still had not managed to get three dollars to each new mother to prevent five million deaths. The West spent $2.3 trillion, and children are still carrying firewood and not going to school. It's a tragedy that so much well-meaning compassion did not bring these results for needy people.[2]

An Oxford-trained African economist, Dambisa Moyo of Zambia, argues that foreign aid is actually the main cause of continuing poverty in Africa. She explains that aid has prevented Africa from moving toward economic growth:

---

[1] Daron Acemoglu and James A. Robinson, *Why Nations Fail: The Origins of Power, Prosperity and Poverty* (New York: Crown Publishers, 2012), 452–54. We explain what they mean by "inclusive" institutions in a later section (310, note 2).

[2] William Easterly, *The White Man's Burden: Why the West's Efforts to Aid the Rest Have Done So Much Ill and So Little Good* (New York: Penguin, 2006), 4.

But has more than US$1 trillion in development assistance over the last several decades made African people better off? No. In fact across the globe recipients of this aid are worse off; much worse off. Aid has helped make the poor poorer and the growth slower. . . . The notion that aid can alleviate systemic poverty, and has done so, is a myth. Millions in Africa are poorer today because of aid; misery and poverty have not ended but have increased. Aid has been, and continues to be, an unmitigated political, economic and humanitarian disaster for most parts of the developing world.[3]

Moyo goes on to explain that she is not opposed to "humanitarian or emergency aid," which helps people affected by catastrophes, nor is she opposed to "charity-based" aid, which is disbursed by charitable organizations (presumably religious groups and humanitarian agencies). But she is opposed to "aid payments made directly to governments," either through government-to-government transfers or through agencies such as the World Bank.[4] In what she calls "systematic aid," Moyo includes both cash transfers and loans at below-market interest rates, because, she says, "policymakers in poor economies may come to view [these loans] as roughly equivalent to grants." Therefore, she says, "For the purposes of this book, aid is defined as the sum total of both concessional loans and grants."[5]

Moyo then traces the history of aid given to African nations from 1940 to the present and shows why, overall, it has been more harmful than helpful. This is true whether the aid was given to help industrial projects, to alleviate poverty, or to encourage economic "stabilization and adjustment" (with economic reform conditions attached), and whether it was contingent on reform of government corruption, tied to increasing democratic reforms in governments, or was "glamour aid" promoted by famous entertainers and government leaders.[6]

She explains that "one of the underlying problems of aid" is "that it is fungible—that monies set aside for one purpose are easily diverted

---

[3] Dambisa Moyo, *Dead Aid: Why Aid Is Not Working and How There Is a Better Way for Africa* (New York: Farrar, Straus & Giroux, 2009), xix.

[4] Ibid., 7.

[5] Ibid., 8–9.

[6] Moyo traces the history of these kinds of aid on pages 10–28. Similar criticisms are advanced with the support of more detailed research in William Easterly, *The Elusive Quest for Growth: Economists' Adventures and Misadventures in the Tropics* (Cambridge, MA: The MIT Press, 2001), esp. chaps. 2–7.

towards another," often including "private pockets, instead of the public purse." But, she explains, "when this happens, as it so often does,
no real punishments or sanctions are ever imposed. So more grants
mean more graft."[7]

Angus Deaton, the Dwight D. Eisenhower Professor of Economics
and International Affairs at Princeton University, writes:

> The historical record tells us that it is possible to grow and eliminate
> poverty without foreign aid; all of the now-rich countries did so. We
> also know that some of the most successful poor countries, such as
> India and China, grew with very little aid relative to their size, or with
> aid that was dictated by their own priorities rather than donors'. . . .
> *Aid as we have known it has not helped countries to grow.*[8]

Likewise, economist James Peron writes:

> For almost half a century the countries of Africa have been awash in
> aid. Hundreds of billions of dollars have been given to African govern-
> ments. More billions were lent to these same governments. Countless
> tons of food have inundated the continent, and swarms of consultants,
> experts, and administrators have descended to solve Africa's problems.
> Yet the state of development in Africa is no better today than it was
> when all this started. Per capita income for most of Africa is either
> stagnant or declining. . . .
>
> A World Bank report admitted that 75 percent of their African
> agricultural projects were failures. . . .
>
> The Marxist dictatorship of Ethiopia's Mengistu Haile Mariam
> was a major recipient of donor funds. . . . Relief aid was intentionally
> kept away from some of the most severely affected areas because it
> suited Mengistu's regime to starve its opponents. . . . President Mobotu
> of Zaire managed to build a fortune in his Swiss bank account that
> was estimated as high as $10 billion. . . . Marxist autocratic regimes
> were often heavily financed by European governments. . . . The Ital-
> ian Socialist Party gave heavy financial backing to Somalia's Marxist
> government of warlord Said Barre. . . . *The New York Times* reported that
> when President Julius Nyerere of Tanzania announced a radical Marx-
> ist program, "many Western aid donors, particularly in Scandinavia,

---

[7] Moyo, *Dead Aid*, 46.
[8] Angus Deaton, writing in Abhijit Vinayak Banerjee et al., *Making Aid Work* (Cambridge, MA: The MIT Press, 2007), 56–57, emphasis added.

gave enthusiastic backing to this socialist experiment, pouring an esti-mated $10 billion into Tanzania over 20 years". . . . The Marxist regime of Samora Machel in Mozambique similarly destroyed that country's agricultural output through price controls. . . . The continent itself is rich in resources, but the incentive to produce has been destroyed by government policies.[9]

However, economist Paul Collier, while recognizing that much aid is harmful and fails to reach its goal, still thinks that in very limited situations aid is necessary and can sometimes be helpful.[10] He specifies that such aid should be given not to the already-developing countries that receive most foreign aid today, but to the countries in which the absolute poorest people of the world ("the bottom billion") reside, and that it must be given with very well defined restrictions and much more effective supervision.

Collier also recognizes that in some situations foreign aid can make a military coup more likely and can actually detract from necessary reforms that have to be made in a nation.[11] Even then, Collier does not see aid as the primary means by which poor nations can emerge from poverty, but rather as a necessary help for particularly dire situations.

2. The reasons foreign aid is harmful

Why is aid so harmful? Moyo explains that foreign aid props up cor-rupt governments—providing them with freely usable cash:

> These corrupt governments interfere with the rule of law, the es-tablishment of transparent civil institutions and the protection of civil liberties, making both domestic and foreign investment in poor countries unattractive. Greater opacity and fewer investments reduce economic growth, which leads to fewer job opportunities and in-creasing poverty levels. In response to growing poverty, donors give more aid, which continues the downward spiral of poverty. This is the vicious cycle of aid. The cycle that chokes off desperately needed investment, instills a culture of dependency, and facilitates rampant

---

[9] James Peron, "The Sorry Record of Foreign Aid in Africa," in *The Freeman*, 51, no. 8 (August 2001), ac-cessed August 28, 2012, www.thefreemanonline.org/features/the-sorry-record-of-foreign-aid-in-africa/.
[10] See Paul Collier, *The Bottom Billion: Why the Poorest Countries Are Failing and What Can Be Done About It* (Oxford: Oxford University Press, 2007), 99–123.
[11] Ibid., 104–5, 116.

and systematic corruption. . . . [It] perpetuates underdevelopment and guarantees economic failure in the poorest aid-dependent countries.[12]

Moyo adds, "Aid supports rent-seeking—that is the use of governmental authority to take and make money without greater production of wealth."[13] She quotes Rwandan President Paul Kagame, who explains, "Much of this aid was spent on creating and sustaining client regimes of one type or another, with minimal regard to developmental outcomes on our continent."[14]

Why, then, do Western governments continue to give aid to poor countries? Moyo calculates that in the world today there are around five hundred thousand people who work for aid agencies, and "they are all in the business of aid . . . 7 days a week, 52 weeks a year, and decade after decade. Their livelihood depends on aid, just as those of the officials who take it. For most developmental organizations, successful lending is measured almost entirely by the size of the donor's lending portfolio."[15]

Ruth Levine, senior fellow at the Center for Global Development, writes about "a hard truth":

> There is a lack of rigorous impact evaluation in foreign aid. We collectively lack the will to learn systematically from experience about what works in development programs. . . . The rewards for institutions and for individual professionals within them come from doing, not from building evidence or learning. . . . There are, frankly, disincentives to finding out the truth. . . . The temptation to avoid impact evaluation and concentrate instead on producing and disseminating anecdotal success stories is high. The aversion to recognizing unfavorable results is woven into the fabric of most bureaucracies.[16]

Abhijit Banerjee agrees: "The community of aid giving (and using) has shown no great empathy for evidence."[17]

Ian Vásquez, director of the Cato Institute's Center for Global Lib-

---

[12] Moyo, *Dead Aid*, 49.
[13] Ibid., 52.
[14] Ibid., 27.
[15] Ibid., 54.
[16] Ruth Levine, writing in Banerjee et al., *Making Aid Work*, 105–9.
[17] Banerjee, writing in ibid., 114.

erty and Prosperity, has little hope for change: "Is more money really going to improve the discouraging record of aid conditioned on policy change when a major problem (well recognized by borrowers) continues to be the aid agencies' institutional urge to lend?"[18]

Moyo also writes that "foreign aid foments conflict. The prospect of seizing power and gaining access to unlimited aid, well, is irresistible. . . . The underlying purpose of rebellion is the capture of the state for financial advantage," and "aid makes such conflict more likely."[19] She explains that many of the civil wars in Africa in recent decades have been basically conflicts over control of large amounts of aid money coming from other countries.

In addition, little of this aid really helps the poor. Acemoglu and Robinson say:

> Many studies estimate that only about 10 or at the most 20 percent of aid ever reaches its target. . . . Throughout the last five decades, hundreds of billions of dollars have been paid to governments around the world as "development" aid. Much of it has been wasted in overhead and corruption. . . . Worse, a lot of it went to dictators such as Mobutu.[20]

Moyo recognizes that someone might object by saying that some aid has been successful, such as the Marshall Plan from 1948 to 1952, which was instrumental in rebuilding Western Europe after World War II. But this was not economic development of a poor country. Germany (like other Western European countries) had been a wealthy nation with a developed economic infrastructure, legal traditions and systems, and immense human capital (skilled workers) before it was destroyed by the war. It just needed a massive infusion of cash to repair the destruction and get back to its previous condition.[21]

---

[18] Ian Vásquez, writing in ibid., 52.

[19] Moyo, Dead Aid, 59.

[20] Acemoglu and Robinson, Why Nations Fail, 452. They add, however, that if 10 percent of aid reaches the poor, "it might still be better than nothing" (ibid., 454). "Mobutu" is Mobutu Sese Seko, who was president of the Democratic Republic of the Congo (formerly Zaire) from 1965 to 1997, and is thought to have embezzled more than $5 billion from the country; see The Guardian (UK), March 26, 2004, accessed October 12, 2012, http://www.guardian.co.uk/world/2004/mar/26/indonesia.philippines. This article reported, "By the time he was overthrown in 1997, Mobutu had stolen almost half of the $12bn in aid money that Zaire—now the Democratic Republic of Congo—received from the IMF during his 32-year reign, leaving his country saddled with a crippling debt."

[21] Moyo, Dead Aid, 35–37.

3. Biblical teaching about dependence on donations from others

From the standpoint of the Bible, it is not surprising that nations cannot become prosperous by means of aid from other countries. Dependence on donations is not God's ideal for human life on the earth. God's purpose from the beginning has been for human beings to work and create their own goods and services, not simply to receive donations.

God put Adam and Eve in the garden of Eden and told them to work and develop it: "Be fruitful and multiply and fill the earth and subdue it and have dominion" (Gen. 1:28). Then we read, "The LORD God took the man and put him in the Garden of Eden *to work it* and keep it" (2:15).

In the history of Israel, when God promised multiple economic blessings to his people, it was clear that these blessings would not come to inactive Israelites simply living off donations from other people; instead, they would be blessed when their work brought fruitful results:

> For the LORD your God is bringing you into a good land, a land of brooks of water, of fountains and springs, flowing out in the valleys and hills, a land of wheat and barley, of vines and fig trees and pomegranates, a land of olive trees and honey, a land in which you will eat bread without scarcity, in which you will lack nothing, a land whose stones are iron, and out of whose hills you can dig copper. And you shall eat and be full, and you shall bless the LORD your God for the good land he has given you. (Deut. 8:7–10)

The Israelites would have to harvest the wheat and the barley; they would have to tend and pick the vines and the fig trees; they would have to bake the bread; and they would have to dig copper out of the ground to make tools and implements. God's blessing came through *productive work that created new goods and services*. It did not come by dependence on donations.

Far from being the continual recipients of donations from other countries, the people of Israel were to be lenders: "You shall lend to many nations, but you shall not borrow" (Deut. 15:6). (Note the similar blessings that were promised for the people's work in Deut. 28:6, 11–12).

Even the poor people in Israel were not to become dependent on donations from others, for they had to *work* to gather their food from the "gleanings" that were left in the fields after the first harvesting (see Deut. 24:19–22).

Another provision for the poor in Israel was that others were to lend to them without charging interest (see Ex. 22:25; Lev. 25:37; Deut. 23:19; Prov. 28:8; Neh. 5:7–10). But the fact that God spoke of a *loan* (even one without interest) assumed that it would be repaid, not that the recipient would depend on donations year after year.[22]

Still another solution for poverty was the provision that a poor person could become an indentured servant to a wealthier person for a specified period of time, after which his debts would be considered repaid and he would obtain his freedom (Lev. 25:39–43; Deut. 15:12–18; compare the story of Jacob serving Laban in Gen. 29:18–27). Indentured servants automatically had their debts paid off in the seventh year of their servitude (see Deut. 15:12–15) or in the Year of Jubilee (Lev. 25:28, 40).

The important point is this: there is no thought in the Bible that poor people would become permanent recipients of gifts of money, ~~missionaries?~~ year after year, or would become dependent on such gifts. The only exceptions were people who were completely unable to work due to permanent disabilities, such as a blind beggar (Mark 10:46; Luke 18:35) or a lame beggar (Acts 3:2–10).[23]

In the New Testament, Paul rebuked those who were "idle" (1 Thess. 5:14; 2 Thess. 3:7), stipulating, "If anyone is not willing to work, let him not eat" (2 Thess. 3:10).

The Bible's expectations that people must work to earn their living should not be seen as harsh or unkind. The fact that God gave Adam and Eve work to do before there was sin in the world (see Gen. 1:28; 2:15) indicates that we should see work as a *blessing*, a valuable gift from God. Although God has now added a dimension of pain and difficulty to our work because of the sin of Adam (see Gen. 3:17–19), the ability to work and create useful goods and services is still seen as a positive gift

---

[22] However, see Deut. 15:1–3 for debt payments that were temporarily suspended every seven years. For a discussion of this passage, see E. Calvin Beisner, *Prosperity and Poverty* (Westchester, IL: Crossway, 1988), 58–62, arguing that the release from payments was temporary, for that year only, and not a permanent cancellation, as in the Year of Jubilee.

[23] Modern technology even allows many physically disabled people to provide for themselves through information-processing work or intellectual creativity. One example is Stephen Hawking, a renowned physicist who is almost completely paralyzed and communicates by means of speech-generating technology.

throughout the rest of the Bible and something that God commands his people to do for their good (see Ex. 20:9; Eph. 4:28).

4. "Earned success" is more important than money

The importance of productive work for all human beings was emphasized in a recent book by Arthur C. Brooks, former professor of business and government policy at Syracuse University. As a result of his extensive studies of causes of human satisfaction in life, Brooks argues that the primary economic factor that makes people happy is not money but what he calls "earned success," that is, having a specific responsibility and then doing good work to fulfill that responsibility. Brooks writes, "The secret to human flourishing is not money but earned success in life."[24] He explains:

> Earned success means the ability to create value honestly—not by winning the lottery, not by inheriting a fortune, not by picking up a welfare check. It doesn't even mean making money itself. Earned success is the creation of value in our lives or in the lives of others.[25]

One example of this that I (Wayne Grudem) know of involved a recent student of mine at Phoenix Seminary. He was an outstanding student, getting straight As in his classes. He worked for me for two years and was highly responsible in every task. He had a stable marriage, and I expect him to do very well in his career.

When I got to know him, I found that several years prior to this his life had been going entirely downhill. He had a history of crime and substance abuse, and had spent time in jail for drug dealing. But after he got out of jail, he got a job at a Wendy's fast-food restaurant. One day his manager told him, "You're doing a good job of keeping the french fries hot."

He remembers that remark as a turning point in his life. Suddenly he realized that he was able to do something well. He had experienced a touch of the joy of "earned success." He began to think that if he worked hard he might eventually become a shift manager, or even the

---

[24] Arthur C. Brooks, *The Battle: How the Fight between Free Enterprise and Big Government Will Shape America's Future* (New York: Basic Books, 2010), 71.
[25] Ibid., 75.

manager of the restaurant itself. It was not money that gave him this happiness and sense of satisfaction, but rather "earned success."

It is not surprising that God created us with the ability to create goods and services, and commanded us to work in order to do this. And it is not surprising that he also created us so that we would have a great sense of happiness when we followed his plan, worked to create goods and services, and then achieved earned success.

This reinforces the importance of the primary goal: a poor nation should not focus on trying to gain more aid from other countries, but on how it can produce more goods and services, and therefore have a higher GDP.

B. Redistribution of wealth from the rich to the poor

Several Christian writers who are concerned for the poor have emphasized "reducing inequalities" between the rich and the poor. Their solution has been to work for greater "equality" because "God hates inequality." This equality can be promoted, we are told, by "more just" policies that take more from the rich and give more to the poor.

"Taking from the rich" may simply refer to rich countries giving more development aid to poor countries. We discussed the futility of that approach in the previous section. It does not solve the problem of poverty.

But this drive for more equality may refer to governments levying heavy taxes on the rich and giving much of that money to the poor *within* poor countries. That approach needs careful analysis. What would happen? It depends on the individual nation.

1. In some nations, people are rich because of abuse of government power

There is a small group of wealthy people within every poor country on earth. The ways in which these wealthy people came to be wealthy vary from country to country.

In communist countries, such as Cuba and North Korea (or in Russia, which still has many vestiges of communism), a few people are "wealthy" in terms of much better housing, cars, shopping privileges at restricted stores, travel and vacation privileges, and other protections and benefits. They receive these privileges because they have high offices in government.

Likewise, in many African nations, the wealthy people are those who have high government positions and have helped themselves to money from the public treasury, sometimes amassing huge fortunes that they have used to buy homes overseas or stored in Swiss bank accounts. Sometimes it seems to people in the country that most of the wealthy people are liars, thieves, extortionists, and even murderers.

In many oil-rich Arab countries, the ruling families and their friends have access to vast amounts of oil wealth that they spend on vacations, yachts, airplanes, luxury cars, and palatial homes.

In some Latin American countries, a few wealthy families have amassed vast amounts of land, money, and power with the help of special privileges and restrictive laws made by friendly government officials. In some cases, their wealth has come from the drug trade, theft, bribery, and extortion. These few wealthy families typically own nearly all the land, have government-protected monopolies for the products of their companies, and habitually violate the law while knowing that they will never be convicted by their friends, who are the powerful judges. These families might own the only businesses that receive huge government contracts. If this situation does not change, ordinary poor citizens have no hope. They will never be able to own land, license a competitive business, get a fair trial in the courts, have their contracts enforced, or win a government contract. Sometimes this system is called "crony capitalism" or "oligarchic capitalism."[26]

In all of these cases, there are significant *structural evils* in the ways the governments function. These evils must be addressed before such countries can emerge from poverty. (We will address such changes in detail in subsequent chapters, especially the chapters on the freedoms of the system and the government of the system.) In addition, those who have profited from criminal activity must be prosecuted and punished for their crimes.

---

[26]See William J. Baumol, Robert E. Litan, and Carl J. Schramm, *Good Capitalism, Bad Capitalism, and the Economics of Growth and Prosperity* (New Haven: Yale University Press, 2007), 71–79, for a discussion of what they call "oligarchic capitalism." They say that in these societies, "Economic growth is not a central objective of the government, whose main goal is instead to maintain and enhance the position of the oligarchic few (including government leaders themselves) who own most of the country's resources" (ibid., 71).

However, the solution to these structural evils is not simply to "take from the rich and give to the poor." To do that is to address a *symptom* of the problem rather than the *cause*. The cause of the problem is not inequality in wealth in the nation; rather, it is the selective use of government power to protect only the wealthy few and effectively prevent others from increasing their own prosperity through hard work and thrift.

The reason that merely redistributing wealth from the rich to the poor does not solve the problem of poverty is that it does not achieve the primary goal: becoming a nation that continually creates more goods and services. Redistributing wealth in itself does not create new goods and services in a nation.

Imagine that the total value of all the goods in a nation (all the houses, cars, clothing, trucks, tractors, buildings, livestock, and money) is $3 billion on January 1, and the rich have almost all that wealth and the poor have almost nothing. Now suppose that on January 2 the government takes half of the wealth of the rich people and distributes it among the poor people of the country. The total value of all the goods in the country on January 2 is still $3 billion, because no new product of value has been produced.

Of course, the poor people are able to buy better food and clothing for a while, and perhaps even able to buy cars or small houses. But if the governmental system that trapped them in poverty in the first place is not corrected, the food soon is eaten, the new clothes worn out, the cars broken down, and there will be no permanent solution. This is because the goal of continually producing more goods and services is forgotten in this "solution." Once again, this approach attacks only a symptom, not the cause.

2. In other nations, people are rich because they have rightfully worked and earned more money

We definitely believe that all governments, to the extent that they are able, should provide a "safety net" so that no one in the nation lacks food, clothing, and shelter. Such a provision should come from the general tax revenue of the nation, so that everyone who pays taxes contributes to this general social good. The Bible says that part of a ruler's responsibility is to show "mercy to the oppressed" (Dan. 4:27) and to serve the people as "God's servant for [their] good" (Rom. 13:4). This is the idea behind the gleaning law in Deuteronomy 24:19–22. It is part of caring for "the fatherless" for whom God cares, but who have no one to provide for and protect them (Deut. 10:18; 14:29; 24:17; Ps. 82:3).

On the other hand, the Bible does not support the idea that governments should forcibly take from the rich simply because they are rich and give to the poor (beyond basic needs) simply because they are poor. In fact, the laws that God gave to Israel specified that government officials (such as judges) were not to show favoritism either to the rich or to the poor, but were simply to enforce the law fairly: "Nor shall you be *partial to a poor man* in his lawsuit. . . . You shall not *pervert the justice due to your poor* in his lawsuit" (Ex. 23:3, 6; see also Deut. 16:19–20). Similarly: "You shall do no injustice in court. You shall not be partial to the poor or defer to the great, but in righteousness shall you judge your neighbor" (Lev. 19:15).[27]

In the New Testament, the role of government is never said to be one of equalizing differences between rich and poor. Rather, the government "is to punish those who do *evil* and to praise those who do *good*" (1 Peter 2:14). The government is to punish only those who "do wrong" (Rom. 13:4), whether they are rich, poor, or in between.

Taking from the rich simply because they are rich penalizes both rich people who have broken the law and rich people who have *not* broken the law. This is unjust, because it commits an injustice against those who have legally and justly earned their money: "To impose a fine on a righteous man is not good, nor to strike the noble for their uprightness" (Prov. 17:26).

Jay Richards sees an analogy between poverty and illness:

> We rightly see poverty as a problem, just as disease is a problem. But the problem isn't that some people are rich and some are poor, any more than the problem of disease is that some people are healthy. The problem is quite simply that some people are poor. . . . If we really want to help the poor, we need to get our eyes off decoys and

---

[27] For further discussion, see Wayne Grudem, *Politics—According to the Bible* (Grand Rapids: Zondervan, 2010), 278–84.

focus on the real problem—*poverty*—and its only known solution: creating wealth.[28]

Nowhere does the Bible teach that it is the responsibility of the government to attempt to *equalize* incomes between the rich and the poor. That is not a legitimate purpose of government, according to the Bible.

No nation should focus on overcoming poverty and gaining wealth by forcibly redistributing wealth from the rich to the poor. The goal must be production, not redistribution. The nation must continually produce more goods and services so as to increase its GDP.

C. Depletion of natural resources

David S. Landes explains the fatal mistake that Spain made in the mid-1500s by placing all of its hopes of fortune on the gold that it could find and extract from the New World, especially from Central America. Soon after Christopher Columbus brought news of the discovery of America in 1492, Spanish expeditions began to explore the New World, looking for gold. "For a quarter of a century the Spanish sailed about the Caribbean. . . . And always they asked after gold."[29]

Finally, in 1519, Hernando Cortez conquered the Aztec Empire in Mexico, and the Spanish had found the gold they longed for. Then, in 1532–1539, Francisco Pizarro captured the Incan Empire in Peru, and again the conquerors found fabulous amounts of gold that could be taken back to Spain.

But what was the result of this fabulous wealth? Landes writes, "In retrospect the Spanish passion for gold was a big mistake."[30] He explains: "The wealth of the Indies went less and less to Spanish industry because the Spanish did not have to make things anymore; they could buy them. . . . Nor did the American treasure go to Spanish agriculture; Spain could buy food."[31]

The increasingly wealthy people of Spain hardly had to make anything or learn to earn a living anymore. There was no need to train

---

[28] Jay W. Richards, *Money, Greed, and God: Why Capitalism Is the Solution and Not the Problem* (New York: HarperOne, 2009), 110.
[29] David S. Landes, *The Wealth and Poverty of Nations: Why Some Are So Rich and Some So Poor* (New York: W. W. Norton, 1999), 101.
[30] Ibid., 114.
[31] Ibid., 172.

skilled craftsmen, because the wealthy could buy the best of goods made by the best craftsmen in any other nation. People failed to learn good work habits because they hardly needed to work. Fewer and fewer Spaniards travelled abroad to build and establish businesses because they had no need to trouble themselves with such work, and therefore these skills were lost for succeeding generations.

The result was tragic. Although Spain was the wealthiest and most powerful nation on the earth in the sixteenth century, its wealth was not destined to last. Landes explains:

> Spain . . . became (stayed) poor because it had too much money. The nations that did the work learned and kept good habits, while seeking new ways to do the job faster and better. The Spanish, on the other hand, indulged their penchant for status, leisure, and enjoyment. . . . By the time the great bullion inflow had ended in the mid-seventeenth century, the Spanish Crown was deep in debt. . . . The country entered upon a long decline. Reading this story, one might draw a moral: Easy money is bad for you. It represents short-run gain that will be paid for in immediate distortions and later regrets.[32]

Landes notes a modern parallel in Middle Eastern nations that have gotten easy wealth from oil. He says:

> The best comparison is with sixteenth- and seventeenth-century Spain, cursed by easy riches and led down the path of self-indulgence and laziness. So with the oil-rich. . . . These countries simply haven't developed an advanced economy. Like the Spain of yesteryear, they've purchased the skills and services of others rather than learn to do things for themselves.[33]

Landes sees a similar situation in the early days of independence for many Latin American nations (the early nineteenth century, for the most part). He says that many of the key sectors of the economies of these new nations were dependent on commodities, such as silver, copper, and forestry products, but "Little was done for industry, and little in industry was done. . . . So the nations of South America re-

---

[32] Ibid., 173.
[33] Ibid., 408–9. To this observation we would add a word of counsel from the Bible: "Wealth gained hastily will dwindle, but whoever gathers little by little will increase it" (Prov. 13:11).

mained, after independence as before, economic dependencies of the advanced industrial nations."[34]

William Bernstein agrees:

> There may well be an inverse correlation between wealth and natural endowment. Cast your gaze upon the Hapsburg Empire, as well as modern Nigeria, Saudi Arabia, and Zaire, and it is difficult not to conclude that abundant natural resources are a curse. The production of wealth from commercial enterprise born of risk taking and sweat encourages healthy governmental institutions and begets further wealth. The production of wealth from a limited number of holes in the ground, owned or controlled by the government, begets rent seeking and corruption.[35]

Of course, resource wealth can be used wisely.[36] For example, Norway, for the most part, has managed its vast oil reserves well.[37] Norway has high levels of literacy, excellent elementary and secondary schools, clearly titled lands, protected property rights, and a culture of hard work and frugality. With all of these positive factors, Norway has a very high per capita income ($54,200).

Another positive example is Botswana. According to Acemoglu and Robinson:

> At independence, Botswana was one of the poorest countries in the world; it had a total of twelve kilometers of paved road, twenty-two citizens who had graduated from university, and one hundred from secondary school . . . yet over the next forty-five years, Botswana would become one of the fastest growing countries in the world.[38]

Yes, Botswana's discovery of diamond mines helped, but that was only part of the story:

> Inclusive economic and political institutions [were set up] after independence. Since then, it has been democratic, holds regular and

---

[34] Ibid., 314.
[35] William J. Bernstein, *The Birth of Plenty: How the Prosperity of the Modern World was Created* (New York: McGraw-Hill, 2004), 289–90.
[36] Collier, *The Bottom Billion*, 140–146, suggests some rules that could go into an "international charter" by which wealthy nations would adhere to certain principles of clarity and accountability when they export resources from poor nations (or from any nation).
[37] "From Hero to Knave," *The Economist*, August 25–31, 2012, 40, accessed January 3, 2013, www.economist.com/node/21560872.
[38] Acemoglu and Robinson, *Why Nations Fail*, 409.

competitive elections, and has never experienced civil war or military intervention. The government set up economic institutions enforcing property rights, ensuring macroeconomic stability, and encouraging the development of an inclusive market economy.[39]

Before the discovery of the diamond mine was announced, King Khama instituted a change in law so that all subsoil mineral rights were vested in the nation, not the tribe. This ensured that diamond wealth would not create great inequalities in Botswana.[40]

Resource wealth, therefore, can help an economy, but it is dangerous. It can take a country's eyes off the primary goal that must be kept in mind: the continual creation of more goods and services, more products of value. If resource wealth helps achieve that goal, then it is beneficial. But if it distracts a nation from that goal, and if it causes the people to see no need to develop crucial skills and work habits, when the resources eventually run out or are no longer in demand, poverty looms on the horizon and the citizens increasingly focus on the non-productive task of fighting over control of a diminished resource base.

No nation should focus its hope of overcoming poverty on depleting natural resources. The goal must be to become a nation that continually creates more goods than just extracted resources, and more services as well.

D. Blaming poverty on outside factors or entities

Sometimes people think that poor nations are poor because of things done by outside factors and entities, such as colonialism, large banks, large corporations, rich nations, or the world economic system. The basic problem with blaming poverty on such outside factors is that it does nothing to solve the problem. It does not help to create new goods and services within a poor country. Blaming outside factors or entities is looking backward, not forward.

Even if some of this blame is well placed (and we agree that it is; see below), the question still remains: What can be done now? What is the solution going forward?

---

[39] Ibid., 410.
[40] Ibid., 412.

In addition, this question must be answered: Are factors or entities from *outside* a poor nation really responsible for poverty *within* that nation? In subsequent chapters of this book, we will discover at least seventy factors *within* poor nations that determine whether they remain in poverty or grow in prosperity year after year. Our argument in this book is that these internal factors in poor nations are the primary causes of remaining poverty. Therefore, even if external factors or entities have had *some* negative effect in poor nations, they are still secondary causes of poverty today, not the primary causes. We will attempt to demonstrate this point in the following sections.

However, there is one outside factor that can impoverish a country. When one nation conquers and oppresses another, reducing it to poverty and virtual slavery, this is the primary cause of poverty in that nation. This happened to the people of Israel when the Philistine armies subdued and enslaved them again and again:

> The people of Israel did what was evil in the sight of the LORD, and the LORD gave them into the hand of Midian seven years. And the hand of Midian overpowered Israel, and because of Midian the people of Israel made for themselves the dens that are in the mountains and the caves and the strongholds. For whenever the Israelites planted crops, the Midianites and the Amalekites and the people of the East would come up against them. They would encamp against them and devour the produce of the land, as far as Gaza, and leave no sustenance in Israel and no sheep or ox or donkey. (Judg. 6:1–4)

A similar tragic oppression was suffered by the countries of Eastern Europe after World War II, when they came under the enslaving domination of the former Soviet Union and remained trapped in poverty while Western Europe experienced great economic prosperity.

In such cases, poverty is rightly blamed on an outside entity—that is, on the oppressing nation. Nations impoverished by conquest can emerge from poverty only by somehow being delivered from their oppressors.

But what about the other factors and entities mentioned above as causes of poverty in poor nations? We can now examine them one at a time: colonialism, banks that lend money to poor countries, the world economic system and international terms of trade, and rich nations and multinational corporations.

1. Colonialism

During the sixteenth to twentieth centuries, a few powerful European nations ruled other countries (in Africa, Southeast Asia, and Latin America) as dependent "colonies." The main countries that engaged in colonization were France, the Netherlands, Britain, Spain, Portugal, Germany, and Belgium.

Did these countries merely plunder the wealth of their colonies and so impoverish them? Should we think that such colonialism was a major cause of the poverty that remains in these nations today, sometimes more than a hundred years after they gained independence? (Colonialism is also sometimes called "imperialism" because it built "empires" for European nations.)

Not surprisingly, colonialism was disliked everywhere it had influence. In Africa especially, colonialists were seen as occupiers and looters of natural resources. The anti-colonialists believed that colonialism represented a system of economic plunder, and that it was racist and exploitive.

Academic studies of the effects of colonialism have reached widely varying conclusions. We will mention first some studies that are more positive, then others that are more negative. All parties seem to agree that while the history is complex, the results varied according to the specific policies of the different European nations.

Landes, the Harvard economic historian, says that some former colonies have prospered economically, such as Canada, the United States, Singapore, and Hong Kong (former British colonies); Finland (a former part of the Russian Empire); and Norway (formerly under Sweden). He also notes that (South) Korea and Taiwan, which are now prosperous, were once colonies of Japan.[41]

Landes concludes that around the world, colonies experienced suffering, but he also points to gains:

> Almost all imperialisms have brought material and psychological suffering for the subject people; but also material gains, direct and indirect, intended and not. Some of these gains flowed from opening and trade. . . . The colonials typically built useful things—roads,

---

[41] Landes, *Wealth and Poverty*, 436–37.

railroads, port facilities, buildings, water supply, waste disposal units, and the like. . . .

Would more of these facilities have been built if these countries had been free? Under the pre-colonial regimes, unlikely. . . . Worse, successor regimes have allowed the colonial legacy to deteriorate. The great exceptions have been the postcolonial societies of East and Southeast Asia: South Korea, Taiwan, Singapore.[42]

Colonial powers varied in their effects on colonies, largely because they varied in how they related to the colonies and in the cultural influences they brought to them. In this regard, Landes writes:

Some imperial nations were better rulers than others and their colonies did better after independence. This criterion would have the Spanish and Portuguese bad, the Dutch and French less bad, and the British least bad because of their willingness and ability to invest in social overhead (railways in India, for example) and their reliance on local elites to administer in their name. In 1900, India had thirty-five times the railway mileage of nominally independent China—a salute to Britain's sense of imperium and duty.[43]

Britain's two centuries of rule in India included several beneficial and enduring consequences. The nationwide spread of the English language no doubt enhanced the communication between the hundreds of castes and tribes of differing languages. The British also left behind a workable education system and a system of laws and contracts, giving India both rule of law and the idea of protected property rights. The extensive infrastructure of roads, railways, ports, schools, hospitals, and other large developments all came about because of British influence.

Even Indian Prime Minister Manmohan Singh recalled some of the benefits of British colonialism in a speech at Oxford University in the early twenty-first century:

Today, with the balance and perspective offered by the passage of time and the benefit of hindsight, it is possible for an Indian Prime Minister to assert that India's experience with Britain had beneficial

---

[42] Ibid., 434–35.
[43] Ibid., 437.

consequences too. Our notions of the rule of law, of a Constitutional government, of a free press, of a progressive civil service, of modern universities and research laboratories have all been fashioned in the crucible where an age old civilization met the dominant Empire of the day.[44]

Here is Niall Ferguson's recent description of colonialism:

Each European power had its own distinctive way of scrambling for Africa. The French favored railways and health centers. The British did more than just dig for gold and hunt for happy valleys; they also built mission schools. The Belgians turned the Congo into a vast slave state. The Portuguese did as little as possible. The Germans were the latecomers to the party. For them, colonizing Africa was a giant experiment to test, among other things, a racial theory. According to the theory of "Social Darwinism," Africans were biologically inferior. . . . The British and the French had a point of abolishing slavery in the colonies during the nineteenth century. The Germans did not.[45]

One of the twentieth century's widely-respected experts on the economic consequences of colonialism was P. T. Bauer, economics professor at the London School of Economics. His summary of the impact of British colonial rule in Africa shows both positive and negative results. He summarizes the positive results as follows:

Before colonial rule, conditions in the Gold Coast [in West Africa] were extremely primitive and life was short and perilous. People's circumstances improved out of all recognition during the colonial period. . . . In the Gold Coast, there were about 3,000 children at school in the early 1900s, whereas in the mid-1950s there were over half a million. In the early 1890s there were in the Gold Coast no railways or roads, but only a few jungle paths. Transport of goods was by human porterage or canoe. By the 1930s there were railways and wood roads; journeys by road required fewer hours than they had required days in 1890. In British West Africa public security and health improved out of all recognition over the period. Peaceful travel became possible;

---

[44] Prime Minister Dr. Manmohan Singh at Oxford University, July 8, 2005, in a speech given on acceptance of an honorary degree. A transcript of this talk appeared in *The Hindu*, the online edition of India's national newspaper, http://www.hindu.com/nic/0046/pmspeech.htm.
[45] Niall Ferguson, *Civilization: The West and the Rest* (New York: Penguin, 2011), 176–177.

slavery, slave trading and famine were practically eliminated, and the incidence of the worst diseases greatly reduced.[46]

Bauer also recognizes negative consequences: "Colonial conquest was usually attended by bloodshed."[47] And Bauer also acknowledges at least one terribly destructive export that the British brought to Africa: the socialist idea that the government should control the economy of a nation. For example, governments began to adopt measures for "state monopoly of export of all major crops."[48] This meant that African governments could pay local farmers "far less than world market prices" for their agricultural goods, then sell them at high prices on world markets, and pocket the difference for themselves.[49]

Bauer attributes this exportation of socialist ideas to the popularity of socialist theories among British government officials in the 1930s and 1940s:

> The emergence and spread of the belief that state control of economic life was desirable on social, political and economic grounds was a major factor behind the burgeoning of controls. The most influential British civil servants in charge of African affairs in the 1930s and 1940s shared this belief. They also welcomed policies which enhanced their power and status. By restricting competition the measures often benefitted influential private interests, both expatriate and African. . . .
>
> The principal effects of state economic control are familiar . . . they politicize life and provoke tension. They restrict the movement of people, ideas, commodities and financial resources. They curtail the volume and diversity of external contacts, and inhibit productive capital formation and obstruct both economic change and the effective deployment of human, financial and physical resources. They divorce economic activity from consumer demand. . . . Their operation confers monopolistic or windfall profits and benefits on some people and inflicts losses on others. . . . Much of the cost falls on farmers who are discouraged from producing for the market when their terms of trade deteriorate. . . . They may . . . revert to subsistence production.[50]

---

[46] P. T. Bauer, *Equality, the Third World, and Economic Delusion* (Cambridge, MA: Harvard University Press, 1981), 163–65.
[47] Ibid., 170.
[48] Ibid., 173.
[49] Ibid., 179; Bauer discusses state export monopolies that were known as "marketing boards" on 177–82.
[50] Ibid., 174–75.

If such government control of the economy is so harmful, why did it persist? Bauer has no doubts about the reason:

> The various economic controls . . . were not designed specifically to benefit ordinary Africans, but have always been useful to the politicians and civil servants who impose and administer them. . . . The departing colonialists bequeathed a political and financial bonanza to the incoming African politicians.[51]

Acemoglu and Robinson express a similar view when they speak of the "extractive institutions" that colonial rulers left in poor countries. They say that "extractive political institutions" are those that "concentrate power in the hands of a narrow elite and place few constraints on the exercise of this power."[52] The parallel to extractive political institutions is "extractive economic institutions," which "are designed to extract incomes and wealth from one subset of society to benefit a different subset."[53] They argue that colonial influence left destructive "extractive institutions" that perpetuated themselves in the Dutch colonies in Southeast Asia (250), in Africa generally (250–73), in South Africa in particular (259), in India (272–73), in Sierra Leone (342), and in Ghana, Kenya, and Zambia (343).

William Easterly, in *The White Man's Burden*, argues:

> The old conventional wisdom was correct—the previous imperial era did not facilitate economic development. Instead it created some of the conditions that bred occasions for today's unsuccessful interventions: failed states and bad government.

However, he continues:

> This is not to say that the West was the only driving force that created bad governments in the Rest—this would exaggerate the West's negative impact . . . there was plenty of despotism and vicious politics before the West ever showed up. Nor is the West the only source of imperial conquest—remember, say, the Aztecs, the Muslims, and the Mongols?[54]

---

[51] Ibid., 175, 183.
[52] Acemoglu and Robinson, *Why Nations Fail*, 81.
[53] Ibid., 76.
[54] Easterly, *The White Man's Burden*, 272. See also 278–83 for an evaluation of both positive and negative impacts of colonialism.

Easterly explains that when European nations began to abandon colonial rule and grant colonial nations independence, more mistakes were made:

> First, the West gave territory to one group that a different group already believed it possessed. Second, the West drew boundary lines splitting an ethnic group into two or more parts across nations, frustrating nationalist ambitions of that group and creating ethnic minority problems in two or more resulting nations. Third, the West combined into a single nation two or more groups that were historical enemies.[55]

The conclusion is that colonialism brought significant economic benefits to some countries, but fewer benefits to others and lingering destructive effects on government to many. Where colonialism brought socialist or "extractive" theories for government control of the economies in poor countries, the legacy has been a wealthy and corrupt governing class living above the majority of the population, who are oppressed by their own governments and trapped in poverty for generation after generation.

We realize that historians today will have widely differing assessments of the benefits and harmful consequences of European colonialism. It is not our purpose in this book to settle that question. The crucial question for today is, what can a poor country do now, looking forward?

It does not seem to us, however, that looking to the past and blaming colonialism does much of anything to solve the current problems, all of which have complex causes. The correct approach is to look forward and seek solutions. In particular, wherever planned, government-directed, largely unfree socialist economies remain, wherever there are what Acemoglu and Robinson call "extractive institutions," the solution is to seek to introduce increasing measures of genuine economic freedom (see chaps. 4, 5, 7, 8).

Finally, perhaps there are citizens of former European colonial powers reading this book, and perhaps they now recognize some of the destructive consequences that, intentionally or unintentionally, were inflicted on colonized nations by their own nations. Is there anything they can do to help alleviate some of the harm, even today?

---

[55] Ibid., 291.

One step would be to speak out and encourage their own nations to change any import tariffs that are still hindering poor nations from selling products in their nations (see 98–99). Another step would be to encourage their nations to stop the agricultural price support programs that depress world prices for crops (see discussion at 97–98). A third step would be for them individually or as groups to invest in starting for-profit companies that will increase jobs and economic productivity in poor nations (see 185–86). But we do not think they should encourage any more government-to-government aid from wealthy countries to poor countries, because it is generally more harmful than helpful, as we explained earlier (65–75).

2. Agencies that lend money to poor countries

What about international agencies, such as the World Bank and the International Monetary Fund, that have made loans to poor countries? Is the cost of repaying these loans so great that it constitutes an unbearable burden on these poor nations? Are these nations poor because the cost of servicing these loans is too high?

The main point to remember here is that these loans represent *assets* that were transferred *to* the poor countries, not taken *from* them, and almost all of the loans were made at very favorable rates, far below the market rates for loans in ordinary international financial markets. The loans were presumably made in order to finance projects that would be profitable and would pay a substantial rate of return.

Bauer explains:

> The external debts of the Third World are not the result or reflection of exploitation. They represent resources supplied. . . . Difficulties of servicing these debts do not reflect external exploitation or unfavorable terms of trade. They are the result of wasteful use of the capital supplied, or inappropriate monetary and fiscal policies.[56]

The Bible is emphatic that borrowers should repay their debts:

> The wicked borrows but does not pay back, but the righteous is generous and gives. (Ps. 37:21)

---

[56] Bauer, *Equality*, 78.

Pay to all what is owed to them: taxes to whom taxes are owed, revenue to whom revenue is owed. . . . *Owe no one anything*, except to love each other, for the one who loves another has fulfilled the law. (Rom 13:7–8)

Some Christians have campaigned for "debt forgiveness" for poor nations. This is really a plea that loans be cancelled without declaring them in default. But then someone else has to pay for them, usually the taxpayers in the nations that have made the loans. Therefore, the plea for debt forgiveness is essentially a plea for more foreign aid to be given to the heavily indebted countries, so the arguments given above with respect to aid apply directly to this question.[57]

Easterly devotes an entire chapter to debt forgiveness in his book *The Elusive Quest for Growth* (123–37). He concludes:

Our heart tells us to forgive debts to help the poor. Alas, the head contradicts the heart. Debt forgiveness grants aid to those recipients that have best proven their ability to misuse that aid. Debt relief is futile for countries with unchanged government behavior. The same mismanagement of funds that caused the high debt will prevent the aid sent through debt relief from reaching the truly poor.[58]

Since the loans represent assets that were *transferred to* a poor country, they cannot rightly be considered the source of poverty in such a nation. *Some* people in the poor nation have gained massive amounts of money from those loans, and those who have received the benefits should repay the costs. Princeton economics professor Angus Deaton says, "According to the European Community, the total value of stolen assets in individual foreign accounts is equivalent to half of Africa's outstanding debt."[59]

If corrupt leaders who have stolen huge fortunes from loan money are now taxing the poor people of their nation to repay the stolen money, then the blame should be laid squarely on the shoulders of those leaders. They are making their country poor. The loans themselves did not make the country poor.

However, what if the corrupt leader who stole the funds has been

---

[57] See also the more detailed analysis of debt forgiveness in Grudem, *Politics*, 451–56.
[58] Easterly, *Elusive Quest*, 136.
[59] Deaton, writing in Banerjee et al., *Making Aid Work*, 59.

deposed, and there seems to be no way of recovering the stolen money? Easterly thinks (and we agree) that in certain very limited cases such as this one, debt relief might be justified:

> A debt relief program could make sense if it meets two conditions. (1) It is granted where there has been a proven change from an irresponsible government to a government with good policies; (2) it is a once-for-all measure that will never be repeated. . . . It could be that the debt is inherited from a bad government by a good government that truly will try to help the poor. We could see wiping out the debt in this case. . . . A debt relief program that fails either of these two conditions results in more resources going to countries with bad policies than poor countries with good policies.[60]

3. The world economic system and international terms of trade

What about the world economic system? Do wealthy nations get together and conspire to pay unfairly low prices to farmers in poor countries for their agricultural products?

This common suggestion shows a misunderstanding of the way in which prices for agricultural products are determined. We will discuss coffee here, but the same arguments apply to hundreds of other crops.

a. No one can control commodity prices on world markets

First, nations do not buy coffee, companies do. There are thousands of large and small companies in the world that seek to buy coffee for their customers. These include (in the United States) the companies that market Starbucks, Seattle's Best, Nestle, Maxwell House, Folgers, Dunkin Donuts, Yuban, Melitta, and thousands of other coffee brands. These are not nations, such as Britain, France, Germany, or the United States. These are independent companies, and they are found in nearly every country of the world.

Second, the price of coffee is mainly determined by two factors—supply and demand. When customers around the world drink more coffee, the coffee companies need to buy more, which means that the quantity demanded in coffee markets goes up. This pushes the price

---

[60] Easterly, *Elusive Quest*, 136–37. However, being aware of decades of past failures with aid, readers might well be skeptical as to whether such a situation as he describes will actually occur.

upward. But if people drink less coffee, the quantity demanded goes down, and this pushes the price down. With many thousands of buyers throughout the world, no one company or nation can determine the overall *demand* for coffee.

What about the supply? If it is a bad year for coffee crops, less coffee is supplied, coffee is scarce, and buyers are willing to pay more or drink less so they do not run out. The smaller amount supplied pushes prices up. But if there is a bumper crop of coffee, then more coffee is supplied, and there is more to sell than the companies were planning on buying. Sellers have to cut their prices in order to sell their coffee. A larger supply drives the price of coffee down.

Every year around the world, thousands upon thousands of small and large coffee growers decide how much they are going to plant and try to bring to harvest. (They have to plan in advance because the coffee tree grows for three to five years before it bears coffee beans.) With so many thousands of growers, no one company or nation can determine the overall *supply* of coffee.

As I (Wayne Grudem) am writing this chapter, the world price of coffee is 210 cents per pound (this is the "composite" price among several varieties and markets). In coffee exchanges in various cities around the world, 210 cents per pound is the price at which supply and demand intersect. Farmers are willing to *sell* their coffee at that price (supply) and coffee companies are willing to *buy* it at that price (demand). (In this discussion, we are holding other factors constant and omitting transaction costs for the sake of simplification.).

In such a system, with a world market and prices determined by hundreds of thousands of individual decisions, there is no way a wealthy company or a wealthy nation could say: "We want to pay coffee farmers an unfairly low price, an *unjust* price. We don't think they should get 210 cents per pound for coffee. We're just going to pay 150 cents per pound!"

Suppose a powerful company, say, Starbucks, decided it would pay only 150 cents per pound. Starbucks buyers would go to coffee exchanges in cities around the world and announce, "We are offering to buy coffee at 150 cents per pound!" What would happen?

The traders would laugh them out of the room. No one would sell coffee to the Starbucks buyers. Why should they sell to Starbucks at 150 cents a pound when they could sell to anyone else in the world for 210 cents per pound? If no one would sell to Starbucks at that price, Starbucks would soon run out of coffee, and their customers would get fed up and leave. Starbucks knows this, so its buyers have no choice but to offer 210 cents per pound, the world price for coffee. So, no individual, no government, and no powerful company is able to "set" the world price for agricultural products.

But what about the campaign to encourage people to buy "fair-trade" coffee that carries a higher price? The promise of the fair-trade movement is that coffee growers in poor nations will receive a higher price for coffee if it is produced in better working conditions with higher wages. Then coffee that is marketed as "fair-trade coffee" is sold at a higher price to consumers in wealthy nations.

At first, such a simple system seems to be a sensible way to help poor coffee growers earn more money. But the general consensus of economists is that it does not do much good and might even do some harm.

Economist Victor Claar points out, "Fair trade coffee roughly represents just one percent of the coffee markets in the United States and Europe."[61] But Claar points out an economic harm that comes from an artificial increase of the price of some coffee above what the world market will bear (that is, higher than the price set by the world supply and demand). Paying some growers a higher price than the world market price for coffee encourages them to grow more coffee than the market actually demands. Claar writes:

> Thus, while there is too much coffee being grown relative to global demand in general, there is also not sufficient demand to purchase, at the fair trade price, all of the coffee being grown as fair trade coffee. In both cases, there is simply too much coffee.[62]

The larger supply of coffee then *depresses* the price for other coffee growers that are not part of the fair-trade movement. (This is some-

---

[61] Victor Claar, *Fair Trade? Its Prospects as a Poverty Solution* (Grand Rapids: Poverty Cure, 2012), 39. Even if fair-trade coffee represented 3 percent or 4 percent of the coffee market in the United States and Europe, that would not take into account the rest of the world, so it is doubtful that fair-trade coffee accounts for even 1 percent of the world market.
[62] Ibid., 40.

thing like what occurs because of the agricultural subsidies that the United States pays to certain farmers, giving them a price above the world market price for their crops, and then ending up with surplus crops which it "dumps" on the world market, depressing agricultural prices for other countries.)

Claar goes on to say that artificially raising the price for coffee just prolongs the problem of too much coffee on the world market:

> If the fundamental problem with the coffee market is that prices are low because there is too much coffee, then it would appear that the fair trade movement may be making matters worse rather than better because it increases the incentives to grow more coffee.[63]

An additional problem is that, by paying a higher price than the world market price for coffee, the fair-trade movement encourages farmers to keep producing coffee when they would be much better off shifting to alternative crops for which there is more demand (he shows how Costa Rica shifted its production to new exports and significantly increased the value of its exports).[64]

We noted earlier that Paul Collier is professor of economics at Oxford University and former director of development research at the World Bank. He writes this about fair-trade coffee (but the arguments apply to "fair-trade" campaigns for other products as well):

> The price premium in fair trade products is a form of charitable transfer, and there is evidently no harm in that. But the problem with it, as compared with just giving people the aid in other ways, is that it encourages recipients to stay doing what they are doing—producing coffee. . . . They get charity as long as they stay producing the crops that have locked them into poverty.[65]

We agree with these economic assessments, and therefore we cannot recommend that people support the "fair-trade" movement. Charitable contributions to the poor are more efficiently given by other means, and such charitable transfers will never lead to a long-term solution for world poverty.

---

[63] Ibid., 43–44.
[64] Ibid., 53.
[65] Collier, *The Bottom Billion*, 163.

b. Governments of poor countries sometimes keep farmers from receiving the world price for their crops

Governments of poor countries can force poor farmers in these countries to accept unfairly low prices, far below the world market price, by means of taxes, fees, licensing restrictions, tariffs, quotas, and other distortions of the market. Bauer explains how this can happen:

> The world prices of coffee and cocoa . . . are determined by market forces and not prescribed by the West. On the other hand, the farmers in many of the exporting countries receive far less than the market prices, because they are subject to very high export taxes and similar government levees.[66]

Bauer adds that after the end of British colonial rule, "the great bulk of agricultural exports from British colonies in Africa, including practically all exports produced by Africans, *was handled by state export monopolies known as marketing boards*. . . . [They] became the most important single instrument of state economic control in Africa."[67] The marketing boards received the world price for a crop, took much of it for themselves, then paid the local farmers a far lower price from what was left over.

Though many such marketing boards have now been abolished, it is still important to determine in each nation whether there are government-imposed tariffs or quotas or local dealer monopolies that mean that growers receive much less than the world market price for their crops—and whether government officials are skimming off profits from these tariffs, quotas, or monopolies.

On the other hand, if growers are receiving something close to the world market price for crops, then we do not think there is anything else a poor nation can do to bring about a higher price. If growers do not think the world market price is enough for them to live on, they have to make the decision to find some other crop that is more profitable. Blaming something that cannot be changed does not help a nation produce more goods and services of value.

---

[66] Bauer, *Equality*, 68–69. See also 173, 177–82.
[67] Ibid., 177, emphasis added.

c. Rich nations "dump" excess agricultural products on the world market, wrongfully depressing world prices

"Commodity dumping" also negatively impacts the prices farmers in poor nations receive. This happens when governments (usually in wealthier nations in Europe and the United States) pay huge subsidies to farmers in their countries, which means that many farmers are paid above the world market prices for crops such as wheat, peanuts, sugar beets, and many others. The government makes a "support price" guarantee, so the farmers grow more of a product (for example, wheat) than the world market demands. The government then buys the wheat from these farmers at the promised price and stores it in huge grain silos. This happens in the United States, for example, year after year.

What is to be done with this excess wheat? The U.S. government can either give it away to other countries of the world (in which case it would destroy the market for locally grown wheat in those countries, because the farmers cannot compete with a price of zero) or can offer it for sale on the world market at less than the world market price (in which case the large influx of supply depresses the world market price for wheat, and again the farmers in poor countries receive less than they otherwise would).

Many economists believe this system of farm subsidies is economically harmful and would like to see it abolished. We agree. When wealthy nations "dump" massive amounts of a crop on the world market, they definitely harm farmers in poor countries. We also think such subsidies are economically harmful for the countries where they occur. However, there are political reasons why these subsidies continue in various nations, which one of us has written about elsewhere.[68] Both of us have argued publicly that these subsidies should be abolished.[69]

But the crucial question for poor nations is this: What can be done about this practice?

Quite honestly, it is unlikely that any poor nation or group of poor nations can stop the dumping of excess products on the world

---

[68] See the discussion of farm subsidies in Grudem, *Politics*, 528–33.
[69] See Barry Asmus and Donald B. Billings, *Crossroads: The Great American Experiment: The Rise, Decline, and Restoration of Freedom and the Market Economy* (Lanham, MD: University Press of America, 1984), 224–27 (on agricultural price supports); Grudem, *Politics*, 528–33.

market in the foreseeable future. The practice can be changed only by internal political powers within each country that does this, and that might or might not happen soon. We certainly hope it does. The only step (for now) that poor countries can take seems to be to adapt to the circumstances as they are.

It is important to keep the main goal in mind: producing more goods and services. If the world market for wheat is unpredictable, and if growing wheat therefore proves unlikely to provide farmers with a good income year after year, then the only solution (short of producing much more wheat) is to shift to other crops. In other words, poor nations can successfully adapt to foreign dumping of commodities by growing other crops or producing other products that are not subject to such "dumping."

The important point is that poverty cannot be solved by blaming it on other factors or entities, even the nations that dump subsidized commodities on the world market. Recognizing this practice as one cause of poverty does nothing to solve the problem (unless the dumping nations change their policies as a result, which we hope they will someday do). People in poor nations *can* look forward and discover how they can continually create more products—other products— of value.

d. Rich nations wrongfully impose harmful tariffs and quotas on products that they import from poor nations

We think that when wealthy countries place restrictive tariffs or quotas on goods imported from poor countries, they wrongfully hinder those poor countries. If a Latin American country can grow tomatoes more cheaply than producers in the United States, then U.S. consumers benefit from the lower prices and the Latin American growers benefit from earning more income. The U.S. government should not prevent the Latin American growers from realizing this benefit by forcing them to pay high tariffs when they bring tomatoes into the United States, just so American tomato growers are protected. Free trade brings benefits to both nations.[70] (See the discussion below on

---

[70] Ron Sider, *Rich Christians in an Age of Hunger* (Nashville: Thomas Nelson, 2005), 143–47, 240–44, offers disturbing statistics about the harm that such tariffs impose on poor nations.

comparative advantage, 169–72.) It is important for citizens and leaders in rich nations to work to remove such harmful tariffs and quotas. In fact, the first two legislative recommendations of the HELP Commission's report to the U.S. Congress in 2007 included "Grant duty-free, quota-free access to U.S. markets" to many poor countries, especially "those countries with a per capita Gross Domestic Product (GDP) under $2000."[71]

However, apart from participating in trade negotiations that can take years to bring a resolution, poor nations have no way to remove such tariffs. The abolition of any tariff requires the agreement of the country that has imposed it. For the present, it is important for the poor nations to focus on things they can change on their own, especially the main goal of producing more goods and services of value.

4. Rich nations and multinational corporations

Finally, it is claimed that rich nations, or perhaps large multinational corporations, have made countries poor by stealing their wealth. This is the claim that rich nations have become rich by making poor nations poor. Is there merit in this charge?

a. Poor nations were poor before rich nations became rich

First, the nations that are poor today were not prosperous in the past.[72] Second, countries that are rich today became so by producing their own goods and services. In general, they did not get rich by making the poor nations poor.[73] Third, the factual evidence of history shows that the accusation that rich countries in general are responsible for poverty in poor countries is simply not true.

---

[71] The HELP (Helping to Enhance the Livelihood of People Around the Globe) Commission Report on Foreign Assistance Reform (Dec. 7, 2007), 24, accessed March 20, 2013, http://www.americanprogress .org/wp-content/uploads/issues/2007/12/pdf/beyond_assistence.pdf.

[72] Someone might object that China was relatively rich in the fifteenth century. Yes, or at least a few people were quite wealthy, but then China went through centuries of backwardness and poverty before it recently began to develop rapidly.

[73] However, we recognize that Spanish explorers forcibly stole vast quantities of gold from the Aztec and Inca empires in Latin America in the early sixteenth century, and Spain gained vast amounts of wealth in the process, which was ultimately destructive not only to the conquered peoples but also to Spain itself: see 79–81. Spanish explorers also forcibly enslaved native Indians in Central and South America to work in their mines, inflicting great suffering, and they left behind a destructive legacy that continues to some extent even today: see the comments of Acemoglu and Robinson, *Why Nations Fail*, 9–19, 114–15, 432–33. These actions were not the initial cause of poverty, however, because the common people in Central and South America were extremely poor even before the Spanish arrived.

Until about 1700, there was very little difference in the lives of ordinary people in the richer and poorer countries of the world. Most of the people worked hard, obtained enough food, clothing, and shelter to survive, and saw little change in their standard of living century after century. Living on less than a dollar a day was common.

But around 1770, the Industrial Revolution began in Britain and soon spread to other countries. Landes notes that British income per head "doubled between 1780 and 1860, and then multiplied by six times between 1860 and 1990."[74] In short, some nations produced tremendous new prosperity and other nations stayed poor. Landes says, "The Industrial Revolution made some countries richer and others (relatively) poorer; or more accurately, some countries made an industrial revolution and became rich; and others did not and stayed poor."[75]

b. Sometimes poor nations sell their natural resources rather than manufactured goods

We recognize that sometimes poor nations make agreements to sell some of their natural resources (such as oil and minerals) to large corporations in other countries. If these are voluntary transactions and the corporations pay money for the resources, this practice should not be called "stealing" but "buying" resources. Because there is a world market for commodities, with many companies competing to purchase the resources of a poor nation, any given company must pay the world market price or the country will seek another buyer that will. (But it is possible a company might bribe officials in a poor nation to get an agreement below the world price, in which case there is moral wrongdoing both on the part of the corporation and on the part of the government officials.)

As we discussed above (see 79–82), we do not think that depleting a country's natural resources is a good path toward increasing GDP and overcoming poverty. But unless the resources are plundered as a result of military conquest or bribery, it is incorrect to refer to the transfer of resources as stealing.

---

[74] Landes, *Wealth and Poverty*, 194.
[75] Ibid., 169.

c. Economic contacts with the West have mostly benefitted poor nations

Bauer explains the results of economic transactions between rich and poor nations:

> Far from the West having caused the poverty in the Third World, contact with the West has been the principal agent of material progress there . . . the level of material achievement usually diminishes as one moves away from the foci of Western impact. The poorest and most backward people have few or no external contacts; witness the aborigines, pygmies and desert peoples.[76]

> The prosperity of the West was generated by its own peoples and was not taken from others.[77]

> The West has not caused the famines in the Third World. These have occurred in backward regions with practically no external commerce. [This backwardness at times] reflects the policies of the rulers who are hostile to traders . . . and often to private property.
>
> Contrary to the various allegations and accusations . . . the higher level of consumption in the West is not achieved by depriving others of what they have produced. Western consumption is more than paid for by Western production.[78]

Bauer also points out that the frequent accusation that wealthy countries have "exploited" the poor nations of the world began with Marxist ideology and has become a standard claim put forth by Marxist scholars. He says:

> The notion of Western exploitation of the Third World is standard in publications and statements emanating from the Soviet Union and other communist countries. . . . [According to] Marxist-Leninist ideology . . . any return on private capital implies exploitation. . . . The principal assumption behind the idea of Western responsibility for Third World poverty is that the prosperity of individuals and societies generally reflects the exploitation of others. . . . According to

---

[76] Bauer, *Equality*, 70.
[77] Ibid., 75.
[78] Ibid., 82.

Marxist-Leninist ideology, colonial status and foreign investment are by definition evidence of exploitation.[79]

But Bauer's conclusion is quite the opposite. He writes:

In fact, foreign private investment and the activities of the multi-national companies have expanded opportunities and raised incomes and government revenues in the Third World. Reference to economic colonialism and neo-colonialism both debase the language and distort the truth.[80]

We must recognize that some economic interactions between rich and poor nations have caused harm. Sometimes wealthy multinational corporations have bribed government officials in poor nations to secure monopoly privileges that have oppressed those countries' ordinary people and prevented free markets from functioning (we discuss this evil in the next section). In such cases, both the companies that paid the bribes and the officials who took them share in the moral blame. But we view that as the breakdown of free markets, not the fault of the free-market system itself. (And many countries, such as the United States, make such practices illegal for American companies that do business in other countries.)

In general terms, however, Bauer has no doubt that the economic interaction between rich and poor nations has been immensely beneficial for the poor nations:

Altogether, it is anomalous or even perverse to suggest that external commercial relations are damaging to development or to the living standards of the people of the Third World. They act as channels for the flow of human and financial resources and for new ideas, methods and crops. They benefit people by providing a large and diverse source of imports and by opening up markets for exports.[81]

 The poorest areas of the Third World have no external trade. Their condition shows that the causes of backwardness are domestic and that external commercial contacts are beneficial. Even if the terms of

[79] Ibid., 74–76.
[80] Ibid., 76.
[81] Ibid., 79.

trade were unfavorable on some criterion or other, this would only mean that people would not benefit from foreign trade as much as they would if the terms of trade were more favourable. People benefit from the widening of opportunities which external trade represents.[82]

d. Do multinational corporations pay unfair wages in poor countries?

What about the claim that large multinational corporations come to poor countries and pay unjustly low wages, thereby taking advantage of workers in those countries? In answering this question, it is important to distinguish between a labor market in a country that is completely free and a labor market that is constrained by laws and restrictive hiring permits.

Just as the government of a poor country can restrict coffee exports so that local farmers receive much less than the world price for their product (and the government officials pocket the huge difference when they sell the coffee on the world market), so the government can keep wages artificially low. For example, the government might give only one company a permit to build a factory and hire workers in a certain region.

Suppose government officials in a poor country sign a lucrative agreement with World Famous Running Shoes to build a shoe factory in a certain area, and as part of the agreement they guarantee (because of money they receive) that they will deny all other companies permits to build factories in that area. World Famous Running Shoes has a monopolistic control on the hiring of local workers, and it can pay extremely low wages and allow horrendous working conditions.

In this situation, much of the blame must be placed with the government officials who set up and protect World Famous's monopoly in the local labor market. But if the conditions and pay are inhumane, World Famous shares in the blame. The New Testament says, "Masters, treat your bondservants justly and fairly, knowing that you also have a Master in heaven" (Col. 4:1).

On the other hand, if there are no such government-imposed restrictions on hiring, then any company in the world is free to come and hire workers, and an element of competition enters the labor market. Then wages are set by the prevailing market price. If World

---

[82] Ibid., 76.

Famous offers people only $1 per hour, then Saucony is free to come and offer people $1.50 per hour, and Jockey is free to build a shirt factory and offer people $1.75 per hour, and so forth. With a free labor market, every company that manufactures goods in the world is free to compete for local workers.

In such a labor market, local workers are free to work for any company they want, and no one can "set" the price of labor; rather, it is regulated by the interplay of supply and demand in the free market. If a company offers $1.50 per hour for five hundred jobs and finds that it has five hundred qualified applicants, the labor supply is certainly meeting the demand, and $1.50 is a "fair" and "just" wage. It is the price at which workers are willing to work in that labor market. Presumably they have decided that they are far better off working for $1.50 per hour than not working at all or working at subsistence-level farming.

Does the factory that pays $1.50 per hour make these workers poor? No. It makes them more prosperous than they were before, and the increased prosperity of these workers no doubt brings benefits to the rest of the economy as well.

One of the economic advantages that poor nations have today is a supply of inexpensive labor. Low labor costs make it economically attractive for companies to build factories and invest in poor countries, and thereby help them create goods and services, and move toward prosperity.

When people object that companies should not pay such low wages (suggesting that something like American or Western European wages would be more "fair"), they fail to understand that any regulation that requires companies to pay higher wages in a poor country tends to take away that country's economic advantage, making it more difficult for that country to compete on the world market and attract the factories and investments needed for economic growth.

e. The Bible does not blame the rich in general for the poverty of the poor

We agree that the Bible sometimes blames the poverty of poor people and nations on rulers and countries that oppress others by military power. It also blames powerful, wealthy people who wrongly withhold wages (see James 5:4: "Behold, the wages of the laborers who mowed your fields, which you kept back by fraud, are crying out against you, and the cries of the harvesters have reached the ears of the Lord of hosts"). But it never blames wealthy people or wealthy nations *in general* for the situations of those in poverty.[83]

In fact, the Bible lists numerous causes for poverty. Some poverty is caused by war, crime, disease, accidents, or natural disasters. And some poverty is caused by evil governments that rob their people, or by wealthy, powerful people who cheat others:

> The fallow ground of the poor would yield much food, but it is swept away through injustice. (Prov. 13:23)

> Whoever oppresses the poor to increase his own wealth . . . will only come to poverty. (Prov. 22:16; see also James 5:4, cited above)

At other times, the Bible sees poverty as the result of laziness or too much love for pleasure:

> How long will you lie there, O sluggard? When will you arise from your sleep? A little sleep, a little slumber, a little folding of the hands to rest, and *poverty* will come upon you like a robber, and want like an armed man. (Prov. 6:9–11)

> In all toil there is profit, but mere talk tends only to *poverty*. (Prov. 14:23)

> Whoever loves pleasure will be a poor man; he who loves wine and oil will not be rich. (Prov. 21:17)

> Whoever works his land will have plenty of bread, but he who follows worthless pursuits will have plenty of *poverty*. (Prov. 28:19)

Sometimes God in his sovereignty even brings poverty on greedy, stingy people:

> One gives freely, yet grows all the richer; another withholds what he should give, and only suffers want. (Prov. 11:24)

---

[83] See Darrow L. Miller and Stan Guthrie, *Discipling Nations: The Power of Truth to Transform Cultures* (Seattle: YMAM, 1998), 57. The authors say that the view that poverty is caused by Westerners who consume too much of the world's resources is a "secular" viewpoint, not a biblical one.

A stingy man hastens after wealth and does not know that poverty will come upon him. (Prov. 28:22)

But the important point here is that the mere fact that some people are rich is never in itself said to be a cause of poverty.

Claiming that rich countries are responsible for the poverty of poor countries, or that poverty is the result of rich companies "exploiting" poor countries, is often contrary to fact, and is certainly counterproductive. It does nothing to increase the prosperity of a poor nation. It does nothing to help it to create more goods and services.

No nation can hope to overcome poverty and increase in prosperity by blaming its poverty on outside factors or entities. Such a focus on blame does nothing to solve the problem. The goal must be to become a nation that continually creates more goods and services.

E. Conclusion: what the goal is not

Producing more goods and services does not happen by depending on donations from other countries; by redistributing wealth from the rich to the poor; by depleting natural resources; or by blaming factors and entities outside the nation, whether colonialism, banks that have lent money, the world economic system, rich nations, or large corporations. None of the wrong goals surveyed in this chapter will move a nation toward what should be its primary economic goal: continually producing more goods and services, and thus increasing its GDP.

3

WRONG SYSTEMS

Economic Systems That Did
Not Lead to Prosperity

If a country decides to move from poverty to ever-increasing prosperity, the next question is: What kind of economic system best brings about regular increases in gross domestic product (GDP)? In very simple terms, the question can also be phrased in terms of human motivation and ability: What kind of economic system best motivates and enables people to create more goods and services of value?

We need to emphasize that the right kind of economic system does not *by itself* bring a nation out of poverty. The causes of both poverty and prosperity are complex, and single-cause explanations are always deficient. Therefore, leaders of poor nations need to consider *all* of the factors explained in chapters 3 to 9. Some of these factors (such as property rights and the rule of law) are more influential than others, but every one of them has some effect, for good or ill, on a nation's economy—and this includes government actions, laws, and cultural beliefs and values of the nation (see chapters 7–9 below).

David S. Landes, in the conclusion of his study of the causes of wealth and poverty in nations, writes: "Economic analysis cherishes the illusion that one good reason should be enough, but the determinants of complex processes are invariably plural and interrelated. Monocausal explanations will not work."[1]

This means that the solution to poverty can never be *merely* a free market, private property ownership, the rule of law, government accountability, the absence of bribery and corruption, a good work ethic, or superior education. These factors, and many others, provide *some* economic benefit to a nation. But a nation that genuinely desires to escape from poverty will seek to implement *as many as possible* of the steps we recommend in the following chapters.

Still, the right kind of economic system is crucial. Without the right economic system, no nation can find a lasting solution to poverty. An inappropriate economic system only exacerbates the problems of corruption, oppression, poor education, poor public services, and lack of opportunity. Without incentives, no one wants to work, and without work, all is lost.

We are going to argue (in the next chapter) that a free-market economic system is the best for bringing nations out of poverty. In that chapter, we define a free-market system as one in which economic production and consumption are determined by the free choices of individuals rather than by government, and this process is grounded in private ownership of the means of production (see 131–32).

But someone might object: "What about *other* economic systems? Aren't there other options that should be considered?" In response to that question, in this chapter we review eight other economic systems that have been tried at various points in human history, some of which persist even today:

A. Hunting and gathering
B. Subsistence farming
C. Slavery
D. Tribal ownership
E. Feudalism
F. Mercantilism
G. Socialism and communism
H. The welfare state and equality

---

[1] David S. Landes, *The Wealth and Poverty of Nations: Why Some Are So Rich and Some So Poor* (New York: W. W. Norton, 1999), 517.

Unfortunately, none of these systems has ever opened the door to really significant economic growth or permanent poverty reduction.

A. Hunting and gathering

In many primitive societies, women did the gathering, preparing, and cooking, while men did the hunting. The women focused on the fruits and vegetables, and the men on the protein. It was an early form of specialization and trade that kept human beings going for thousands of years, but there was no significant economic development.[2]

Those primitive attempts at specialization could never produce increasing standards of living because of the time involved in hunting and in extracting and processing food from plants and trees.[3] There was little progressive innovation. Centuries passed with most hunters and gatherers enduring at mere subsistence levels. Because so much time and energy were devoted to securing food, "women would not maintain a sufficient surplus to keep themselves fertile for more than a few prime years."[4] Famines of food and epidemics of disease made hunting and gathering a very precarious way to live.

An economy based on hunting and gathering could never bring a country from poverty to prosperity.

B. Subsistence farming

Subsistence farming is an economic system in which each family grows enough food to feed itself. For much of the world's history, subsistence farming was the most common means of food production. It was also practiced in the early years of the settling of the American Midwest and West, and the sparsely populated parts of Canada and Australia. It persists today in large sections of rural Africa, Asia, and Latin America. While subsistence farmers generally did not starve, they usually remained poor.

A subsistence farmer prepared the soil with a rock or stick, worried constantly about water and weeds, and harvested his own wheat to make his own bread. It was backbreaking work. Every task was

---

[2] This summary is derived from the treatment in Matt Ridley, *The Rational Optimist: How Prosperity Evolves* (New York: HarperCollins, 2010), 61–65.
[3] Ibid., 29.
[4] Ibid., 45.

extremely time-consuming, and often the farmer and his family were only one crop failure away from starvation.

It is surprising that many environmentalists still believe that subsistence farming is soulful, organic, and proper. These earnest and well-meaning people believe that a community's economic security would be enhanced if all the people grew their own food and produced the necessities of their lives. Then, markets would become irrelevant and families could ensure their own survival. If only this were true.

Subsistence farmers were not only dependent on their own muscle power for cultivation and transport, but also seldom participated in markets that would have exposed them to specialization and trade. Days spent on subsistence farming were always long, sunup to sundown, with no time to invest in trade relationships or tools, or, better yet, create tools that would produce other tools. The effort was always toward today's sufficiency.

Demographic experts estimate that the life span for early man was the mid- to late 20s. That did not change much until very recently. "Average global life expectancy at birth as late as 1800 A.D. was just 28.5 years. Two centuries later, in 2001, it had more than doubled to 66.6 years,"[5] thanks to the agricultural and industrial revolutions, which fully trumped the idea of subsistence farming.

Subsistence farming tends to breed other problems. British economic writer Matt Ridley observes:

> Wherever anthropologists look, from New Guinea to the Amazon and Easter Island, they find chronic warfare among today's subsistence farmers. Preemptively raiding your neighbours lest they raid you is routine human behavior As Paul Seabright has written: "Where there are no institutional restraints on such behavior, systematic killing of unrelated individuals is so common among human beings that, awful though it is, it cannot be described as exceptional, pathological or disturbed."[6]

Christians would describe this conduct as being the result of man's inherent sin nature, and surely morally wrong.

---

[5] Niall Ferguson, *Civilization: The West and the Rest* (New York: Penguin, 2011), 146.
[6] Matt Ridley, *The Rational Optimist*, 138.

Subsistence farming did not permit people to be either economically or morally better off. It failed economically because populations were sparse, markets were few, and people were so involved with the daily concern for food that they could not work on much of anything else. Large-scale division of labor, specialization, and trade were yet to be understood or embraced.

However, someone today might object: "But weren't people who lived on subsistence farming happier than people are today? Their lives were much simpler. They didn't have to cope with the stress of modern life. If people are content with subsistence farming, we shouldn't interfere with their lives."

We simply do not know that people living by means of subsistence farming were happier. We tend to paint an idealized picture in our minds, forgetting the short life spans (often under thirty years), the crippling diseases and frequent deaths, the anxiety of never knowing whether there would be enough to eat next month, the weariness of dawn-to-dusk manual labor for one's entire lifetime, the unfulfilled longing of parents for better lives for their children, the yearning after the option of choosing another way of life, and so on.

If individuals want to choose subsistence farming today, they are free to do so, even within a wealthy nation, by purchasing a remote plot of land and raising their own food. But if our goal is to help whole nations rise from poverty to greater prosperity, then we should not impose poverty-producing subsistence farming on them.

In addition, we think the Bible encourages human beings not just to *survive* but to *flourish* on the earth. This is implied by the Bible's teaching about stewardship, as we explain below (see chapter 6, 144–45).

Subsistence farming is also an inadequate solution to the moral challenge of feeding the world's poor. Economies based only on individual subsistence farming would not be sufficient to feed more than a small portion of the world's 7 billion people.

In short, an economy based on subsistence farming can never bring a country from poverty to prosperity.[7]

---

[7] Someone might object that these first two systems were the basis on which subsequent systems were founded, so they did in fact lead to economic growth. But this objection misses the point. These systems had to be abandoned because they did not produce growth. Only after they were replaced by better systems did genuine economic growth occur.

C. Slavery

No one seriously considers slavery as a legitimate economic system today, but we include it here because it was highly significant to numerous societies in past centuries. Even some early hunting-and-gathering societies employed slaves.[8]

Slavery is a system in which a person is forced to work by another person who has legal ownership either of the slave's work for a certain period of time or of the slave himself.

Ancient civilizations thought slavery was normal. Egypt's glory was literally built on the backs of slave laborers. Chinese slavery in the Chang Dynasty was not questioned. Athens in the fifth and sixth centuries BC practiced slavery that continued into the Greek and Roman empires two thousand years ago. "Both slavery and prolonged conscription were too deeply ingrained in the Roman system to be seriously questioned. . . . The Greeks also sanctioned slavery."[9]

Sheldon M. Stern, a curator at the John F. Kennedy Library and Museum, says:

> [The] Islamic slave trade had thrived since the eighth century and . . . millions of Africans had been captured for sale to Egypt, Arabia, Mesopotamia, and the Ottoman Empire.[10]

> At least 90 percent of the slaves in the Atlantic trade from Africa to the Americas were sold in the Caribbean or South America. The British colonies that became the United States imported no more than 8 percent. Brazil alone imported over six times the number of Africans sold in the British American colonies and didn't abolish slavery until a quarter century after emancipation in the United States.[11]

According to M. Stanton Evans:

> Servitude was so common in the ancient world, indeed, that hardly anyone thought to question it. . . . While we don't know the exact

---

[8] Ridley, *The Rational Optimist*, 92.

[9] William J. Bernstein, *The Birth of Plenty: How the Prosperity of the Modern World was Created* (New York: McGraw-Hill, 2004), 66.

[10] Sheldon M. Stern, "The Atlantic Slave Trade—The Full Story," *Academic Questions* (Summer 2005), 17, citing Giles Milton, *White Gold: The Extraordinary Story of Thomas Pellow and Islam's One Million White Slaves* (New York: Farrar, Straus & Giroux, 2004).

[11] Stern, "The Atlantic Slave Trade," 17, citing Seymore Drescher and Stanley L. Engerman, eds., *A Historical Guide to World Slavery* (Oxford: Oxford University Press, 1998), 374.

number of slaves in Attica at the time of Pericles, there is no question that it was large—and that the workaday economy depended on it. Tocqueville cites an estimate of 20,000 free men versus upwards of 300,000 slaves, though this seems excessive.[12]

There are two major reasons why slavery must be rejected as a suitable system for economic growth. First, there is a moral reason: slavery is dehumanizing and fails to recognize the full dignity of every human being as someone created "in the image of God" (Gen. 1:27). Its cruelty and abuse do not respect the value of human freedom and the divinely granted right to "liberty" that belongs to every person.

The Bible emphasizes the importance of human freedom, as God set the Jewish people free from "slavery" in Egypt (Ex. 20:2) and promised his people yet greater liberty in a more wonderful age to come (Isa. 61:1). Paul encourages slaves in the Roman Empire to gain their freedom if possible (1 Cor. 7:21) and emphasizes freedom as a crucial part of a Christian's life (Gal. 5:1).

Second, there are considerable economic reasons to reject slavery. Slavery was profitable up to a certain point for a slave owner (he was getting the benefit of people's work at far below the level of "free-market" wages), but the benefits did not accrue to the whole population, especially not to the slaves. In addition, economic systems eventually evolved to the point where mechanical productivity was more economical than human muscle. The benefits to the slave owners became increasingly hard to justify.

By the very nature of slavery, its profitability is always limited. People forced to work against their will are never going to do their best work or put out their best effort. They do just enough to get by and avoid being punished. Innovative productivity and creativity cannot be exacted, and therefore technological advancement in slave societies is minimal. Without economic and personal freedom, national poverty rather than prosperity is the result.

The movement to end slavery, beginning with voluminous amounts of anti-slavery writing and self-criticism in the West, was mainly initiated by Christians, and they were surely right to take up this cause.

---

[12] M. Stanton Evans, *The Theme Is Freedom: Religion, Politics, and the American Tradition* (Washington: Regnery, 1994), 138–39.

The persistent efforts of the church to mitigate and do away with slavery were recounted by Harold Berman in his book *Law and Revolution*.[13] Hundreds of Quakers in 1783 presented the British Parliament with petitions calling for the elimination of slavery, and wealthy individuals such as Josiah Wedgwood (a merchant) and William Wilberforce (an evangelical Christian parliamentarian and the son of a merchant) financed and led the anti-slavery movement before and after 1800 in Britain.[14] About two-thirds of the abolitionist leaders in the United States in the 1830s were Christian clergymen.[15]

Tragically, there have been reports of continuing slavery even in recent decades in a number of countries.[16] Slavery is a deeply immoral system that must be rejected on every count. Both the moral and economic arguments strongly suggest that an economy based on slavery can never bring a country from poverty to genuine, lasting prosperity.

D. Tribal ownership

Tribal ownership is a system in which all the land is owned by the tribe or social community, not by individuals. Many places in Africa, Asia, and North and South America have practiced tribal ownership. Even today it is a common economic system for many of the countries in sub-Saharan Africa and is the dominant economic system on Native American reservations.

It sounds like a good idea: we all own everything together. But over the centuries, tribal ownership has trapped its victims in perpetual poverty. How could such a widely-used system turn out to be so inept?

The lack of private ownership, discussed in the next chapter, is the main problem. When no particular owner has responsibility for property, there is little individual incentive to improve or steward it. Simply put, people need to be able to own things. When everyone's business becomes no one's business, commonly held property is neglected and the tribally owned enterprise deteriorates as if stricken

---

[13] Harold Berman, *Law and Revolution: The Formation of the Western Legal Tradition* (Cambridge, MA: Harvard University Press, 1983).

[14] Ridley, *The Rational Optimist*, 105

[15] See Wayne Grudem, *Politics – According to the Bible* (Grand Rapids: Zondervan, 2010), 50, citing Alvin Schmidt, *How Christianity Changed the World* (Grand Rapids: Zondervan, 2004), 279.

[16] Jim Powell, *The Triumph of Liberty* (New York: Free Press, 2000), xiv, citing Milton Meltzer, *Slavery: A World History* (Cambridge, MA: Da Capo Press, 1993).

by a plague. Tribal ownership eliminates individual incentives and reduces the tribe members to primitive economic activities and burdensome tribal duties. When personal responsibility is widely shared, personal responsibility is lost and growth curtailed.

Such a lack of personal property rights is highly significant because a crucial key to economic growth is enabling individuals to obtain clearly documented ownership to property. This is best demonstrated by Peruvian economist Hernando de Soto, who shows that when individuals own a piece of land that belongs to them and no one else, they care for, improve, and develop it.[17]

Ownership also allows a person to use his property's value as the basis for borrowing money to start a business or make other investments. When property is owned and ownership is documented, an economy then has the potential to grow and lift itself from the clutches of poverty. People find meaningful employment and opportunities for providing their children and grandchildren with a better life.

As we will explain more fully in the next chapter, the Bible itself regularly assumes and reinforces a system in which property belongs to individuals, not to a government, a tribe, or, in some vague sense, a "society" as a whole. In the Bible, property belongs to *individuals* (see 142–44).

Defenders of tribal ownership typically speak of self-reliance, bravado, and courage, all good things. But the "self" they mean is a tribal self, one that is continually de-emphasizing individuals while stressing the larger community. Everyone's heart must beat as one and all must work for the tribe's benefit. Since personal economic freedoms have low priority, the important habits of saving, investment, frugality, and ownership are marginalized.

Aristotle said, "Property that is common to the greatest number of owners receives the least attention; men care most for their private possessions, and for what they own in common less, or only so far as it falls to their own individual share."[18]

This is precisely why there is graffiti on the walls of public rest-

---

[17] Hernando de Soto, *The Mystery of Capital: Why Capitalism Triumphs in the West and Fails Everywhere Else* (New York: Basic Books, 2000). We discuss de Soto's research in chapter 4, 149–54.
[18] Aristotle, *Politics*, trans. H. Rackham, Loeb Classical Library (Cambridge, MA: Harvard University Press, 1932), 2.1.10, 76–77.

rooms but not in our homes. It explains the overgrazing of grass in the public domain, and why buffalo almost became extinct yet Hereford cows multiplied. Everyone's responsibility becomes no one's responsibility; this is what Garrett Hardin called "The Tragedy of the Commons."[19]

As long as the tribal structure gives the chief both executive and judicial power, any progress toward the rule of law and an independent judiciary is highly unlikely.

The inevitable consequences of holding resources in common—the proposition that everyone in "the tribe" owns the forests, lands, oceans, and wildlife—are readily evident. The results are inefficient exhaustion of the resources, deterioration of the environment, and social conflict among those who compete for resource use. While it may seem emotionally pleasing to believe that land, oceans, and wildlife belong to everyone as a common heritage, the economic consequences are typically tragic (see Photograph 1 following page 192).

Although abandoning tribal ownership and instituting private property are necessary for economic growth in countries that retain tribal ownership, each generation's leaders unfortunately seem to resist such fundamental change, and the tribe remains caught in a self-inflicted poverty trap, ending up as subsistence farmers (or, in the United States, working in casinos for low wages). Federal government entitlements in the United States continue to encourage this ineffective and destructive way of life.

The inevitable result of common ownership is the opposite of what everyone desires, for the verdict of world economic history remains the same: an economy based on tribal ownership of property can never bring a country from poverty to prosperity.

E. Feudalism

Feudal societies flourished in much of Europe from the ninth to the fifteenth centuries, lasting longer in certain Eastern European countries and some Asian countries such as Japan. In a feudal system, the "serfs" were tenant farmers who made a formal agreement with the "lord" of a large estate to give him some of their labor each year for his crops, as

---

[19] Garrett Hardin, "The Tragedy of the Commons," *Science* 162, no. 3859 (1968): 1243–48.

well as some "taxes" from their own crops, in exchange for the right to live on the land and farm a portion of it as their own. While the serfs were bound to the land, they had no ownership rights in the property.[20]

Early in the second millennium, however, money increasingly replaced bartering, producing a new social mobility along with rising productivity in agriculture and an increase in trade. Now a peasant could sell his labor to the highest bidder. The servant/master relationship began to dissolve as serfs discovered new employers who provided them a way to escape from the low pay and quasi-slavery of the feudal system. According to Dudley Dillard, "this growth of commerce was the chief dissolvent of the feudal system and serfdom, despite the fact that feudalism existed side by side with commerce throughout the medieval period."[21] Basically, the new social mobility encouraged serfs to become freemen.

As the feudal status of reciprocal obligation in an unchanging economic system of tradition started to fall, the expression of people's acquisitive nature began to rise. The opportunity to improve one's material condition and status in life finally became a natural human aspiration.

An important technological change that also contributed to the breakdown of the feudal system was the transition from a two-field to a three-field crop-rotation system. Under this innovation, a farmer divided his land into three parts. He planted each third with crop A one season, crop B the second season, and let it lie fallow for the third season (rather than letting each half lie fallow every other year, as in a two-field rotation system). Now a farmer could harvest not 50 percent but 67 percent of his land each year. As with modern multi-cropping, agricultural efficiency increased dramatically as trade was embraced and wealth grew. Dillard writes:

> The body of law practiced at the fairs became known as the "law merchant," which forms the basis of modern commercial law, including the law of contracts, negotiable instruments, agency, sale and auction. This was the "private international law of the Middle Ages." Mer-

---

[20] For more discussion, see Douglass C. North and Robert Paul Thomas, *The Rise of the Western World: A New Economic History* (Cambridge: Cambridge University Press, 1976), 9.

[21] Dudley Dillard, *Economic Development of the North Atlantic Community: Historical Introduction to Modern Economics* (Inglewood Cliffs, NJ: Prentice Hall, 1967), 59.

chants became privileged characters exempt from the common and canon law of the time.[22]

As the production and distribution of economic goods for more than mere subsistence commenced, the exchange of property for profit became common. Now cities would grow, more goods could be exchanged, and the standard of living—$2 a day under feudalism—doubled and then doubled again. The growing economies produced a middle class of merchants and shopkeepers in Britain, Holland, and Northern Europe, who busied themselves with commerce, manu-facturing, and finance. Economic growth, because of better defined property rights and population growth, became the order of the day. It started in Europe and then spread throughout Western civilization, where global dominance would last for more than five hundred years.

All this change showed feudalism to be a stagnant system that was increasingly undermined by improving economic opportunities outside the feudal system. Once again, the economic verdict was the same: an economy based on feudalism could never produce the growth necessary for prosperity.[23]

F. Mercantilism

After the decline of feudalism, an economic system called mercantil-ism was dominant throughout Europe for most of the seventeenth and eighteenth centuries. Its main goal was the accumulation of gold and silver bullion in a nation by exporting more and importing less. The idea behind mercantilism was that, just as a family's wealth can be measured by the amount of money it possesses, so a nation's wealth could be measured by the amount of gold and silver it accumulated. Laura LaHaye explains:

> Mercantilism is economic nationalism for the purpose of building a wealthy and powerful state. Adam Smith coined the term "mercantile system" to describe the system of political economy that sought to en-rich the country by restraining imports and encouraging exports. This

---

[22] Ibid., 19.
[23] For additional reading on feudalism and mercantilism, see North and Thomas, *The Rise of the Western World*; Eli Heckscher, *Mercantilism*, 2 vols. (New York: Macmillan, 1955); Dillard, *Economic Development of the North Atlantic Community*.

system dominated Western European economic thought and policies from the sixteenth to the late eighteenth centuries. The goal of these policies was, supposedly, to achieve a "favorable" balance of trade that would bring gold and silver into the country and also to maintain domestic employment.[24]

Under mercantilism, manufacturing and mining companies were emphasized so as to produce products for export, and often colonies and shipping companies were established to bring more money and goods into the nation.[25] Governments in Europe embraced it, as did business exporters. Murray Rothbard concludes that it was really a conspiracy against consumers and in favor of subsidized merchants, with the goals of enriching governments and penalizing competitors. Governments had the power to pass the laws to benefit monopolistic producers and extract considerable taxes for doing the favor.[26]

Adam Smith put it this way:

> Consumption is the sole end and purpose of all production; and the interest of the producer ought to be attended to, only so far as it may be necessary for promoting that of the consumer. . . . But in the mercantile system, the interest of the consumer is almost constantly sacrificed to that of the producer; and it seems to consider production, and not consumption, as the ultimate end and object of all industry and commerce.[27]

Jacob Viner, an economics professor at the University of Chicago and Princeton in the first half of the twentieth century, wrote:

> The laws and proclamations . . . were the product of conflicting interests of varying degrees of respectability. Each group, economic, social, or religious, pressed constantly for legislation in conformity with its special interest. The fiscal needs of the crown were always an important and generally a determining influence on the course of trade legislation.[28]

---

[24] Laura LaHaye, "Mercantilism," in *The Concise Encyclopedia of Economics*, ed. David R. Henderson (Indianapolis: Liberty Fund, 2008), 340.
[25] See Murray Rothbard, "Mercantilism: A Lesson for Our Times?" *The Freeman* 13, no. 11 (November 1963).
[26] Ibid.
[27] Adam Smith, *An Inquiry into the Nature and Causes of the Wealth of Nations*, ed. Edwin Cannan (1776; repr., New York: Modern Library, 1994), 715.
[28] Jacob Viner, *Studies in the Theory of International Trade* (New York: Harper and Brothers, 1937), 58–59.

In other words, governments granted special favors and privileges, and were paid for this with taxes. But this just made governments and their favored special interests more powerful.

The weakness of mercantilism was that while a nation was busy accumulating money, the more important goal of providing more and better goods and services for the people was neglected. Just as a reclusive miser might have a million dollars in cash but wear tattered clothing and live in a beat-up shack, so money itself does not truly enrich a nation. People eat, drink, and sleep on goods and services, not gold.

As mercantilism spread, merchants and labor guilds formed special-interest groups to restrict competition and game the system. While desiring competition for others and monopoly for themselves, the mercantilists (merchants) sought and received government protection. Favoring restrictive trade practices and government-granted monopoly charters for their specific interests, they focused on exports and gold. "In exchange for paying levies and taxes to support the armies of the nation-states, the mercantile classes induced governments to enact policies that would protect their business interests against foreign competition."[29]

European countries in particular adopted extensive export and import regulations, all with the goal of improving their balance of payments and accumulating money. "By the mid seventeenth century, then, Britain was ready to impose a general system of mercantile restriction on the colonists. The most general of the mercantile acts are those known as the Navigation Acts . . . [which were] passed over the years from 1651 through 1663."[30] Government regulations would also control wages, rule on the quality of goods, supervise the hiring and firing practices of different occupations, and specify the conditions of employment. Even though entrepreneurship and markets were slowly gaining ascendancy, the state controlled most of the economic power.

Not surprisingly, principal European countries tried to exclude the merchants and traders of other countries from their own colonial empires. Potential competitors were denied access so that those with

---

[29] LaHaye, "Mercantilism," 340.
[30] Clarence B. Carson, "The Founding of the American Republic: 6. The Mercantile Impasse," *The Freeman* 22, no. 1 (January 1972).

monopoly charters would benefit. It was not a good time for free trade or for economic freedom.

Protests began to mount against this kind of government protection, however, and by the 1860s, Britain had finally removed the last vestiges of the mercantile era. "Industrial regulations, monopolies, and tariffs were abolished, and emigration and machinery exports were freed. In large part because of its free trade policies, Britain became the dominant economic power in Europe."[31]

Since mercantilism does not seek the best economic interests of the people of a nation, it could never bring a country from poverty to prosperity.

G. Socialism and communism

The twentieth century witnessed several experiments with Marxian socialism (Germany, parts of South America, Africa) and Soviet/Sino communism (the Soviet Union, Eastern Europe, China). Both systems were committed to abolishing private ownership, belief in God, and inequality. Since these two economic systems are similar in many ways, we will examine them together.

Socialism is an economic system in which the government owns the means of production (the businesses and farms), and goods are almost entirely produced and distributed by government direction. Communism is an economic system in which the government owns not only the means of production but also all other property, including people's labor; in addition, communism is a political system that claims that genuine socialism must be brought about by violent revolution as a step toward an eventual utopian society that is classless and moneyless. In countries such as the Soviet Union and China, violent communist revolutions were followed by reigns of mass murder and terror to keep the population submissive, which was thought necessary until the population could eventually realize the benefits of the communist system.

The communist movement of Karl Marx was inaugurated by the publication of a small pamphlet titled *The Communist Manifesto* (London, 1848), in which he and Friedrich Engels summarized the fundamental

---

[31] LaHaye, "Mercantilism," 341.

proposition of communism and the Marxist framework. They introduced their ideas this way:

> All history has been a history of class struggles, of struggles between
> exploited and exploiting, between dominated and dominating classes
> at various stages of social development; . . . this struggle, however,
> has now reached a stage where the exploited and oppressed class
> (the proletariat) can no longer emancipate itself from the class which
> exploits and oppresses it (the bourgeoisie), without at the same time
> forever freeing the whole of society from exploitation, oppression
> and class struggles.[32]

The idea was that rival nations and rival economic classes were
pitted against each other in a fundamental and historic struggle for
supremacy. Collectivism, authoritarianism, and command-and-control
government planning would all be interconnected and mutually re-
inforcing, and would work together as a liberating force. Greedy
"capitalist" profit takers would finally be defeated.

The essence of the Marxist system was the concept of surplus
value,[33] the proposition that the worker is cheated because he is not
paid the full value of his labor, and that interest, rent and profit are
simply forms of theft of that which actually belongs to labor.

Marx claimed that the value of a commodity could be measured
by the labor hours put into it.[34] If one item took twice as many hours
to produce as another, it was worth twice as much. His call to abolish
property ownership (from which owners derived profit when laborers
came to work in their factories) came from his ill-conceived theory
that the value of a product was determined by the amount of labor put
into it. He thought that the owner of a factory or farm did not deserve
to gain any profit simply as a result of his ownership. Marx did not
understand that value is subjectively determined by the preferences
of buyers, not simply by the hours of labor invested, and that owners
of property deserve to profit from their investment of time, effort,
planning, and risk.

---

[32] Friedrich Engels, preface to the 1883 German edition of Karl Marx and Friedrich Engels, *The Communist Manifesto*, in *The Marx-Engels Reader*, ed. Robert C. Tucker (New York: W. W. Norton, 1972), 334.
[33] Karl Marx, "The Critique of Capitalism," in, 232–49.
[34] See Karl Marx, *Das Capital* (Washington: Regnery, 2000), parts 1–2.

Marx's theory initiated policies that inevitably took from the more productive to subsidize the less productive. Although the theory is demonstrably false, it prevailed in many countries at the end of the nineteenth century and then through most of the twentieth century.

Marxian theory also gave government the primary role of producing equality of material conditions. Only communist government planners could occupy the commanding heights of society to manage the herculean task of planning an entire economy according to abilities and needs, and make it all come out equal. In order for government to be empowered, coercion would be necessary, and, yes, eggs would be broken to make the omelet. But even Marx could not have anticipated how many eggs.

In their later three-volume book *Das Kapital* (Hamburg, 1867), Marx and Engels tried to enumerate the main principles of communism—value, exploitation, and class struggle—and to show how a communist order would work. They claimed that history was moving inevitably toward an ever larger "proletariat" (oppressed working class) in which, according to *Das Kapital*, "along with the constantly diminishing number of the magnates of capital, who usurp and monopolize all advantages of the process of transformation, grows the mass misery, oppression, slavery, degradation, exploitation."[35]

Eventually the proletariat would take over and a new (communist) economic order would emerge, with no oppression by one class of another.[36] In this new state, the wealth of the nation would finally be used for the good of all, "from each according to his ability, to each according to his needs."[37]

People under communism would no longer have the freedom to decide whether to work or not, for everyone would be compelled to work. But the problem (experienced now by all communist countries) is that people under communism have no incentive to work harder or be more innovative, because they cannot keep the fruits of their

---

[35] Ibid., 355.
[36] Communist revolutions never occurred where Marx said they would, in developed capitalist economies. They occurred only in mainly undeveloped economies (Russia, China, Cuba, North Korea, and some African nations). Marx's assumption that employers (the bourgeoisie) and workers (the proletariat) were enemies was false, for in modern developed economies they usually work together for the common good of companies.
[37] Karl Marx, *Critique of the Gotha Program* (Rockville, MD: Wildside Press, 2008), 27.

extra labor. Productivity inevitably falls. Abolishing private property destroys incentives.

Yet Marx did not see this. He believed that private property damaged human nature, and if private property could be abolished, people would naturally work for the good of the whole. He wrote, "The theory of the Communists may be summed up in the single sentence: Abolition of private property."[38]

The same objections that we raised in the section on tribal ownership also apply here. The teachings of the Bible clearly support a system of private ownership of property, reflected in the command "You shall not steal" (Ex. 20:15), as well as in numerous laws that regulated ownership of property. (On the incorrect claim that the early church practiced a primitive form of communism, see below, 143–44.)

More than a century before Marx, John Locke wisely observed, "As much land as a man tills, plants, improves, cultivates, and can use the product of, so much is his property. He by his labour does, as it were, enclose it from the common."[39] Then, in dozens of paragraphs, Locke proceeded to describe the rights of man to his property.

It is not surprising that Marx's predictions of a communal society did not materialize and the uprising of oppressed workers followed by a communist utopia did not happen. But it is not because the Soviet Union of the twentieth century did not try to realize them. The U.S.S.R. was the first country to apply Marxist principles and a rational communist plan to operate an entire economic system.

"Gos" is an abbreviation for the Russian word for government. Thus, in the Soviet Union, "Gosplan" determined the plan; "Gosten" set prices; "Gosnab" allocated supplies; and "Gostude" set labor assignments and wages. Smart, experienced government planners meshed local economic plans into regional economic plans, which, in turn, were meshed into a national economic plan.

This elaborate structure explains: (1) why the Soviet economy was so cumbersome it could not function efficiently (a critic might say it was one great big mesh); and (2) why Soviet planners had to rewrite five-year plans on an annual basis. Why didn't it work? Because, once

---

[38] Karl Marx and Friedrich Engels, *The Communist Manifesto* (New York: Monthly Review Press, 1968), 27.
[39] John Locke, *Concerning Civil Government*, in *Locke, Berkeley, Hume*, Great Books of the Western World, Vol. 35, ed. Robert Maynard Hutchins and Mortimer J. Adler (London: Oxford University Press, 1952), 51.

again, when everyone owns something, no one owns it. Farmers have a bad habit of not working very hard when they do not own the lands they farm. In addition, Gosplan was not good at predicting demand for the products it forced workers to produce.

The Soviet experience, as well as those of the People's Republic of China, Cuba, North Korea, and Cambodia, has shown that the hoped-for "dictatorship of the proletariat" has, in fact, always meant the tyrannical dictatorship of party leaders over the masses. *There has not been one real-world success story under the communist banner.* State power is absolute, government power is arbitrary, and the most elementary human freedoms are denied to the average citizen.

Even worse, the death toll from authoritarian, totalitarian communist regimes was staggering. "Measured by such basic standards as respect for human life and personal freedom, ours has been the most barbaric era in the history of the planet. More than 100 million people have been exterminated by the totalitarian powers, with millions more locked up in slave camps or subject to other organized repression."[40]

Jay W. Richards recounts in a few pages the horrible evils imposed under communism in the Soviet Union under Vladimir Lenin and Joseph Stalin, in China under Mao Tse-tung, and in Cambodia under Pol Pot.[41] Then he summarizes how communist regimes killed *85 million to 100 million* of their own people in the twentieth century:

China	65 million
U.S.S.R.	20 million
North Korea	2 million
Cambodia	2 million
African nations	1.7 million
Afghanistan	1.5 million
Vietnam	1 million
Eastern European nations	1 million
Latin American nations	150,000
The international communist movement	about 10,000[42]

---

[40] Evan M. Stanton, *The Theme Is Freedom: Religion, Politics, and the American Tradition* (Washington: Regnery, 1994), 5.

[41] See Jay W. Richards, *Money, Greed, and God: Why Capitalism Is the Solution and Not the Problem* (New York: HarperOne, 2009), 11–19.

[42] Ibid., 21; Richards quotes these statistics from *The Black Book of Communism* (Cambridge, MA: Harvard University Press, 1999), 4.

What about socialism? Since the essential economic element of government ownership of the means of production is the same, full-fledged socialism faces the same obstacles as communism: lack of sufficient incentive, loss of human productivity, loss of private ownership of businesses, and a corresponding loss of human and economic freedoms to be productive. Instead of consumers freely deciding which products are best and what should be produced, government officials make all those decisions. Socialism thus diminishes human freedom, choice, and opportunity to excel. No matter the plan, it has not been and cannot be made to work.

Political philosopher Michael Novak criticizes these destructive "-isms," writing in his landmark book *The Spirit of Democratic Capitalism*:

> Socialism was from the beginning a mythic force. Socialists adopted the red flag as a dramatic simplifying device, deliberately contrasting their single color (at first black, then red) with the conventional tricolor of existing democratic revolutions. They wished to represent a simple universal idea transcending any one nation. The color red glowed ominously by torchlight, Victor Hugo observed, signifying fire, danger, struggle, and a universality of shared blood.[43]

The total failure of both the Soviet Union and China to make communism work has forced Marxist-Leninist advocates to fall back on the unproven proposition that communism is still "inevitable" and that their utopian dream is still someday going to be built. However, a century of promises that resulted only in horrible dehumanization and economic failures leads us to conclude that an economy based on socialism or communism can *never* bring a country from poverty to prosperity.

But is there a "third way" between socialism and the free market? Some have proposed this in the modern welfare state.

H. The welfare state and equality

Many European governments now provide extensive benefits to their citizens from cradle to grave. The continent is now populated with

---

[43] Michael Novak, *The Spirit of Democratic Capitalism* (New York: Simon and Schuster, 1982), 319, citing James H. Billington, *Fire in the Minds of Men* (New York: Basic Books, 1980), 203–4.

people who believe their governments owe them a list of "human rights": education, secure jobs, long vacations, early retirements, generous pensions, subsidized housing, and free health care. They have built what many believe to be the best welfare states in the world. But what was the cause? And can it continue?

We must recognize that the wealth of European countries was created under structures much like free-market systems, not under the modern welfare state. Northern Europe became prosperous during the Industrial Revolution (about 1770–1870) and the century that followed, and the modern welfare state did not come into being until the prosperity that followed World War II (ended 1945). Governments then found that they could implement state ownership and/or massive subsidies for health care, housing, education, unemployment payments, and compulsory long vacations and early retirements.

Because the welfare state assures people of lifetime jobs and largely protects them from market forces and change, it has increasingly produced a continent of equal achievers, slow economic growth, and an entitlement mentality. British historian Niall Ferguson, in his book *Civilization: The West and the Rest*, says, "Europeans today are the idlers of the world."[44] On average, they work less than most people on any continent, enjoy protracted education and early retirement, have shorter work days and longer holidays, and are much more likely to go on strike. Ferguson also writes:

> Europeans not only work less; they also pray less—and believe less. There was a time when Europe could justly refer to itself as "Christendom." Europeans built the continent's loveliest edifices to accommodate their acts of worship. . . . As pilgrims, missionaries, and conquistadors, they sailed to the four corners of the earth, intent on converting the heathen to the true faith. Now it is Europeans who are the heathens.[45]

When the reality of entitlements outgrew the wealth being created, Europe finally hit a wall. According to financial expert and author John Mauldin and co-author Jonathan Tepper:

---

[44] Ferguson, *Civilization*, 265.
[45] Ibid., 266.

> We are coming to the end of a 60-year debt supercycle. Not just con-
> sumers but banks borrowed (and not just in the United States but all
> over the developed world) like there was no tomorrow. . . . European
> banks still remain highly leveraged. . . . Why is Greece important?
> Because so much of their debt is on the books of European banks.
> Hundreds of billions of dollars worth. . . . But those European banks?
> When that debt goes bad, and it will, they will react to each other
> just like they did in 2008. Trust will evaporate. . . . There are other
> countries in Europe, like Spain and Portugal, that are almost as bad
> as Greece.[46]

How long can economic freedom survive the underlying mass rage and the potential loss of the economic security that is now considered a basic human right? The European Union's welfare states, with their attempt to split the difference between free-market capitalism and government-directed socialism, appear to have run their course.

But at this moment, much of the continent remains in denial. Because debt, deficits, and unfunded social entitlements will not go away, dozens of countries in the European Union are facing either a Euro-zone breakup or a continent-wide fiscal union that constrains or eliminates the welfare state and big labor unions, but also collectivizes fiscal policy and governments.

Economists recognize that their discipline is about harnessing the power of incentives. Their helpful insights include: "When you reward an economic activity, you get more of it; when you penalize it, you get less." "Taxes matter." "Incentives matter." "You cannot spend your way out of a debt crisis or tax your way into prosperity." Europe must decide. Many of its policies to this point have disregarded these basic economic truths.

The main pillars of the European welfare states are no longer viable. A country could legislate significant entitlements when its population demographics were young, but now, with populations aging fast, and fewer workers (the "makers") supporting more and more retired ones (the "takers"), those generous entitlements for health and retirement are becoming impossible.

---

[46]John Mauldin and Jonathan Tepper, *Endgame: The End of the Debt Supercycle and How It Changes Everything* (Hoboken, NJ: John Wiley & Sons, 2011), 40–42.

Unless high deficits and debt are brought under control, it is inevitable that skyrocketing borrowing costs and credit rationing downgrades are inevitable. Labor flexibility in Europe needs serious fixing. Employers must be given the freedom to hire and fire as economic conditions change; union closed-shop protection of dozens of professions is no longer affordable. Competitive labor costs and increasing productivity are all necessary to compete in a global economy.

Germany's role is key. It cannot be expected to bankroll Europe's existing welfare states, but neither can it believe that Europe can get out of its financial hole without German help and economic aid. However, there will soon come a limit. Germany cannot continue to run large trade surpluses while the rest of Europe runs trade deficits. Gradual adjustments must be made everywhere. It now seems that European politicians will either deal with the European Union's serious flaws in their long march to recovery or experience the potential pain of bankruptcy and devaluation.

I. A better solution: the free-market system

The final economic system to consider is a free-market system. A free-market system is one in which economic production and consumption are determined by the free choices of individuals rather than governments, and this process is grounded in private ownership of the means of production. In very simple, practical terms, a free-market system means that people, not the government, own the farms, businesses, and properties in a nation ("the means of production").

"Fundamentally," says Nobel laureate Milton Friedman, "there are only two ways of co-ordinating the economic activities of millions. One is central direction involving the use of coercion—the technique of the army and of the modern totalitarian state. The other is voluntary co-operation of individuals—the technique of the market place."[47]

We describe such a free-market system in the next chapter.

---

[47] Milton Friedman, *Capitalism and Freedom: A Leading Economist's View on the Proper Role of Competitive Capitalism* (Chicago: University of Chicago Press, 1962), 13.

4

THE ECONOMIC
SYSTEM

The Free Market

We explained in the last chapter that many previous economic systems have failed to produce human prosperity. Hunting and gathering, subsistence farming, tribal ownership, feudalism, mercantilism, and socialism and communism all ended in failure. The modern welfare state is still living off earlier prosperity, but it is quickly discovering that current tax income falls massively short of promised obligations. The entitlement state is collapsing.

These systems neglected many (and sometimes all) of the factors that matter most for economic growth: the rule of law, private ownership of property, specialization and free trade, economic freedom, and the incentives necessary to create wealth and the hope of reward.

In this chapter, we will discuss various advantages of the free market. But first, what is a free-market system?

A. The free-market system defined

1. Definition

In the previous chapter, we defined a free-market system in this way:

> A free market system is one in which economic production and consumption are determined by the free choices of individuals rather

than by governments, and this process is grounded in private ownership of the means of production.

In this definition, the phrase "means of production" refers to all
the non-human factors that go into making goods and services, such
as factories, equipment, agricultural land, and mines. In very simple
terms, in a free-market system, *people*, not the government, own the
farms and the businesses. In addition, the people "own" themselves
in the sense that they have freedom to choose where to work. The
government does not decide where they work (as in slavery or in
communism).

By calling this a "free-market system," we also intend to distinguish it from various undesirable forms of "capitalism" that are really
not free-market systems, such as "state capitalism" and "oligarchic
capitalism" (explained in chapter 6, 211–15).

But what, then, is the "market" part of a free-market system? Can
we define a *free market*? Economist Murray Rothbard offers this definition: "'Free market' is a summary term for an array of exchanges
that take place in society. Each exchange is undertaken as a voluntary
agreement between two people or between groups of people represented by agents."[1] He adds that this "array of exchanges" has more
complexity: "The market, then, is not simply an array; it is a highly
complex, interacting latticework of exchanges. . . . The free market and
the free price system make goods from around the world available to
consumers."[2]

Writing from the perspective of a Christian theologian, one of us
(Wayne Grudem) elsewhere explains the free market in a similar way,
but viewing it as a divinely ordained process that is built into human
nature and emphasizing the beneficial results of the entire process of
voluntary exchanges:

> The free market is a wonderful, God-given process in human societies
> through which the goods and services that are *produced* by the society
> (supply) continually adjust to exactly match the goods and services

---

[1] Murray N. Rothbard, "Free Market," in *The Concise Encyclopedia of Economics*, ed. David R. Henderson
(Indianapolis: Liberty Fund, 2008), 200.
[2] Ibid., 200–201.

that are *wanted* by the society (demand) at each period of time, and through which the society assigns a measurable value to each good and service at each period of time, entirely through the free choices of every individual person in the society rather than through government control.[3]

Another writer, Jay W. Richards, also sees the providential hand of God in the free market:

Rather than despising the market order, Christians should see it as God's way of providentially governing the actions of billions of free agents in a fallen world. . . . The market is, as [F. A.] Hayek said, "probably the most complex structure in the universe." It deserves our admiration . . . a stunning example of God's providence over a fallen world.[4]

The functioning of such a free market is important for the main point of this book, that countries that want to move from poverty toward prosperity must produce more goods and services of value. But how can governments get their people to produce more? Some nations tried to force productivity through slavery, but it did not work. Nations that adopted socialism and communism also tried government planning and compulsion to make people work, but their economies failed miserably.

The genius of a free-market system is that it does not try to *compel* people to work. It rather leaves people *free to choose* to work, and it rewards that work by letting people keep the fruits of their labor. In a free market, no government officials have to force people to work. The government simply has to get out of the way and let the free market work all by itself (with some appropriate restraints on crime; see the next section).

The reason that market freedom produces prosperity was explained in 1776 by Adam Smith:

---

[3] This definition is taken from Wayne Grudem, *Politics—According to the Bible* (Grand Rapids: Zondervan, 2010), 276, emphasis in original.

[4] Jay W. Richards, *Money, Greed, and God: Why Capitalism Is the Solution and Not the Problem* (New York: HarperOne, 2009), 214–15. E. Calvin Beisner uses lengthy citations from Adam Smith's earlier writings to argue that by the phrase "invisible hand" Smith was referring to divine providence: see "Stewardship in a Free Market" in *Morality and the Marketplace*, ed. Michael Bauman (Hillsdale, MI: Hillsdale College Press, 1994), 26–29.

> That security which the laws in Great Britain give to every man that he shall enjoy the fruits of his own labour, is alone sufficient to make any country flourish. . . . The natural effort of every individual to better his own condition, when suffered to exert itself with freedom and security, is so powerful a principle, that it is alone, and without any assistance . . . capable of carrying on the society to wealth and prosperity.[5]

Smith's oft-repeated statement has been demonstrated again and again in subsequent history. In today's world, there is a strong correlation between economic freedom and prosperity. Those countries that have the highest levels of economic freedom (which can be calculated statistically using at least ten different factors) also have the highest per capita incomes. This can be seen when we plot the countries of the world on a graph comparing their economic freedom with their average per capita income (see Figure 1 following page 192).

The rest of this chapter and the next will explain just how the free market produces such amazing results—or, rather, how *the free people* in a free market produce such amazing results.

2. The rule of law

The rule of law is important to a free-market system. It prevents thieves and other criminals from taking away people's economic freedom by taking their property through fraud, deceit, or force. A free-market system must have laws to prevent crime. No one who defends a free-market system believes that the word *free* means that there should be anarchy. In fact, some laws are necessary to protect the *idea* of a free market, because the idea of free, voluntary exchanges is violated when people steal from, cheat, or deceive others, or when people do not have the information they need to make informed decisions. (We explain the rule of law more fully in chapter 7, 225–26; see also 154–55.)

Therefore, a proper understanding of a free market includes laws against theft, fraud, the violation of contracts, and the sale of defective and dangerous products. A country can have such laws and remain a free-market system because the decisions about what to produce and consume are left to individual people, not the government.

---

[5] Adam Smith, *An Inquiry into the Nature and Causes of the Wealth of Nations*, ed. Edwin Cannan (1776; repr., New York: Modern Library, 1994), 581.

3. Are all economies "mixed"?

From time to time when we mention free markets in our seminars, someone in the audience objects: "There is no such thing as a *free-market* system today, because all economies have a *mixture* of private ownership and government ownership and control. Therefore, what you are really arguing for is a *mixed* economy, and almost all nations have mixed economies today." The discussion then becomes confused because the relabeling implies that different economic systems are mostly the same.

So, does it even make any sense to talk about a "free-market system"? We think it does make sense, because there are real differences between economic systems from country to country. Of course, most nations with free-market economies have a few elements of government ownership or control over production, but that does not make them socialist countries by any means. For example, in the United States, the government has quasi-ownership of the massively tax-subsidized Postal Service, but this is the exception, not the rule. Most decisions about production and consumption in the United States are still made by individuals and private companies, not by the government.

In fact, the national economies of the world can be numerically arranged along a scale from "free" to "unfree." One such ranking has been published annually for the last eighteen years by the Heritage Foundation and *The Wall Street Journal*. The current volume is called *2012 Index of Economic Freedom*.[6] In order to determine how free an economy is, each year the researchers score 179 countries according to ten factors grouped in four categories:

A. Rule of law
   1. Property rights
   2. Freedom from corruption
B. Limited government
   3. Fiscal freedom
   4. Government spending

---

[6] Terry Miller, Kim R. Holmes, and Edwin Feulner, eds., *2012 Index of Economic Freedom* (Washington, DC: Heritage Foundation/New York: *The Wall Street Journal*, 2012). The index is also available at www.heritage.org/index/default. Another excellent source on this topic is James Gwartney, Robert Lawson, and Joshua Hall, *Economic Freedom of the World: 2012 Annual Report* (Vancouver, BC: Fraser Institute, 2012). It is also available at www.freetheworld.org.

    C. Regulatory efficiency
        5. Business freedom
        6. Labor freedom
        7. Monetary freedom
    D. Open markets
        8. Trade freedom
        9. Investment freedom
       10. Financial freedom

Each country is ranked on an economic freedom scale from 0 to 100, accompanied by a brief analysis according to the ten factors. In the 2012 *Index of Economic Freedom*, Hong Kong scored the highest (89.9), then Singapore (87.5), Australia, (83.1), New Zealand, (82.1), and Switzerland (81.1). These five are considered "free" by this publication (see inside its front cover).

The researchers then listed twenty-three countries that are "mostly free," including Canada (79.9), Chile (78.3), Mauritius (77.0), Ireland (76.9), the United States (76.3), and eighteen others. For purposes of our study, these top twenty-eight countries may be considered to have free-market systems or mostly free-market systems.

Sadly, eighty-eight countries still fall at the lower end of the scale: sixty countries rank as "mostly unfree," and below them another twenty-eight rank as "repressed." These countries score poorly in all ten categories of economic freedom. Such countries do not have free-market systems. The lowest ten are Equatorial Guinea (42.8 out of 100), Iran (42.3), the Democratic Republic of the Congo (41.1), Myanmar (38.7), Venezuela (38.1), Eritrea (36.2), Libya (35.9), Cuba (28.3), Zimbabwe (26.3), and North Korea (1).

4. Are we really talking about capitalism?

Some people refer to a free-market system as a "capitalist" system. If the word *capitalism* is understood to refer to a free-market system as we it describe here, then we certainly support such a description. However, we do not commonly use the term *capitalism* in this book because in speaking to audience after audience we have found that the term *capitalism* can mean many different things to different people—sometimes many positive things and sometimes quite a few negative things.[7] It does not seem wise to us to refer to the system we are proposing with a term that, in the minds of many readers, means several things that we do not intend. When speakers and hearers mean different things by a key term, clarity in analysis and discussion is hindered. Definitional clarity is important. In any case, the term *capitalism* does not convey the essential idea of a free-market system, which is that decisions about economic production and consumption are made by the free choices of individuals, not by the government.

Still, we do use *capitalism* from time to time, especially in interacting with quotations from other writers, and we find ourselves in agreement with the excellent defenses of genuine capitalism that have been published by writers such as Milton Friedman,[8] Michael Novak,[9] Jay W. Richards,[10] Steve Forbes and Elizabeth Ames,[11] and Austin Hill and Scott Rae.[12]

Sometimes a free-market system is also called a "free-enterprise system." This term has mostly positive connotations, but we have chosen the term "free-market system" because "free enterprise" places too much focus on business (what people think of when they hear the term *enterprise*) to the exclusion of *personal* economic choices made by millions of people who do not think of themselves as being in the business world or in any sort of "enterprise."

Not everyone connected with foreign aid today agrees with our recommendation that a free-market system (what some call "capitalism") is the solution to poverty in poor nations. In particular, many people working in NGOs (non-government organizations that are set up to help the poor in various ways) have a worldview that prevents them from seeing the benefits of a free-market system. Respected development economist Paul Collier writes bluntly:

---

[7] Robert Hessen says that *capitalism* is "a term of disparagement coined by socialists in the mid-nineteenth century" and that it is "a misnomer for 'economic individualism'" ("Capitalism," in *The Concise Encyclopedia of Economics*, 57).

[8] Milton Friedman, *Capitalism and Freedom: A Leading Economist's View on the Proper Role of Competitive Capitalism* (Chicago: University of Chicago Press, 1962).

[9] Michael Novak, *The Spirit of Democratic Capitalism* (New York: Simon and Schuster, 1982).

[10] Richards, *Money, Greed, and God.*

[11] Steve Forbes and Elizabeth Ames, *How Capitalism Will Save Us: Why Free People and Free Markets Are the Best Answer in Today's Economy* (New York: Crown Business, 2009).

[12] Austin Hill and Scott Rae, *The Virtues of Capitalism: A Moral Case for Free Markets* (Chicago: Northfield, 2010).

When I give the message to an NGO audience they get uneasy for a different reason. *Many of them do not want to believe that for the majority of the developing world global capitalism is working. They hate capitalism and do not want it to work.* The news that it is not working for the billion at the bottom is not good enough: they want to believe that it does not work anywhere. . . . The left needs to move on from the West's self-flagellation and idealized notions of developing countries. Poverty is not romantic. The countries of the bottom billion are not there to pioneer experiments in socialism; they need to be helped along the already trodden path of building market economies. The international financial institutions are not part of a conspiracy against poor countries; they represent beleaguered efforts to help. The left has to learn to love growth.[13]

Collier explains, for example, how Christian Aid, an influential charity in Britain, used the obscure research of someone who had never published an academic article on trade, and who was studying at a solidly Marxist institution, to support a deeply harmful call for maintaining high trade barriers in poor nations, and to crudely demean "capitalism" as a force of oppression for the poor.[14]

Why do organizations such as Christian Aid promote such harmful advice? Collier says, "As I write it is too early to tell which situation it is—confused Christians, infiltrating Marxists, or corporate marketing executives."[15]

5. The economic success of free-market systems

Has the free-market system proved to be a productive economic system? Yes, it has been far more successful than any of the other systems discussed above. In fact, except for a few oil-rich Middle Eastern nations, all nations with high per capita income today have become wealthy through various forms of a free-market system. (China's per capita income for 2012 was still only $9,100, which puts it in the middle of the income range. It ranks as no. 118 in per capita income out of the 228 countries of the world. And China's remarkable eco-

---

[13] Paul Collier, *The Bottom Billion: Why the Poorest Countries Are Failing and What Can Be Done About It* (Oxford: Oxford University Press, 2007), 190–91, emphasis added.
[14] Ibid., 157–59.
[15] Ibid., 159.

nomic growth was itself the result of introducing significant elements of economic reform in a free-market direction.)[16]

No other economic system has brought any country from poverty to prosperity. A free-market system is the only type that offers a workable alternative and resilient counterforce to the failed -isms and systems discussed in the previous chapter.

6. Biblical support for human freedom in economic systems

In a later chapter, we discuss the biblical support for the idea that governments should protect human freedom (see 189–90), but here we can say briefly that support for the idea of freedom in the market comes from various strands of thought:

(1) *The teaching about private property in the Bible.* Property is seen as belonging not to the government or to society as a whole but to individuals (see Ex. 20:15; Lev. 25:10; Deut. 19:14; 1 Sam. 8:10–18; 1 Kings 21; and the discussion later in this chapter, 142–44).

(2) *The biblical concept of personal stewardship responsibility to God for the property we have (Ps. 24:1, and see below, 144–45).* This stewardship can be exercised only when individuals are free to choose how to use their property.

(3) *The biblical teaching that all human beings are created in the image of God (Gen. 1:26–27; 9:6; James 3:9),* and therefore should have equal rights before the law. The opposing view is that a small group of rulers has superior rights to dictate everyone else's economic decisions.

(4) *The biblical teaching of a limited role for government.* Government is to punish wrongdoers, reward those who do good, and maintain order in society. There is no biblical teaching that government has the right to manage the economic decisions of a nation (see Rom. 13:1–6; 1 Peter 2:13–14 on the responsibilities of the state).

(5) *The absence of any clear biblical support for the idea that government should control the economy of a nation and should not allow economic freedom.* In fact, government does not need any special warrant to leave people alone and leave the economy alone (except for punishing criminal activity).

---

[16] The World Factbook, accessed March 7, 2013, https://www.cia.gov/library/publications/the-world
-factbook/rankorder/2004rank.html.

We do not want government leaders to think they somehow have to "create" a free market. If government stays out of the way and simply prevents people from wrongfully harming one another, economic freedom just happens. In that sense, freedom already exists wherever people begin to enter into voluntary exchanges with one another, which is everywhere in human society. Governments do not have to create free markets. But governments do have to protect free markets in various ways, as we explain in the chapters that follow.

B. The wonder of a pencil: the free market, without a human director, makes complex products that no one knows how to make

Does a free market need a central planner to know what goods to make? The answer is no. No one person possesses enough expertise to plan all the facets of a free economic system. In fact, there is not one person on the planet who knows how to make even a simple pencil, yet pencils are manufactured with great success. This is illustrated in the story *I, Pencil*, by Leonard Read, the late former president of the Foundation for Economic Education.[17]

"Not a single person knows how to make me," the pencil says. Could that be true? Compared to a house, a car, or a computer, a pencil seems so easy to make. But then Read (speaking through "the pencil" as if it were a person) proceeds to tell all the things that go into the making of a pencil. First, the wood comes from a cedar tree of straight grain that grows in certain forests. To cut down the tree and transport the logs to the railroad siding requires saws, ropes, trucks, and countless other pieces of machinery. Thousands of people and hundreds of skills go into making just the "wood" part of a pencil. The mining of ore, the manufacture of steel, and its eventual refinement into chain saws, axes, and motors are just the start. Hemp is grown and brought through all the production stages that produce a strong rope. Even the logging camps, with their beds, mess halls, and untold thousands of people making many components represent a process full of more details.

Think about all the skills that are needed to bring the logs to the

---

[17] Leonard Read, *I, Pencil: My Family Tree as Told to Leonard E. Read* (Irving on the Hudson, New York: The Foundation for Economic Education, 2006), 3–9.

mill and all the trucks that move them from place to place. Think about all the millwork involved in converting the logs to slats. Vast amounts of machinery and expertise are needed just to secure the wood for a pencil. But that is just part of what you see.

The "lead" of a pencil is not lead at all. It starts as graphite mined in Sri Lanka, which passes through many complicated processes before it ends up in the center of a pencil. The bit of metal—the ferrule—near the top of the pencil is brass. Think of all the energy and technology it takes to mine the zinc and copper, then all the skills involved in making the shiny sheet brass from these products of nature.

What we call the eraser is known in the trade as the "plug." We think of it as rubber, but the rubber is only for binding purposes. The erasing is actually done by "factice," a rubberlike product made by reacting rapeseed oil from Indonesia with sulfur chloride.

Do you know how to mine graphite? Are you a chemical engineer? Do you know how to make yellow paint and hydraulically blast it through a spray gun? Do you know how to run a lumber mill, a smelter, a Caterpillar logging machine, or an injection-molding machine? None of us knows how to do all of these tasks. But all of us as a combined world economy do. After all of this and much more, the pencil says, "Does anyone wish to challenge my earlier assertion that no single person on the face of this earth knows how to make me?"[18] I, *Pencil* leaves us amazed at what can be accomplished despite the absence of a mastermind.

The seemingly "invisible hand" of a free market, in which everyone attempts to do at least one thing well, produces the coordination, harmony, and resources to make exactly what people want. When all people specialize on what they do best and then exchange their efforts, markets work effectively, quietly, and profoundly.

C. The economic foundation of a free market: private ownership of property

It is widely recognized that private ownership of property is the foundation of a free-market economic system, in distinction from communism (which has no private ownership of any property) or socialism

---

[18] Ibid., 6.

(which has no private ownership of the means of production). But what is the justification for a belief in private property?

We find one justification for private property in the teachings of the Bible on this topic. We find other justifications in recent economic studies that have demonstrated how crucial private ownership of property is for successful economic development.

1. The justification of private property from the Bible

In the Ten Commandments, the eighth commandment, "You shall not steal" (Ex. 20:15), assumes that there is something to steal—something that belongs to someone else and not to me. I should not steal your ox or donkey—or your car, cell phone, or iPad—because these things belong to you and not to me. Therefore, the command "You shall not steal," assumes private ownership of property.[19]

Other passages in the Old Testament show that God was concerned to protect the private ownership of property. Property was to be owned by individuals, not by the government or by society as a whole. For instance, God told the people of Israel that when the Year of Jubilee came, "It shall be a jubilee for you when *each of you shall return to his property* and each of you shall return to his clan" (Lev. 25:10).

Many other laws defined punishments for stealing and appropriate restitutions for damages to another person's farm animals or agricultural fields (see, for example, Ex. 21:28–36; 22:1–15; Deut. 22:1–4; 23:24–25). These were properties that belonged to individual people, and the Israelites were to honor the rights of those people to their property.

Another commandment protected property boundaries: "You shall not move your neighbor's landmark, which the men of old have set, in the inheritance that you will hold in the land that the LORD your God is giving you to possess" (Deut. 19:14). To move a landmark was to move the boundaries of a piece of land, and thus to steal land that belonged to one's neighbor (compare Prov. 22:28; 23:10).[20]

---

[19] This paragraph and the following seventeen paragraphs are adapted from Barry Asmus and Wayne Grudem, "Property Rights Inherent in the Eighth Commandment Are Essential for Human Flourishing," in *Business Ethics Today: Stealing*, ed. Philip J. Clements (Philadelphia: Center for Christian Business Ethics Today, 2011), 119–34. See notes 20 and 22 for earlier sources of some sections.
[20] The previous two paragraphs have been adapted from Grudem, *Politics—According to the Bible*, 262.

The Old Testament also shows an awareness that governments can wrongly use their immense power to disregard property rights and steal what they should not have. At the urging of wicked Queen Jezebel, King Ahab wrongfully stole Naboth's vineyard, and had Naboth killed in the process (1 Kings 21).

The prophet Samuel warned the people of Israel of the evils of a king who would "take" and "take" and "take":

> So Samuel told all the words of the Lord to the people who were asking for a king from him. He said, "These will be the ways of the king who will reign over you: he will *take* your sons and appoint them to his chariots and to be his horsemen and to run before his chariots. And he will appoint for himself commanders of thousands and commanders of fifties, and some to plow his ground and to reap his harvest, and to make his implements of war and the equipment of his chariots. He will *take* your daughters to be perfumers and cooks and bakers. He will *take* the best of your fields and vineyards and olive orchards and give them to his servants. He will *take* the tenth of your grain and of your vineyards and give it to his officers and to his servants. He will *take* your male servants and female servants and the best of your young men and your donkeys, and put them to his work. He will *take* the tenth of your flocks, *and you shall be his slaves.* And in that day you will cry out because of your king, whom you have chosen for yourselves, but the Lord will not answer you in that day." (1 Sam. 8:10–18)

God later spoke through the prophet Ezekiel, prohibiting exactly this kind of confiscation of property by a ruler:

> The prince *shall not take* any of the inheritance of the people, thrusting them out of their property. He shall give his sons their inheritance out of his own property, so that none of my people shall be scattered from his property. (Ezek. 46:18)[21]

Sometimes people claim that the early church practiced a form of "early communism" because it is said in the book Acts, "All who believed were together and had all things in common" (Acts 2:44). But

---

[21] For further discussion of private property, see ibid., 137–39, 261–68.

this situation was far different from communism, because (1) the giving was voluntary and not compelled by a government, and (2) people still had personal possessions and owned property, as we see from the fact that they continued to meet in "their homes" (Acts 2:46), and that many other Christians after this time owned homes (see Acts 12:12; 17:5; 18:7; 20:20; 21:8, 16; Rom. 16:5; 1 Cor. 16:19; Col. 4:15; Philem. 2; 2 John 10). Peter even told Ananias and Sapphira that they did not have to feel any obligation to sell their house and give away the money, because it belonged to them (see Acts 5:4).[22]

2. Private property implies an obligation for responsible stewardship

Private property itself implies some stewardship responsibilities. If human beings were alone in the universe, with no accountability to any God, then people might assume that private ownership of property carried no obligations. Conversely, people might assume that "society" or government should take the property away, lest people use it for selfish purposes. This is the view of communist societies.

But if *God himself* has commanded, "You shall not steal," and if in that commandment *God himself* establishes the legitimacy of private property, this leads us to think that God has probably entrusted property to us for a purpose. This is certainly the Bible's perspective. In biblical terms, our ownership of property is not absolute, but we are "stewards" who will have to give an account of our stewardship. This is because, ultimately, "The earth is the LORD's and the fullness thereof, the world and all those who dwell therein" (Ps. 24:1).

We now have greater insight into the wisdom of God in the eighth commandment. "You shall not steal" implies, in the context of the entire Old Testament, a system of private ownership of property. And private ownership of property, which is given by God, implies responsible stewardship and accountability for the use of that property. Once I realize that *God* commands others not to steal my land, my ox, my donkey, my car, or my laptop, then I realize that I also have a responsibility for how those things are used. I have been *entrusted* with these

---

[22] The previous paragraph was adopted from the *ESV Study Bible*, Wayne Grudem, gen. ed. (Wheaton: Crossway, 2009), note on Acts 2:44, 2085.

things by the God who created the universe, and I must act as a faithful steward to manage what he has entrusted to me.

3. Governments both violate biblical principles and hinder economic development when they prevent people from owning property

What if a government takes away this right to own property? Then I am no longer free to act as a steward in deciding how that property is to be used, for I can no longer control the use of that property. Likewise, if a government places burdensome restrictions on how I can use my property, then my ability to exercise stewardship is also diminished.

We must acknowledge at the outset that governments have a proper authority to collect taxes for legitimate government functions. Paul says that because the civil authority is "God's servant for your good, . . . you also pay taxes, for the authorities are ministers of God attending to this very thing. Pay to all what is owed to them: taxes to whom taxes are owed . . ." (Rom. 13:4, 6–7). Legitimate government functions include encouraging good and punishing evil, and establishing order in society, for Peter says that governors are sent "to punish those who do evil and to praise those who do good" (1 Peter 2:14).

However, too often in history governments have gone far beyond these legitimate functions. We cannot here define in detail the exact limits of government's legitimate power of taxation, but we can point to several examples of governments that have so diminished or abolished private property that they have destroyed human flourishing in their nations. This is because, if people are to exercise stewardship fully, they must have freedom to use their property as they think best. But if government owns, controls, or over-regulates all the property, people no longer have freedom to use their property as they think best and to be rewarded for their effort. Human achievement is thereby stifled and true human excellence occurs rarely, if ever.

4. Historical evidence of the economic damage that occurs when governments prevent private ownership of property

It is not difficult to find examples of governments that severely hindered economic development by denying people the right to own property:

a. Communist countries

Communist countries regularly and by conviction prohibit private ownership of land. Karl Marx and Friedrich Engels said, "The theory of the Communists may be summed up in the single sentence: abolition of private property."[23]

Communist countries such as North Korea, China, Cuba, and the former Soviet Union have prohibited private ownership of property such as land and buildings. Therefore, it is no surprise that these nations have uniformly trapped their people in horrible poverty. China's remarkable economic growth began only when it instituted significant economic changes in a free-market direction under Deng Xiaoping beginning in 1978.

b. Tribal ownership

In some nations, all property is owned by a tribe, not by individuals. Every nation that has tribal ownership of property is poor, and will always remain poor. This is because tribal ownership of property prevents private ownership, and thus takes away the incentives necessary for human economic development.

In the United States, tribal ownership of land characterizes most of the reservations where many Native Americans (also called "American Indians") live (see above, 114–16). There are about 310 Indian reservations in the country, representing about 2.3 percent of the nation's total land area. But the economic and educational situations on these reservations are terrible, with about one-third of Native Americans living below the poverty line. There are few jobs, and unemployment rates are often more than double the national average. Alcoholism and drug abuse abound. Lack of private ownership of property traps Native Americans in poverty and economic despair, and alienates them from the prosperous society that surrounds them (see Photograph 1 following page 192).[24]

Tribal customs in Africa also can effectively prevent private ownership of property, or at least the accumulation of any significant amount

---

[23] Karl Marx and Friedrich Engels, *Communist Manifesto* (1848; repr. New York: Monthly Review Press, 1968), 27.
[24] Fortunately, some progress is being made, especially in Canada, in establishing private property rights in Native American lands. See, for example, Terry Anderson, "The Right to Own Property on Reservations," *PERC Reports* 30, no. 2 (Summer/Fall 2012): 4.

of property. Ethnologist David Maranz writes that in many sub-Saharan Africa countries:

> A major factor in people's use of money is the expectation that friends and relatives will ask to "borrow" from them . . . [so] expenditures need to be made without delay. If this is not done, the cash will appear to be available for borrowing.[25]

> Not all Africans follow the normal and accepted financial principles of the sharing that society dictates, but people who do not do so pay a very heavy social price: they are shunned and marginalized by friends and relatives.[26]

> People who have many possessions or a "surplus" of money are pre-judged to be selfish egoists who are insensible to the needs of others.[27]

This social expectation that possessions must be shared equally effectively prevents people from accumulating any capital to build or expand businesses. The social pressures of this tradition can become so strong that people are effectively denied the right to decide how their property is to be used. Maranz explains:

> The person requesting a thing or money from a friend or relative has a dominant role in determining whether his or her need is greater than that of the potential donor, and consequently, of whether or not the potential donor should donate. . . . If the owner does not give into the demand for something, a refusal may well result in an immedi-ate verbal lashing in which the person refused angrily calls the other selfish. . . . It is virtually the right of a self-defined poorer person to be given what is asked for from a relative or a close friend, if what is asked for appears to be "donatable." I have heard many Africans complain about this, but all have said they are powerless to stop it, to condemn it openly, or to challenge the system.[28]

Lack of respect for private property rights also extends to smaller possessions. Maranz explains that, in much of sub-Saharan Africa:

---

[25] David Maranz, *African Friends and Money Matters* (Dallas: SIL International, 2001), 18.
[26] Ibid., 27.
[27] Ibid., 37.
[28] Ibid., 33–34.

Loans of goods or things are tantamount to gifts. Generally, the lender must ask for the return of a loaned item if there is to be any likelihood of it being returned. . . . Articles loaned may be: books, tape recorders, carrying bags, articles of clothing, tools, dishes, and such items. There seems to be a strong sense that if the person believes he needs a thing more than you do, you owe it to him/her and should not expect it back. The greater need is defined by the one without the thing.[29]

c. Other examples

There are many other examples of nations that have prevented private ownership of property.

In India prior to the advent of British rule in 1757, local Mogul princes had unquestioned regional authority and essentially took from the people whatever they wanted. This system effectively prevented private ownership of property, and thus greatly hindered human flourishing for centuries.[30]

In China for many centuries, the emperor had absolute rule and took whatever he wanted from the people.[31] Once again, this practice prevented a workable system of private ownership of property, and thus hindered human flourishing. In fact, it kept vast numbers of Chinese people in destitute poverty.

David S. Landes points to "the lack of free land" (that ordinary people could buy) in Argentina as "one of the worst legacies of the colonial regime." Although Argentina had immense natural resources, including rich agricultural land, it failed to develop economically because "vast domains had been given away, assigned to the Church and to men of respect and power, and the leftovers were grabbed up during the troubles that followed the revolution [of 1810]."[32]

Similar problems have plagued much of the rest of Latin America, where a few wealthy families control essentially all the land, and the legal process for purchasing and registering a piece of property is

---

[29] Ibid., 160.
[30] David S. Landes, The Wealth and Poverty of Nations: Why Some Are So Rich and Some So Poor (New York: W. W. Norton, 1999), 156–57. The extractive institutions that Daron Acemoglu and James A. Robinson discuss (absolutism in the case of North Korea) are forms of restriction of private ownership of property. See Acemoglu and Robinson, Why Nations Fail: The Origins of Power, Prosperity and Poverty (New York: Crown Publishers, 2012), 79–83.
[31] Landes, Wealth and Poverty, 31, 35–36.
[32] Ibid., 324.

so complex that it has effectively been made impossible for the vast majority of the population. This has been extensively documented by Peruvian economist Hernando de Soto.[33]

Similarly, under the feudal system in Eastern Europe for several centuries, a few wealthy lords owned all the property, trapping everyone else in poverty. The lack of an easily accessible means to gain ownership of property meant that human flourishing was effectively prevented for centuries.

Another way in which governments prevent people from owning property is by failing to resolve conflicting property claims that often occur after civil wars or changes of government. This is still a problem, for example, in modern-day Albania.[34] Collier points out that after a civil war or other conflict, nations need to "sort out conflicting and confused property claims quickly."[35]

5. The importance of legal titles to property

In a widely-acclaimed book, Hernando de Soto explains why documented ownership of property is so important. He says that most poor people of the world "have houses but not titles; crops but not deeds; businesses but not statutes of incorporation."[36] Without titles, deeds, and articles of incorporation, people have no chance to borrow money based on the value of their property, build wealth, and grow in prosperity.

Such a system, even if it is sometimes called "capitalism," is a dead one, and it is surely in no sense a "free-market" system. Poverty is inevitable. When individuals and businesses do not possess verifiable addresses or documented and protected property rights, their assets are rendered useless. They cannot use the small houses they live in or the land they occupy as a basis for borrowing money and starting a small business. Only when people have legal titles can they borrow, invest, and expand from the value of their property.

---

[33] See Hernando de Soto, *The Mystery of Capital: Why Capitalism Triumphs in the West and Fails Everywhere Else* (New York: Basic Books, 2000).

[34] "Albania still lacks a clear property rights system, particularly for land tenure. Security of land rights remains a problem in coastal areas where there is potential for tourism development" (Miller, Holmes, and Feulner, *2012 Index of Economic Freedom*, 82).

[35] Collier, *The Bottom Billion*, 152.

[36] De Soto, *Mystery of Capital*, 7.

Yes, the world's three billion poor do have some savings, according to de Soto. In fact, the total value of the real estate held but not legally owned by the poor of the Third World and former communist nations is at least $9.3 *trillion*.[37] This astounding amount is equal to more than 10 percent of the annual economic production of the entire world ($70 trillion GDP in 2011).

The problem is the need for ownership rights that are publicly documented, so that people have legal protection for their property. Lacking titles to their houses and other assets, and blocked by their local governments from ever getting them, the poor remain squatters. Without legal titles to property, they have no publicly confirmed value to add security to their economic situation. Poverty becomes permanent since their assets provide no capacity against which to borrow. One can hardly mortgage what one does not officially own or convince an electric company to deliver power to a non-verifiable address. Turning assets into liquid capital is thus an insurmountable hurdle for these poor people, a hurdle that Westerners do not face.[38]

De Soto explains the problem this way:

In the West, by contrast, every parcel of land, every building, every piece of equipment, or store of inventories is represented in a property document that is the visible sign of a vast hidden process that connects all these assets to the rest of the economy. Thanks to this representational process, assets can lead an invisible, parallel life alongside their material existence. They can be used as collateral for credit. The single most important source of funds for new businesses in the United States is a mortgage on the entrepreneur's house. These assets can also provide a link to the owner's credit history, an accountable address for the collection of debts and taxes, the basis for the creation of reliable and universal public utilities, and a foundation for the creation of securities (like mortgage-backed bonds) that can then be rediscounted and sold in secondary markets. By this process the West injects life into assets and makes them generate capital. Third World and former communist nations do not have this representational process. . . . Without representation, [the assets of the poor]

---

[37] Ibid., 35. See also C. K. Prahalad, *The Fortune at the Bottom of the Pyramid* (Upper Saddle River, NJ: Wharton, 2005).
[38] De Soto, *Mystery of Capital*, 35.

are dead capital. The poor inhabitants of these nations—five-sixths of humanity—do have things, but they lack the process to represent their property and create capital.[39]

6. Government rules that make property ownership impossible

But assume that you are a poor person who somehow gets a title to some land, which gives you a legal basis for borrowing money to start a small business. You still might not get any money. Borrowing money requires filling out numerous government forms and getting permissions and permits from government bureaus. Poor treatment can be expected. But that is just the start. You must show proof that you meet numerous qualifications to afford a loan. This procedure alone could take weeks, even months. Then you must show tax records, at least three years of income earned, credit records (oh, you haven't borrowed before?), a driver's license, and anything else government officials can think of.

The nastiness of the process resembles a person pleading innocence while everyone presumes he is guilty. Even when you do pass muster, officials may still refuse your application unless you are willing to pay a bribe. It is humiliating and embarrassing, and it breaks most people. In free countries, the entire process of getting a legal title for a business takes only days or weeks. In countries that are not free, the process might take years or even decades.

The research team headed by de Soto tried opening a small garment workshop (with one worker) on the outskirts of Lima, Peru. The team members worked at the registration process six hours a day, and it took 289 days! The cost was $1,231, or thirty-one times the monthly minimum wage (approximately three years' salary). De Soto writes: "To obtain legal authorization to build a house on state-owned land took six years and eleven months requiring 207 administrative steps in fifty-two government offices. . . . To obtain a legal title for that piece of land took 728 steps."[40]

According to De Soto:

---

[39] Ibid., 6–7.
[40] Ibid., 20.

> [The procedure to formalize urban property in the Philippines] could necessitate 168 steps, involving fifty-three public and private agencies and taking thirteen to twenty-five years. . . . In Egypt, the person who wants to acquire and legally register a lot on state-owned desert land must wend his way through at least 77 bureaucratic procedures at thirty-one public and private agencies. . . . This can take anywhere from five to fourteen years. . . . Total time to gain lawful land in Haiti: nineteen years. . . . Yet even this long ordeal will not ensure that the property remains legal.[41]

Developing countries create such a maze of procedures that drain both time and money that most citizens choose to go underground and deal in the informal, illegal economy. They do not want to break the rules, but the rules break them.[42]

De Soto writes:

> Imagine a country where nobody can identify who owns what, addresses cannot be easily verified, people cannot be made to pay their debts, resources cannot conveniently be turned into money, ownership cannot be divided into shares, descriptions of assets are not standardized and cannot be easily compared, and the rules that govern property vary from neighborhood to neighborhood or even from street to street. You have just put yourself into the life of a developing country or a former communist nation.[43]

When this bogus kind of "capitalism" cannot be made to work (bogus, for it is surely not a "free-market" system), people keep beating on the dead horse of a "third way" (between capitalism and socialism) until they sadly learn that the third way is a trip to the third world. Meanwhile, a majority of the adults on the planet are caught in the morass of inability to own, title, or securitize property.

7. Establishing an easy path to documented property ownership

How did developed nations establish their systems of documented property rights? De Soto spent years researching the history of this

---

[41] Ibid., 20–21.
[42] Ibid., 20–27.
[43] Ibid., 15.

development and concluded that in every nation that has well-established, easily obtained legal and public property rights, "this property revolution was always a *political* victory. In every country, it was a result of a few enlightened men deciding that official law made no sense if a sizeable part of the population lived outside it."[44]

For example, in the United States, local governments accepted the fact that improving a piece of soil was enough to establish property rights, so squatters were allowed to purchase land at prices set by local juries. This innovative legal provision was called preemption.[45] Remarkably, instead of laws coming first and then pioneers settling later, the pioneers settled first and then the law was established.

The immense economic benefit is summarized under the term *collateralization*. The term *collateralization* means using a piece of land (or land and a house or other asset) as security ("collateral") for a loan. When someone owns land, he can collateralize that land—borrow money equal to some part of the value of the land.

When the western part of the United States was being settled, legalization and protection of property rights effectively produced collateralization and thereby unlocked the additional legal property arrangements to make the free-market system work.

On a personal level, both of my (Barry Asmus's) grandparents benefitted from this law, as described in my book *The Best Is Yet to Come*.[46]

Developing countries could choose to do the same today. Once appropriate laws and access to titles are in place, squatters can make the system work for them. It is just a matter of making the law conform to what people are already doing. (De Soto explains this process in much more detail.)

Establishing easy, quick access to clearly documented property rights is of utmost importance for any country that seeks to move from poverty toward increasing prosperity. Massachusetts Institute of Technology professor Abhijit Banerjee writes, "There is an extremely

---

[44] Ibid., 106.

[45] A treatment of the complex and highly disputed matter of the conflicts between white settlers and Native Americans over property rights is beyond the scope of this book.

[46] Barry Asmus, *The Best Is Yet to Come* (Phoenix: Ameripress, 2001), 129–31.

strong and positive relation between the security of private property in a country and its per capita income."[47]

Land laws like these, with documented property rights, must be duplicated in developing countries. This is the basic foundation necessary for free markets to work. The difficulty of purchasing and titling property must be eased. Inefficient, overworked, bribery-ridden titling offices must be reformed so that it is easy and inexpensive for people to gain clear legal titles to property. Governments must protect property rights rather than blocking or even confiscating them.

D. The legal foundation for a free market: the rule of law

In order for a free-market system to work, everyone in the nation must be subject to the rule of law. This means that all the people in the nation, including the highest government officials, are accountable to the laws and will be punished if they break them.

The classic example of this in the history of the nation of Israel is the story of David and Bathsheba. David was the king, the most powerful person in Israel. But he violated the law that God had given to the nation by committing adultery with a woman named Bathsheba and then by arranging to have Bathsheba's husband, Uriah, killed in battle (2 Samuel 11). Afterward, God sent the prophet Nathan to David. Nathan told David a parable about a rich man who had committed great wrong against a poor man, and David was outraged. Then Nathan said to David, "You are the man!" (2 Sam. 12:7). He went on to tell David how God was going to punish him for his sins (2 Sam. 12:8–15).

Here a principle was established: not even the king is above the law that God gave to the nation. In order for the king to be reminded of this fact, God decreed that he "shall write for himself a copy of this law . . . and he shall read in it all the days of his life" (Deut. 17:18–19).

As we explained earlier (134–35), the very idea of a free-market system carries with it the need for some laws to prevent crime. If people are going to be able to make voluntary, well-informed economic choices, then there must be laws against stealing and cheating others (for these are not free or voluntary exchanges). There must also

---

[47] Abhijit Vinayak Banerjee, writing in Abhijit Vinayak Banerjee et al., *Making Aid Work* (Cambridge, MA: The MIT Press, 2007), 133.

be laws against fraud, the violation of contracts, and causing harm to others by selling defective and dangerous products. Everyone in the nation must be subject to these laws.

When some government officials and their friends are above the law, it is a tremendous disincentive to economic growth. Why would you want to build a business when you know that if you become successful, the local governor can impose arbitrary fines and drive you out of business—or the country can just confiscate ("nationalize") your business? Or when your largest customer turns out to be the judge's nephew, who might suddenly refuse to pay for any of the large orders he has received from you with no fear of repercussions? When a few people can violate the law with impunity, tremendous uncertainty is introduced into the business climate, and people do not want to take risks. This, in turn, tends to paralyze any growth in production of goods and services in the nation. A free-market system cannot function effectively apart from the rule of law in a nation. (We discuss the rule of law more fully in chapter 7, 225–26.)

E. Two crucial economic factors for a free market

If a nation establishes a clear and simple path to private ownership of property, and if it establishes the rule of law, two other economic policies are crucial for a free-market system to function effectively: (1) a stable currency, and (2) low tax rates. This is because a stable currency ensures that the prices in the market give accurate signals about value and supply and demand, and low tax rates guarantee that people are genuinely free to decide how to use their money themselves rather than a government agency that has taken their money deciding this for them.

1. The government must establish a stable currency

The free-market economy we have described, based on private property and voluntary exchange, can be viewed as a massive auction of buyers and sellers responding to a vast array of prices. Everyone gets what they want when they exchange money for a good or service. This means that prices are the signaling system. But how are prices going to be measured? In what kind of money or currency?

It is a remarkable fact that market *prices*, if they can be measured and fairly compared, produce actions by both selfish and unselfish individuals that benefit everyone. While an entrepreneur might intend to promote only his enlightened (or even unenlightened!) self-interest and personal gain, the secondary effect of a voluntary exchange is a significant benefit to the buyer. The agreement of a seller and a buyer on a price is voluntary, and therefore both must think it is mutually beneficial. But it is the currency used that provides a mutually under-stood means of exchange, and allows both seller and buyer to evaluate whether the deal is a good one for them. In order for the system to work correctly, the currency used in a transaction must have a known and stable value.

More efficient than barter, a system of currency—whether it be furs, stones, shells, beads, copper, or fiat paper—reduces the cost of all our exchanges because it provides a common denominator into which all goods and services can be converted. Paper currency that is truly backed by gold (or sometimes silver) has often worked well, because individuals are confident they can exchange their currency for an equivalent value in gold if they wish.

When money consists of printed paper that is not backed by gold (or a similar valuable metal), it is called *fiat currency*. (The term *fiat* is a Latin verb form that means "let it be done," and it communicates the idea that paper money has value because the government *declares* that it has value.) Fiat currency is vulnerable, however, because it has value only as long as people trust the government enough to think that it has value. It is easier to debase a fiat currency that the government merely *says* is valuable than a currency backed by gold.

Money has power only because it can be used to purchase some-thing, so its value is measured in terms of what it can buy. Money allows us to engage in exchanges, even ones of long duration. It gives us a way to store purchasing power for future use. It also acts as a unit of account that keeps track of all costs and revenues by telling us what we need to know now and for future time periods. Without money, exchange would be difficult. It definitely qualifies as one of the best social inventions ever.

But the productive contribution of money to the exchange is directly related to the *stability* of its value. The pieces of paper that government authorize as money have value because everyone thinks they have value. If you destroy that belief, you destroy the value of money.

Underlying every piece of paper money are the industry, ingenuity, resources, and economic capacity of a nation's citizens. In this regard, money is tied to an economy as much as language is tied to communication. Without definitions, words could mean anything. So it is with money. If money does not have a stable and predictable value, the price-signaling system breaks down.

The loss of the purchasing power of money through inflation, for example, makes it more costly for lenders and borrowers to conduct exchanges, as uncertainty continually alters the meaning of the agreed exchange. Saving and investing also have additional risks under inflation, and time-dimension transactions (such as paying for a house or an automobile over time) are fraught with additional dangers because the real value of the agreed-upon price constantly changes. When the value of money is unstable, everything economic—supply, demand, profits/losses, specialization, trade, production, social cooperation—is less clear and less efficient, and this causes uncertainty and confusion in decision making.

Milton Friedman explains how this happens:

> Inflation occurs when the quantity of money rises appreciably more rapidly than output, and the more rapid the rise in the quantity of money per unit of output, the greater the rate of inflation. There is probably no other proposition in economics that is as well established as this one.[48]

When a government increases the money supply faster than the productivity of the economy, too much money chasing too few goods produces inflation. (Actually, what "inflates" first is the supply of money.) Inflation is an ongoing rise in the general level of prices— and thus it is a fall in the overall purchasing power of a unit of currency. Inflation causes the signaling system of a market system to inaccurately reflect buyer and seller intentions. "It is like a country

[48] Milton and Rose Friedman, *Free to Choose: A Personal Statement* (New York: Harcourt Brace Jovanovich, 1980), 254.

where nobody speaks the truth."[49] Likewise, it is a disease that nearly destroys nations: for example, Russia and Germany after World War I, and China, Chile, and Argentina after World War II.[50]

Inflation gives the illusion that we have more money than we really do—we never quite catch up with how fast prices are climbing. When people know that their future buying power is being reduced, lenders raise interest rates, reduce loan periods, and eliminate fixed mortgages. In short, credit becomes less available. Everyone loses, except government.

Hundreds of years of economic history indicate that prices and the stock of money have moved together. Since governments control the money supply, their policies are the main causes of inflation. They inflate the money supply because it is easier to pay off massive government debt with cheaper money created by printing it. If the policy makers' alternatives are (1) to default on the government's debt, (2) to devalue their currency, (3) to declare national bankruptcy (all of which are very painful), or (4) to inflate the nation's currency, is it any wonder they often choose inflation?

The famous British economist John Maynard Keynes said: "There is no surer means of overturning the existing basis of society than to debauch the currency. By a continuing process of inflation, governments can confiscate, secretly and unobserved, an important part of the wealth of their citizens."[51]

Likewise, Friedman writes, "Inflation distorts price signals, undermines a market economy, and is a form of taxation that can be imposed without legislation."[52]

2. The government must maintain relatively low tax rates

It is entrepreneurs and workers seeking to be more productive in free markets that produce prosperity. This means that tax rates matter. People produce, innovate, and create more when they are permitted to keep more of what they earn. When people do not get to keep much

---

[49] Walter B. Wriston, *Risk and Other Four Letter Words* (New York: Harper and Row, 1986), 106.
[50] Milton and Rose Friedman, *Free to Choose*, 253.
[51] John Maynard Keynes, *Economic Consequences of the Peace* (New York: Harcourt, Brace, and Howe, 1920), 235.
[52] Friedman and Friedman, *Free to Choose*, 225.

of what they earn, they tend not to try to earn very much. If economic efforts are penalized with high taxes, efforts diminish, opportunities for employment fall, the number of economic exchanges diminishes, and economic growth rates fall.

Alvin Rabushka of Stanford University reconstructed the tax and growth rates of fifty-four developing countries over a thirty-year period in the latter half of the twentieth century.[53] His data showed that lower tax rates were generally associated with more rapid rates of growth. The average growth rate of per capita income for the eight countries classified as "low tax" was 3.7 percent *annually*. (This rate would double per capita income in twenty years.)

By contrast, the eight countries that had the highest tax rates had annual growth rates of only 0.7 percent, less than one-fifth of the average growth rate for the eight countries with the lowest tax rates. (This rate would take one hundred years to double per capita income!) Rabushka says that good economic policy, including tax policy, fosters economic growth, and that the key in any system of direct taxation is to maintain low tax rates.

Rabushka also gives developing countries a concrete formula for how to structure a tax code. The tax system should 1) raise sufficient revenue for a limited government, 2) be fair and neutral, 3) be revised from time to time, 4) be simple and easy, and 5) be used to achieve non-fiscal objectives only in exceptional conditions.[54]

Unfortunately, the developing countries in Asia, Africa, and South America frequently levy high rates to raise revenue to finance government-directed projects. This is the opposite of what they need to do if they want to foster economic growth.

Economic history is clear: high tax rates retard progress, reduce capital investment, and hold back economic growth. When governments over-tax work, production, savings, and investment, and subsidize leisure and consumption, it is not surprising that we get less of the first four items and more of the last two.

Developing countries should be especially aware of the Laffer

---

[53] Alvin Rabushka, "Taxation, Economic Growth, and Liberty," *Cato Journal* 7, no. 1 (Spring/Summer 1987), accessed January 3, 2013, www.cato.org/pubs/journal/cj7n1/cj7n1-8.pdf.
[54] Ibid.; see esp. 131, 136, 141.

Curve. Named for its originator, Arthur Laffer, the curve shows the relationship between tax rates and tax revenue.

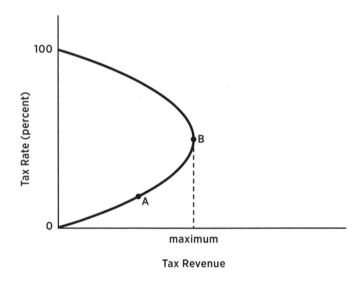

The Laffer Curve

The curve reflects the fact that tax revenues (the money actually collected by government) are low for both very high and very low tax rates. Beyond some point A, an increase in tax rates may actually cause tax revenues to fall (that is, when a government raises taxes, it collects less money).

James Gwartney and Richard L. Stroup explain how this works:

Obviously, tax revenues would be zero if the tax rate was zero. What is not so obvious is that tax revenues would also be zero (or at least very close to zero) if the tax rates were 100 percent. Confronting a 100 percent tax rate, most individuals would go fishing or find something else to do rather than engage in productive activity that is taxed, since the 100 percent tax rate would completely remove the material reward derived from earning taxable income. Production in the taxed sector would come to a halt, and without production, tax revenues would plummet to zero.

As tax rates are reduced from 100 percent, the incentive to work and earn taxable income increases, income expands, and tax revenues rise. Similarly, as tax rates increase from zero, tax revenues expand. Clearly, at some rate greater than zero but less than 100 percent, tax revenues will be maximized (point B [in graph]). This is not to imply that the tax rate that maximizes revenue is ideal. In fact, as the maximum revenue point (B) is approached, relatively large tax rate increases will be necessary to expand tax revenues. In this range, the excess burden of taxation will be substantial.[55]

Neither should it be assumed that the maximum revenue point is 50 percent. Most economists argue that the tax rate should be closer to 15 percent to 20 percent, nearer to point A.[56]

Another complication arises in many countries: people do not pay taxes. In some countries, tax evasion is widely practiced and tax laws are not effectively enforced. But in such countries, the solution is not to keep raising tax rates to higher and higher levels, but to reduce them to reasonable levels and then enforce compliance with the laws. Lower tax rates are an incentive for more widespread tax compliance.

Where people regularly disobey the law and ignore their tax obligations with impunity, pastors and church leaders can influence society toward greater tax compliance, for the Bible teaches:

> Because of this you also pay taxes, for the authorities are ministers of God, attending to this very thing. Pay to all what is owed to them: taxes to whom taxes are owed, revenue to whom revenue is owed, respect to whom respect is owed, honor to whom honor is owed. (Rom. 13:6–7)

History provides evidence for the validity of the Laffer Curve. The twentieth century saw three major tax reductions in the United States: the Calvin Coolidge tax cuts in the mid-1920s (creating the "roaring 20s"); the John F. Kennedy tax cuts in the early 1960s ("the country gets going again"), and the Ronald Reagan tax cuts of the early 1980s ("morning in America" and the beginning of an economic expansion

---

[55] James Gwartney and Richard L. Stroup, *Economics: Private and Public Choice* (New York: Harcourt Brace Jovanovich, 1987), 115–116.

[56] We recognize that not all economists agree with this recommendation, but we maintain it is important because what matters for the productivity of an economy are incentives to work, save, invest, and take risks. All of these are affected negatively by higher tax rates and positively by lower tax rates. Relatively low tax rates are an important factor for economic growth.

that lasted twenty-five years). Each of these tax cuts stimulated growth, created employment, raised per capita GDP, and helped balance the national budget.[57]

To be more specific, when Reagan succeeded in lowering tax rates from 70 percent to 28 percent, the result was a doubling of tax revenues from $500 billion in 1980 to $1 trillion in 1988, including a huge expansion of the economy.

Governments must recognize that work effort (and therefore national production) is very sensitive to tax rates. *The Wall Street Journal* noted, "Every major marginal rate income tax cut of the last 50 years—1964, 1981, 1986, and 2003—was followed by an unexpectedly large increase in tax revenues."[58]

F. Does your country have a free-market system?

We have now completed a basic overview of the essentials of a free-market system. At this point, readers may be wondering, "Does my country have a free-market system?"

If you want to know, it is easy to check the most recent issue of the *Index of Economic Freedom* to see where your country ranks in degree of freedom among the countries of the world, as we explained above (see 135–36).[59] A brief analysis is given for each country. The *Economic Freedom of the World* index is also an excellent source.[60]

---

[57] Summarized from Arthur Laffer, "The Laffer Curve: Past, Present, and Future," *The Heritage Foundation Backgrounder* 176 (June 1, 2004): 1–16.

[58] "The Romney Hood Fairy Tale," *Wall Street Journal*, Review and Outlook section, Aug. 8, 2012, A14.

[59] The rankings are also available at http://www.heritage.org/index/.

[60] James Gwartney, Robert Lawson, and Joshua Hall, *Economic Freedom of the World: 2012 Annual Report* (Vancouver, BC: Fraser Institute, 2012). Available online at http://www.freetheworld.com/release.html.

5

THE MECHANICS
OF THE SYSTEM

How Does a Free Market Work?

Just how does a free-market system work? Who decides what is produced, how much, and of what quality? How does the system guarantee that the goods produced are what people want? In this chapter,
we will seek to answer these questions as we examine seven features
of a free-market system.

A. "No one" decides what, how, and for whom a national economy will produce

Nobel economic laureate Milton Friedman very simply answered the
question of who decides what is produced: no one.[1]

Friedman explains that this fact can be seen even in the production
of a simple lead pencil. After summarizing the *I, Pencil* story that we
mentioned above (140–41), he writes:

> No one sitting in a central office gave orders to these thousands of
> people. No military police enforced the orders that were not given.
> These people live in many lands, speak different languages, practice

[1] Milton Friedman and Rose Friedman, *Free to Choose: A Personal Statement* (New York: Harcourt Brace Jovanovich, 1980), 13.

different religions, may even hate one another—yet none of these differences prevented them from cooperating to produce a pencil.[2]

This process is even more remarkable when we realize that economic knowledge does not exist in concentrated form. In fact, the more complex the system, the less amenable it is to individual direction, because no one person can know all the relevant facts. Because economic knowledge is in dispersed, incomplete, and even contradictory pieces, only the wisdom of the many can ever possess it. That wisdom is dispensed through the millions of free exchanges in the market. "No one" decides in an overall way what an economy produces.

The thousands of people involved in producing each piece of a pencil perform their individual tasks not because they want a pencil or even know what a pencil is for. They simply see their work as a way to get the goods and services they do want.

Every time you buy a pencil, you exchange a little bit of your money for the thousands of small services that multitudes have contributed toward producing it. All the exchanges in the production and distribution of a product create a mosaic of unity and coherence in which self-interest tends to be cooperative, economically beneficial, and productive.[3]

The mystery of the market is that it is an exquisitely complicated process that emerges spontaneously from the enlightened self-interest of billions of people who specialize, exchange, and produce wealth. The market is a complex, brainlike organism that evolves over decades. The immense requirement that someone consciously plan, manage, and list all the resources available, formulate all the tasks to be done, and answer all the questions of "Who?" "What?" "Why?" and "When?" is literally beyond the ability of any one human being or any designated group of central planners. Instead, it is directed by what Adam Smith called an "invisible hand":

> As every individual . . . neither intends to promote the public interest, nor knows how much he is promoting it . . . by directing [his work] in such a manner as its produce may be of the greatest value, he intends

---

[2] Ibid., 13.
[3] Ibid., 13–18.

only his own gain, and he is in this, as in many other cases, led by *an invisible hand* to promote an end which was no part of his intention. . . . By pursuing his own interest he frequently promotes that of the society more effectually than when he really intends to promote it.[4]

From the standpoint of the Christian faith, we can add that the miracle of human creativity can best be understood in light of the fact that man is created in the image of God. Both individually and as a human society corporately, we are able to create remarkable products of value from the resources of the earth. The amazing functionings of the so-called "invisible hand," of markets, and of creativity are a few of the many expressions of our likeness to our Creator, abilities bestowed by a sovereign God filling society with evidences of his common grace.

Human creativity honors God as but a faint reflection of his infinite wisdom and power in his act of creation: "In the beginning, God created the heavens and the earth" (Gen. 1:1). Then "God created man in his own image" (v. 27). After that, he told Adam and Eve to "subdue" the earth, which implied a responsibility to make useful products from the earth's natural resources—to create products of value to human beings. In creating such products, they acted like "imitators of God, as beloved children" (Eph. 5:1).

Because God is pleased with such human creativity, he appointed skilled craftsmen to work in making the furnishings of the tabernacle: "Bezalel and Oholiab and every craftsman in whom the Lord has put skill and intelligence to know how to do any work in the construction of the sanctuary shall work in accordance with all that the Lord has commanded" (Ex. 36:1).

From the godly wife, who "makes linen garments and sells them" (Prov. 31:24); to Jesus, who worked as a "carpenter" (Mark 6:3); to Aquila, Priscilla, and the apostle Paul, who worked as "tentmakers" (Acts 18:3); to the Christian whom Paul commanded not to steal but to do "honest work with his own hands" (Eph. 4:28), God approves of those who create useful goods from the resources of the earth.

George Gilder writes about what he sees as a divine origin behind human creativity:

---

[4] Adam Smith, *An Inquiry into the Nature and Causes of the Wealth of Nations*, ed. Edwin Cannan (1776; New York: Modern Library, 1994), 485, emphasis added.

Because economies are governed by thoughts, they reflect not the laws of matter but the laws of mind. One crucial law of mind is that belief precedes knowledge.[5]

Creative thought is not an inductive process in which a scientist accumulates evidence in a neutral and "objective" way until a theory becomes visible in it. Rather the theory comes first and determines what evidence can then be seen.[6]

Imagination, intuition, and hypothesis are merely the first steps of learning. . . . Creative thought requires an act of faith. The believer must trust his intuition, the spontaneous creations of his mind, enough to pursue them laboriously to the point of experiment and knowledge. . . . It is love and faith that infuse ideas with life and fire. . . . But the essence of the universe is creative consciousness continually generating new energy and thought.[7]

Many of the most significant intellectual, scientific, and economic breakthroughs of the last three centuries were, in fact, driven by Christian beliefs. Niall Ferguson in his 2011 book *Civilization: The West and the Rest*, quotes a fellow of the Chinese Academy of the Social Sciences as saying,

We were asked to look into what accounted for the . . . pre-eminence of the West all over the world. . . . At first, we thought it was because you had more powerful guns than we had. Then we thought it was because you had the best political system. Next we focused on your economic system. But in the past twenty years, we have realized that the heart of your culture [the United States] is your religion: Christianity. That is why the West has been so powerful. The Christian moral foundation of social and cultural life was what made possible the emergence of capitalism and then the successful transition to democratic politics. We don't have any doubt about this.[8]

---

[5] George Gilder, *Wealth and Poverty* (New York: Basic Books, 1981), 261.
[6] Ibid., 262, citing John E. Sawyer, "Entrepreneurial Error and Economic Growth," *Explorations in Entrepreneurial History*, Vol. 4 (May 1952), 199–200.
[7] Gilder, *Wealth and Poverty*, 262, 263.
[8] Niall Ferguson, *Civilization: The West and the Rest* (New York: Penguin, 2011), 287, citing David Aikman, *The Beijing Factor: How Christianity Is Transforming China and Changing the Global Balance of Power* (Oxford: Monarch, 2003), 5.

While some might disagree, we believe that what this Chinese scholar is saying is basically true.

The free-market system allows creativity to flourish and produce great value through free human decisions, not through government direction and control. A free-market system is a spontaneous order that arises out of natural liberty. It is also a circuit of never-ending ideas.

While wealth might reside in some resources, not all resources are wealth. Gilder reminds us:

> The market, as it generates the "news"—its ceaseless play of prices and ideas—passes its wand over the world of human possessions, conferring capital gains as some things become profitable in a new light of time and knowledge, and casting giant shadows of loss over looming wealth works of the past. . . . Qualities of thought and spirit in an economy can overshadow all the quantities of capital and contracts of labor. . . . Work indeed is the root of wealth, even of the genius that mostly resides in sweat.[9]

Entrepreneurs continually demonstrate that faith and imagination are the most important capital goods in a changing economy, and that wealth is a product less of money than of the mind to create, produce, invest, and, in the often-repeated expression of Austrian economist Joseph Schumpeter, to creatively destroy (to shut down businesses that are not working).

B. Specialization is the key to greater prosperity

1. The benefits of specialization

All countries want to use land, labor, and capital productively. The question is, how can people become more productive? How can people who already work very hard produce *more goods* of *greater value* while working the same number of hours? The answer is specialization, followed by mutually beneficial exchange (or trade).

Adam Smith, in his 1776 book *An Inquiry into the Nature and Causes of the Wealth of Nations*, observed that the output of a pin factory is much greater when everyone specializes in a particular task. The division of labor helps people become proficient at performing small but essential

---

[9] Gilder, *Wealth and Poverty*, 51.

functions. When everyone acts as a specialist, more is produced than if each makes the final product from start to finish. (Making pins might appear to us to be a trivial example, but before staplers—invented and patented only in 1866—people often used pins to fasten papers together in businesses. Most people also made their own clothing at home, using pins in the process, so pins were a crucial part of an economy.)

Here is Smith's famous description of the division of labor in a pin factory.

> To take an example, therefore, from a very trifling manufacture; but one in which the division of labour has been very often taken notice of, the trade of the pin-maker; a workman not educated to this business (which the division of labour has rendered a distinct trade), nor acquainted with the use of the machinery employed in it (to the invention of which the same division of labour has probably given occasion), could scarce, perhaps, with his utmost industry, make one pin in a day, and certainly could not make twenty. But in the way in which this business is now carried on, not only the whole work is a peculiar trade, but it is divided into a number of branches, of which the greater part are likewise peculiar trades. One man draws out the wire, another straights it, a third cuts it, a fourth points it, a fifth grinds it at the top for receiving the head; to make the head requires two or three distinct operations; to put it on, is a peculiar business, to whiten the pins is another; it is even a trade by itself to put them into the paper; and the important business of making a pin is, in this manner, divided into about eighteen distinct operations, which, in some manufactories, are all performed by distinct hands, though in others the same man will sometimes perform two or three of them. I have seen a small manufactory of this kind where ten men only were employed, and where some of them consequently performed two or three distinct operations. But though they were very poor, and therefore but indifferently accommodated with the necessary machinery, they could, when they exerted themselves, make among them about twelve pounds of pins in a day. There are in a pound upwards of four thousand pins of a middling size. Those ten persons, therefore, could make among them upwards of forty-eight thousand pins in a day. Each person, therefore, making a tenth part of forty-eight thousand pins, might be considered as making four thousand eight hundred pins in a day. But if they had all wrought separately and independently, and without any of them having been

educated to this peculiar business, they certainly could not each of them have made twenty, perhaps not one pin in a day; that is, certainly, not the two hundred and fortieth, perhaps not the four thousand eight hundredth part of what they are at present capable of performing, in consequence of a proper division and combination of their different operations. In every other art and manufacture, the effects of the division of labour are similar to what they are in this very trifling one.[10]

Specialization encourages innovation because it forces people to invest time making tools that make tools. It fosters productivity because more is done in less time. Less fishing with a pole and more fishing with a net is always productive. Planting, harvesting, threshing, and baking grain became more efficient when individuals concentrated on particular aspects of the many-faceted production process. In short, self-sufficiency is inefficient, while specialization always produces more.[11]

Matt Ridley reminds us in *The Rational Optimist* that raising standards of living has always involved more specialization and more trade. He uses an example from an earlier century that must have amazed consumers:

> Nobody in China can blow glass; nobody in Europe can reel silk. Thanks to the middleman in India, however, the European can wear silk and the Chinese can use glass. The European may scoff at the ridiculous legend that the lovely cloth is made from the cocoons of caterpillars; and the Chinese may guffaw at the laughable fable that this transparent ceramic is made from sand. But both of them are better off and so is the Indian middleman. All three have acquired the labour of others . . . and lifted the standard of living at both ends.[12]

2. Specialization works because everyone has some comparative advantage

Economists disagree on many issues, but all concur that a nation's best route to success is to specialize on the basis of comparative advantage

---

[10] Smith, *Wealth of Nations*, Book I, chap. 1, 4–5.
[11] The danger that comes with specialization, which must be guarded against, is that people can become isolated in their own narrow specialties and lose sight of their responsibility also to contribute to the larger good of society, to relate in a genuine way to people outside their specialties, and also ultimately to honor God in their specialized work. Universities also can become centers of minute specializations, with very few people even thinking there can be a larger unified and unifying kind of knowledge.
[12] Matt Ridley, *The Rational Optimist: How Prosperity Evolves* (New York: HarperCollins, 2010), 175.

and then trade with others. In our personal affairs, we all do this. In a modern developed economy, we let others grow most of our food, cut our hair, build our homes, provide our health care, manufacture our cars, and even do our dry cleaning. Common sense tells us to specialize and trade, and the more we do, the better off we all become.

Smith trumpets this theme:

> It is the maxim of every prudent master of a family, never to attempt to make at home what it will cost him more to make than to buy. . . . If a foreign country can supply us with a commodity cheaper than we ourselves can make it, better buy it of them with some part of the produce of our own industry, employed in a way in which we have some advantage.[13]

If Spain, South Korea, or China, for example, can produce better shoes more cheaply than your country, buy them. Let everyone do what he or she does best. Nations only hurt themselves by not specializing and trading.

But what if another country can potentially make *everything* better and cheaper than your country? Do you still specialize and trade? Yes. The law of comparative advantage is an indisputable truth that could do more to reduce poverty than any manmade law. It is worth explaining with a simple example.

Suppose there is a doctor who can type 120 words per minute.[14] He is trying to decide whether to hire a secretary who types only sixty words per minute. If the doctor does the typing, it takes him four hours. If a secretary is hired, the job takes eight hours.

Yes, the doctor has an *absolute advantage* in typing skills compared to the prospective employee. He is "better at everything" because he is better at treating patients and better at typing. This is like one nation that is "better at making everything" than another nation. But absolute advantage is not the important issue. The question is, who has the *comparative advantage*?

The doctor's time is worth $100 per hour when he is working as a

---

[13] Smith, *Wealth of Nations*, Book IV, chap. 2, 485–486.
[14] Friedman and Friedman, *Free to Choose*, 45; this idea is mentioned by the Friedmans but expanded with our details for illustration purposes.

doctor, whereas the typist's time is worth $15 per hour as a typist. Even though the doctor is twice as fast at typing as the person he is about to hire, when we *compare* what it costs him to do the typing with what it costs him to pay the secretary, doing the typing does not give him a comparative advantage.

If the doctor types the documents he needs, the job costs $400, which is the income he loses by doing typing instead of working as a doctor (4 x $100 = $400). In economic terms, $400 is his "opportunity cost" of four hours of lost time as a doctor—the lost "opportunity" of earning $400.

Alternatively, if he hires the typist, the cost of having the documents typed is only $120 (eight hours of typing service at $15 per hour). It is obviously a wise choice to get the typing done for $120 instead of $400. The doctor's *comparative advantage* lies in practicing medicine. He gains by hiring the typist and spending his time specializing in his area of comparative advantage. The typist also has a comparative advantage in doing typing (at $15 per hour) rather than, say, retail sales (at $10 per hour). Everyone becomes better off by specializing and then trading (selling) their products and services.

In addition, society is better off. Instead of typing for four hours, the doctor produces for society four hours more of medical work, valued at $100 per hour, or $400 more of value. When he did not do four hours of typing, the society lost only 4 x $15, or $60 of value. So the society is still $340 better off ($400 gained – $60 lost). But the secretary has added eight hours worth of work, or 8 x $15 = $120, minus the 8 x $10 per hour she did not work in retail sales. She has added $40 more of work to the society. Together, by specializing, they added $340 + $40 = $380 of value to the society.

Name a job. Name a person. It is always to a person's advantage to specialize in the thing he does best, even though someone else, somewhere, could possibly do it better. The other person (or the other country) cannot make everything all at the same time. The other country also has to specialize in something. A poor country might not have an *absolute* advantage in making any product, but it always has a *comparative advantage* in making some products.[15]

---

[15] Donald J. Boudreaux, "Comparative Advantage," in *The Concise Encyclopedia of Economics*, ed. David R. Henderson (Indianapolis: Liberty Fund, 2008), 69–71.

The idea of specialization and trade, probably one of the three most important concepts in all of economics, is absolutely necessary for a nation to improve its standard of living.

This principle is so important because currently two billion people on the planet are making less than $2 a day. Most do not hold titles to property and are practicing subsistence farming. Can the twenty-first century be different for them? Yes. People from all over the world can take advantage of specialization and gains from trade, largely because of world-shrinking inventions such as cellular phones and the Internet, which have opened up more access to world markets. It is a matter of many people in a nation looking at the reasons their economy is working and seeing how to benefit from the division of labor by specializing and then trading through voluntary exchange. When people decide to specialize and then trade (or buy and sell), this greases the wheels of the economy by opening opportunities and helping the economy run properly.

3. Specialization in a nation changes over time

As a nation becomes more efficient in its specialization, its growing surplus can then be traded for win/win exchanges, which again enhance the standard of living.

Most poor countries start with agriculture, then move to simple manufacturing, then to more complex manufacturing, and finally to services, consumer goods, and information of every stripe. When a poor country begins to produce more complex products, then the more developed countries that were making those products have to shift to other products.

For example, after World War II, Japan began to produce small toys and other simple manufactured products. Later, it produced automobiles, and it did this better and more efficiently than the United States. Many American autoworkers then had to retrain for jobs in construction, heating and air conditioning, information technology, cell phone sales and services, restaurants, health care, and many other fields. As noted above, Joseph Schumpeter calls this process "creative destruction,"[16]

---

[16] See W. Michael Cox and Richard Alm, "Creative Destruction," in *The Concise Encyclopedia of Economics*, ed. David R. Henderson (Indianapolis: Liberty Fund, 1980), 101–4.

noting that free markets' pain and gain are closely linked, and that new ideas cannot be instituted without sweeping away the old order.

Will the world run out of new products to make and new job opportunities? No, because human beings have limited needs (food, clothing, and shelter) but unlimited wants. The increasing standard of living throughout the world comes about partly because people continually invent new products that people want, products that no one knew about before they were invented: Think of, in the last one hundred years, the invention of automobiles, airplanes, air conditioning, telephones, televisions, computers, snowmobiles, cell phones, iPods, iPads, Starbucks coffee, bottled water, and FedEx and UPS. In another fifty years, we will have an entirely different list. (We agree that some of these new wants reflect wrongful greed, while others are morally healthy, but the basic idea of wanting new and better products is not wrong in itself. It is part of how God created the human race—with a drive to continually subdue the earth.)

There will always be something new to invent, something new to produce. At first, highly developed countries will start to produce these new inventions. When this happens, the theory of comparative advantage tells us that to do this they will have to move out of production of some older products (perhaps textiles, small manufactured housewares, or some food crops), and this opens up new areas of comparative advantage for less-developed countries.

All this will happen again and again in a free-market system without central planning or government direction. Providing for the *unlimited wants* of mankind happens spontaneously in free markets because they allow people and nations the freedom to concentrate on what they do best. However, this process happens hardly at all, if ever, in communist or socialist economies (except when they allow some measure of free-market principles). Providing for the unlimited wants of mankind is what free markets do best. (Importantly, the truth of mankind's unlimited wants also implies, in a competitive free market, that *there will always be some jobs* for those who want them—if government does not interfere with the functioning of the free market.)

As the world becomes more networked and as entrepreneurial free markets operate more widely, innovation to discover new products, new services, and new markets increasingly emerges. This is why specialization in individual nations constantly changes.

C. The remarkable signaling system of the free market

The free market also does something else very well: it signals to workers what jobs need to be done and it signals to businesses what products need to be made.[17] It does this with no central clearinghouse for information, no hourly nationwide report on every product that has been bought, and no government planner telling factories what to make. The market does this spontaneously through an amazing signaling system: "The price system transmits only the important information and only to the people who need to know."[18]

What if the world had a futuristic Star Wars technology that could instantaneously give us the information we need to make economic decisions or mutually beneficial trades? What if this technology could also register countless personal preferences and then use that information to miraculously determine the market value of every one of millions of items? What if this technology could also calculate the supply and demand of millions of products and people, telling people what to do, where to work, and what to produce and how. What if it could also signal prices, wages, interest rates, profits, losses, and other important information that humans need to make good choices? What if it could register literally billions of opinions per minute and produce nonstop signals that every nation and every language would understand and act upon? What if it could accomplish the additional service of determining how land, labor, and capital could best be used to produce just what people want, just when they want it? What if, traveling at the speed of light, these signals could coordinate the actions of all world participants and produce a profoundly cooperative process in which everyone benefits, commerce thrives, and creativity flourishes?

You might think this could happen only in a utopian dream. But the free market is such a system, even though no one controls it.

---

[17] For a further description of the signaling function of prices in a free market, see Barry Asmus and Donald B. Billings, "The Price System and Economic Coordination" and "Entrepreneurship and the Competitive Process," in *Crossroads: The Great American Experiment: The Rise, Decline, and Restoration of Freedom and the Market Economy* (Lanham, MD: University Press of America, 1984), 202–6.
[18] Friedman and Friedman, *Free to Choose*, 15.

Consider this: there are sixty thousand items in a modern hardware and lumber store, and there are forty-five thousand items in a large food supermarket, and whenever the stock on hand diminishes, these products arrive on time, when and where they are needed, each and every day (including pencils). But there is not too much, for if a surplus arises, the store must lower prices to clear the excess, and this lower price tells the manager not to buy so much next time. Each item requires a human touch—inventing, producing, marketing, distributing—and each item requires the management skills to ensure that the right product arrives at the right time. Is that possible? Who directs it all? Any person seeing a store like this for the very first time would probably stare in disbelief, calculating its impossibility and wondering how such a miracle could happen. Yet it happens in tens of thousands of such stores around the world every day.

Friedrich A. Hayek, a Nobel Prize recipient in economics, wrote a relatively short but profound article in 1945 entitled "The Use of Knowledge in Society." In that piece, he summarized the necessary conditions for an efficient and socially beneficial economic system:

> The peculiar character of the problem of a rational economic order is determined precisely by the fact that the knowledge of the circumstances of which we must make use never exists in concentrated or integrated form, but solely as the dispersed bits of incomplete and frequently contradictory knowledge which all the separate individuals possess. . . . It is rather a problem of how to secure the best use of resources known to any of the members of society, for ends whose relative importance only these individuals know. Or, to put it briefly, it is a problem of the utilization of knowledge not given to anyone in its totality.[19]

So, can people ever obtain such knowledge, which no one individual has? Yes, says Hayek. It arises spontaneously through the competitive price system of the free market.

Israel Kirzner writes in his book *Competition and Entrepreneurship* that anyone who proposes systems other than the free market "calmly

---

[19] Friedrich A. Hayek, "The Use of Knowledge in Society," *American Economic Review* 35, no. 4 (September 1945): 519–20.

assumes that the critically important social task of making all the scattered bits of information available to those making decisions has already been performed."[20] In other words, system planners think that knowledge of relative scarcities, consumer tastes, production costs, and the most recent technologies is immediately and inexpensively available to anyone. However, this is incorrect, for we are largely ignorant of what we would like to know.

This lack of necessary economic information is a matter of utmost importance for the outlook of nations seemingly condemned to poverty. And it is the competitive price system that offers the best opportunity for maximizing the quantity and quality of information that would eventually lead to poverty's eradication.

Try any kind of command-and-control socialism you like—we guarantee it does not work efficiently or for the long term: "A society that chooses between capitalism and socialism does not choose between two social systems; it chooses between social cooperation and the disintegration of society."[21] Socialist systems can never generate the kind of supply and demand information that enables individuals and companies to be successful. But *the price system of free markets* provides this information instantly, continually, throughout nations and around the world.

Governments might know how to direct armies and win wars, but the complicated and unlimited wants of a consumer society are infinitely more difficult to determine. This is why nations today are slowly realizing that the crucial economic structure must be a bottom-up free market and not a top-down command-and-control system. Hayek said the problem of utilization of knowledge that is not given to anyone in its totality makes rational planning of an economy impossible. The free market is needed to produce, transmit, and make available all the knowledge needed for beneficial outcomes. The answers are in the actions of the market, not the dreams and schemes of the planners.

Some have called this system the "magic" of the market. Yes, the market is a wondrous instrument of communication and a computerlike transmitter of opinions, as well as a determiner of value. It is

---

[20] Israel Kirzner, *Competition and Entrepreneurship* (Chicago: University of Chicago Press, 1973), 214.
[21] Ludwig Von Mises, *Human Action: A Treatise on Economics* (Chicago: Henry Regnery, 1966), 680.

incredible. But the market process is not really magic. It is far cleverer than that, because no one *designs* the market, *manages* it, or *controls* it. The market just happens. Just as we can say, "Gravity is," whether we can explain it or not, so "the market is." It does not need to be created by conscious human design. Wherever human beings exist, have freedom of choice, and have a desire to improve their own condition, the market exists.

The market economy and its price system are gifts to the world. People did not intentionally create a complex array of exchanges and price signals. Their only goal was simply to improve their lot in life. The free market was the result.

At this point, we can explore in more detail just what makes the signaling system of the market work so effectively. The answer is prices.

D. Prices are an amazing worldwide source of instant economic information

The chief virtue of a functioning market is in dispersing and applying socially useful information. Prices and competition, as we will see, do that. Buyers prefer to buy low and sellers prefer to sell high. The prices that are signaled by the market determine their choices.

Supply and demand determine the prices of goods and services, as well as wages, interest rates, profits, and losses. The market is the arena in which all these interacting decisions are made. The pricing system of the market is a continual process with an overall tendency toward coordination. It is a process for the discovery and correction of error through multiple exchanges inducing decision makers to produce and sell just what the customer wants.

The market is constantly signaling "do more," "do less," or "do it differently," because supply and demand are never constant. The market is a constant discovery procedure that generates large amounts of information about new products, product improvements, and the latest technologies. In all of these areas, prices are needed before buyers and sellers can make decisions.

The essential function of changes in relative prices is to provide new information on relative scarcities, resource availability, consumer preferences, technology, and the constant flux of a hundred other factors continually producing altered circumstances. The price system is the only reliable and efficient system that can "keep track" of all this complexity. Market prices generate information about changes in personal tastes, in the relative availability of different raw materials, and in the comparative expense of capital and labor. In addition, they signal the reactions of market participants to these changes. For example, an increase in gasoline prices induces at least some consumers to reduce their amount of driving. Higher prices also signal producers to increase their efforts and supply more. Lower prices, on the other hand, lead to increases in the amount of gasoline purchased and the amount of driving while telling producers to supply less.

According to Israel Kirzner, "The activity of these pure entrepreneurs (economic actors) can then explain how prices and input and output quantities and qualities change."[22]

The market also acts as a window on the future by permitting individuals to *register their expectations* about tomorrow's relative scarcities. If a frost destroys a part of a Colombian coffee crop, the price for the future delivery of coffee on the Chicago commodities market immediately rises.

Prices are the language of the market economy. They are the summation of a vast amount of knowledge and information not known to most market participants. As the price of bauxite rises, a producer of aluminum may not know why. Nonetheless, it is clear that the real cost of an important material has risen and production plans have to be altered. Nothing conveys information faster than prices.

Prices convey *objective information* on the *subjective attitudes and feelings* of buyers and sellers. As relative prices change, options are altered and decisions are made. Perceived benefits and costs are continuously affected by changing circumstances, including many important variables that are never constant. In other words, not a person in the world knows how to make a market work or how to make even a simple thing like a pencil. But it still happens, because enormous complications are simplified when decentralization and prices take charge. In these ways, prices serve as an amazing, worldwide source of instant economic information.

---

[22] Kirzner, *Competition and Entrepreneurship*, 42.

E. Profits and losses are the green and red lights of the system, by which customers signal "go" or "stop"

Two other signaling components of a free-market system are profits and losses. Profits and losses tell entrepreneurs whether their ideas are succeeding or failing. So, if entrepreneurs represent the engine of the competitive market process, then profits and losses are the green lights and red lights, signaling "go" or "stop."

Even in a free market, our knowledge is imperfect and incomplete. In the absence of perfect coordination of the independent plans of decision makers, opportunities for improvement in products and services are always present. Profits are an excellent incentive for such improvement.

On the other hand, losses can stop everything, forcing a business model to be reassessed and another option tried. Entrepreneurs invent, create, envision the future, produce things, feed people, save lives, and enhance others' well-being by risking their money and time. If their ideas do not work, they can lose everything. Once losses set in, the process must change or be terminated.

Recognizing what the consumer wants and calculating the costs of making it available, while still earning a profit, is no easy task. Profits are the rewards, losses are the pain. Even good ideas might not align properly with what people want, and therefore losses might be incurred. Yet losses are as important as profits. Cleansing an economic system, losses remove what consumers do not want and signal producers to change, improve, or fail. Businesses must be constantly attentive to consumer preferences. The system of profits and losses encourages enterprises to cast their bread upon the waters of uncertainty with the hope that it might return with rewards. But this is risky, because the system requires entrepreneurs to give first and get later, maybe. Risking personal money and time with the hope of profitability drives the whole process.

But if the hope of making and keeping a reasonable profit is taken away (through higher tax rates, for example), then fewer people will take risks, and the economy will falter.

Business profit is the incentive that permits people to believe with a good deal of confidence that market forces work. Do people always guess right? No, there are lots of mistakes and unforeseen costs. In fact, many people fail and have to try again. But over the long run, those who succeed continually produce goods and services that consumers value, and thus they increase a nation's GDP.

F. Competition leads to interpersonal cooperation, better products, more choices, and lower prices

We have talked about several factors in the mechanics of how free markets work: (1) decentralized decision making ("no one" decides), (2) specialization and trade, (3) the signaling system of the market, (4) prices as the language of the signaling system, and (5) profits and losses as the green lights and red lights of the system. But there is still another factor: (6) competition and voluntary cooperation.

We include competition and cooperation together because they naturally occur together and reinforce each other. First, think of how competition happens. We have seen it again and again in the cellular telephone market in the past twenty years. Companies have competed to make a better cell phone: Smaller. Thinner. Lighter. More reliable. More rugged. More instinctive to use. More features. A better camera. Better apps. Longer battery life. Better Internet connectivity.

At first, everyone wanted to have a Palm Pilot, then a Blackberry, then an iPhone, then an Android, or something else. On and on it goes.

No central government planner could ever make this happen: "The characteristic mark of economic history under capitalism is unceasing economic progress, a steady increase in the quantity of capital goods available, and a continuous trend toward an improvement in the general standards of living."[23]

This kind of market competition is the father of innovation and a constant force for making progress happen. Competition works to lower costs and prices, and to vet all rival approaches for improvement.

But why do we combine competition *and cooperation?* It is because saying they are mutually exclusive is like saying that the fingering hand and the bow hand of the violinist are adversaries. Could it be that competition in fact *encourages*, even *requires* cooperation? Yes. This is because no one can succeed in the market today—that is, no one can be

---

[23] Von Mises, *Human Action*, 565.

truly competitive—without the *voluntary cooperation of many other people*. For products such as the iPhone, the necessary cooperation extends not only to remarkable teamwork within Apple itself, but also to the cooperation of hundreds of other suppliers of parts, advertisers, sellers, employees in phone networks, and even to people in many other countries. The need to *compete* and produce a better product remarkably leads people to decide to *cooperate* with many other people, or their product could not be produced.

For a simpler example, think of a woman who has a number of children to feed and earns her money by weaving baskets. Someone must supply the bamboo and another the twine. Someone must make signs and advertise her business. Someone must provide her a space in the local market or agree to sell her baskets for a commission. She might also need a babysitter or a helper during certain parts of the day. If she can afford it, she buys some food that others have produced, cooked, and transported for her children and herself. What else do they need? Medicine? Water? Protection? The point is that everyone, no matter how small his or her contribution to the overall economy, still needs the cooperation of many others. In order to compete with other vendors for her share of the woven basket market, even this poor woman has to cooperate with many others.

Progress and improvement naturally occur when competition and cooperation work together. The result is better service, better quality, and better products provided faster and cheaper to approving customers. When it comes to service and quality, for many products there is no "finish line," and "good enough" never is good enough for long. When it comes to customers, an entrepreneur can never stop thinking about them. Everyone must be constantly alert to what customers want, when they want it, how they want it, and where they want it. It takes unbelievable effort to make customers the first priority. Only the free market does all that and more, through the voluntary choices of individuals participating in the market.

Imagine the millions of bits of know-how that must come together to serve but one customer. The complex process of human cooperation that comes together in a transaction that leads to consumer possession is somehow both mysterious and awesome. In a very real sense, producers and consumers are not enemies, because they need each other. They both do best when they cooperate.

Cooperation and competition generate untold examples of socially beneficial results. Consumers show their preferences by their purchases, while the voluntary nature of exchange in the market guarantees that both parties benefit. When the consumer chooses one store or one service provider over another, that decision gives signals to both buyer and seller, and it even gives important notice to the one not making the sale to lower his price, give faster service, or do something better to compete. The consumer is again the winner.

As customers find out what is best and cheapest, and producers discover how they might lower costs and make their product more attractive to the buyer, the end result is a greater range of choice and increased opportunities for everyone. In a free market, enlightened self-interest produces continued exchanges that vastly exceed anyone's deliberations. The market is a "higher-level order" that outstrips the knowledge in any one of us: "Competitors aim at excellence and pre-eminence in accomplishments within a system of mutual cooperation. The function of competition is to assign every member of the social systems that position in which he can best serve the whole of society and all its members."[24]

G. Entrepreneurship: many try, few succeed, but all of society benefits

We now turn to the final component of the free market, but this one is not a process but a person: the entrepreneur.

The importance of the entrepreneur to make the free-market system work has become more and more evident as innovation has become so necessary. When a nation first begins to develop, it can pick the low-lying fruits to produce growth. Urbanization, low labor costs for manufacturing, and producing goods for export all have initially served developing countries well. But individuals and businesses must innovate to get to the next stage, and entrepreneurs are the key to innovation.

Competition naturally produces a process of entrepreneurial discovery, pulling and prodding markets in new directions. Alert to the

---

[24] Ibid., 117.

changes always occurring, entrepreneurs must then earn profits by innovating and turning problems into opportunities. They must create new products or services, calculate the best ways to utilize resources and deliver them, and constantly look for new and better productive techniques. It is entrepreneurs who seldom fear failure but see new ways to do things by breaking the mold: builders, creators, dreamers, doers, opportunists, and future builders. Entrepreneurs attempt to read the market signals, anticipate previously undeveloped consumer demands, and then take risks, usually with their own money.

Sometimes entrepreneurs get rich, sometimes their ideas fail, and often they have to start all over again. Successful entrepreneurs have to be proactive. "Economic progress, in a capitalistic society, means turmoil," according to Joseph Schumpeter (born in Austria-Hungary in 1883 and an economics professor at Harvard from 1932 to 1950).[25] He said that entrepreneurship always involves a process of "creative destruction" in which newer, better ideas displace the old.

This is, overall, a good process that continually brings benefits to society as a whole. When entrepreneurs begin striving to create a better product than someone else, "Competition . . . wrests progress, as fast as it is made, from the hands of the individual and places it at the disposal of all mankind."[26]

But "creative destruction" soon forces those on top down, if not out, because their once-dominant products become obsolete (witness Palm Pilots). It is no wonder that so many forces array themselves against anything new. As new sectors attract resources away from existing ones and new firms threaten established ones, economic and political realities are often reversed. Since both political power and economic power are radically changed, existing institutions fight for the status quo. "I love change, but don't change me," seems to be everyone's credo. People who will lose because of change in a dynamic economy often want laws to protect them from the change. But protecting all members of a society from any losses stifles the innovations and change needed to create new wealth in a society.

---

[25] Joseph A. Schumpeter, *Capitalism, Socialism, and Democracy* (London: Taylor & Francis e-Library, 2003), 31–32.
[26] Frédéric Bastiat, *Economic Harmonies* (Irvington-on-Hudson, NY: Foundation for Economic Education, 1997), 289.

History repeatedly shows not only the decline of great ideas, companies, and empires, but also the constant pressure for change. Blink and the opportunities are gone, passing by those who waited too long. Yet unrealized opportunities exist for anyone who keeps looking. Given that humans possess unlimited wants (see discussion above, 173–74), every person can be encouraged to use his or her personal gifting to meet new possibilities and unfilled needs. The competitive process can be joined by anyone who wants to work, because there is always work to do.

H. Summary of how a free-market system functions

In the previous chapter, we discussed four necessary foundations for a free-market system: (1) private ownership of property with easy legal documentation of ownership, (2) the rule of law, (3) a stable currency, and (4) low taxes.

In this chapter, we have discussed briefly the seven key components in the working of a free-market system: (1) decentralized decision making ("no one" decides what is made); (2) specialization and trade, by which people multiply their productivity; (3) the signaling system of the market, which indicates continually changing supply and demand; (4) prices as the language of the signaling system; (5) profits and losses as the green lights and red lights that signal success or failure for businesses; (6) competition and voluntary cooperation as the interpersonal dimension that leads to continual improvement; and (7) the risk-taking of the entrepreneurs who drive innovation.

This, then, is how a free-market system works. With no central director or planner, it still enables vast amounts of wealth to be created, and benefits to be widely distributed, in every nation where it is allowed to function. No other system encourages everyone to compete and cooperate, and gives people such economic freedom to choose and produce, and thus enhances prosperity. Slowly but surely, countries around the world are seeing the win-win nature of a free-market system.

I. How wealthy people in rich nations can genuinely help poor nations

If our preceding analysis is correct, then the only permanent solution to poverty in any poor nation is for that nation to increase its GDP by producing more goods and services of value. And the only economic system in history that has successfully brought about such increased prosperity is the free-market system.

What can we say, then, to a wealthy person in a rich country who wants to help the poor and wants to promote a permanent, sustainable solution in poor countries? There are several practical steps such a person can take.

One very practical step would be for a wealthy person to invest in for-profit businesses in poor nations, especially nations that are beginning to move in a free-market direction with more effective rule of law. As we indicated in the last several chapters, GDP will grow when entrepreneurs risk their money to try producing some product or service. The only way to know if that product or service is truly meeting a need is to see whether customers will buy it—and profits are the "green lights" that will signal customer approval of the product. A new business that is truly making a profit in a poor country helps the poor country by (1) making products that increase the GDP, (2) making products that meet people's needs, and (3) providing jobs that enable poor people to support themselves. (See our discussion of freedom to start a business, 269–71.)

In addition, investing in a business that makes a profit treats the people in that country with utmost dignity, both the employees who create products of value and the customers who buy them. It enables the employees to experience the joy of earned success (see 193–95). It also avoids paternalism (see 27–28) and dependency.

While many organizations have promoted microloans (typically under $250) to start one-person businesses, we are also aware of encouraging cases in which Christians have decided to invest in for-profit businesses in the "small and medium enterprise" (SME) range, where $25,000 to $1 million is required to start a business. Such businesses are crucial for larger economic growth in poor nations, but they are more difficult to launch due to high start-up and due-diligence costs, and the challenge of providing a reasonable risk/return model for investors.

A wealthy person also could support:

• Educational programs in poor countries that promote free markets (as we explain in chapters 4–6) and promote the kinds of gov-

ernmental policies and cultural beliefs that we will explain below (chapters 7–9).
- Literature distribution programs that promote the same policies.
- Seminaries in poor countries that train pastors in the cultural beliefs and values that we outline in chapter 9.
- Financial-assistance programs to enable future leaders in poor countries to travel abroad to study in institutions that promote free-market economics, sound government policies, and beneficial cultural beliefs.

But readers must keep in mind that all of the activities we mention in this list promote theory and abstract knowledge more than they directly promote needed economic growth. Investing in for-profit businesses directly promotes economic growth, and those who work to make such businesses succeed will learn real-life lessons that could never be learned from any book or taught in any classroom.

Should wealthy people also give money to charities that provide things such as food, clean water, sanitation, and medical care for poor countries? Yes, those things are also beneficial in the short run, and especially in crisis situations, as we mentioned earlier (67). But donors must avoid charities whose policies promote dependency rather than productivity (see 27–28, 65–75). And even beneficial charities by themselves will not bring about a permanent solution. That will come about only through supporting private investment and the educational activities that we mention here, so that the entire economic system, governmental system, and belief system of a poor nation can be transformed.

6

THE MORAL ADVANTAGES OF THE SYSTEM

A Free Market Best Promotes Moral Virtues

While some people have raised moral objections to free-market systems, we think it is important to mention an alternative perspective: there are many moral advantages to free markets.

In saying this, we must guard against a possible misunderstanding. In the following pages, we are going to list several moral virtues that are encouraged by free-market systems. But we do not believe that free markets make morally perfect people!

As Christians, we believe that there is a sinful inclination to do evil in the heart of every person on earth (as well as, by God's "common grace," an opposite inclination to do good). We believe that "all have sinned and fall short of the glory of God" (Rom. 3:23), and that, except for Jesus Christ, no sinless person has walked the earth since the time of Adam and Eve.

Therefore, every economic system on earth has sinful people in it, people who do morally wrong things. There are people who lie, cheat, and steal, and hope to get away with it. In addition, in every society there are a few very evil people whose repeated wrong choices have deepened and strengthened the hold of sin in their hearts.

Neither are we saying that free markets are the cure for every conceivable human defect. They do not eliminate stupidity, obliterate selfishness, eradicate greed, or control the behavior of companies to everyone's satisfaction. Flawed human beings could never create a flawless system.

The question, then, is not, "Do free-market systems still have some evil people in them?" Of course they do. The proper question is, "Does a free-market system tend to discourage and punish wrong behavior and tend to encourage and reward virtuous behavior, and does it do these things better than other economic systems?" We believe it does, and that is what we explain in the rest of this chapter. We list what we see as sixteen advantages of free markets in four categories, then close the chapter by looking at five moral objections to these systems.

A. Promoting personal freedom

1. Promoting freedom of choice for moral actions

A free-market system is consistent with certain fundamental moral principles—that we should respect the dignity and individuality of each person, that governments should not manipulate people as objects but recognize each person's rights and values, and that economic decisions should be directed by means of persuasion and voluntary exchange rather than coercion and force. These ideas are summarized by the concept of individual freedom.

Free markets thrive on the non-aggression principle that protects human freedom. The requirement that transactions in the private sector of the economy must be voluntary ensures that, if such a system is working properly, the moral and physical autonomy of people is protected from violent attack by others. Force is inadmissible in human interpersonal relationships under a system of free markets, because the free market depends on people making *voluntary* exchanges.

Economist F. A. Hayek said it this way in his classic book *The Road to Serfdom*: "Individualism, in contrast to socialism and all other forms of totalitarianism, is based on the respect of Christianity for the individual and the belief that it is desirable that men should be free to develop their own individual gifts and bents."[1] Everyone should be able to make choices free of external intimidation and coercion. The free-market system, in which only voluntary and mutual exchange is permitted, thus promotes freedom of choice.

The Bible places a high value on human freedom and voluntary choices. God gave Adam and Eve a choice in the garden of Eden before there was sin in the world: "But of the tree of the knowledge of good and evil you shall not eat, for in the day that you eat of it you shall surely die" (Gen 2:17). Other passages emphasize the importance of such freedom of choice:

"I have set before you life and death, blessing and curse. Therefore *choose life*, that you and your offspring may live." (Deut. 30:19)

"*Choose* this day whom you will serve." (Josh. 24:15)

The Spirit and the Bride say, "*Come*." And let the one who hears say, "*Come*." And let the one who is thirsty come; let *the one who desires* take the water of life without price. (Rev. 22:17)

In the Old Testament, slavery and oppression (the opposites of freedom) are always viewed negatively. In fact, the Ten Commandments begin with God's declaration, "I am the LORD your God, who brought you out of the land of Egypt, *out of the house of slavery*" (Ex. 20:2).

Later, when the people of Israel turned against the Lord, he gave them into the hands of oppressors who enslaved them and took away their freedom (see Deut. 28:28–29, 33; Judg. 2:16–23). Loss of freedom was a curse, not a blessing.

That is why one blessing God promised was that a deliverer would come who would free the people from oppression by their enemies, for he would come "to proclaim *liberty* to the captives" (Isa. 61:1).

Throughout the Bible, from the beginning of Genesis to the last chapter of Revelation, God honors and protects human freedom and human choice. This is an essential component of our humanity, and it ultimately is a clear reflection of our creation in the image of God

---

[1] Friedrich A. Hayek, *The Road to Serfdom* (Chicago: The University of Chicago Press, 1944; repr., Washington: Heritage Foundation, 1994), 6.

(Gen. 1:27) and our desire to imitate God (Eph. 5:1), who has absolute freedom to do whatever he pleases as long as it is consistent with his own righteous and holy nature.

Freedom of choice is important for building other virtues in a nation, virtues that together make up a person's character. Yes, the more choices we have, the more opportunities there are to choose wrongly. But being deprived of choice does not build character; choosing rightly among many choices does. Punctuality, courtesy, truthfulness, trust, and productive efficiency are all strengthened when their opposites are options. So are other virtues that are encouraged and developed in a free-market system. These virtues improve the quality of personal relationships and increase respect for other people in a society.[2]

2. Promoting freedom for abstract or spiritual pursuits

Unfortunately, people who are not materially oriented—for example, those who might want to pursue lives of much personal contemplation or prayer, of ministry to others, or of artistic creativity—are seen as laggards in statist, government-planned economies, and they could be jailed or even killed for refusing to perform government-mandated jobs. But they are free to pursue such lives with no fear of government penalty in a free-market system.

Mark Zupan, dean and professor of economics and public policy at the University of Rochester's William E. Simon School of Business, notes that only in a decentralized, pluralistic, private-property order can the inalienable rights of everyone be secure.[3] This includes the right to pursue non-material activities.

Robert Sirico, in his thoughtful book *Defending the Free Market*, shows how material and non-material pursuits are naturally interconnected:

> Private property demonstrates the interpenetration between our physical bodies and our capacity for transcendence. We engage nature with labor that our reason plans and directs—and produce something that

---

[2] Mark A. Zupan, "The Virtues of Free Markets," *Cato Journal* 31, no. 2 (Spring/Summer 2011): 171–94, mentions a much longer list of positive moral virtues that are encouraged by free markets: integrity, trust, morality, cooperation, ethical behavior, legality, honoring one's word, honoring informal contracts, generating prosperity, punctuality, civil behavior, fidelity, win-win relationships, voluntary philanthropy, civic mindedness, social well-being, social harmony, minimal envy and resentment, freedom of choice, expanded options, and less selfishness.

[3] Ibid., 177.

did not previously exist. Not just another beaver dam exactly the same as the ones beavers have been building for millennia, but a Chartres Cathedral, a Mona Lisa, or an electric light bulb, a smallpox vaccine, a revolution in agriculture that lifts millions of people out of dire poverty or, more modestly, a garden or orchard that feeds a family and expresses a particular gardener's thoughtful stewardship of the land.

These things are possible because we don't just relate to the material world in an immediate or temporary manner. The relationship of human beings is not merely a relationship of consumption. It is also one of reason and creativity—and it is that relationship that makes the institution of private property possible. "The right to private property" is not merely control over a physical object, as my dog Theophilus might possess a bone. Rather the right to property is wrapped up in a person's capacity to apply his intellect to matter and ideas, to look ahead, to plan and steward the use of that possession. Just as other fundamental human rights are not created by the state but are possessed by virtue of a person's existence and nature, so also the right to private property is recognized rather than granted by the government. . . . It is sacred because it has such close connection to human beings as creatures made in the image of God, creatures placed in the context of scarcity and given a capacity to reason, create, and transcend.[4]

Therefore, the freedom to use the income we earn, the property we possess, and our time and effort to focus on abstract and spiritual pursuits is a moral advantage of a free-market system.

B. Promoting personal virtues

3. Promoting personal integrity and truth-telling

Zupan writes that the virtues of free markets produce an underlying morality. He argues that because of the repeated nature of exchanges, free markets create—or at least provide incentives for—integrity and other cooperative virtues.[5]

When future exchanges are expected, individuals are more willing to do the right things today. Free markets, he says, should be praised for fostering integrity and cooperative behavior through their promotion of ongoing mutually beneficial exchanges. Integrity in this case,

---

[4] Robert Sirico, *Defending the Free Market: The Moral Case for a Free Economy* (Washington: Regnery, 2012), 31.
[5] Zupan, "The Virtues of Free Markets," 177.

according to Zupan, is not about good or bad, or what should be or not be, but is about truth-telling. You either keep your word or you don't, and using that definition, he shows that free markets, as compared to other economic systems, more fully promote the practice of integrity and other desirable virtues.

It is not surprising that free markets tend to produce truth-telling, especially for established businesses in a relatively stable population. The very nature of repeated, even frequent, voluntary exchanges reinforces truthfulness. (You won't likely return to a grocer who lied to you about the freshness of the bread or milk, or an auto mechanic who lied to you about a repair that he did.) Lying destroys trade.[6]

The overwhelming levels of corruption seen in non-free-market economies throughout the world compare unfavorably with the greater honesty of free-market, private-property economies where repeated exchanges take place. For example, India still ranks as "mostly unfree" in the 2012 Index of Economic Freedom (54.6 points out of 100): "Despite India's high economic growth, the foundations for long term economic development remain fragile in the absence of an efficiently functioning legal framework. Corruption, endemic throughout the economy, is becoming even more serious."[7]

The 2012 Index of Economic Freedom[8] ranks "freedom from corruption" in 179 countries around the world.[9] The countries that rank at the lowest end of the scale for freedom from corruption (with a horrible score of 14–25 out of 100) include many unfree, government-controlled economies, such as Myanmar (14 out of 100), Uzbekistan (16), Venezuela (20), Russia (21), the Democratic Republic of the Congo (20), and Zimbabwe (24). By contrast, the highest ranking nations in freedom from corruption are all free-market economies, such as Denmark (93), New Zealand (93), Singapore (93), Canada (89), The Netherlands (88), Australia (87), Switzerland (87), and Hong Kong (84). There

---

[6] However, in cases where it is difficult for consumers to obtain adequate information to make a decision, there is a proper role for government regulation (for example, regulating sanitary conditions in food production facilities, which consumers could not personally investigate).

[7] Terry Miller, Kim R. Holmes, and Edwin Feulner, eds., 2012 Index of Economic Freedom (Washington: Heritage Foundation/New York: The Wall Street Journal, 2012), 225.

[8] Ibid., 8–12.

[9] The information on corruption is derived mostly from the Corruption Perception Index published periodically by Transparency International; see Miller, Holmes, and Feulner, 2012 Index of Economic Freedom, 456–457.

Photograph 1: Tribal Lands in Scottsdale, Arizona

In Scottsdale, Arizona, prosperous suburbs surround a largely barren area that is part of the Salt River Pima-Maricopa Indian Community, which is under tribal ownership. Except for the green areas surrounding a casino/golf resort and a new Major League Baseball spring training facility, the tribal land is largely unproductive. Tribal ownership of land traps people in poverty (see pages 116, 146).

Figure 1: Per Capita Income by Region

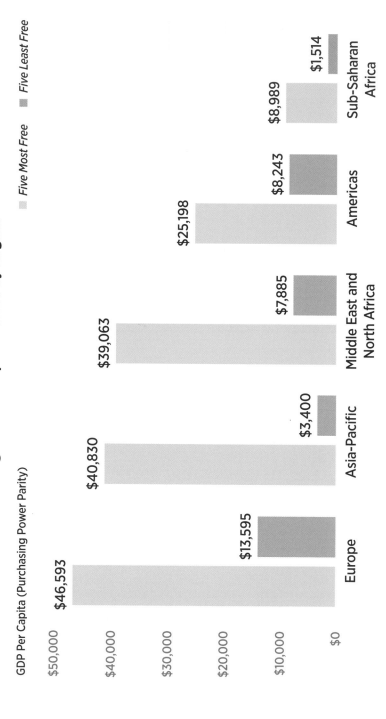

GDP Per Capita (Purchasing Power Parity)

Five Most Free   Five Least Free

Europe
- $46,593
- $13,595

Asia-Pacific
- $40,830
- $3,400

Middle East and North Africa
- $39,063
- $7,885

Americas
- $25,198
- $8,243

Sub-Saharan Africa
- $8,989
- $1,514

$50,000
$40,000
$30,000
$20,000
$10,000
$0

Nations that have the highest levels of economic freedom also have the highest per capita incomes. The chart above compares the economic freedom of the countries of the world (as measured by the 2012 *Index of Economic Freedom*) with their average per capita income (see page 134).

Figure 2: 2011 Corruption Perceptions Index

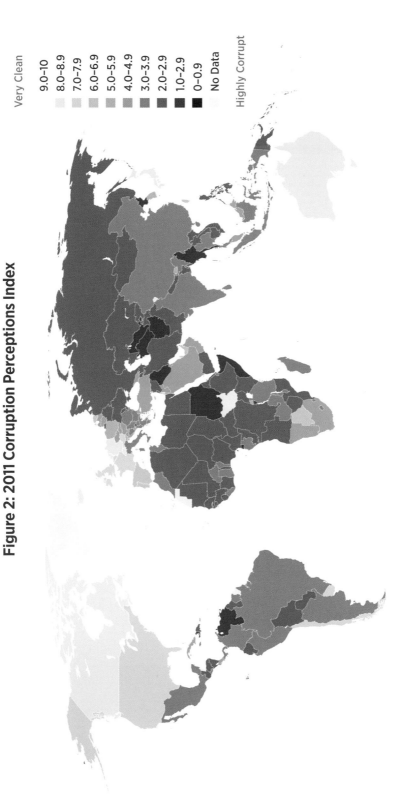

Very Clean
- 9.0–10
- 8.0–8.9
- 7.0–7.9
- 6.0–6.9
- 5.0–5.9
- 4.0–4.9
- 3.0–3.9
- 2.0–2.9
- 1.0–2.9
- 0–0.9
- No Data

Highly Corrupt

Transparency International's Corruption Perceptions Index measures the perceived level of public-sector corruption in countries and territories around the world. Such corruption is a major hindrance to economic development and therefore a contributing factor to lingering poverty (see page 275).

Figure 3: Income Mobility, 1975–91

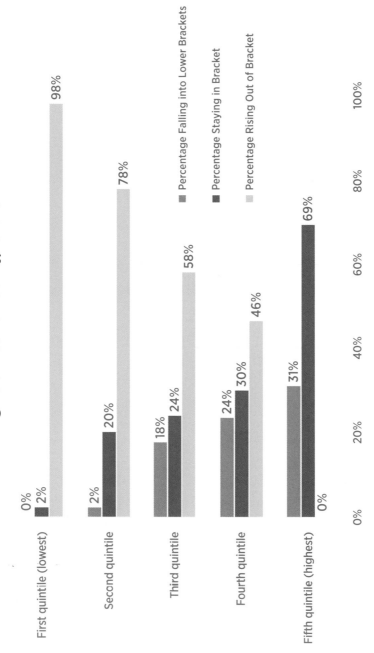

A study of the U.S. population from 1975 to 1991 showed that many people made significant economic gains. The population was divided into five income levels at the beginning of the study period. By the end of the period, very high percentages of the lower groups had moved to higher brackets. Smaller percentages of the upper-income groups had fallen to lower brackets. The study indicates that in the United States, most people are not mired in poverty but can and do progress economically (see page 299).

may be some countries with free markets and significant corruption due to various cultural or legal factors, but the general pattern is clear: countries with higher economic freedom tend to have lower levels of perceived corruption.

4. Promoting accountability

Well-defined free-market procedures and property rights also promote accountability for one's actions. The only exchanges people desire in such a system are positive-sum ones in which they benefit from the voluntary exchange. When both parties find that they are better off, they will make repeated exchanges because accountability for one's product is the norm.

The absence of free markets and property rights, on the other hand, often encourages dishonesty, thievery, or use of the heavy hand of government to coercively extract wealth from its rightful owner. Government redistribution becomes legalized thievery, giving rightfully gained property to other people. When government hands out favors, more effort is expended on redistributing wealth than on producing it, and political solutions (force) drive out market ones (peaceful resolution). When people are held accountable by the voluntary personal interactions of the free market, they are typically more responsible.

5. Promoting earned success

As we mentioned in chapter 2, recent research has confirmed what many people already knew by experience and instinct: the primary economic factor in making people happy is not money but "earned success" (see 74–75). This is the term used by American Enterprise Institute President Arthur C. Brooks to describe the joy and satisfaction that comes from having a specific responsibility and then doing good work to fulfill that responsibility. Brooks writes, "The secret to human flourishing is not money but earned success in life."[10]

We include the opportunity to attain "earned success" as a moral issue because it is consistent with the Bible's teaching about the responsibility of human beings to work and be productive. Even before

---

[10] Arthur C. Brooks, *The Battle: How the Fight between Free Enterprise and Big Government Will Shape America's Future* (New York: Basic Books, 2010), 71.

there was sin in the world, God put Adam in the garden of Eden "to work it and keep it" (Gen. 2:15), thus demonstrating the moral goodness of productive work and its necessity for fulfilling God's purpose for us here on earth. Later in the Old Testament, the book of Ecclesiastes speaks often about joy in one's work, as in this passage:

> There is nothing better for a person than that he should eat and drink and find enjoyment in his toil. This also, I saw, is from the hand of God, for apart from him who can eat or who can have enjoyment? (Eccl. 2:24–25).

In the New Testament, Paul told the Thessalonian church, "With toil and labor we *worked* night and day," and this was "to give you in ourselves an example to imitate" (2 Thess. 3:8–9). Then he added, "If anyone is not willing to *work*, let him not eat" (v. 10; see also 1 Thess. 4:11–12; Ex. 20:9).

Therefore, the Bible views productive work as *morally good*, and even commands that Christians should "work heartily for the Lord, and not for man" (Col. 3:23, teaching that a person's highest motivation for doing good work is to please God).

When this viewpoint is affirmed by a society, working at a regular job is seen as a rightful source of personal fulfillment and dignity. Also, the culture in general assumes that honorable people will strive to become diligent, faithful, and cheerful workers, and do a bit more than what is required because they view productive work as a moral good. Another reason to expect faithful, diligent work arises when people really believe that God will be pleased if they strive for excellence in their work. A society that provides greater opportunities to achieve such a sense of "earned success" therefore has a moral advantage.

Johan Norberg, in his book *In Defense of Global Capitalism*, emphasized this advantage of a free-market system:

> The growth of world prosperity is not a "miracle" or any of the other mystifying terms we customarily apply to countries that have succeeded economically and socially. Schools are not built, nor are incomes generated, by sheer luck, like a bolt from the blue. These things happen *when people begin to think along new lines and work hard to bring their ideas to fruition.* But people do that everywhere, and there is

no reason why certain people in certain places during certain periods of history should be intrinsically smarter or more capable than others. *What makes the difference is whether the environment permits and encourages ideas and work, or instead puts obstacles in their way.* That depends on whether people are free to explore their way ahead, to own property, to invest for the long term, to conclude private agreements, and to trade with others. In short, it depends on whether or not the countries have capitalism.[11]

Therefore, another moral advantage of a free-market system is that it allows everyone the freedom to try various ideas and occupations, with most eventually ending up in a job they do well. This is in contrast to a collectivist, state-controlled economy that assigns jobs, regulates wages, and squelches individual initiative. Allowing freedom of individual occupational choice also gives a greater sense of earned success, which is a big factor in human satisfaction with life.

A related consideration is that a free market encourages good work by allowing people to take pride in the quality of their work rather than just meeting a government-assigned quota for number of units produced. A free market promotes and rewards satisfaction in a job well done.

6. Moderating selfishness and greed, and using them for good

While some say free markets promote selfishness and greed, we think another perspective on this question is helpful. Because of the way free markets work, they also exercise a moderating force on greed, if not in everyone, at least in many successful people. (We discuss the difference between greed, which is wrong, and ordinary self-interest, which is often morally right, in a later section: see 208–9.)

Wherever a free-market system (under the rule of law) is allowed to function, life, health, liberty, and prosperity are all improved because countless individuals seem to be able to take an idea, act on it, and begin to produce something (perhaps by starting a small business). The ideas that are most successful are those that best meet the needs

---

[11]Johan Norberg, *In Defense of Global Capitalism* (Washington: Cato Institute, 2003), 64, emphasis added. What Norberg calls "capitalism" is similar to what we are calling a "free-market system" (see our discussion above, 136–38).

of others. Therefore, successful business people are often those who, over the course of a lifetime, have become habitually accustomed to recognizing and meeting the needs and desires of others.

Short-sighted selfishness, in fact, makes it impossible for a business to flourish. In order to develop a successful business, individuals must forgo present spending on themselves by saving, by exercising self-control, and by investing wisely. If there is no saving and no capital formation, the business does not grow.

We do not pretend that free markets eliminate human selfishness. But a free-market system can *channel* selfishness into work and investment activities that actually bring good to other people. Thus, someone's initial short-sighted selfishness can be modified over time to long-term enlightened self-interest, and thus it is turned to beneficial ends for society. As for those who are not greedy and selfish, but simply want to work and invest because of healthy, normal self-interest (not greed) and a proper desire to provide for their families, the free market also channels their work in a productive direction.

Finally, even for those people who do not give a moment's thought to earning money and whose sole purpose is just to serve others through new, useful inventions (such as smart phone apps), the free market often provides a financial reward that frees up more of their time and enables them to go on inventing and creating.

Again, we repeat that free markets will not rid the world of selfishness, greed, or other defects of human nature. But the actual working of a free-market system moderates and directs those tendencies in a socially beneficial direction more than any other economic system.

7. Promoting wise use of the environment

A free-market society with a combination of private ownership of most land and resources, and public ownership of some designated national and state parks, seems best suited to preservation of resources and wise use of the environment. We discuss this more fully in chapter 7, where we note that a productive society must protect the environment from destruction (see 250–52), and in chapter 8, where we note that government must also protect people's ability to use the earth's resources wisely (see 280–84). By contrast, socialist societies have often been the most destructive to the environment (see 250–52).

8. Curbing materialism and promoting personal charity

It is strange that people who favor state-controlled economies criticize free-market economies as materialistic. It is socialist countries that place almost all of their economic emphasis on the production of material goods, while free-market economies voluntarily support hundreds of thousands of organizations and people that clothe the naked and feed the hungry. Many people work as pastors, church staff members, missionaries, or employees of non-profit charitable organizations.

Charity for the poor, educational endowments, donations for medical research, and other kinds of private giving have experienced significant growth in the past two hundred and fifty years, during the most explosive period of the market economy. This is because:

> Capitalism honors and promotes charity and virtue. True charity cannot be compelled. Universities, hospitals, social agencies are more satisfactory and more fun when they derive from voluntary support. Money taken by force and bestowed by formula is no gift. . . . Capitalism honors the liberty and dignity of every person. . . . He is regarded as a free citizen under God and under the law—able to make his own choices.[12]

By contrast, socialism discourages and (by excessive governmental confiscation of people's money) makes more difficult any individual contributions to charitable causes. More and more of the whole energy of society is forced to focus on material production at the direction of the state.

In this way, socialism is not only more materialistic than a free-market system, but also has a generally detrimental moral influence. Claire Berlinski, in her important book on Margaret Thatcher, summarized Thatcher's view that state-controlled economies uniformly exert a corrupting moral influence on their people:

---

[12] Perry E. Gresham, "Think Twice Before You Disparage Capitalism," in *The Freeman* 27:3 (March 1977), accessed October 5, 2012, http://www.thefreemanonline.org/features/think-twice-before-you-disparage-capitalism/.

In all its incarnations, wherever and however it was applied—[socialism] was morally corrupting. [It] turned good citizens into bad ones; it turned strong nations into weak ones; it promoted vice and discouraged virtue; and . . . it transformed formerly hardworking and self-reliant men and women into whining, weak and flabby loafers. Socialism was not a fine idea that had been misapplied; it was an inherently *wicked* idea. This was Thatcher's single contribution to the debate. It was a point she emphasized again and again: "In the end, the real case against socialism is not its economic inefficiency, though on all sides there is evidence of that. Much more fundamental is its basic immorality." . . .

To a Western world preoccupied with guilt, decline and decay, Thatcher's message has a particularly significant resonance. It is hardly a secret that many of us are still wondering whether capitalism is the right path. It is the *only* right path, says Thatcher, and the only one men and women of virtue—not greed, but *virtue*—should take.[13]

C. Promoting interpersonal virtues

In one sense, the advantages listed in this category could be included with the "personal virtues" listed in the previous section. But we thought it useful to have this separate category of virtues that have more of an effect on other people than on oneself.[14]

9. Meeting the needs of others

Many scholars remind us that a competitive free market was the first social system in human history to direct man's desire toward peacefully supplying greater quantities of goods and services for his fellow human beings.[15] Hayek clearly explained the efficacy of the free market in his 1944 book *The Road to Serfdom*. Other good books followed, but Milton Friedman's 1962 book *Capitalism and Freedom* then produced a

---

[13] Claire Berlinski, *There Is No Alternative: Why Margaret Thatcher Matters* (New York: Basic Books, 2008), 7–8, 13. We first saw this statement about Thatcher in Dennis Prager, *Still the Best Hope* (New York: HarperCollins, 2012), 417.

[14] There is some overlap between the categories because the personal virtues also influence other people, and the interpersonal virtues flow from a person's own character. It is a distinction in emphasis, not an absolute distinction, and which virtues go in which list makes no difference to our argument.

[15] See, for example, Robert Axelrod, *The Evolution of Cooperation* (New York: Basic Books, 1984); J. R. Clark and Dwight R. Lee, "Markets and Morality," *Cato Journal* 31, no. 2 (Winter 2011); Milton Friedman, *Capitalism and Freedom: A Leading Economist's View on the Proper Role of Competitive Capitalism* (Chicago: University of Chicago Press, 1962); Charles A. Murray, *In Pursuit of Happiness and Good Government* (New York: Simon and Schuster, 1989); Matt Ridley, *The Rational Optimist: How Prosperity Evolves* (New York: Harper Collins, 2010).

veritable flood of scholarly books, essays, and other materials on the beneficial implications of free markets. Frank Knight, Henry Simons, James Buchanan, Gordon Tullock, George Stigler, Yale Brozen, Harold Demsetz, Murray Weidenbaum, Thomas Sowell, and George Gilder are just a few of those contributing to understanding and instituting the free-market order. Most mention that the working class and the poor are its chief beneficiaries, for in generation after generation the poor take advantage of the opportunities available in a free-market system to rise out of poverty.

10. Prioritizing the wants of others

Providing customers with products they want at lower prices naturally makes a business more profitable. Most companies are responsive to the consumer because they recognize that, in terms of determining sales of products, the consumer reigns. IBM declared this viewpoint in a 2012 advertisement entitled "Welcome to the Era of the Chief Executive Customer":

> On a smarter planet, we've seen how predictive analytics can help transform everything from how we fight crime to how we improve things like healthcare, food safety, and utility grids. . . . The proliferation of new mobile devices . . . [is helping us] understand [consumers] not just as segments or targets, but as actual individuals. And those individuals expect more from the brands they do business with—not just service, but hyperpersonalized service . . . that can give customers what they want, when they want it.[16]

By its very nature, competition prompts a company to improve everything it can to satisfy a customer. Jay W. Richards correctly says: "The logic of competition in a market is not about destroying enemies. It's about serving consumers better than your competitors."[17]

The alternative to serving other people's wants through voluntary exchange is to try to control their lives through the use of force by

---

[16]IBM advertisement, "Welcome to the Era of the Chief Executive Customer," in *The Wall Street Journal*, June 6, 2012, A16.
[17]Jay W. Richards, *Money, Greed, and God: Why Capitalism Is the Solution and Not the Problem* (New York: HarperOne, 2009), 81.

government, invariably producing lower living standards and the sub-jugation of the many by the privileged few.

11. Treating others humanely

The morality and justice of the free-market system cannot be fully appreciated until its alternatives are observed and evaluated. British economist Arthur Shenfield reminds us, "It is a plain historical fact that the treatment of man by man became conspicuously more hu-mane side by side with the rise of capitalism."[18]

British author Matt Ridley similarly writes:

> Unimaginable cruelty was commonplace in the pre-commercial world: execution was a spectator sport, mutilation a routine punish-ment, human sacrifice a futile tragedy and animal torture a popular entertainment. The nineteenth century, when industrial capitalism drew so many people into dependence on the market, was a time when slavery, child labour, and pastimes like fox tossing and cock fighting became unacceptable. The late twentieth century, when life became still more commercialised, was a time when racism, sexism, and child molesting became unacceptable. In between, when capital-ism gave way to various forms of state-directed totalitarianism and their pale imitators, such virtues were noticeable by their retreat—while faith and courage revived.[19]

What about violence? Countries with considerable experience with free markets and commercialization also have found that "random vio-lence makes the news precisely because it is so rare; routine kindness does not make the news precisely because it is so commonplace."[20]

12. Truly helping the poor

Since free-market systems are economically the most productive, they are also the systems that bring the most genuine, long-term help to the poor. Other economic systems might have short-term welfare pro-grams for the poor, but the best kind of help is not welfare but lasting,

---

[18] Arthur Shenfield, "Capitalism Under the Tests of Ethics," *Imprimis* 10, no. 12 (December 1981): 4.
[19] Ridley, *The Rational Optimist*, 104.
[20] Ibid.

productive jobs in which the poor can support themselves and begin to advance out of poverty.

For example, fully 98 percent of the poorest people in the United States (the bottom 20 percent of income earners) in 1975 had moved to higher income brackets by 1991. Among those in the next-highest 20 percent of earners, 78 percent had moved to higher brackets.[21] (We discuss such income mobility in more detail at 297–300.) In a productive, growing economy, jobs are available and many poor people are able not only to begin to support themselves and get ahead economically, but also to have the satisfaction of getting a job and doing well at it, the happiness that comes from "earned success."

Whatever the level of concern for the poor on the part of individuals who live in different economic systems, the free market still seems to be the most humane way mankind has found for dealing with the economic problems of scarcity. Whenever the barriers to the exercise of free personal choice are removed and economic freedoms are granted, prosperity begins to occur. When more goods are produced and more jobs are available, people at every level of society, from rich to poor, are helped. It is also important to note that very few people go hungry under such a system.

13. Promoting "lesser virtues" such as punctuality, courtesy, tidiness, and a job well done

✱ what about customer service?
incentives necessary

Lawrence Harrison's extensive studies of progress-prone cultures (those that have higher economic development) and progress-resistant cultures (those that are poorer) showed that the productive, progress-prone cultures tend to place a higher value on what he calls the "lesser virtues": "A job well done, tidiness, courtesy, punctuality."[22]

This makes perfect sense once we understand that free markets depend on voluntary exchanges. If I had a small plumbing company and wanted a customer to hire me more than once, I would be motivated to do my best work ("a job well done"), to leave the customer's fixed kitchen sink neat and clean ("tidiness"), to treat him with politeness

---

[21] "Income Mobility 1975–91," in Stephen Moore and Julian Simon, *It's Getting Better All the Time: Greatest Trends of the Last 100 Years* (Washington: Cato Institute, 2000), 79.
[22] Lawrence E. Harrison, *The Central Liberal Truth: How Politics Can Change a Culture and Save It from Itself* (Oxford: Oxford University Press, 2006), 36.

and respect ("courtesy"), and to show up at his house when I said I would ("punctuality"). I would also want the plumbers who work for me to show the same high standards.

Harrison is insightful when he calls these "lesser virtues." They do not rise to the level of refraining from murdering, stealing, or committing adultery, for example, nor is neglecting one of them a criminal offense, but they are still important. They reflect the way we would want others to treat us, so they reflect the Golden Rule: "Whatever you wish that others would do to you, do also to them, for this is the Law and the Prophets" (Matt. 7:12). These virtues show genuine concern for the interests of others, so they are one way of obeying Jesus's command, "You shall love your neighbor as yourself" (Matt. 22:39). A free-market system encourages these virtues.

In addition to these specific virtues, free markets tend to reinforce general habits of respect for the convictions and preferences of others. One of the great advantages of a social system characterized by cooperation through mutually beneficial exchange is that the freedoms of the system provide the opportunity and scope for sympathy, beneficence, sharing, and even tolerating people with whom we have major disagreements. Indeed, it is far more likely that feelings of friendship and cooperation are the *effects* of a system of contractual social cooperation rather than the cause. Since each individual is unique, it is difficult for anyone else to know what does or does not lead to another's fulfillment. The free market tends to favor those who respect the sanctity of other people's freedom of choice.

D. Promoting societal virtues

14. Promoting a peaceful and harmonious society

The social harmony that results from a market order should be of great interest to those concerned with moral issues. Dinesh D'Souza offers New York City as an example:

> We see the evidence in New York, which presents an amazing sight to the world. Tribal and religious battles, such as we see in Lebanon, Mogadishu, Kashmir, and Belfast, don't happen here. In New York restaurants, white and African-American secretaries have lunch together.

In Silicon Alley, Americans of Jewish and Palestinian descent collaborate on e-commerce solutions and play racquetball after work. Hindus and Muslims, Serbs and Croats, Turks and Armenians, Irish Catholics and British Protestants, all seem to have forgotten their ancestral differences and joined the vast and varied parade of New Yorkers.[23]

Adam Smith was among the first to see how the impersonal, non-discriminatory free market seemed to protect everyone. Edward Coleson writes:

> Smith had discovered to his amazement that the true long-range self-interest of each individual was compatible with everyone else's welfare, that what was good for one was best for all. . . . As Smith said, the businessman in seeking his own interest is "led by an invisible hand" to promote the general welfare, "an end which was no part of his intention." . . . What is good for the farmer is good for the consumer, what is good for labor is good for management, what is good for Russia, Red China, Cuba and other friendlier neighbors is good for the United States and vice versa.[24]

But isn't the free market competitive and overly ambitious? Yes, the free market does encourage strong competition. But, remarkably, it also encourages strong cooperation and social harmony.

It is enlightening to contrast the differences between *market solutions* and *political solutions* concerning two potentially contentious issues. P. J. Hill, professor emeritus of economics at Wheaton College and senior fellow at the Property and Environment Research Center (PERC) in Bozeman, Montana, explains why arguments over creationism versus evolution are so heated, but not arguments over meat-eating versus vegetarianism:

> There have always been conflicts over teaching the origins of mankind. School boards, which must make collective decisions, generally have to decide to teach either that human beings were created or that they evolved. Such decisions are fraught with conflict. People who disagree with a board's decision march, write letters to the newspaper,

---

[23] Dinesh D'Souza, *What's So Great About America* (New York: Penguin, 2002), 93.
[24] Edward Coleson, "Capitalism and Morality," in *The Morality of Capitalism*, ed. Mark W. Hendrickson (Irving-on-Hudson, NY: Foundation for Economic Education, 1996), 20.

lobby, hire lawyers, and in general become quite exercised. This is almost inevitable when highly emotional issues are involved since any collective decision (political), including one made by a majority vote, is likely to be contrary to the wishes of the minority. Thus the decision makers are in a no-win situation. If the board allows creationism to be taught, evolutionists will be irate. If they decide to teach evolution, creationists will be outraged.

In contrast, consider the decision to be vegetarian or carnivorous. There are individuals who feel every bit as strongly about these issues as those involved in the origins of mankind debate. Nevertheless there is little chance that a decision about diet will generate public controversy. Diet is not determined by a collective decision making process. The point is, leave it in the private sector market and people will interact peacefully about it. The person who believes that avoiding meat is healthier or morally correct can pursue such a diet without arguing with the meat eater. Advocates of a meat diet can find producers and grocers eager to satisfy their desires. In fact, vegetarians and meat eaters can shop at the same stores, pushing their carts past each other with no conflict. It is the absence of collective decision making that permits this peaceful proximity.

The social harmony that results from a market order should be of great interest to those concerned with moral issues. People of very different cultures, values, and world views can live together without rancor under a system of private rights and markets. A market order requires only minimal agreement on personal goals or social end states.[25]

Peaceful, fair, accountable, and harmonious societies all flowing from property rights and a system of free markets under law? Remarkable.

Here is one more story on the efficacy of property rights—in this case, among children. Have you ever seen two children quarreling over a toy? Such squabbles were commonplace in Katherine Hussman Klemp's household. But in *The Sesame Street Parents' Guide*, she tells how she created peace among her eight children by assigning property rights to toys.

As a young mother, Klemp often brought home games and toys from garage sales. "I rarely matched a particular item with a particu-

---

[25] P. J. Hill, "Markets and Morality," in Hendrickson, *The Morality of Capitalism*, 97.

lar child," she says. "Upon reflection, I could see how the fuzziness of ownership easily led to arguments. If everything belonged to everyone, then each child felt he had a right to use anything."

To solve the problem, Klemp introduced two simple rules. First, she would never bring anything into the house without assigning clear ownership to one child. The owner would have ultimate authority over the use of the property. Second, the owner would not be required to share. Before the rules were in place, Klemp recalls, "I suspected that much of the drama often centered less on who got the item in dispute and more on who Mom would side with." Now, property rights, not parents, would settle the arguments.

Instead of teaching selfishness, the introduction of property rights actually promoted sharing. The children were secure in their ownership and knew they could always get their toys back. Adds Klemp, "'Sharing' raises their self-esteem to see themselves as generous persons."

Not only do her children value their own property rights, but they also respect the property of others. "Rarely do our children use each other's things without asking first, and they respect a 'No' when they get one. Best of all, when someone who has every right to say 'No' to a request says 'Yes,' the borrower sees the gift for what it is and says 'Thanks' more often than not," says Klemp.[26]

Since private property rights are human rights, every person has the right to use his property or exchange it. Any restriction on private property increases the probability of disagreement. Private property rights not only protect individual liberty, but as Dr. Hill's and Mrs. Klemp's examples point out, all humans, young or old, benefit when everyone knows who owns what, and public ownership and collective decisions are minimized. Economic history also shows that without property rights, human rights deteriorate and are often lost. The loss of economic freedom seriously affects all the other rights individuals desire.

15. Promoting a fair society

"Another reason that a system based on private property rights encourages social harmony," says Hill, "is that it holds people accountable for

---

[26] Janet Beales Kaidantzis, "Property Rights for 'Sesame Street,'" summarized from *The Sesame Street Parents' Guide*, in *The Concise Encyclopedia of Economics* (Indianapolis: Liberty Fund, 2008), 424.

what they do to others. Under a private property regime, a person who injures another or damages another's property is responsible for the damages, and courts enforce their responsibility. The mere knowledge that damage must be paid for leads people to act carefully and responsibly. When people are accountable for their actions, individual freedom can be allowed."[27] This idea is consistent with what we mentioned earlier about a free-market system requiring the rule of law in order to restrain and punish wrongdoing that harms other people (see 134–35).

This awareness of accountability is consistent with the protection of private property found in the Bible. People who damaged the property of others, whether by taking something from a neighbor or by allowing an animal to ravage or a fire to burn a neighbor's grain, had to repay the neighbor, and, if the damage was intentional, had to pay an additional penalty (Ex. 22:1–6). Such respect for the property of others reflects an awareness of each person's equal value before God, based on equal creation in the image of God (Gen. 1:26–27; 9:6; James 3:9).

16. Promoting a productive society

If free-market systems result in the greatest economic productivity for nations, this also must be seen as a moral advantage. Productive societies not only have more resources to help the poor, they also have more resources for the benefit of everyone in those societies.

Someone might object that we already have enough material goods. Why should we continually strive to produce more? Isn't this a wrongful kind of materialism? We answer this objection below, in the section, "Objection: we don't need more 'stuff'" (215–21). The short answer is this: we do not need more "stuff" to *survive*, but we need it for *human flourishing*, which is God's intention for us on the earth.

Increased wealth is a net addition to a country's GDP and hence to the economic well-being of that society. The moral virtue of an economic system of greater productivity surely must be weighed against the poverty, starvation, and degradation of a system that does not produce.

---

[27] Hill, "Markets and Morality," in Hendrickson, *The Morality of Capitalism*, 98, citing "Markets and Morality," in *The Freeman*, 39, no. 2 (February 1989).

E. Moral objections

1. Objection: free markets do not work

In light of the remarkable productivity of free-market economies in the last two centuries, it is somewhat surprising to us that people still raise the objection that free markets do not work. For example, President Barack Obama, in a speech in Kansas on December 6, 2011, argued for more government spending and more regulation:

> The market will take care of everything, they tell us. . . . But here's the problem: it doesn't work. It has never worked. It didn't work when it was tried in the decade before the Great Depression. It's not what led to the incredible postwar booms of the '50s and '60s. And it didn't work when we tried it during the last decade. I mean, understand, it's not as if we haven't tried this theory.[28]

We disagree. Neither the president of the United States, the president of Venezuela, a brilliant movie producer such as Steven Spielberg, nor any of the thousands of critics of free markets before or after the 2008 financial meltdown have proposed a more decent, moral, and uplifting system. Compared to perfection, the free market is easy to criticize. Utopia is always a better idea. But compared to any real-world example ever tried in the past, its virtues of greater economic productivity, of lifting the masses from poverty, of promoting virtuous behavior, and of frequent personal benevolence are unsurpassed.

On the other side, we are reminded of the historical fact that systems other than economic freedom trample liberty, spawn totalitarian political regimes, and make a mockery of economic efficiency. Despite the evidence that socialism, in all of its manifestations, leads to government intervention in private actions and often ruthless dictatorship, the hope for a welfare state or a "third way" lives on. President Obama's suspicions about free markets are not new, but they must be challenged. If poverty is to be overcome and the preciousness of human beings living as free moral agents is to be realized, the free-market system now being tried successfully by countries on every continent needs to be morally defended.

---

[28] James R. Oheson, "An Audacious Promise: The Moral Case for Capitalism," *Manhattan Institute*, no. 12 (May 2012), 1.

2. Objection: free markets depend on greed

We often hear people object that free-market economic systems are "based on greed." We doubt that those who make such an objection have given this subject serious thought, because they fail to make a crucial distinction between "greed" and ordinary self-interest. It is true that in an ordered market people are better off appealing to someone else's *self-interest* than to that person's kindness, but this is not necessarily a bad thing. Smith said it this way: "It is not from the benevolence of the butcher, the brewer, or the baker that we expect our dinner, but from their regard to their own interest."[29]

Jay W. Richards explains self-interest as follows:

> Every time you take a breath, wash your hands, eat your fiber, take your vitamins, clock in at work, look both ways before crossing the street, crawl into bed, take a shower, pay your bills, go to the doctor, hunt for bargains, read a book, and pray for God's forgiveness, you're pursuing your self-interest. . . . In fact, proper self-interest is the basis for the Golden Rule. . . . "In everything do to others as you would have them do to you."[30]

British economist Brian Griffiths writes perceptively:

> From a Christian point of view therefore self-interest is a characteristic of man created in the image of God, possessed of a will and a mind, able to make decisions and accountable for them. It is not a consequence of the Fall. Selfishness is the consequence of the Fall and it is the distortion of self-interest when the chief end of our lives is not the service of God but the fulfillment of our own ego.[31]

Notice that self-interest and greed are not the same thing. Self-interest is unavoidable. Self-interest might even lead someone to give generously to the needs of others because giving carries its own rewards—Jesus said, "It is more blessed to give than to receive" (Acts 20:35).

Greed, on the other hand, is excessive self-interest. It is wanting

---

[29] Adam Smith, *An Inquiry into the Nature and Causes of the Wealth of Nations*, ed. Edwin Cannan (1776; repr., New York: Modern Library, 1994), 15.

[30] Richards, *Money, Greed, and God*, 121. Darrow L. Miller and Stan Guthrie, *Discipling Nations: The Power of Truth to Transform Cultures* (Seattle: YWAM, 1998), 253–54, also rightly distinguish self-interest (which is biblical) from wrongful greed (which is not).

[31] Brian Griffiths, *The Creation of Wealth* (London: Hodder and Stoughton, 1984), 69.

more than you rightfully deserve or failing to care for the needs of others as well as yourself. But greed cannot be prevented by human laws, since it is an internal attitude. It can be reduced only with a change of heart coming from inside a person.

When greed manifests itself through violations of the rights of others, a free-market system is most likely to limit its harmful effects through the reactions of consumers (who will soon refuse to buy from a merchant they perceive to be greedy) and through the protections provided by the rule of law and legal protections of others' rights.

Has any economic system ever *eliminated* greed from every person in a society? No. So what shall we do? Why not favor a system that *utilizes* people's healthy self-interest and even their sinful greed in a socially beneficial way by rewarding those who best serve the needs of others? That is what a free-market system does.

Instead of despising self-interest and the free market's untold goods and services, we wish that people would see the role of self-interest in a free-market system as God's providential method of guiding the actions of billions of fallible humans to decisions and choices that benefit all mankind.

In every potential sale, purchase, or trade, if the initial inquiry ends in a *voluntary* exchange, everyone benefits. A voluntary exchange meets not only our own concerns but others' concerns as well, so these mutual gains represent a win-win situation. As we have seen, trading with others adds value even when nothing new is produced, and, therefore, the more trading partners, the more wealth produced. The economic freedom to specialize, trade, own, and produce is powerful because it is driven by enlightened self-interest and not by a national planner.

Admittedly it is not easy to understand the remarkably beneficial nature of free-market systems and to appreciate the nature of a competitively determined structure of relative prices. Yet free markets, neither created nor planned by mortals, and evolving over many centuries, have produced fantastic increases in the standard of living where they have been allowed to operate. As economist Thomas Sowell has said, "Individually we know so pathetically little, and yet socially we use a range and complexity of knowledge that would confound a computer."[32] The economic system of entrepreneurial free markets makes this all possible.

3. Objection: free markets result in inequality

Another objection sometimes raised against free markets is that they result in unfair economic inequality, that a few people become very rich while many others remain poor.

In response, we must distinguish various kinds of equality. One great benefit of a free-market system is that it best protects two crucial kinds of equality: (1) equality before the law and (2) equal opportunity to attempt to succeed and improve one's situation in life. These understandings of equality are implications of the biblical teaching that every human being is created in the image of God (Gen. 1:26–27; 9:6; James 3:9).

But (3) economic equality is a different question. Individuals have differing skill sets, levels of willingness to work hard, intelligence, desires, preferences, and even luck (or rather, from a Christian point of view, divine providence). Because of this, complete economic equality is impossible to create, and efforts to do so are destructive and cause havoc.

In fact, no society or economic system has ever produced strict economic equality among its population, and those that have tried the hardest (the Soviet Union, Cuba, and China under Mao Tse-tung) produced nothing but bloodshed and the tyranny of oppressive governments. Among the masses of the population, there was equality in misery, but among the elite leaders there was still vast privilege, with better vacations, homes, and cars. No system can guarantee equal outcomes.

People generally recognize that not all economic inequality is wrong. Can you sing like Luciano Pavarotti, play football like the Manning brothers, play tennis like the Williams sisters, or create a software company like Bill Gates or a computer company like Steve Jobs? It is a fact of life that people are unequal in their abilities, interests, and motivations. Is Bill Gates really worth billions of dollars? Or is that the wrong question? Could it be there is nothing inherently wrong with *some* inequality?

---

[32] Thomas Sowell, *Knowledge and Decisions* (New York: Basic Books, 1980), 3.

We should be thankful there are some who make larger amounts, save larger amounts, and invest larger amounts than we do. Otherwise, economic productivity and growth would be dismal, and we all would be much poorer than we are now. Inequality of talent, beauty, and luck may be unfortunate, but isn't it envy that tells us they are always wrong or unfair?

Unfortunately, legislating economic equality does not work because it shifts capital from investment and jobs to unearned transfers and entitlements in developed economies, and to zero-sum, unproductive relationships in developing economies. Attempting to legislate economic equality usually gives more power to the political ruling class, who retain access to all the privileges the society affords.

But we must add that some economic inequality is very wrong. We have already mentioned a common pattern in poor countries, where small, powerful elites manipulate laws, property ownership, and business licenses to keep the vast majority trapped in poverty (75–77). Such cases are not representative of a free-market system, for they nullify the crucial elements of equality before the law and equal opportunity to attempt to succeed and improve one's situation in life.

4. Objection: in some countries, free markets become "bad capitalism"

The twentieth century provided abundant proof that the communism of the Soviet Union, China, and North Korea, and the Marxian socialism practiced in many sub-Saharan African countries, did not work. More and more countries are now navigating toward free markets, sometimes calling it "capitalism." But the term *capitalism* can be misleading. Unfortunately, some of the systems that pass as "capitalism" are really highly-controlled economies and not free markets at all.

William J. Baumol, Robert E. Litan, and Carl J. Schramm's book *Good Capitalism, Bad Capitalism, and the Economics of Growth and Prosperity*[33] discusses two kinds of capitalism that they define as bad (neither of which would qualify as a "free market" in our understanding). First, they list *state-guided capitalism*, in which a government tries to guide

---

[33] William J. Baumol, Robert E. Litan, and Carl J. Schramm, *Good Capitalism, Bad Capitalism, and the Economics of Growth and Prosperity* (New Haven: Yale University Press, 2007), 60–92.

the market, most often by supporting particular industries and even individual firms that it wants to become winners. As examples, they mention China, Russia, Japan, other Southeast Asian countries, and, to an extent, India.

They give many reasons why this approach does not work in the long term. Though initially it can produce handsome economic numbers, the hard questions of planning an industry—such as "Who?" "What?" "Why?" and "When?"—cannot be answered by top-down government controllers, and attempts to do so usually end in inefficiency, even chaos.

After the low-hanging fruit is picked, such as low-cost manufacturing workers producing products for export, problems multiply as the economic questions get harder. As examples, Baumol and his coauthors cite the following: excessive investment in unproductive sectors continues but no one pulls the plug; the country is unable to come up with the necessary innovation needed to compete successfully in a global economy; the system proves susceptible to ongoing and growing corruption; and planners are reluctant to channel resources from low-yielding activities toward potentially more rewarding ventures.[34] State capitalism, in the authors' opinion, does not work long-term, and its drawbacks heavily outweigh its advantages.[35]

The second kind of bad capitalism they describe is *oligarchic capitalism*, under which the bulk of the power and wealth in a nation is held by a few individuals and families. Government policies are designed mainly for promoting a few very wealthy land-holders and power brokers.

Baumol, Litan, and Schramm say that oligarchic capitalism is common in Latin America, as well as in many of the nations that were part of the former Soviet Union, in much of the Arabic Middle East, and now in some parts of Africa.

To support their argument, they refer to the Gini coefficient, which

---

[34] Ibid., 62–71.
[35] We do not find our own nation blameless in this regard. For example, we find it unfortunate that many of the policies pursued by President Obama's administration from 2008 to 2012 represented this kind of state capitalism, with government picking winners and losers in the private sector and trying to control segments of the economy, such as energy (pouring millions of dollars into wind and solar, but blocking oil and coal), automobiles (essentially bailing out General Motors from bankruptcy), and much of the banking industry (with thousands of new regulations), while turning the entire health-care industry into a government enterprise (the Affordable Care Act).

is a standard statistical measure of income inequality within a nation.[36] The higher the Gini number, the greater the inequality. The Gini coefficient is distressingly high in many Latin American countries. Whereas most prosperous nations today have a Gini coefficient between 25 and 40, the score for many Latin American countries is in the very high 40s or even in the 50s, indicating huge disparities between a very rich but tiny minority and a very poor majority in those nations. Such countries do not have meaningful equality before the law or equality of opportunity. Here are some of the scores:

Chile[37]	57.1
Colombia	57.6
El Salvador	53.2
Guatemala	59.9
Honduras	55.0
Mexico	54.6
Panama	56.4
Peru	49.8
Venezuela	49.1[38]

This brand of so-called "capitalism" is not genuine free-market capitalism because it breeds corrupt leaders who manage to preserve wealth and income for the inside few. It inevitably produces an extensive "informal" black-market economy in which economic exchange is corrupt, secret, and works only for those determining policy.[39]

Daron Acemoglu and James A. Robinson, in their 2012 book *Why Nations Fail: The Origins of Power, Prosperity and Poverty*, do not use the categories of "state-guided capitalism" and "oligarchic capitalism," but both of these types, especially the first, are similar to what they call an

---

[36] We do not mean to imply that the Gini coefficient is the only legitimate measure of fairness in a society. As we explained above (210–11), we believe that some economic inequality is inevitable if an economy fairly rewards people for the value of their efforts and skills. Therefore, a very low Gini coefficient might indicate that a society is unjustly penalizing its more productive workers, and some wealthy nations might have a relatively high Gini coefficient while the low-income people are still wealthy by world standards. But the higher Gini coefficients shown here for poorer Latin American countries seem to us to indicate systemic factors that have wrongly trapped most people at a very low income level.

[37] We noted earlier that Chile ranks high on a scale of economic freedom. Chile has also been the fastest growing and most pro-free-market country in Latin America (see 46, 58, 136). Though Chile still retains a high score in overall economic freedom, its present high Gini coefficient indicates that large income differentials between the very rich and the very poor have not yet been overcome.

[38] Baumol et al., *Good Capitalism*, 72–73.

[39] Ibid., 71–79.

economy guided by "authoritarian" institutions. Acemoglu and Robinson say:

> Current policy recommendations encouraging "authoritarian growth" based on the successful Chinese growth experience of the last several decades . . . are misleading and . . . unlikely to translate into sustained economic development.[40]

> Growth under authoritarian, extractive political institutions in China, though likely to continue for a while yet, will not translate into sustained growth, supported by truly inclusive economic institutions and creative destruction.[41]

> Authoritarian growth is neither desirable nor viable in the long run, and thus should not receive the endorsement of the international community as a template for nations in Latin America, Asia, and sub-Saharan Africa.[42]

In short, they say a country cannot engineer its way out of poverty by means of the government picking winners and losers. These authors argue that the attempts of policy makers and bureaucrats to rectify a country's inefficiencies (bad economic policies, for example) may backfire precisely because those in charge are not grappling with the institutional causes of poverty.[43]

A good example, Acemoglu and Robinson argue, is China's authoritative brand of state capitalism that is crucially dependent on the government's authority to control the media. A Chinese commentator said there are three requirements to make this kind of capitalism work: the party must control the armed forces; the party must control all the political and economic cadres and committees; and the party must control the news.[44]

This distorted model of capitalism might be of great interest to the Communist Party, but it does not appeal to the Internet-savvy youth or to the vast hundreds of millions of poor citizens. The majority of the

---

[40] Daron Acemoglu and James A. Robinson, *Why Nations Fail: The Origins of Power, Prosperity and Poverty* (New York: Crown, 2012), 437.
[41] Ibid., 445.
[42] Ibid., 446.
[43] Ibid., 437–50.
[44] Ibid., 462.

Chinese people have not realized economic growth and are becoming restive, resistant, and revolution-prone.

By contrast, in countries that distribute political power widely, that have the rule of law and limited government, and that engage in an entrepreneurial economy with genuinely free markets where both small and large firms are proactive and innovative, the twenty-first century will be exciting indeed. When economic power is widely diffused and millions of people can play a part in the free marketplace of goods and services, poverty has little chance to survive.

5. Objection: we don't need more "stuff"

Finally, some people might object that all of this emphasis on the *economic* productivity of free markets is in itself morally objectionable. It places too much emphasis on prosperity and wealth. It seems "unspiritual," especially from the standpoint of Christian values and the teachings of Jesus, who said, "Blessed are you who are poor, for yours is the kingdom of God" (Luke 6:20).

We have three things to say by way of response:

First, we must reaffirm here what we stated at the beginning of this book: we do not believe that material wealth should ever become our highest goal, nor does material prosperity ever provide lasting happiness or rewarding fellowship with God. This is taught repeatedly in the Bible:

> He who loves money will not be satisfied with money, nor he who loves wealth with his income; this also is vanity. (Eccl. 5:10)

> For what will it profit a man if he gains the whole world and forfeits his soul? Or what shall a man give in return for his soul? (Matt. 16:26)

> You cannot serve God and money. (Luke 16:13)

Second, this book is about a very specific topic: we are seeking a solution to the economic poverty in many nations. The only way for millions of poor people in these nations to escape from poverty is through the production of more goods and services of value. This means that it is crucial to understand what kind of economic system is most productive. Poverty can be solved only when nations adopt *productive* economic systems. When a society moves from poverty to increased prosperity, it provides immense advantages to the poor, the powerless, and the dispossessed in that society. We dare not abandon that hope out of a fear of increased materialism.

Acemoglu and Robinson remind us of the incredible differences in the lives of people in rich countries and very poor ones:

> In rich countries, individuals are healthier, live longer, and are much better educated. They also have access to a range of amenities and options in life, from vacations to career paths, that people in poor countries can only dream of. People in rich countries also drive on roads without potholes, and enjoy toilets, electricity, and running water in their houses. They also typically have governments that do not arbitrarily arrest or harass them; on the contrary, the governments provide services, including education, health care, roads, and law and order. Notable, too, is the fact that the citizens vote in elections and have some voice in the political direction their countries take. The great differences in world inequality are evident to everyone, even to those in poor countries.[45]

Third, God wants human beings not just to survive on the earth, but to flourish. According to the Bible, everything on earth ultimately belongs to God: "The earth is the LORD's and the fullness thereof, the world and all those who dwell therein" (Ps. 24:1). We own what God has entrusted to us as "stewards" of that which is ultimately his. This means that we are accountable to him for how we use our possessions.

This idea of stewardship is also implied in the Ten Commandments. If *God himself* has commanded, "You shall not steal" (Ex. 20:15), that implies that God is interested in protecting my stewardship of what he has entrusted to me.

As we noted earlier, the fact that God commands others not to steal my land, my ox, my donkey, my car, or my laptop shows that I have an individual responsibility for how those things are used. The God who created the universe has entrusted these things to me, and I must act as a faithful steward to manage them.

---

[45] Ibid., 40–41.

But stewardship implies even more.[46] [If God *entrusts* me with something, then he expects me to do something with it, something worthwhile, something that he finds valuable.] This was evident from the very beginning, when God placed Adam and Eve on the earth. He said:

> "Let us make man in our image, after our likeness. And *let them have dominion* over the fish of the sea and over the birds of the heavens and over the livestock and *over all the earth* and over every creeping thing that creeps on the earth."

> So God created man in his own image,
> in the image of God he created him;
> male and female he created them.

> And God blessed them. And God said to them, "Be fruitful and multiply and fill the earth *and subdue it* and have dominion . . . over every living thing that moves on the earth." (Gen. 1:26–28)

The Hebrew word translated "subdue" (Hebrew *kabash*) means to make the earth useful for human beings' benefit and enjoyment. In this way, God was entrusting Adam and Eve, and by implication the entire human race, with stewardship over the earth. He wanted them to create useful products from the earth, for their benefit and enjoyment. This means that God wanted them to progress far beyond subsistence farming.

The command to subdue and have dominion "over all the earth" implies that God wanted Adam and Eve to discover, create, and invent products from the earth—at first, perhaps, simple structures in which to live and store food, and later, more complex forms of transportation, such as carts and wagons, then eventually modern homes, office buildings, and factories, as well as cars and airplanes—the entire range of useful products that could be made from the earth.

Stewardship implies an expectation of human achievement. When God entrusts us with something, he expects us to *do* something worthwhile with it. (This is clearly taught later by Jesus in the parable of the talents, Matt. 25:14–30.)

---

[46] The rest of this section is taken from "Property Rights Inherent in the Eighth Commandment Are Essential for Human Flourishing," by Barry Asmus and Wayne Grudem, in *Business Ethics Today: Stealing*, ed. Philip J. Clements (Philadelphia: Center for Christian Business Ethics Today, 2011), 119–34.

Therefore, the eighth commandment—"You shall not steal" (Ex. 20:15)—understood in the fullness of its implications, gives both the *opportunity* for human achievement (by entrusting property to us) and the *expectation* of human achievement (by making us accountable stewards).

What do we mean by human achievement? The range of human activity is vast; it includes the physical sciences, technology, industry, commerce, the arts, and all of the social sciences and the relationships that we find in family, community, nation, and church. Human activity also includes bearing and raising children, with all the challenges unique to each child. All of these are areas of human activity in which we have been entrusted with a stewardship.

In addition, the human drive to understand and to create from the world is unlimited. Rabbits and squirrels, birds and deer, are content to live in the same kinds of homes and eat the same kinds of food for thousands of generations. But human beings have an innate desire to explore, to discover, to understand, to invent, to create, to produce— and then to enjoy the products that can be made from the earth. This innate human drive to subdue the earth has never been satisfied throughout the entire history of mankind. This is because God created us not merely to survive on the earth but to flourish.

God has created us with very *limited needs* (food, clothing, shelter) for our physical survival, but he has also created us with *unlimited wants*. We think this is a good thing, part of God's original creation (though it can be distorted by sin—see below).

For many centuries, human beings did not know that they wanted cell phones, because such things did not exist. (In fact, both of the authors of the book lived quite happily without cell phones for more than forty years of our lives). But now we have realized that we want them and we are willing to spend money to buy them. When I (Wayne Grudem) was growing up as a child in Wisconsin, I didn't realize that I wanted Cherry Garcia ice cream or pomegranate raspberry frozen yogurt, because those products did not exist. The only ice cream store in my childhood town sold vanilla, chocolate, and strawberry, and what a treat they were! Now people want dozens of varieties.

The same is true of electric lightbulbs, plastic water bottles, gas furnaces, air conditioners, refrigerators, washing machines and dryers, antibiotics, automobiles, computers, and airplane travel. For thousands of years, human beings did not know they wanted these things, because no one knew they could be made.

But today, in these and countless other areas, human achievement continues to progress, and thereby human beings give more and more evidence of the glory of our creation in the image of God. With such inventions, we demonstrate creativity, wisdom, knowledge, skill in use of resources, care for others who are distant (through the use of telephones or e-mail), and many other Godlike qualities.

We recognize, certainly, that every situation of life carries unique temptations. The abundant productivity of modern wealthy economies provides strong temptations to sins such as greed, materialism, and insensitivity to the needs of others. God warned the people of Israel through Moses that when he blessed them with material prosperity, there would be greater temptations to be proud and to forget about God and his commands (see Deut. 8:11–18, quoted below).

There are also other temptations that come with modern prosperity. The increased labor mobility that comes with prosperity carries with it temptations to neglect or break important ties of family and community interaction, and to live isolated lives in which it is easier to violate long-established moral standards. The lure of ever-higher salaries can lead to a workaholic mentality that distorts every other part of life. The abundance of material things can make people feel self-sufficient, insensitive to their need for God. And the temptations of wealth can turn people's hearts from God. The apostle Paul said, "Those who desire to be rich fall into temptation, into a snare, into many senseless and harmful desires that plunge people into ruin and destruction" (1 Tim. 6:9). Likewise, Jesus said, "You cannot serve God and money" (Luke 16:13). Increasing wealth can easily lead to wasteful, excessive spending on luxuries and gaudy trinkets while neglecting the desperate needs of those in poverty. The apostle James was unsparing in his condemnation of the self-indulgent rich:

> Come now, you rich, weep and howl for the miseries that are coming
> upon you. Your riches have rotted and your garments are moth-eaten.
> Your gold and silver have corroded, and their corrosion will be evi-
> dence against you and will eat your flesh like fire. You have laid up

treasure in the last days. . . . You have lived on the earth in luxury and in self-indulgence. You have fattened your hearts in a day of slaughter. (James 5:1–5)

In addition, when a wealthy society provides freedom of opportunity for people, some people choose to use that freedom badly, in ways that harm others and dishonor God.

However, it is important to remember that these evils are not *caused* by increased prosperity, but are *temptations* that come along with the prosperity, and they need to be guarded against. They are best countered not by returning to poverty (which is not God's intention for human beings), but by strong moral examples and teaching in the culture. This is something that churches are especially well-equipped to do.

Regarding the temptations that come with the blessings of prosperity, God did not tell the people of Israel that they should seek to return to poverty, but warned them to guard their hearts:

✱ Take care lest you forget the LORD your God by not keeping his commandments and his rules and his statutes, which I command you today, lest, when you have eaten and are full and have built good houses and live in them, and when your herds and flocks multiply and your silver and gold is multiplied and all that you have is multiplied, then your heart be lifted up, and you forget the LORD your God, who brought you out of the land of Egypt, out of the house of slavery, who led you through the great and terrifying wilderness, with its fiery serpents and scorpions and thirsty ground where there was no water, who brought you water out of the flinty rock, who fed you in the wilderness with manna that your fathers did not know, that he might humble you and test you, to do you good in the end. Beware lest you say in your heart, "My power and the might of my hand have gotten me this wealth." *You shall remember the LORD your God*, for it is he who gives you power to get wealth. (Deut. 8:11–18)

Then why do we need more "stuff"? Because increased productivity and increased prosperity are not in themselves evil. They are morally good, and they provide another way we can glorify God.

Plants and animals show a measure of God's glory by merely surviving and repeating the same activities for thousands of years, while human beings glorify God by *achieving* much more than mere survival. We glorify him by understanding and ruling over the creation, and then producing more and more wonderful goods from it for our enjoyment, with thanksgiving to God. He is the one who "richly provides us with everything to enjoy" (1 Tim. 6:17). Also, "everything created by God is good, and nothing is to be rejected if it is received with thanksgiving, for it is made holy by the word of God and prayer (1 Tim. 4:4–5). The commandment "You shall not steal," together with the entire Bible's teachings on stewardship, implies that God created us not merely to survive but to achieve much and to flourish on the earth.

God gives us these various stewardship responsibilities so that through them we have unlimited potential for glorifying him through discovery, creation, production, distribution, and use of potentially limitless material and intellectual resources. All these are good things (though they can be distorted and misused by sin), and it is right for us to pursue them, with gratitude to our wise Creator for making such an excellent, resourceful earth and giving us the wisdom to develop its resources and flourish as we live on it.

7

THE GOVERNMENT OF THE SYSTEM

Leaders Who Use Their Power for the Benefit of the People as a Whole

Up to this point, we have argued that a poor country that wants to move from poverty toward greater prosperity must adopt the right goal (produce more goods and services) and the right economic system (a free market). Now we turn to another, equally important topic: it must have the right kind of government.

The main principle that we hope to establish regarding government is this: If a country is going to move from poverty toward ever-greater prosperity, its leaders must use government power for the benefit of the people as a whole rather than for themselves, their families, and their friends.

The apostle Paul makes this point in the New Testament when he explains that the civil authority "is God's servant *for your good*" (Rom. 13:4). God's intention is that government officials work to do "good" to the people under their authority rather than making it their goal to enrich themselves while in office or to use government power simply to increase their own power.

Unfortunately, the idea that rulers can just "take" money from the government's treasury for their own benefit and for the benefit of friends is a cultural value deeply entrenched in some poor societies. What we would call "corruption" is widely accepted as just "the way government works."

Dr. David Maranz, an ethnologist who lived for more than twenty-five years in several sub-Saharan African countries, describes what he observed in many of those nations:

> A major function of government is to provide money and other resources to those members of society who are in power or have a close relationship to those who are in power. This unofficial role of government is widely observed in Africa. Many of the conflicts, the wars, and leaders' clinging to power are a direct result of the practice. . . . The pressure is immense, from above and from below, on individuals in government and business to use their positions for the direct benefit of themselves and family members.[1]

> Leaders in society (religious, political, and business) are expected to be people . . . who distribute resources and in other ways provide for their followers when they have needs.[2]

Economic historian David S. Landes sees that such government corruption is one of the primary causes of poverty in most of sub-Saharan Africa:

> The governments produced by . . . strong-man rule have proved uniformly inept, with a partial exception for pillage. In Africa the richest people are heads of state and their ministers. Bureaucracy has been inflated to provide jobs for henchmen; the economy, squeezed for its surplus. Much (most?) foreign aid ends in numbered accounts abroad.[3]

Such corruption of government officials is not limited to Africa. Landes gives many other examples throughout economic history. For example, for centuries in China, the emperor ruled over all and took what he wanted. When Western Europeans discovered mechanical clocks, they proved to be a great boon for increasing productivity

---

[1] David Maranz, *African Friends and Money Matters* (Dallas: SIL International, 2001), 112–14.
[2] Ibid., 132.
[3] David S. Landes, *The Wealth and Poverty of Nations: Why Some Are So Rich and Some So Poor* (New York: W. W. Norton, 1999), 504.

and helping people make wise use of time. But when Western mechanical clocks were brought to China, they were simply thought of as instruments to entertain the emperor and other favored officials rather than as tools to be used for the benefit of the population generally.[4] We have already mentioned, from history, similar self-serving behavior on the part of Mogul princes in India, Spanish conquerors in Central and South America, and feudal lords in Eastern Europe (see 148). Powerful kings in Britain, France, and the Holy Roman Empire similarly used their power to enrich their families for many generations.

The cultural value that rulers have a right to take people's money (such as tax revenue) and use it for themselves is a violation of the biblical view of property. As we explained in an earlier chapter (see 142–144), the Bible itself regularly assumes and reinforces a system in which property belongs to individual people, not to the rulers, the government, a tribe, or "society" as a whole in some vague sense.

In the rest of this chapter, we describe seventeen specific characteristics of a government that functions for the good of the people rather than the benefit of the rulers. (In the next chapter, we will list another twenty-one freedoms that the government must protect.)

A. Protections against corruption in the government

1. Rule of law: all people are equally accountable to the laws

The most basic safeguard against corruption in government is a system that holds everyone in the nation, including the highest government officials, equally accountable before the law. This is the most basic guarantee that leaders will use their power for the benefit of the people as a whole. Even if the president or the king violates the law, he will be brought to trial and, if he is found guilty, he will be punished. In addition, the rule of law means that poor, powerless individuals will receive just treatment from the law.

The rule of law, ideally, does not merely mean that an arbitrary set of laws is in place. It also includes the idea that the law has moral authority. This is because the laws are derived from higher principles

---

[4] Ibid., 336, 339.

of justice and impartiality, so that all people are treated equally before the law.[5]

As we saw earlier (154–55), the classic example of this in the biblical history of Israel is the story of David and Bathsheba (2 Samuel 11–12). Even David the king was held accountable before the laws of God that he had violated.

This idea of the rule of law was increasingly held in Britain and in Northern Europe more generally during the Industrial Revolution, and the growing respect for this principle was one of the keys to Northern Europe's remarkable economic development. Both British statesmen and clergymen imprinted on British constitutional theory the idea that "the king is under God—and under the law. This was the essence of Christian teaching about the state."[6]

One good recent example of the highest official being made subject to the law happened in Honduras in 2009. President Manuel Zelaya attempted to change the constitution of the nation so that he could stay in office for another term (or more). But the constitution specified that the term limit for the president could not be changed. So the Honduran Supreme Court ordered him removed from office, and the military did so. In a subsequent election, his party was soundly defeated. Even the president was not above the law.[7]

But if government officials are able to violate the law without punishment, then there are no external restraints on their use of their power. In such cases, many officials will become corrupt, using government power not to enforce justice fairly but to gain privileges and riches for themselves, their relatives, and their friends.

There are numerous examples of countries where certain officials have been or are above the law, including the communist nations of the Soviet Union, Cuba, and North Korea; Iraq under the former dictatorship of Saddam Hussein; and several countries in sub-Saharan Africa.

---

[5] We believe that the requirement to treat people justly and impartially is itself anchored in the idea of the equal creation of all people in the image of God. This idea of equality by creation (that is, the idea that all people are equal *because they were created equal* by God) was widely believed in Colonial American society; see Thomas Kidd, *God of Liberty: A Religious History of the American Revolution* (New York: Basic Books, 2010), 131–46. The Founding Fathers of the United States proclaimed it a "self-evident" truth that "all men are created equal" and therefore have been given "by their Creator" certain "inalienable rights," including the rights to "life, liberty, and the pursuit of happiness" (Declaration of Independence, paragraph 2).

[6] M. Stanton Evans, *The Theme Is Freedom: Religion, Politics, and the American Tradition* (Washington: Regnery, 1994), 32.

[7] See details in Wayne Grudem, *Politics—According to the Bible* (Grand Rapids: Zondervan, 2010), 445–48.

2. Fair court system: courts show no favoritism or bias, but enforce justice impartially

The courts are the primary means for guaranteeing that everyone in a nation is subject to the rule of law. But if the judges are corrupt and use their power to favor certain people (such as government officials or wealthy and powerful friends), then business investment is discouraged (because of the risk that the relative of a judge could defraud a business owner without fear of punishment) and the economy is hindered from producing more goods and services. Therefore, a fair court system is important for guaranteeing that leaders will use their power for the benefit of the people as a whole.

The Bible strongly emphasizes that judges must be fair and not pervert justice:

> You shall appoint judges and officers in all your towns that the LORD your God is giving you, according to your tribes, and they shall judge the people with righteous judgment. You shall not pervert justice. *You shall not show partiality, and you shall not accept a bribe*, for a bribe blinds the eyes of the wise and subverts the cause of the righteous. Justice, and only justice, you shall follow, that you may live and inherit the land that the LORD your God is giving you. (Deut. 16:18–20)

Judges were not to show favoritism to the poor: "nor shall you be partial to a poor man in his lawsuit" (Ex. 23:3). However, neither were they to show favoritism to the rich and thus act with bias against the poor: "You shall not pervert the justice due to your poor in his lawsuit" (v. 6).

3. Absence of bribery and corruption in government offices

Again and again in the Bible, officials are warned against taking bribes: "And you shall take no bribe, for a bribe blinds the clear-sighted and subverts the cause of those who are in the right" (Ex. 23:8; see also Pss. 26:10; 82:2; Prov. 15:27; 17:23; 24:23; Isa. 33:15; Ezek. 22:12).

If a nation is going to move from poverty to prosperity, government officials should be reasonably compensated for their service, but laws should prevent them from becoming wealthy through "gifts" or promises received while they are in office. Corruption (especially using government office for private gain) in a country with such laws will be rare and, when it is discovered, it will be publicly exposed and quickly punished. This is another safeguard to insure that leaders will not use power for personal gain but for the benefit of the people as a whole.

On the other hand, when nations are trapped in poverty, it is almost always the case that government officials and their relatives and friends increasingly become wealthy because of the power of their offices. Corruption will be widespread, and when it is discovered, it will be covered up and punished lightly, if at all. In such cases, government officials will show favoritism to some people and show bias against others. Nepotism will be common.

Landes points out how such corruption continually hindered economic development in Eastern Europe (where feudal lords and nobles could take property and violate people's legal rights at will),[8] in pre-British India (where the Mogul princes could take whatever they wanted from the people),[9] and in many African societies (where the strongman or tribal chief could confiscate what he wanted).[10] Similar corruption is common in communist countries generally (the former Soviet Union, North Korea, or Cuba for example) and in many Islamic countries (where wealthy ruling families control the riches from oil and everyone else is subject to their whims). We are not saying that free-market systems are completely free of bribery and corruption, but the societal response to it is substantially different (see below, 358–59).

Such corruption is one of the primary reasons that poor nations remain trapped in poverty today. Economist Paul Collier writes: "Why is bad governance so persistent in some environments? One evident reason is that not everyone loses from it. The leaders of the poorest countries in the world are themselves among the global superrich. They like things the way they are."[11]

The opposite of such corrupt systems is found in nations where government officials are fair and impartial, and do not take bribes. This

---

[8] Landes, *Wealth and Poverty*, 251–53.
[9] Ibid., 156–57.
[10] Ibid., 504–5.
[11] Paul Collier, *The Bottom Billion: Why the Poorest Countries Are Failing and What Can Be Done About It* (Oxford: Oxford University Press, 2007), 66. Collier cites the tragic example of Madagascar, where the president, Adm. Didier Ratsiraka, reacted to an election loss by blockading the port, destroying the economy of the nation (83–84).

encourages anyone who wants to invest money and time in the hope that a farm or factory will grow and prosper. In such a country, contracts are surely enforced, and theft, vandalism, and other wrongdoing are regularly punished. The Old Testament warned against a powerful official such as a king becoming wealthy while in office: "And he shall not . . . *acquire for himself excessive silver and gold*" (Deut. 17:17). Sadly, a tragic violation of this law was seen in the reign of King Solomon. The king accumulated fabulous amounts of gold for himself and built great houses and a spectacular throne (1 Kings 10:14–20).

By contrast, the Old Testament narrative holds up Samuel as an example of a good ruler who did not accept bribes and did not show partiality. At the end of Samuel's reign as judge over Israel, he stood before the people and proclaimed his freedom from corruption:

> "Here I am; testify against me before the LORD and before his anointed. Whose ox have I taken? Or whose donkey have I taken? Or whom have I defrauded? Whom have I oppressed? Or from whose hand have I taken a bribe to blind my eyes with it? Testify against me and I will restore it to you." They said, "You have not defrauded us or oppressed us or taken anything from any man's hand." (1 Sam. 12:3–4)

Samuel is an example of a biblical leader. As noted above (223), the New Testament teaches that a government official is to serve God for the good of the people, not himself: he "is God's servant *for your good*" (Rom. 13:4).

Paul also wrote to Timothy, who had been given authority over the church in Ephesus, "I charge you to keep these rules without prejudging, *doing nothing from partiality*" (1 Tim. 5:21). In the government of the church, leaders are to be fair and impartial, showing no favoritism. Certainly that should be true of government officials as well.

4. Adequate power of government

Poor nations sometimes face the problem of weak, unstable governments. Governments must have enough power to maintain their own stability, and to prevent crime and flouting of their authority, if their nations are to move toward prosperity. This will allow them to effectively use their power for the benefit of the people as a whole.

Italy, Spain, and Portugal in the nineteenth century were "plagued by political instability,"[12] and economic development was stunted as a result. Similarly, Latin America in the nineteenth century experienced all of the problems of unstable and ineffective government, such as repeated "conspiracies, cabals, coups and countercoups—with all that these entailed in insecurity, bad government, corruption and economic retardation."[13]

Daron Acemoglu and James A. Robinson emphasize that a "lack of centralization" in a government, which leaves the government too weak to control the nation, leads to disorder and prolonged poverty. They say, "Inclusive political and economic institutions [which lead to economic growth] necessitate some degree of political centralization so that the state can enforce law and order, uphold property rights, and encourage economic activity when necessary by investing in public services." But they report that several African nations and a few outside Africa have failed to achieve this centralization of effective authority: "Afghanistan, Haiti, Nepal, and Somalia . . . have states that are unable to maintain the most rudimentary order, and economic incentives are all but destroyed."[14]

The Bible recognizes the evil that results when there is no effective government and anarchy prevails. The history of Israel, as recorded in Judges 17–21, shows what happens when there is no effective government at all, for "in those days there was no king in Israel. Everyone did what was right in his own eyes" (Judg. 17:6; cf. 18:1; 19:1; 21:25). This portion of Scripture contains stories about the most horrible kinds of sin and corruption as evil ran rampant.

5. Limited power of government

On the other hand, if a nation wants to move from poverty to prosperity, the power of its government must be *limited* enough so that it does not take too much freedom from the people. This is true for two reasons.

First, there is always a tradeoff between government power and individual freedom. When government power increases, personal free-

---

[12] Landes, *Wealth and Poverty*, 249.
[13] Ibid., 313.
[14] Daron Acemoglu and James A. Robinson, *Why Nations Fail: The Origins of Power, Prosperity and Poverty* (New York: Crown Publishers, 2012), 243–44; see also 115, 253.

dom must decrease. Such powerful governments then make more and more decisions for people. These kinds of governments are oppressive and destroy the incentives for economic growth.

However, when government power is smaller, individual freedom is greater. And when people are free, they are able to try thousands of different ways to increase economic productivity. They might try a new method of farming (hoping they can grow more and better crops). They might invent new products (hoping that they can gain rewards from their inventions). They might build small shops to bake bread or manufacture clothing. They might start carpentry businesses or auto repair shops. Greater freedom in a society encourages more and more of such activity.

Second, greater power tends to have a corrupting influence on government officials because they think they can get away with more and more wrongdoing. Landes refers to governmental corruption as "tyranny" when he says that economically productive societies "secure rights of personal liberty—secure them against both the abuses of *tyranny* and private disorder."[15] He adds that such societies "provide moderate, efficient, *ungreedy government.*"[16] He then cites Adam Smith, writing in 1776 about the misuse of government power: "Great nations are never impoverished by private, though they sometimes are by public, prodigality and misconduct. The whole or almost the whole, public revenue is, in most countries, employed in maintaining unproductive hands."[17]

Landes notes several historical examples of excessive governments preventing economies from growing. These are egregious examples of leaders using their power not to benefit the people as a whole but to benefit themselves and their friends. One example is China, which had many early inventions but remained in abject poverty for many centuries. Part of the explanation is "the absence of a free market and institutionalized property rights. The Chinese state was always interfering with private enterprise—taking over lucrative activities, prohibiting others, manipulating prices, exacting bribes, curtailing private enrichment."[18]

---

[15] Landes, *Wealth and Poverty*, 218.
[16] Ibid., emphasis added.
[17] Ibid., 519–20, citing Adam Smith, *An Inquiry into the Nature and Causes of the Wealth of Nations*, Book II, chap. 3.
[18] Ibid., 56.

The government in China had monopolies on necessary items, such as salt, iron, tea, alcohol, education, and foreign trade. There were regulations regarding the kind and color of clothing that people could wear, the sizes of houses they could build, and the music and festivals in which they could participate. Quiet despondency overcame daily life, such that Landes says: "In short, no one was trying. Why try?"[19]

In Russia, the all-powerful czars controlled all of life and thereby kept the nation in poverty. From the sixteenth to the eighteenth centuries, as Western Europe moved steadily toward greater freedom, Russia reduced its peasants to "near-slave status." The result was that "Russia became in effect a huge prison, and with the exception of some months in 1917, and the few years since 1990, it has remained a prison ever since."[20]

In many African nations, tribal chiefs exercised nearly unlimited rule. In Africa, "the legacy was rule by a strongman, autocratic embodiment of the popular will, hence slayer of democracy."[21] However, there were notable exceptions, such as the participatory, representative tradition of government in Botswana.[22]

How can government power be limited to allow economic growth to occur? Government officials must be effectively accountable to the will of the people.

While many nations today have healthy structures that limit the powers of their governments, the one that we know the best is the United States, so we include a brief discussion of its limitation of powers at this point. Part of the reason the United States has endured as a representative democracy for so long is that there are many provisions in the Constitution designed to limit the power of government and protect the people from the government. Some of these are:

(1) *Freedom of speech, freedom of the press, freedom of religion, and freedom of assembly.* These constitutional provisions guarantee that open political dialogue and criticism of the government are guaranteed rights and are not subject to legal sanctions:

[19] Ibid., 57.
[20] Ibid., 240.
[21] Ibid., 504.
[22] See discussion in Acemoglu and Robinson, *Why Nations Fail*, 404–14.

Congress shall make no law respecting an establishment of religion, or prohibiting the free exercise thereof; or abridging the freedom of speech, or of the press; or the right of the people peaceably to assemble, and to petition the Government for a redress of grievances. (First Amendment)

(2) *The freedom to petition the government for redress of grievances.* This means that no one can be punished for simply asking the government to correct some wrong that has been committed against a citizen (First Amendment).

(3) *The right to bear arms.* This provision means that no tyrant can take over the powers of the central government in Washington, DC, and thereby gain control of all weapons in the nation, for citizens have the right to own weapons, even to defend themselves against a potential tyrannical ruler: "A well regulated Militia, being necessary to the security of a free State, the right of the people to keep and bear Arms, shall not be infringed" (Second Amendment).

(4) *Term limits for the office of president.* This article of the Constitution provides another safeguard against abuse of power by a tyrant. A limit of two four-year terms for presidents was inserted into the Constitution by the Twenty-second Amendment (ratified in 1951).

(5) *Regular election of members of Congress.* Members of the House of Representatives must stand for re-election every two years, thus making them more accountable to the people. In addition, all revenue bills (involving levels of taxation) must originate in the House of Representatives, which is most accountable to the people because of its two-year terms, rather than in the Senate. Senators are also accountable, but less often, for they must stand for re-election every six years. (We will come back to the idea of regular elections in section 7 below, on the accountability of government to the people.)

Another set of protections against excessive government power falls under the category of the separation of powers in government, which we discuss in the next section.

Other nations have similar provisions. Such limitations on government power provide an immense protection against government officials becoming corrupt or the nation being taken over by an oppressive tyrant or powerful national army.

6. Separation of powers in government

One of the most effective means of limiting government power and protecting against corruption is a governmental structure in which power is separated among several branches. According to Stephen Haber, Douglass North, and Barry Weingast of the Hoover Institution at Stanford University:

> No simple recipe for limiting government exists. Yet two principles are clear. First, a country must create mechanisms *and* incentives for different branches and levels of government to impose sanctions on one another if they exceed the authority granted to them by the law. Second, these sanctions cannot be imposed in an arbitrary or ad hoc fashion: The sanction mechanisms themselves must be limited by the law. This is not to say that the sanctions cannot be harsh (indeed, if they are not harsh they are not credible sanctions).
>
> There are essentially two ways to create these sanction mechanisms and incentives. One is a system of checks and balances that limits a strong central government. In a system like this, political competition among actors in different *branches* of government provides incentives for actors to police one another's actions. . . . A second way to limit government is federalism, in which different levels of government limit one another.[23]

They note that the United States represents an unusual combination of both of these methods of limiting the power of government.

The United States Constitution mandates a separation of powers designed to prevent any one branch from becoming too powerful and therefore becoming overly corrupt. The separation of powers established in the Constitution includes the following provisions:

(1) *A three-way separation of powers at the national level.* Power is divided between three branches of government: (a) the legislative branch, which makes laws, (b) the executive branch, which enforces laws, and (c) the judicial branch, which interprets and decides the correct application of laws.

(2) *A separation of powers between the national government and the state governments (originally thirteen, now fifty states).* All powers not expressly

---

[23] Stephen Haber, Douglass C. North, and Barry R. Weingast, "The Poverty Trap," *Hoover Digest*, no. 4 (2002): 77–78.

given to the national government remain with the state governments: "The powers not delegated to the United States by the Constitution, nor prohibited by it to the States, are reserved to the States respectively, or to the people" (Tenth Amendment).

(3) *The prohibition of national military forces from doing any law-enforcement work within the nation*. In addition, police power inside the nation is greatly divided. The FBI functions nationwide, but its jurisdiction is limited to certain kinds of federal crimes, not crimes against state and local laws. Local city police forces are subject only to the city governments that employ them. County sheriffs are responsible only to their individual counties. State police are accountable only to individual states. In this way, no individual can take over the army, as in some countries, and immediately gain control of the whole nation, because the national army has no authority over state and local police, and neither does the national government.

In the Bible, several passages support the ideas of limitation of governmental power and separation of powers in a governing authority.[24] The Old Testament narratives give many examples of kings who had unchecked power and abused it. Saul repeatedly put his own interests ahead of those of the people. David misused his royal authority in his sin with Bathsheba (see 2 Samuel 11). Solomon wrongfully accumulated "700 wives, princesses, and 300 concubines. And his wives turned away his heart" (1 King 11:3–4). In addition, he had excessive silver and gold, even though that was prohibited (1 Kings 10:14–20; Deut. 17:17). During the divided monarchy, most kings abused their power and did evil (see 1–2 Kings; 1–2 Chronicles). Many other examples of unchecked power throughout human history confirm the idea that when power is combined with sin in the human heart, it has a corrupting influence on people and is easily misused.

The Bible also contains a number of positive examples of various kinds of divided power, reflecting the wisdom of God in protecting against the abuse of power by one person. In the Old Testament, the king had *some* checks on his power because of the existence of the offices of prophet and priest, and the heads of tribes, clans, and families (even though the king often disregarded them).

---

[24] This paragraph and the next are taken from Grudem, *Politics*, 102.

In the New Testament, it is noteworthy that Jesus called not *one* apostle with authority over the church but *twelve* apostles (see Matt. 10:1–4; Acts 1:15–26). Although Peter at first served as spokesman for the apostles (see Acts 2:14; 3:12; 15:7), James later seems to have assumed that role (see Acts 15:13; 21:18; Gal. 1:19; 2:9, 12). Moreover, the Jerusalem Council made its decision based not on the authority of the apostles alone, but on a decision that "seemed good to the apostles and the elders, *with the whole church*" (Acts 15:22). Finally, every New Testament indication of the form of government that local churches followed shows that they were not governed by a single *elder* but by pluralities of *elders* (see Titus 1:5; James 5:14; this was an imitation of the plurality of elders in Israel in the Old Testament).

7. Government accountability to the people

A final kind of "separation of powers" was implied in our section on limited powers in government, but it is so important that we list it separately here: the government must be accountable to the will of the people in the nation. Regular, fair elections, free access to information about government actions and spending, and term limits for the most powerful offices all help to insure such accountability. This is the most effective, enduring method for guaranteeing that government officials use their power for the benefit of the people as a whole rather than for the benefit of themselves, their relatives, and their friends.

Acemoglu and Robinson argue that nations succeed economically only when they have "inclusive" political institutions, that is, "institutions that distribute power broadly in society and subject it to constraints."[25] By contrast, they say bluntly that the reason for poverty in poor nations is intentional wrongdoing on the part of the leaders: "Poor countries are poor because those who have power make choices that create poverty. They get it wrong not by mistake or ignorance but on purpose."[26]

A number of examples in Scripture indicate that government seems to work best with the consent of those who are governed. Even

---

[25] Acemoglu and Robinson, *Why Nations Fail*, 80. They also say that, in an inclusive institution, such power has to be sufficiently centralized that leaders can govern effectively.
[26] Ibid., 68.

though Moses had been appointed by God, he sought the assent of the elders and the people of Israel (Ex. 4:29–31), as did Samuel when he stood before all the people in his role as judge (1 Sam. 7:5–6), and Saul after he had been anointed as king (see 1 Sam. 10:24).[27]

When David became king over Judah, he gained the public consent of all the people: "The men of Judah came, and there they anointed David king over the house of Judah" (2 Sam. 2:4). When Zadok the priest anointed Solomon as king, "All the people said, 'Long live King Solomon!'" (1 Kings 1:39; see also 12:1).

In the New Testament, the apostles asked for the consent of the congregation in selecting leaders to oversee the distribution of food to the needy: "Therefore, brothers, *pick out from among you* seven men of good repute, full of the Spirit and of wisdom, whom we will appoint to this duty" (Acts 6:3).

By contrast, there are negative examples in Scripture of tyrants who did not gain the consent of the people but ruled harshly in opposition to the peoples' wishes. "So the king [Rehoboam] did not listen to the people" (1 Kings 12:15), and as a result, the ten northern tribes rebelled against him: "And when all Israel saw that *the king did not listen to them*, the people answered the king, 'What portion do we have in David? . . . To your tents, O Israel!'" (v. 16). Israel was divided into the northern and southern kingdoms from that day onward.

In a similar way, the Old Testament contains several examples of oppressive rulers who subjected the people of Israel to slavery and who certainly did not rule by the consent of those over whom they reigned, including Pharaoh of Egypt (Ex. 3:9–10), the Philistines who ruled harshly over Israel during the time of the judges (Judg. 14:4), and Nebuchadnezzar and the other foreign kings who conquered and eventually carried the people off into exile (2 Kings 25:1–21). These events are all viewed negatively in the biblical narrative.

Therefore, substantial biblical arguments can be given in support of the idea of some form of government chosen by the people themselves (that is, in general terms, a democracy). Such a government seems to be preferable to all other forms of government, such as dictatorship, hereditary monarchy, or government by a hereditary or self-perpetuating

---

[27] This paragraph and the following seven paragraphs have been adapted from Grudem, *Politics*, 107–8.

aristocracy. (Several nations today, such as the United Kingdom and Norway, have retained monarchies that function in a largely ceremonial and symbolic fashion, but they are still democracies because the real governing power rests with the elected representatives of the people.)

In the early history of the American Colonies, the Pilgrims instituted a form of self-government when they established the Mayflower Compact in 1620. They did this with a strong biblical knowledge influenced by many of these passages of Scripture. They also had vivid memories of oppression by the monarchy in England. The Mayflower Compact mandated a government *by the consent of the governed*, and this set a pattern for the subsequent Colonies and for the United States itself in later years. The Pilgrims declared that they were forming a "civil body politik" that would enact "laws" for the general good of the colony, "unto which we promise all due submission and obedience."[28] This was a voluntary submission to a government that they themselves had created. It was not imposed on them from without by a king or some other conquering force. They established a government that would function with the consent of the governed—the core principle of a democracy.

These same principles found fuller expression in the Declaration of Independence of 1776:

> We hold these truths to be self-evident, that all men are created equal, that they are endowed by their Creator with certain unalienable Rights, that among these are Life, Liberty, and the pursuit of Happiness. That to secure these rights, Governments are instituted among Men, *deriving their just powers from the consent of the governed*.[29]

The reasoning was: (1) rights to life, liberty, and the pursuit of happiness are given to people by God (not by governments); (2) governments are established to protect these rights that people already have; and, (3) therefore, a government has no legitimate power on its own authority but only the power that the people agree to give it to protect their rights.

---

[28] Mayflower Compact, see http://mayflowerhistory.com/mayflower-compact.
[29] Declaration of Independence, see http://www.archives.gov/exhibits/charters/declaration_transcript .html, emphasis added.

This principle of the accountability of the government to the people, embedded into the very foundation of the United States on the first day of its existence, explains much of the subsequent prosperity of the United States. On the basis of their extensive research on the economic development of nations, Acemoglu and Robinson say:

> The United States is . . . far richer today than [poor countries] because of the way its institutions, both economic and political, shape the incentives of businesses, individuals, and politicians . . . it is the political institutions of a nation that determine the ability of citizens to control politicians and influence how they behave. This in turn determines whether politicians are agents of the citizens . . . or are able to abuse the power entrusted to them . . . to amass their own fortunes.[30]

When the government officials of a nation are regularly held accountable to the people, they will work most effectively to do good for the nation and to establish policies that will bring the nation from poverty toward greater prosperity. They will be most likely to rule for the good of the people as a whole. Such accountability is implemented through regular, fair, open elections, and also through genuine freedom of the press and freedom of information laws (so that government actions are made known to the general public, with rare exceptions to protect national security).

B. Protections government should provide

A nation that is continually increasing its production of goods and services must recognize that there will always be evil people who will attempt to break the law and take advantage of others. There will also be natural disasters that can cause economic damage. Therefore, a good government must provide protections for its citizens against various kinds of harm in order to foster economic growth.

8. Protection against crime

When there is a notorious high-crime district in any city in the world, very few legitimate businesses locate there, and it is almost impossible

---

[30] Acemoglu and Robinson, *Why Nations Fail*, 42.

to persuade new retail stores or new factories to locate there. It is just too expensive for a business to locate in a high-crime area. Business owners do not want to run the risk of losing their investment because of vandalism, theft, or assaults against their employees.

What is true about cities is also true about nations. When a nation has a high rate of criminal activity, because it is not stopped and punished by the government, no foreign business wants to invest in that country. Neither are the nation's citizens willing to start new factories and open new shops, because they have a legitimate fear that their earnings will simply be lost to criminal activity (or to attempts to protect themselves from it). To take an extreme example today, who would want to invest in any business in Somalia, with its persistent anarchy and the presence of well-armed pirate bands that continually attack ships passing through its coastal waters?

By contrast, one of the factors contributing to the amazing economic growth of the Scandinavian countries throughout the nineteenth century was the atmosphere of "public order" and the perception that the Scandinavian people were among "the most peaceable" in Europe.[31]

Landes says that an ideally productive economy will secure the rights of personal liberty against the abuse of both "tyranny and *private disorder* (crime and corruption)."[32]

The Bible teaches that prevention of crime is a primary responsibility of civil governments. The civil authorities are sent "to *punish those who do evil* and to praise those who do good" (1 Peter 2:14). When a government official punishes crime, he is acting as "God's servant" and as "an avenger who carries out God's wrath on the wrongdoer" (Rom. 13:4).

Therefore, the Old Testament affirms in several places that rulers are to enforce justice against wrongdoers and protect those who are too weak to protect themselves from crime:

> Give justice to the weak and the fatherless;
>   maintain the right of the afflicted and the destitute.
> Rescue the weak and the needy;
>   deliver them from the hand of the wicked. (Ps. 82:3–4)

---

[31] Landes, *Wealth and Poverty*, 248.
[32] Ibid., 218.

But if much of the crime in a nation goes unpunished, evil will simply increase and there will be more and more crime in that nation, creating an environment that is ever more hostile to economic growth:

> Because the sentence against an evil deed is not executed speedily, the heart of the children of man is fully set to do evil. (Eccl. 8:11)

This is why it is important in every nation that the guilty be punished and that the innocent go free. God is watching the affairs of every nation, and his anger is aroused when the innocent are punished or the guilty are released:

> He who justifies the wicked and he who condemns the righteous are both alike an abomination to the Lord. (Prov. 17:15)

In a similar way, Isaiah speaks about evil trends within a nation: "Woe to those . . . who acquit the guilty for a bribe, and deprive the innocent of his right!" (Isa. 5:22–23).

9. Protection against disease

Epidemics of disease are major tragedies in many poor nations. Especially in Africa, HIV/AIDS,[33] cholera,[34] malaria, dengue fever, meningitis, and other diseases cause widespread debilitating illness and even death. These tragedies also have economic implications, for sick and dying people cannot do productive work to help economic growth, but often need time-consuming care.

But such disease epidemics are not the cause of poverty in these nations, but rather the result. Acemoglu and Robinson write:

> Tropical diseases obviously cause much suffering and high rates of infant mortality in Africa, but they are not the reason Africa is poor. Disease is largely a consequence of poverty and of governments being

---

[33] According to a 2010 United Nations report, of the 33.3 million cases of HIV/AIDS globally, sub-Saharan Africa accounted for 22.5 million. AIDS-related deaths in this region resulted in 14.8 million orphans (The United Nations, *UNAIDS Report on the Global AIDS Epidemic 2010*, 180–207, accessed October 16, 2012, http://www.unaids.org/globalreport/Global_report.htm).

[34] Of the thirty-three countries that reported deaths from cholera in 2011, African nations accounted for twenty-two of them and 53 percent of the global deaths. The Dominican Republic and Haiti accounted for 41 percent of deaths globally (World Health Organization, "Weekly Epidemiological Record" (August 2012): 289, accessed October 16, 2012, http://www.who.int/wer/2012/wer8731_32.pdf.

unable or unwilling to undertake the public health measures necessary to eradicate them.[35]

Why do wealthy countries not have epidemics of disease like those in poor countries? It is because these nations have spent enough money to guarantee clean water, sanitary disposal of sewage and waste, healthful regulation of food processing and sales, widespread childhood vaccinations against common diseases, effective air pollution controls, draining of swamps and eradication of disease-carrying mosquitoes,[36] and effective health education of the general population. These nations were able to afford these measures as a consequence of economic growth.

With respect to AIDS in particular, accurate health education within a nation is crucial. It is tragic that absolutely false myths are still believed (such as the hateful lie that having sex with a virgin cures AIDS). The fact that AIDS is spread almost exclusively by sexual intercourse (both heterosexual and homosexual) with an infected person must be more widely reported in poor nations.[37] Both governments and churches should be promoting sexual abstinence outside of marriage, for if sexual intercourse happened only within marriage, the AIDS epidemic would come to an end in a nation.

10. Protection against violations of contracts

Landes says that an economically productive society will seek to "enforce rights of contract, explicit and implicit."[38]

A contract is a legally binding agreement describing an intention to perform some future action, such as pay a fee, deliver some goods or services, or perform a job. For example, I (Wayne Grudem) recently signed a contract to teach for a week at a college in New York City. Fulfillment of the contract was important to both parties. The college counted on

---

[35] Accmoglu and Robinson, *Why Nations Fail*, 51.

[36] Wealthy nations do not distribute mosquito nets. They simply spray mosquito habitats with insecticide and kill the mosquitoes. Then no one gets malaria.

[37] AIDS can also be spread through contaminated blood transfusions or re-use of needles for drugs by different users. AIDS is contracted in these ways in probably less than 5 percent of cases worldwide. Preventative measures should also be taken in these areas, but that should not obscure the fact that if the spread of AIDS through sexual intercourse outside of marriage came to an end, the AIDS epidemic would almost entirely cease.

[38] Landes, *Wealth and Poverty*, 218.

me to arrive on time and deliver the lectures as I had promised to do. The college promised to provide my wife, Margaret, and me with a place to live for the week and to pay me a certain amount. If I had not shown up, the college would have had some very frustrated students and some empty, unused classrooms. But at the end of the week, if the college had not paid me, I would have felt cheated. (They did pay me!)

All businesses rely on the enforcement of contracts in order to survive. An automobile manufacturer signs a contract with a tire company to deliver a certain number of tires by a certain date. If the tires do not arrive on time, the cars cannot be finished and the manufacturer suffers a loss. A builder builds a home just as it was ordered by the customer, and then he depends on the customer to pay the price they agreed to.

Governments must enforce the performance of such contracts, or unscrupulous people will order things and not pay for them, or they will take payment for products and then not deliver them. If people can get away with violating contracts, this creates a very hostile environment for businesses and for business transactions, and this hinders economic growth.

The biblical support for the idea of enforcement of contracts is found in the Ten Commandments, which say, "You shall not steal" and "You shall not bear false witness against your neighbor" (Ex. 20:15–16). These commandments imply an obligation to keep one's word and to keep one's promises.

11. Protection against violations of patents and copyrights

When I (Wayne Grudem) was a young faculty member, it was not easy for my family to live on the income I received. Every summer, I had two choices: I could teach classes during summer school and earn extra cash immediately (summer school teaching was not part of our normal contracts), or I could choose not to teach summer school classes but stay home and try to write books, which I hoped would eventually provide money from royalties once they were in print. For many years, I worked on writing books, and eventually some of those books began to provide significant income, which then freed me to work on even more writing projects.

All of this was possible only because the United States protects patents and copyrights. As an author, each time I wrote a book, I created a new product (for example, my book *Systematic Theology*), and when the United States government allowed me to copyright that book, it allowed me to publicly claim to own the intellectual property that I had created in that book. This process is similar to that by which a farmer grows a truckload of apples and drives them to the market. The apples are his property, and he has a right to sell them and earn an income from them. Although I did not grow apples, I created a book that required several years of my work, and the copyright laws say that I had the right to protect that intellectual property and to sell it to anyone I chose.

The point is this: If my country did not have effective copyright protections, I never would have sat at my desk in the basement of my house, hour after hour, day after day, year after year, working to produce something that anyone could take and use without paying me one cent. I would have just taught summer school year after year and earned immediate cash, because I had a responsibility to work to support my family. If there were no copyright laws and I had just sat in the basement week after week trying to write a free book with no hope of financial reward, my wife would have soon said to me, "Wayne, you need to get a job!"

So it is with artists who paint paintings, composers who write songs, movie directors who produce movies, or inventors who invent devices and then get patents for them. Every year, thousands of people *try* to do these things, and many succeed to some extent, while a few create tremendously successful products that are enjoyed by millions of people. If a nation wants to grow from poverty toward increasing prosperity, it must protect and enforce patents and copyrights so that people will have positive incentives to experiment, create, and invent new products.

But if a nation decides not to protect patents and copyrights (for example, modern-day China), it encourages people to steal. In such countries, copycat companies reproduce inventions cheaply and face no fines or punishments. Works of literature, music, art, and drama are freely copied and distributed by anyone who wishes to do so. Those who make and distribute such copies are not stealing apples from local farmers, but they are stealing intellectual properties that are the product of much more work than loads of apples, and they are not paying the people who created them. The Bible says, "You shall not steal" (Ex. 20:15).

The importance of encouraging innovation and invention in an economy cannot be overestimated, and the need for such invention will never come to an end. "The Industrial Revolution would not have begun in Britain and spread to the rest of the West without the development of a dynamic consumer society characterized by an almost infinitely elastic demand for cheap clothes."[39] But inventions of manufacturing equipment supplied that need; it was "technological innovation that spurred the supply side, and the demand side of the Industrial Revolution was driven by the seemingly insatiable appetite human beings have for clothes."[40]

When a nation does not protect patents and copyrights, most of its truly creative people will eventually move to other countries (if they are able to do so). Those who stay will create very little new artistic, musical, scientific, literary, or other types of intellectual material. Because of their brilliance in one field or another, they sometimes create small bodies of work of middling quality. But without hope of being rewarded for their work in any significant way, few of them will produce material of lasting value, and the nation will be poorer as a result.

A nation can also stifle innovation and invention through price controls that prevent inventors from gaining significant profits from their inventions. This process effectively nullifies the value of the patents.

This kind of price control often occurs in the pharmaceutical industry. After a new medicine has been invented, it might cost a company only 10 cents per pill to produce it in mass quantities. But the company might have spent hundreds of millions of dollars in trying products that did not work, funding expensive research laboratories and trials, and paying the salaries of scientists who worked many years before they invented this medicine:

> Next time you hear about a drug making billions of dollars for its maker, consider this: Currently, bringing one new drug to market takes roughly 14 years, at a cost of about $1.3 billion. For every drug

[39] Niall Ferguson, *Civilization: The West and the Rest* (New York: Penguin, 2011), 198.
[40] Ibid., 201.

that makes it to market, more than 50 other research programs fail. After all that, only two of every 10 newly approved drugs will be profitable. Those profits must fund not only all the research programs that failed, but also all the drugs that are launched but lose money.[41]

If the government of a nation then refuses to allow that product to be sold in the country unless the company agrees to sell it for no more than 11 cents or 12 cents per pill, the company is not able to recover its research-and-development costs or to make a profit on the invention. Thus, over the long term, pharmaceutical research tends to shrivel up and die in that country.

This process has happened so often in most Western countries that now a disproportionate number of new drugs are discovered in only a few countries, including the United States and Switzerland, which have resisted imposing price controls. These countries still allow companies to have some reasonable hope of market-determined gain from their inventions of medicines. Many other governments, even those in wealthy, modernized economies such as France and Canada, have instituted pricing regulations that are so restrictive that they have dried up most pharmaceutical research in their countries.[42] Moreover, government-sponsored research and university research do not seem to provide the answer either, because more than 90 percent of new drugs brought to market have come from private companies.[43]

12. Protection against foreign invasion

One of the most basic responsibilities of a government is to protect the nation's citizens from attack. If any nation is going to move from poverty to prosperity, it must effectively defend its people against foreign invasion and conquest. If a nation is invaded and conquered by a foreign power, its wealth is plundered and its economic growth stymied.

In the Bible, this responsibility is made evident when the apostles declare that government officials are to "punish those who *do evil* and

---

[41]Josh Bloom, "Should Patents on Pharmaceuticals Be Extended to Encourage Innovation? Yes: Innovation Demands It," *Wall Street Journal*, January 23, 2012, accessed October 16, 2012, http://online.wsj.com /article/SB10001424052970204542404577156993191655000.html.
[42]Richard W. Rahn, "Price Controls Can Be Lethal," *Washington Times*, October 28, 2003, accessed January 6, 2013, http://www.washingtontimes.com/news/2003/oct/28/20031028-083515-6228r/?page=all.
[43]Sidney Taurel, "Hands Off My Industry," *Wall Street Journal*, November 3, 2003.

praise those who do good" (1 Peter 2:14), and they are to be a "terror" to bad conduct and to carry out "God's wrath on the *wrongdoer*" (Rom. 13:3–4).

In the Old Testament, when the people of Israel "did what was evil in the sight of the LORD" (Judg. 6:1; see also 2:11–15), he allowed them to be conquered by other nations. For example:

> For whenever the Israelites planted crops, the Midianites and the Amalekites and the people of the East would come up against them. They would encamp against them and devour the produce of the land, as far as Gaza, and leave no sustenance in Israel and no sheep or ox or donkey. For they would come up with their livestock and their tents; they would come like locusts in number—both they and their camels could not be counted—so that they laid waste the land as they came in. And Israel was brought very low because of Midian. And the people of Israel cried out for help to the LORD. (Judg. 6:3–6)

By contrast, when God gave blessing to the people, he delivered them from their oppressors and enabled them to defeat their enemies. This happened, for example, when David defeated Goliath, the giant soldier in the army of the Philistines, who were attacking Israel repeatedly (1 Samuel 17).

The result of the Lord's blessing on the kingships of David and Solomon was that "Judah and Israel lived in safety, from Dan even to Beersheba, every man under his vine and under his fig tree, all the days of Solomon" (1 Kings 4:25). God gave skill and power to the soldiers who defended Israel, so that David could say, "He trains my hands for war, so that my arms can bend a bow of bronze" (Ps. 18:34). In fact, God wants Christians to pray that their government officials will be able to function effectively in office so that Christian citizens (indeed, all citizens) within a nation will be protected and so "may lead a peaceful and quiet life, godly and dignified in every way" (1 Tim. 2:2).

Military conquest and economic destruction came to many of the nations of Europe when they were overrun by Adolf Hitler's armies beginning in 1938. For most Eastern European countries, the oppression continued after they were conquered by Soviet forces, which remained after the war ended in 1945 and kept them in poverty until the breakup of the Soviet Union in 1991. Even today, more than twenty years later, Eastern European countries such as Poland, the Czech Republic, Hungary, Romania, Kosovo, Bulgaria, Macedonia, Serbia, and others are still struggling to overcome the damaging economic effects of these years of foreign domination. Another example is the Ottoman Empire's destruction of much of Armenia in 1915–1916.

In many cases, tragically, smaller nations are simply unable to defend themselves against more powerful aggressors. That was the case when Hitler's armies overran Europe. Centuries earlier, it was true of the conquest of the Aztecs in Mexico by Spanish armies under Cortez in 1519–1521 and of the Incas in Peru by forces under Pizarro in 1532–1533.[44] Acemoglu and Robinson argue that the destructive legacy of such conquests and the extractive institutions they established still remain in Latin America.[45]

13. Avoidance of wars of conquest and civil wars

On the other hand, if a nation is going to move from poverty to prosperity, the government must not launch destructive wars of conquest or revenge against other nations. Landes observes, "War is the most wasteful of uses: it destroys rather than builds; it knows no reason or constraints; and the inevitable unevenness and shortage of resources lead to ruthless irrationality, which simply increases costs."[46] Wars of conquest or revenge often bring destruction not only to the conquered nation but also to the invading nation.

Former Soviet dissident Natan Sharansky reports that a frequent tactic of oppressive dictators is the creation of real or imagined "external enemies" so that the nation remains in a constant state of "emergency," which helps the ruler stay in power. He says, "Nondemocratic rulers find the threat of war a particularly attractive device for justifying the repression that is necessary to control their subjects and remain in power."[47]

He notes that governments in Cuba, North Korea, and Iraq (under Saddam Hussein) "all regard inculcating hatred toward outsiders as

---

[44] The Aztecs and Incas had larger armies, but the Spanish soldiers had guns.
[45] Acemoglu and Robinson, *Why Nations Fail*, 9–19, 114–15, 432–33.
[46] Landes, *Wealth and Poverty*, 171.
[47] Natan Sharansky, *The Case for Democracy* (New York: Public Affairs, 2004), 83.

critical to their rule." In addition, "by waging an ideological war against the West, the Soviet regime was able to find an enemy that would help stabilize its rule for nearly 70 years."[48] Therefore, Sharansky says: *The mechanics of tyranny make nondemocracies inherently belligerent*. Indeed, in order to avoid collapsing from within, fear societies must maintain a perpetual state of conflict."[49] Among other examples, Sharansky mentions North Korea and its continual belligerence toward South Korea. In addition, he believes that the leaders of the hostile Arab nations surrounding Israel find it in their benefit to perpetuate a state of hostility toward the Jewish state as a means of remaining in power.[50]

Other examples of conflicts that have proved detrimental to the aggressor include the horribly destructive war that Sudan is waging against the new nation of South Sudan (including years of conflict that preceded their separation) and the war between Ethiopia and Eritrea (1998–2000) over a still-unresolved border dispute.

Internal civil wars can also destroy nations, as has happened so often in Africa. Acemoglu and Robinson note that in nations with "extractive institutions" (political and economic institutions that are "designed to extract incomes and wealth from one subset of society to benefit a different subset"),[51] there is a huge incentive to wage civil war in order to take over governmental power:

> Because whoever controls the state becomes the beneficiary of this excessive power and the wealth it generates, extractive institutions create incentives for infighting . . . [wars are fought] to capture power and enrich one group at the expense of the rest.
>
> In Angola, Burundi, Chad, Côte d'Ivoire, the Democratic Republic of Congo, Ethiopia, Liberia, Mozambique, Nigeria, Republic of Congo, Brazzaville, Rwanda, Somalia, Sudan . . . Uganda, and . . . Sierra Leone . . . these conflicts would turn into bloody civil wars and would create economic ruin and unparalleled human suffering—as well as cause state failure.[52]

---

[48] Ibid., 84.
[49] Ibid., 88, emphasis in original.
[50] Ibid., 90–95.
[51] Acemoglu and Robinson, *Why Nations Fail*, 76.
[52] Ibid., 344.

Collier also describes conflict for government control as a destructive "conflict trap" that locks many poor nations into poverty.[53]

14. Protection against destruction of the environment

An economically productive nation must protect its natural resources from careless human destruction. One example of such destruction occurred when Lake Erie became so polluted from sewage and industrial waste that in the 1960s and 1970s, whole sections of it were essentially "dead," with no remaining edible fish and occasional fires breaking out in the pollutants on top of the waterways that fed the lake.[54] But in a market economy with governmental accountability to the people, stricter environmental safeguards in place since the early 1970s eventually restored the lake to much of its earlier status as a home for massively abundant marine life.[55]

Regarding the destruction of the environment in socialist economies, P. J. Hill wrote twenty years ago:

> With the collapse of the Soviet Union and the coming of democracy to Eastern Europe, information has flowed much more freely, and the extent of ecological disruption has become more widely known.
>
> Children from the Upper Silesia area of Poland have been found to have five times more lead in their blood than children from Western European cities. Half of the children in that area suffer from pollution related illnesses.
>
> The worst air pollution is in the industrial corridor of the southern part of East Germany, across northern Czechoslovakia, and into southern Poland.
>
> In Leuna, in what was formerly East Germany, at any given time 60 percent of the population suffers from respiratory ailments. Four out of five children in Espenhain develop chronic bronchitis or heart ailments by the age of seven. In Telpice, a town in northwest Czechoslovakia, air pollution keeps children inside for about a third of the winter.
>
> Water pollution has also been a significant problem in numerous Eastern European countries. Drinking water in Hungary is seri-

---

[53] Collier, *The Bottom Billion*, 17–37.

[54] "America's Sewage System and the Price of Optimism," *Time*, August 1, 1969, accessed October 16, 2012, http://www.time.com/time/magazine/article/0,9171,901182,00.html.

[55] Joseph C. Makarewicz and Paul Bertram, "Evidence for the Restoration of the Lake Erie Ecosystem," *BioScience* 41 (January 1991): 216–23, accessed October 16, 2012, http://www.epa.gov/greatlakes/monitoring/publications/articles/restore_lake_erie.pdf.

ously contaminated with arsenic. Sewage treatment is nonexistent or very primitive in many large cities. Bulgarian agriculture suffers from heavy metals pollution through irrigation water of much of its best farming regions.

As deplorable as conditions are in Eastern Europe, the situation in the former Soviet Union is little better. Air and water pollution abound there also.[56]

Although much of that damage has been cleaned up since freedom came to Eastern Europe, the tragic record of the destruction brought by the socialist/communist economy is undeniable.

Two particularly horrible examples of environmental destruction came from the former Soviet Union itself. The Aral Sea in Kazakhstan and Uzbekistan (directly east of the Caspian Sea) was once the fourth-largest body of fresh water on the earth. But the Soviet government diverted the rivers that fed it for use in industrial and agricultural projects, and the Aral Sea began to dry up. Landes writes that it is "today a dying hole—half the original surface, a third of its volume, reeking with chemicals, fish gone, air hot and poisoned. Children in the region die young, one in ten in the first year. Decades of insolent plans, haste and waste, tons of pesticide, herbicide and fertilizer . . . enabled the Soviet Union to grow lots of cotton . . . while reversing gains in life expectancy and leading the way backward."[57]

The second example is the horrible meltdown of the atomic power reactors at Chernobyl (in Ukraine, north of Kiev) in 1986: "The fire burned out of control for five days and spread more than 50 tons of radioactive poison across White Russia (Belarus), the Baltic states, and parts of Scandinavia—far more than the bombs at Hiroshima and Nagasaki combined." Moreover, the cleanup task "was apparently botched: the core was not completely smothered; 'the situation' not stabilized. The area around the plant has become a place of fear."[58] The problem was a flawed design in the plant itself, with inadequate safety protections. But this is not surprising. Landes says, "The socialist command economy was tarred with incompetence, credulity, stupidity and indif-

---

[56] P. J. Hill, "Environmental Problems under Socialism," *Cato Journal* 12, no. 2 (Fall 1992): 321–34.
[57] Landes, *Wealth and Poverty*, 497.
[58] Ibid., 497–98.

ference to the public weal [well-being]." Shockingly, Landes concludes by saying, "A dozen nuclear plants on the Chernobyl model are still in operation."[59]

Other ways of destroying the environment that have been found in many nations include polluting the air, cutting down forests without replanting them, and eroding or depleting the fertile soil.

Economists use the term "tragedy of the commons" to refer to a situation in which many individuals have the right to use a resource that is held in common by all, but no one has the responsibility to care for it. For example, in a small agricultural community, if everyone can allow their cattle to graze on the central plot of grassland, they each have an incentive to put more and more cattle on that plot of land, leading to overgrazing. Then the area soon becomes unsuitable for any cattle to graze. If no one has the responsibility to care for the grassland, this tragedy is likely to occur. This is an argument for other solutions, either more private ownership of grazing land (so that each farmer cares for his own land) or laws that regulate access to some resources (such as river water for irrigation).

The Bible teaches that God has given human beings the responsibility for wise stewardship of the environment. When God created Adam and Eve, he said to them, "Be fruitful and multiply and fill the earth and *subdue it*, and *have dominion* over the fish of the sea and over the birds of the heavens and over every living thing that moves on the earth" (Gen. 1:28). The responsibility to "subdue" the earth and to "have dominion" over it includes an obligation to use the resources of the earth wisely and with adequate care for the needs of future generations as well as our own. This idea is reinforced in Psalm 8, which speaks of God giving man dominion over the earth:

> You have given him dominion over the works of your hands;
>   you have put all things under his feet,
> all sheep and oxen,
>   and also the beasts of the field,
> the birds of the heavens, and the fish of the sea,
>   whatever passes along the paths of the seas. (Ps. 8:6–8)

---

[59] Ibid., 498.

C. Things government should promote

A government not only needs to *protect* its people from certain things, it should also actively *promote* several things. The New Testament indicates that a government official "is God's servant *for your good*" (Rom. 13:4), and the government is supposed to "praise those who *do good*" (1 Peter 2:14), which implies encouraging and promoting things that are good for the society as a whole. In this section, we consider three areas in which government can promote and encourage things that bring great economic benefit: education, marriage and family, and church.

15. Compulsory universal education

Economically productive nations require universal education of all the children in the society. Educated people bring benefits not only to themselves, but also to the society in general, which constitutes a good reason for the government to require some level of educational achievement. Economic progress is closely tied to levels of literacy in an economy and to the attainment of other types of education (such as vocational training) sufficient to enable people to earn a living and contribute positively to society.

By contrast, in nations that remain in poverty, education is often limited to certain favored groups, and it is very difficult for others outside those groups (such as racial, ethnic, or religious minorities; women; and poor people generally) to obtain it. Therefore, poor countries often have widespread illiteracy that is concentrated particularly among women, certain ethnic and religious groups, or certain lower castes.

Regarding the general economic benefits of education, Landes notes that the Scandinavian countries, which were "desperately poor in the eighteenth century," suddenly began to experience spectacular economic growth, more than tripling their per capita incomes from 1830 to 1913. One reason was that "the Scandinavian countries, equal partners in Europe's intellectual and scientific community, enjoyed high levels of literacy and offered a first-class education at higher levels."[60]

This was also true of Protestant Northern Europe in general. Prot-

---

[60] Ibid., 248.

estants placed a "stress on instruction and literacy, for girls as well as boys." A theological belief explains why:

> This is a by-product of Bible reading. Good Protestants were expected to read the holy scriptures for themselves. (By way of contrast, Catholics were catechized but did not have to read, and they were explicitly discouraged from reading the Bible.) The result: greater literacy and a larger pool of candidates for advanced schooling; also greater assurance of continuity of literacy from generation to generation. *Literate mothers matter.*[61]

This Protestant emphasis on education of children is not surprising, because the Bible emphasizes the responsibility of parents to train their children. Immediately after Moses gave the people of Israel the greatest commandment, he encouraged them to educate the next generation:

> You shall love the LORD your God with all your heart and with all your soul and with all your might. And these words that I command you today shall be on your heart. You shall teach them diligently to your children, and shall talk of them when you sit in your house, and when you walk by the way, and when you lie down, and when you rise. (Deut. 6:5–7)

All the people in Israel were expected to imitate the godly man of Psalm 1, who takes "delight . . . in the law of the LORD, and on his law he meditates day and night" (Ps. 1:2).

The Protestant emphasis on education led to rapid economic growth in Protestant Northern Europe, while the Roman Catholic countries of Southern Europe lagged far behind in economic development: "The contrast between Mediterranean and northern Europe is undeniably large. Around 1900, for example, when only 3% of the population of Great Britain was illiterate, the figure for Italy was 48%, for Spain 56%, for Portugal 78%."[62]

Similarly, Russia under the czars failed to develop economically to keep pace with Western Europe, and one reason was "a poorly edu-

---

[61] Ibid., 178, emphasis in original.
[62] Ibid., 250. However, Roman Catholics promote education in many countries today.

cated, largely illiterate population with spots of intellectual and scientific brilliance."[63]

In the Muslim nations of the Middle East, "the rates of illiteracy are scandalously high, and much higher for women than for men."[64] For example, even as late as 1990, 43 percent of the population of Algeria was illiterate, and 55 percent of the women.[65] The only Middle Eastern Muslim nations that are wealthy have much oil and few people (such as Saudi Arabia and Kuwait).[66] This is because the immense wealth generated from oil reserves often remains in the hands of powerful ruling elites, while the majority of the population remains trapped in poverty.

Similarly, there is resistance to universal education in some parts of Hindu culture. Darrow L. Miller and Stan Guthrie note that a development worker who wants to teach poor people in India how to read and write might confront an objection from Hindu culture: "In the Hindu system, encouraging the poor to learn is asking them to sin."[67]

Technological and trade school education is also crucial for a nation's educational progress. Such vocational training must be widely available so that the country has an abundant supply of electricians, plumbers, welders, carpenters, X-ray technicians, lab technicians, secretaries, heavy-equipment operators, and so forth.

Finally, knowledge of a foreign language is important. Because of increasing global opportunities in business, students who cannot speak multiple languages are limited in their economic opportunities. Therefore, it seems that a working knowledge of a worldwide language is increasingly important for children's schooling in every country. In countries where English is not the primary language, prosperous nations today generally require fluency in English for children throughout the nation, because English is now the worldwide language of business and scientific interchange. (English proficiency is now required or strongly encouraged and widely available, for example, in the educational systems in prosperous countries such as Norway, Sweden, Denmark, the Netherlands, and Germany, as well as in the rapidly

---

[63] Ibid., 268.
[64] Ibid., 410–11.
[65] Ibid., 508.
[66] Ibid., 410–11.
[67] Darrow L. Miller and Stan Guthrie, *Discipling Nations: The Power of Truth to Transform Cultures* (Seattle: YWAM, 1998), 68.

growing countries of India and China, and in several of the growing countries in Eastern Europe.)

By contrast, nations that fail to require fluency in English in their educational systems guarantee that each succeeding generation of children grows up to find itself linguistically incapable of participating easily with the commercial, technological, and scientific interactions that occur each day in the most economically advanced countries of the world. The opportunities for these children to escape from poverty themselves, and to help bring their nations out of poverty, are severely restricted. Sadly, many Latin American countries still fail to require their children to have widespread training in English (perhaps because of a nationalistic resistance to becoming "like the United States"). This is also the case with many Muslim countries and with Russia.

16. Laws that give protection and positive economic incentives to stable family structures

The type of family that is most conducive to economic development is one that has both a father and a mother. Studies show that in the United States, where there are (sadly) widespread family breakdown and rampant divorce, children who live with their own two married parents have significantly higher educational achievement and are much more likely to enjoy a better standard of living in their adult lives. In other words, a child growing up in a family with both a father and a mother present is much less likely to end up in poverty.[68]

One of the most important factors for predicting poverty status in the United States is whether a child grows up in a single-parent home:

> Child poverty is an ongoing national concern, but few are aware of its principal cause: the absence of married fathers in the home. According to the U.S. Census, the poverty rate for single parents with children in the United States in 2009 was 37.1 percent. The rate for married couples with children was 6.8 percent. Being raised in a married family reduced a child's probability of living in poverty by about 82 percent.[69]

---

[68] See Grudem, *Politics*, 224.
[69] Robert Rector, "Marriage: America's Greatest Weapon Against Child Poverty," *Heritage Foundation Special Report*, September 5, 2012, paragraph 2, accessed October 16, 2012, http://www.heritage.org/research/reports/2012/09/marriage-americas-greatest-weapon-against-child-poverty#_ftn1.

This is an area in which many poor countries already do much better than many wealthy countries. It is tragic that in many wealthy countries (such as the United States), divorce is more common and children are increasingly born outside of wedlock. Poorer countries that still have stable family structures should count this as a valuable asset and should seek to protect the family against cultural influences that would tear it down.

We also recognize that in many poor countries the reason that children grow up with only one parent or with no parents is not because of divorce but because thousands of parents have died of disease, especially AIDS, and thousands more have been killed in wars. That is another reason why, as we said in previous sections, governments must protect their people against disease, invasions, and unnecessary wars of conquest, if at all possible.

Of course, societies should provide various kinds of assistance to children who grow up with no parents or with single parents. But one of the best safeguards against poverty in the next generation is for children to be raised in two-parent homes.

If a nation wants to move from poverty to greater prosperity, therefore, it should seek to adopt laws that provide positive incentives (such as tax benefits and other legal benefits) to getting married and staying married. Especially in nations where not enough children are being born (such as China), governments should also provide incentives for marrying and raising children, since children are the productive workers of the next generation.

By contrast, we do not think that nations should recognize or promote same-sex relationships as a type of "marriage," because such relationships do not bring the same benefits to society, nor do they adequately bear and nurture the future generation of children.[70] Thus, these same-sex relationships generally contribute to the erosion and shrinkage of the work force in the next generation. We think that encouraging such relationships, in the long run, is economically harmful to a nation. And such relationships are also contrary to the moral standards of the Bible.[71]

---

[70] See Mark Regnerus, "How different are the adult children of parents who have same-sex relationships? Findings from the New Family Structures Study," *Social Science Research* 41 (2012): 752–70, accessed October 2, 2012, http://www.sciencedirect.com/science/article/pii/S0049089X12000610.
[71] For further discussion, see Grudem, *Politics*, 213–38.

17. Laws that protect freedom of religion for all religious groups and give some benefits to religions generally

The United States and many other nations have decided to institute laws that give some protections and benefits to churches and to religious activities in general. This is because these societies have concluded that religions generally teach good moral values to citizens, and this brings good to these societies, including economic benefits. We will discuss this further in chapters 8 and 9, but at this point it is important to note that an economy derives economic benefits from the good moral habits (such as honesty, keeping one's word, not stealing, diligence in work, and thrift) that are taught by churches, temples, and most religious organizations. But denial of freedom of religion (as in the Inquisition in Spain, Portugal, and Italy, or in the bans on Christianity in Japan in 1612 and in Muslim nations today) means that many economically productive people are kept out of a country and so are prohibited from contributing to the economy of that nation.

D. Conclusion

The main point of this chapter is that establishing a free-market economic system is not enough *by itself* to bring a country from poverty to greater prosperity. The government of the nation must also protect against corruption in government; protect its citizens against forces and people who would harm them; and promote universal education, stable family structures, and freedom of religion.

In all of these ways, a country's leaders must use government power for the benefit of the people as a whole rather than for themselves, their families, and their friends. This is what the apostle Paul means when he tells the Christians in Rome that the civil authority "is God's servant *for your good*" (Rom. 13:4).

8

THE FREEDOMS
OF THE SYSTEM

Essential Liberties for Economic Growth

In the previous chapter, we described the kind of government that is most conducive to economic development in a nation that seeks to move from poverty toward increasing prosperity. This is a government in which leaders use power for the benefit of the people as a whole rather than for themselves and their friends. To promote that kind of government, we described safeguards against corruption (rule of law, a fair court system, absence of bribery and corruption, limited power of government, and divided powers of government). We also listed various ways in which governments must protect people from being harmed by others who would take advantage of them (protection against crime, violation of contracts, violation of patents and copyrights, foreign invasion, useless wars of conquest or revenge, and destruction of the environment). Finally, we discussed three beneficial institutions that should be promoted by the government (education, marriage/family, and the church).

There remains one major area of concern that we have not discussed in detail—a *condition* that must be protected by the government. This factor is at least as important as any of those we discussed in the previous chapter, and it influences all of them. It is the general condition of "freedom."

A. The importance of freedom for economic growth

Unless government establishes and guarantees crucial economic and political freedoms, no society can move from poverty to prosperity.[1] The people of a nation must have substantial freedom to try different methods of economic production and business activity so that they can find the most effective methods for themselves and for their nation. But they will not be willing to risk their hard work and resources unless they know that the society will give them the freedom to succeed (or to fail) in their efforts and the freedom to enjoy the fruits of their labor. These freedoms enable the free market to function effectively and to produce continual economic growth.

Adam Smith spoke in 1776 of the absolutely crucial importance of laws that guarantee that each worker can enjoy "the fruits of his own labour." Here is Smith's explanation for the prosperity of Great Britain, which applies to any nation:

> That security, which the laws in Great Britain give to every man that he shall enjoy the fruits of his own labour, is alone sufficient to make any country flourish.[2]

Smith goes on to explain that when people have the freedom to enjoy the fruits of their labor, they naturally work in such a way as to increase the economic well-being of a nation:

> The natural effort of every individual to better his own condition, when suffered to exert itself with freedom and security, is so powerful a principle, that it alone, and without any assistance, not only is capable of carrying on the society to wealth and prosperity but of surmounting a hundred impertinent obstructions with which the folly of human laws too often incumbers its operations; though the effect of these obstructions is always more or less either to encroach upon its freedom or to diminish its security. In Great Britain industry is perfectly secure; and though it is far from being perfectly free, it is as free or freer than in any other part of Europe.[3]

---

[1] This chapter could have been part of chapter 7, since it gives a further description of the kind of government that is needed if a nation is to move from poverty to prosperity. But the list of freedoms the government needs to protect became so long that we thought it useful to devote a separate chapter to these freedoms.

[2] Adam Smith, *An Inquiry into the Nature and Causes of the Wealth of Nations*, ed. Edwin Cannan (1776; repr., New York: Modern Library, 1994), 581.

[3] Ibid.

David S. Landes points to freedom as a crucial aspect of the remarkable growth and prosperity in Great Britain in the seventeenth and eighteenth centuries. He says that Britain "came the closest earliest to this new kind of social order" that would constitute an "ideal growth-and-development society," and then he says that "one key area of change" was "the increasing freedom and security of the people."[4]

Recent studies such as the *Economic Freedom of the World* index and the most recent of the annual volumes of the *Index of Economic Freedom* corroborate these historical observations, because they show a strong correlation between the amount of economic freedom in a nation and the economic prosperity of that country.[5]

Several arguments from the Bible support the idea that governments should protect human liberty.[6] The first consideration is the fact that slavery and oppression are always viewed negatively in Scripture,[7] while freedom is viewed positively.

When God gave the Ten Commandments to the people of Israel, he began by saying, "I am the LORD your God, who brought you out of the land of Egypt, *out of the house of slavery*" (Ex. 20:2). When the people of Israel turned against the Lord, he gave them into the hands of oppressors who enslaved them and took away their freedom (see Deut. 28:28–29, 33; Judg. 2:16–23). Loss of freedom was a judgment, not a blessing. That is why one blessing promised by the messianic prophecy in Isaiah 61 is that a deliverer would free the people from such oppression by their enemies, for he would come "to proclaim *liberty* to the captives" (v. 1).

Individual liberty is also prized in the Bible, for although people would sometimes sell themselves into indentured servitude as a solution to severe poverty, the Jubilee Year, coming once every fifty years, would set free those who had been thus enslaved: "And you shall consecrate the fiftieth year, and *proclaim liberty throughout the land to all its*

---

[4] David S. Landes, *The Wealth and Poverty of Nations: Why Some Are So Rich and Some So Poor* (New York: W. W. Norton, 1999), 219.

[5] Terry Miller, Kim R. Holmes, and Edwin Feulner, eds., *2012 Index of Economic Freedom* (Washington: Heritage Foundation/New York: *The Wall Street Journal*, 2012). The index is also available at www.heritage.org/index/default. For the second volume, see www.freetheworld.com/release.html.

[6] The following twelve paragraphs are taken from Wayne Grudem, *Politics—According to the Bible* (Grand Rapids: Zondervan, 2010), 91–93.

[7] Even when some types of slavery were allowed (as in Leviticus 25:39–46), it was regulated, and slavery was seen as an undesirable situation from which people would ordinarily want to obtain freedom.

inhabitants. It shall be a jubilee for you, when each of you shall return to his property and each of you shall return to his clan" (Lev. 25:10).

Freedom of individual choice is viewed favorably again and again in Scripture. It is a component of full human personhood and is ultimately a reflection of God's own attribute of "will," his ability to approve and bring about various actions as he pleases. Therefore, we have not only God's testing of Adam and Eve in the garden of Eden (they had freedom to choose to obey or not), but also statements such as this:

> I have set before you life and death, blessing and curse. Therefore *choose* life, that you and your offspring may live. (Deut. 30:19)

> *Choose* this day whom you will serve. (Josh. 24:15)

> *Come to me*, all who labor and are heavy laden, and I will give you rest. (Matt. 11:28)

> The Spirit and the Bride say, "*Come*." And let the one who hears say, "Come." And let the one who is thirsty come; let the one who desires take the water of life without price. (Rev. 22:17)

From the beginning of Genesis to the last chapter of Revelation, the Bible honors and protects human freedom and choice. Liberty is an essential component of our humanity. Any government that significantly denies people's liberty exerts a terribly de-humanizing influence on its people.

In founding the United States, the authors of the Declaration of Independence understood the importance of liberty, for they affirmed at the outset not only that "all men are created equal" but also "that they are endowed by their Creator with certain unalienable rights, that among these are Life, *Liberty*, and the pursuit of Happiness" (emphasis added). The unalienable right to "liberty" was listed next to the unalienable right to "life." The next sentence declared that it was the purpose of government to protect rights such as life and liberty: "That *to secure these rights*, Governments are instituted among Men, deriving their just powers from the consent of the governed."[8] The founders

---

[8] Declaration of Independence, see http://www.archives.gov/exhibits/charters/declaration_transcript .html, emphasis added.

regarded protecting human liberty as one of the most important and basic of all the functions of government.

Likewise, the first sentence of the U.S. Constitution declared that one of the most basic purposes of the new government was "to secure the Blessings of *Liberty* to ourselves and our Posterity."[9] The government of the United States was set up to establish and protect human freedom (or liberty), and this protection is one of the most important factors that led to the remarkable economic growth of the nation after its founding.

B. The types of freedom the government should protect

While "freedom" is a broad and somewhat imprecise category, we can list twenty-one specific freedoms (or twenty-one aspects of freedom in general) that should be protected by the government of a nation that desires to move from poverty toward increasing prosperity.

1. Freedom to own property

We discussed this freedom in some detail in chapters 3 and 4 (114–16 and 141–54), but we mention it here again because it is the first and most basic economic freedom that a government must guarantee. The Bible regularly assumes and reinforces a system in which property belongs to individuals, not to the government, to a tribe, or, in some vague sense, to "society" as a whole.   _Israel ??

If a nation wants to grow from poverty toward increasing prosperity, it must establish and protect a system in which people have freedom to buy and own property without excessive hindrances from government. (This also implies the freedom to sell property without excessive interference.)

2. Freedom to buy and sell

Economic growth comes to a nation when individuals are free to buy and sell goods and services in a free market. If government rules say that only certain privileged elites may buy certain goods or if the laws place impossible barriers in the way of those who wish to sell their

---

[9] Constitution of the United States of America, see http://www.archives.gov/exhibits/charters/constitution_transcript.html, emphasis added.

goods, then economic growth is prevented. If there is no market for products, there is no production, and hence no economic growth.

As we mentioned earlier, the system of agricultural marketing boards that was previously in place in a number of African countries prevented everyone except government-licensed agents from buying crops from farmers and selling them to foreign buyers (see discussion in chapter 2, 87–88, 96). The incentive for anyone to try to do better was removed, and economic growth was stifled.

The same thing happens today if only one company, or only one middleman, is given a monopoly for buying products from farmers in a certain area.[10]

3. Freedom to travel and transport goods anywhere within the nation

In order for people and companies to contribute to a growing economy, they need easy access to large markets, which should be at least as large as the entire nation. One of the main reasons Britain prospered so remarkably during the Industrial Revolution was ease of transportation and open access to the entire nation as a large market:

> New turnpike roads and canals, intended primarily to serve industry and mining, opened the way to valuable resources, linked production to markets, facilitated the division of labor. . . . Nowhere else were roads and canals typically the work of private enterprise, hence responsive to need (rather than to prestige and military concerns) and profitable to users.[11]

Merchants could take their wares without hindrance anywhere in Britain, so they had free access to the largest national market in Europe.[12]

By contrast, transportation of goods was difficult and expensive in Germany. While Germany had a large network of rivers that should have provided easy and cheap transportation, merchants encountered frequent river barriers where local tyrants "inspected" goods and ex-

---

[10] However, the ready availability of cell phones and internet access is challenging such monopolies, since growers can now get instant information about world market prices.
[11] Landes, *Wealth and Poverty*, 214–15.
[12] Ibid., 246.

torted tolls while providing no benefits in return. The river tolls were so troublesome and expensive that "haulers were often compelled to use roads, however poor and slow, even for bulk commodities of low value per weight." The entire system "was designed to encourage bribes, including rounds of food and drink for the boys, which did not help the next boat to get through."[13] Of course, tolls soon were collected on the roads as well, slowing industrial growth and bringing benefit only to the local tyrants who collected these tolls, at the expense of both buyers and sellers in the rest of the nation.

Amazingly, Germany did not abolish these tolls effectively until 1834. In France, customs barriers at the entrances of cities did not disappear until the arrival of the automobile in the early twentieth century.[14]

Tragically, such roadblocks and extortion of money persist in a number of African countries today. Robert Guest, the African editor of *The Economist*, got permission to accompany the driver of a large truck that was carrying thirty thousand bottles of beer from the Guinness factory in Douala, the port that is the largest commercial center in Cameroon, to Bertoua, a small town five hundred kilometers (three hundred miles) away. In a country with an open and developed freeway system, such a journey would take five or six hours. In Cameroon, it was supposed to take 18 hours (1½ days), including an overnight rest stop. But Guest explains that the journey took four days, and when the truck arrived, "it was carrying only two-thirds of its original load."

Why did the journey take so long? Guest explains:

> We were stopped at road blocks forty-seven times. These usually consisted of a pile of tyres or a couple of oil drums in the middle of the road, plus a plank with upturned nails sticking out which could be pulled aside when the policemen on duty were satisfied that the truck had broken no laws and should be allowed to pass. . . . At every other road block, they carried out "safety checks." . . . At some road blocks the police went through our papers word by word in the hope of finding an error.

---

[13] Ibid., 245–46.
[14] Ibid., 246–47.

> The pithiest explanation of why Cameroonians have to put up with all of this came from the gendarme at road block number 31 who had invented a new law about carrying passengers in trucks. . . . When it was put to him that the law he was citing did not, in fact, exist, he patted his holster and replied: "Do you have a gun? No. I have a gun, so I know the rules."[15]

In addition, many of the roads were in horrible condition, clogged by wrecks that had not been removed, and at one place a bridge was out, forcing the driver to take an alternative route. At one stop, the truck was detained three and a half hours, and at another one the driver and Guest had to wait twenty-five hours before they were allowed to move again.[16]

As I (Wayne Grudem) read this story, I tried to imagine what would happen in a modern industrialized country if a local police chief decided to set up such a "checkpoint" on a major highway and extort bribes before allowing trucks to continue. Within about ten minutes, he would be arrested by police officers and put in jail.

Any nation that wants to move from poverty to prosperity must understand how much damage these barriers to commercial activity cause to the economy of a nation. Every customer who finally was able to buy one of those bottles of beer in Bertoua, Cameroon, had to pay a much higher-than-necessary price for the beer, because the high transportation costs made the price Guinness had to charge higher.

This is true not only for beer but for every consumer product that has to be brought to that town from anywhere else in the country. The only people who benefit are the local tyrants who collect bribes at the checkpoints. But the tyrants who run the checkpoints also suffer from higher prices because everything they buy has been subject to the same exorbitant transportation costs.

Moreover, these petty tyrants produce no useful economic benefit for Cameroon because they are not employed in productive work of any kind. They could be farming, building houses or roads, or learning some professional skill. Instead, they spend their lives becoming experts in theft. Meanwhile, the driver of the beer truck, who could have

---

[15] Robert Guest, *The Shackled Continent: Africa's Past, Present, and Future* (London: Macmillan, 2004), 172–75.
[16] Ibid., 175–76.

been making other deliveries or working at a second job in his spare time, was forced to do absolutely no work to produce more goods and services for the nation while he was waiting for twenty-five hours at one stop until the man who could give permission for him to go on could be found.

If a country is going to continually produce more goods and services of value and move from poverty toward prosperity, it must guarantee domestic freedom of commerce. The national government must have enough strength and courage to abolish all internal tariffs and extortions. All the people in the nation must have freedom to travel and transport goods anywhere without fees or penalties.

4. Freedom to relocate anywhere within the nation *≠ after college*

If workers are free to move anywhere and take different jobs, they have some ability to bargain for higher pay and thereby improve their status. This was not possible, for example, for most people in Russia from the sixteenth to the eighteenth centuries because the agricultural lords who owned large estates were able to "fix their workers to the soil" through a kind of serfdom that reduced the laborer "to near-slave status," so that "Russia in effect became a huge prison."[17] The government and the aristocracy cooperated in keeping this system in place. But the consequences for Russia's economy were disastrous, and ultimately the system failed because "unfree labor would not work well or honestly."[18]

By contrast, nations that saw rapid economic development, such as Britain, the United States, and the Scandinavian countries, gave people complete freedom to travel and relocate to take different jobs anywhere within those countries.

5. Freedom to trade with other nations

Just as freedom to buy and sell, freedom to travel and transport goods, and freedom to relocate are important within the boundaries of a country, so freedom to trade with people from other countries is vital as a nation seeks to move from poverty to greater prosperity. This is

---

[17] Landes, *Wealth and Poverty*, 240.
[18] Ibid., 241.

because the greater the number of potential trading partners, the more market opportunities there are for gaining better kinds of comparative advantage. Trade is more beneficial with countries that produce far different products than one's own.

One of the main contributors to more than two centuries of poverty in Japan was its self-imposed isolation from foreign trade. In 1616, Japan banned all foreign merchant vessels (except Chinese) from all Japanese ports except two (Nagasaki and Hirado). Beginning in 1633, all Japanese vessels needed official permission to leave the country (this in an island nation). In 1636, all Japanese ships were confined to Japan, and from 1637, "no Japanese was allowed to leave the country by whatever means—no exit. What's more, no return, on penalty of death."[19]

Therefore, while much of the rest of the world was experiencing remarkable economic growth from the seventeenth to the nineteenth centuries, Japan remained isolated. Even though the Japanese people had the benefit of a culture that placed a high value on work and savings, the nation was not open to foreign goods and ideas until a fleet of seventeen British, American, French, and Dutch ships with 305 cannon blasted its way into Shimonoseki harbor in 1864, after which trade with other nations and industrial development based on knowledge of foreign methods began to expand and enrich the nation.[20]

Free trade is as close to a perpetual motion machine as any economic idea of man. Trade produces economic gains; economic gains produce higher incomes; higher incomes allow people to buy more goods and services, which leads to even more efficient production, which leads to ever more trade. The ever-widening circle of wealth causes more division of labor, more specialization, more productivity, and more benefits from mutual exchange and trade. Nations and people get rich when they trade freely.

Quotas and tariffs on trade, however, bring about just the opposite. They always raise the price customers must pay for products. While quotas on products might save a few local jobs, the higher costs to consumers typically far outweigh the amount the winning worker gains.

---

[19] Ibid., 355–56.
[20] Ibid., 373.

Quotas and protective tariffs impose enormous costs on a society, but labor lobbies are too often interested only in how these polices benefit them. The narrow interests of the producer are almost always more powerful than the general interests of the consumer.

Niall Ferguson illustrates this contrast by citing the historical examples of Britain and Japan:

> While the English aggressively turned outwards, laying the foundations of what can justly be called "Anglobalization", the Japanese took the opposite path, with the Tokugawa shogunate's policy of strict seclusion (*sakoku*) after 1640. All forms of contact with the outside world were proscribed. As a result, Japan missed out entirely on the benefits associated with a rapidly rising level of global trade and migration. The results were striking. By the late eighteenth century, more than 25 per cent of the English farm worker's diet consisted of animal products; his Japanese counterpart lived on a monotonous intake, 95 percent cereals, mostly rice. This nutritional divergence explains the marked gap in stature that developed after 1600. The average height of English convicts in the eighteenth century was 5 feet 7 inches. The average height of Japanese soldiers in the same period was just 5 feet 2½ inches.[21]

Economist Paul Collier, from his experience of many years as an economist and director of development research at the World Bank, writes that reform of trade policy is one of the most urgent steps that both wealthy countries and poor countries can take to help the economic development of poor countries. Specifically, he says that poor countries must drop their protectionist tariffs that force their citizens to pay high prices for imported goods simply to protect inefficient homegrown companies (the owners of which are often friends of government officials). In addition, rich countries need to make "unreciprocated reductions" in trade barriers in order to genuinely help very poor countries.[22]

6. Freedom to start businesses

If a nation's goal is to continually create more goods and services, and so move from poverty toward prosperity, it must ask, "Who creates the

---

[21] Niall Ferguson, *Civilization: The West and the Rest* (New York: Penguin, 2011), 45–46.

[22] Paul Collier, *The Bottom Billion: Why the Poorest Countries Are Failing and What Can Be Done About It* (Oxford: Oxford University Press, 2007), 170–72.

most new products of value?" Most such products are not created by government activity, by churches and charitable organizations, or by community garden clubs, bowling leagues, or sports teams. The kind of organization that creates far more products of value than all of these other sources combined is a business.

Businesses produce, distribute, and sell trillions of dollars worth of goods around the world every year. And businesses provide the vast majority of jobs that pay people for their work and thus provide a market in which products can be sold. Therefore, it is crucially important for a society to make it easy for people to start businesses. A new business can try to produce a product that no one has thought of before (such as an electric lightbulb, a telephone, a personal home computer, or a mobile phone). Or a new company can try to produce a better product than what is on the market, or to produce it more cheaply. In these ways, new businesses promote competition, and the company that makes the best product for the least cost will have the most success. Every consumer in the society benefits from this, because we are able to buy higher-quality products at far lower costs than we could without competition in the marketplace.

Therefore, if a country is going to move from poverty toward greater prosperity, it is important that individuals in the society have freedom to start businesses if they want to do so. In a growing economy, the government will make it easy for anyone to start and grow a legally documented business, and few or no monopolies will be allowed.

By contrast, if a government places an unduly high barrier to starting businesses in many industries (perhaps because the businesses that already exist are owned by the wealthy friends of government officials), then competition will be stifled and economic growth will be hindered. Governments can effectively prevent new businesses from starting either by mandating restrictive procedures for getting licenses to operate or by turning a blind eye to theft and violence committed against new businesses by thugs who are secretly funded by established businesses.

Daron Acemoglu and James A. Robinson report how the Mexican government protects the telecommunications monopoly of billionaire Carlos Slim.[23] They write:

---

[23] Daron Acemoglu and James A. Robinson, *Why Nations Fail: The Origins of Power, Prosperity and Poverty* (New York: Crown Publishers, 2012), 39–40.

If you're a Mexican entrepreneur, entry barriers will play a crucial role at every stage of your career. These barriers include expensive licenses you have to obtain, red tape you have to cut through, politicians and incumbents who will stand in your way, and the difficulty of getting funding from a financial sector often in cahoots with the incumbents you're trying to compete against. These barriers can be . . . insurmountable, keeping you out of lucrative areas.[24]

A related and equally important freedom that government must protect is the liberty for people to close down businesses and exit industries if the businesses are not earning money. If government regulations significantly hinder a company from firing employees or going out of business, fewer people will dare to try to start businesses. The possibility of large, long-term indebtedness is too great.

The Peruvian economist Hernando de Soto explains that excessive government restrictions make it almost impossible to start businesses in several poor countries (see example above, 151–52).

7. Freedom from excessive government regulation

If a country wishes to move from poverty toward greater prosperity, the burden of governmental regulations on businesses must be kept relatively small.

Government control of businesses is extremely stifling in planned systems such as communist and socialist economies. Similar problems were evident in the marketing boards that controlled the sale of agricultural goods in a number of African countries (as we explained in chapter 3, 87–88, 96).

Excessive government regulation was seen recently in the United States, where an agency of the state of Louisiana sent a cease-and-desist order to a monastery, St. Joseph Abbey. In order to raise a bit of money to cover their expenses, the monks were making simple wooden caskets and selling them. The state agency notified the monks that the abbey first needed to become a licensed funeral establishment, "which means that St. Joseph's monks would have to hire a funeral director, install embalming equipment, and construct a funeral parlor

---

[24] Ibid., 39.

even though they have no plans to embalm the deceased or perform actual funerals."[25] The monks decided instead to sue the state and won their case on March 20, 2013.

In 2010, a Heritage Foundation report placed the total cost of government regulation on the U.S. economy at an astounding $1.75 trillion per year (in an economy with a GDP of $15 trillion).[26]

8. Freedom from demands for bribes

In many poor countries, government officials are allowed to demand bribes for granting licenses, approving health-and-safety inspections, or giving businesses permission to operate in certain areas. A bribe might be given to a police officer or a judge to persuade him to overlook an offense—or to impose bogus penalties on a competitor! In business transactions, a salesman might offer a bribe to persuade the decision-making officer in another company to buy his company's product rather than the product of some other company. Customs officers might seek bribes before they allow the import or export of a shipment of goods. Or a government inspector might force a factory to stop its production, allegedly because it has violated some obscure health or safety regulation, until he is paid a bribe.

When such practices are allowed in an economy, they form an invisible, all-pervasive net that continually drags down the economy and makes every product more expensive. These practices place unfair disadvantages on honest businesses that do not pay bribes. They also place unproductive costs on businesses that do pay bribes. They encourage routine flouting of health-and-safety regulations because businesses know they can bribe inspectors and pass inspections even if they do not meet the required standards. They discourage product improvement because businesses know that even if they produce low-quality products, they can still sell them by bribing purchasing agents in the government or in other companies. They discourage reductions in the cost of goods because companies' sales are determined not by work-

---

[25] Claire Suddath, "It's Illegal for Monks to Sell Caskets in Louisiana," *Bloomberg Businessweek*, June 1, 2012, accessed October 2, 2012, http://www.businessweek.com/articles/2012-06-01/its-illegal-for-monks-to-sell-caskets-in-louisiana.
[26] James Gattuso, "Red Tape Rises Again: Cost of Regulation Reaches $1.75 trillion," accessed January 3, 2013, http://blog.heritage.org/2010/09/22/red-tape-rises-again-cost-of-regulation-reaches-1-75-trillion/.

ing hard to produce products at better prices but by bribing people to accept higher-priced products of the same quality.

Who benefits when bribes are tolerated? As in the situation of the local thieves who man the "checkpoints" on African roads, the only people who benefit economically under a nationwide system of bribery are the officials who receive the bribe money. They become wealthier, while the cost of doing business for every company in the country is increased, and the prices that everyone pays are higher than they otherwise would be. Therefore, everyone who purchases any product in the country is paying higher prices because at various points the product has been "eased along the way" by bribe money. Once again, it is a situation of the powerful few gaining benefit while the rest of society loses.

But even the people receiving bribes do not profit as much as they might think, because they also have to live in a society where the price of everything is higher and the quality is lower due to the rampant bribery. They, too, pay higher prices for goods of lower quality. Therefore, tolerating bribery is a powerful way for a nation to remain trapped in poverty. It is exactly the opposite of what it should do in order to escape from poverty and move toward greater prosperity.

The Bible very clearly condemns bribery:

And *you shall take no bribe*, for a bribe blinds the clear-sighted and subverts the cause of those who are in the right. (Ex. 23:8)

You shall not pervert justice. You shall not show partiality, and *you shall not accept a bribe*, for a bribe blinds the eyes of the wise and subverts the cause of the righteous. Justice, and only justice, you shall follow, that you may live and inherit the land that the Lord your God is giving you. (Deut. 16:19–20; see also Deut. 10:17; 1 Sam. 12:3; Prov. 17:23; Eccl. 7:7)

What is the solution? Laws against bribery can have some effect, provided they are enforced across the entire nation. But this is an area in which many thousands of individual decisions are made every week nationwide. Each person has to ask himself, "Will I accept this bribe or not?" and, "Will I pay this bribe or not?"

At times in Israel's history, society became very corrupt: "Your princes are rebels and companions of thieves. Everyone loves a bribe and runs after gifts" (Isa. 1:23). Perhaps that is why the Bible at times emphasizes the importance of officials who "hate" bribes:

> Moreover, look for able men from all the people, men who fear God, who are trustworthy and *hate a bribe*, and place such men over the people as chiefs of thousands, of hundreds, of fifties, and of tens. (Ex. 18:21)

> Whoever is greedy for unjust gain troubles his own household, but he who *hates bribes* will live. (Prov. 15:27)

If government officials realize that every bribe that they accept contributes to the economic corruption of the nation, and every instance in which they refuse to demand a bribe contributes to the economic benefit and purification of the nation, bribery is more likely to essentially disappear. People need to understand that accepting bribes is really stealing—it is taking what does not belong to them—and that even if bribes seem to be offered "freely," they are not really gifts, because if bribery were not allowed in the system, no one would be offering bribes.

David R. Henderson explains the general economic concept behind such behavior:

> "Rent seeking" is one of the most important insights in the last fifty years of economics and, unfortunately, one of the most inappropriately labeled. . . . The idea is simple but powerful. People are said to seek rents when they try to obtain benefits for themselves through the political arena. They typically do so by getting a subsidy for a good they produce or for being in a particular class of people, by getting a tariff on a good they produce, or by getting a special regulation that hampers their competitors. They [economists] use the term to describe people's lobbying government to give them special privileges. A much better term is "privilege seeking."[27]

In general, bribery is far more widespread in economically poor countries and far less common in wealthy countries today. For ex-

---

[27] David R. Henderson, "Rent Seeking," in *The Concise Encyclopedia of Economics*, ed. David R. Henderson (Indianapolis: Liberty Fund, 2008) 445.

ample, in Indonesia, the former treasurer of Indonesia's Democratic Party was convicted for bribery in the Southeast Asian Games.[28] Miranda Swaray Goeltom, a former central bank official, was found guilty of bribery in 2012.[29] Although Indonesia has strong scores in several economic freedom areas, according to the 2012 *Index of Economic Freedom*, "corruption continues to be pervasive."[30] Corruption and bribery continue to outscore all other factors in the *Index of Economic Freedom* as worldwide problems that must be overcome (see Figure 2 following page 192).

There are some exceptions. Oil-rich Muslim nations have grown wealthy in spite of the drain that bribery exerts on their economies. And bribery is perceived to be common in China and some other Asian countries that are growing economically due to many other positive factors. But in all of these cases, bribery still exerts a negative influence on economic growth. These countries would have developed even more rapidly if bribery had been largely absent.

This is not to say that there is no bribery at all in the United States, Canada, the United Kingdom, France, Germany, and other prosperous nations. But it is to say that the entire culture in each of these nations agrees that bribery is evil, and if a government official is discovered accepting a bribe, he is immediately removed from office and usually sent to jail. This is far different from the situation in many bribery-drenched nations, where everyone knows that bribery is going on but no one does anything about it and laws against it are not enforced. In every nation, transparency rules for government transactions and "freedom of information" laws that guarantee access to most government records can help alleviate the problem of bribery.

9. Freedom for a person to work in any job

If a society wants to grow from poverty toward greater prosperity, it will give workers freedom to engage in whatever occupation or business they decide to pursue. Prosperous nations have no restrictive

---

[28] BBC News, "Indonesia's Muhammad Nazaruddin Guilty of Corruption," April 20, 2012, accessed January 3, 2013, http://www.bbc.co.uk/news/world-asia-17781379.

[29] iPolitics, "Ex-Indonesia bank official found guilty of bribery," September 27, 2012, accessed January 3, 2013, http://www.ipolitics.ca/2012/09/27/ex-indonesia-bank-official-found-guilty-of-bribery/.

[30] Miller et al., 2012 *Index of Economic Freedom*, 228.

barriers to practicing any craft or occupation except as necessary to protect the quality of the work.

By contrast, if a nation allows the existence of highly-restrictive guilds that limit entrance to certain crafts or occupations, primarily for the purpose of preserving high income for those already in the guild, it is permitting a hindrance to its economic growth.

Douglass North, who shared the 1993 Nobel Prize in economics with Robert Fogel, demonstrated that "England and the Netherlands industrialized more quickly because the guild system, which imposed restrictions on entry and work practices in various occupations, was weaker in those two countries than in other European countries."[31]

Similarly, French economist Anne-Robert-Jacques Turgot (1727– 1781), in his *Reflections on the Production and Distribution of Wealth*, argued against "government intervention in the economic sector." Later, while he was in a high government economic office:

> Turgot abolished the guild system left over from medieval times. The guild system, like occupational licensing today, prevented workers from entering certain occupations without permission. . . . Louis XVI did not welcome Turgot's reforms and dismissed him in 1776. Some historians claim that had Turgot's reforms been kept, the French revolution might not have erupted thirteen years later.[32]

Landes explains that economic development in European countries such as Germany, France, and Italy was hindered by a "medieval legacy" of "the organization of industry into guilds or corporations." These soon became "collective monopolies" that controlled entry into various occupations through required apprenticeships and restrictions on the number of people who were allowed to be considered "masters" in the occupations.[33] The abolition of such guilds finally came as late as 1859 (in Austria) and 1870 (in Germany).

Of course, certain occupations rightly require workers to attain high levels of competence in order to protect the citizens in the society from malpractice. It is appropriate that doctors, dentists, veterinarians,

---

[31] This is explained in the article "Douglass C. North," in *Concise Encyclopedia of Economics*, 575.
[32] Ibid., 599.
[33] Landes, *Wealth and Poverty*, 242–45.

lawyers, and accountants be required to demonstrate extensive knowledge and skill before they are allowed to practice their professions. Many other professions have similar, if less difficult, requirements, and recognized boards that certify them.

But each society must ask, regarding each guild or professional association, whether the current standards are necessary to guarantee the quality of work for the good of the society as a whole or serve merely to preserve high income for those already in the occupation by preventing competition from those who should rightfully be allowed to enter.

10. Freedom for workers to be rewarded for their work

If workers are forced to work as slaves, or in near-slavery conditions, they will not work willingly or well. Also, if workers have no real choice among employers in a region, they will be paid unfairly low salaries because there is no competition for their work, and they will become resentful and discouraged. Creativity and innovative improvements in production will dry up. Economic productivity per worker will be lower than if they were treated fairly.

This was the case, for example, in the feudal plantations in Eastern Europe, where serfs were essentially tied to the soil (see discussion above, 116–18). Another example is Egypt in the early 1800s. Egyptians grew the finest cotton in the world, but the factories depended on forced labor, "scantily fed and housed, much abused by tyrannical superiors." Because of such near-slavery, the Egyptians simply could not compete with British factories, which paid much higher wages. "In spite (or because) of absurdly low wages, Egyptian costs were higher; and for all the fineness of the raw material, the quality of the final product was lower."[34]

Countries today need to protect workers' freedom to be rewarded for their work in a way that motivates them to want to do their best on the job. George Gilder points out: "It is psychological forces that above all shape the performance of the economy with given resources and technology. It is ambition and resolve that foster the impulses of growth, enterprise, and progress."[35]

---

[34] Ibid., 404, 406–7.
[35] George Gilder, *Wealth and Poverty* (New York: Basic Books, 1981), 247.

Incentives matter. Pay and working conditions matter. This is another reason why economic freedom matters.

11. Freedom for employers to hire and fire

Businesses can stay competitive only if they are able to keep their costs down, not wasting money on unnecessary and unproductive expenses. Therefore, they need to have the ability to lay off or fire some employees during slow times. A restaurant that needs four cooks and ten waiters during the busy summer tourist season might need only one cook and three waiters during the winter. If it has to go on paying all four cooks and all ten waiters throughout the year, even when there is no work for them to do, the business will no longer be profitable and will probably fail. So it is with every factory or business, whether it faces seasonal fluctuations in demand or the long-term cycles of expansion and contraction that are always inherent in the business cycle throughout the world.

What is true of a restaurant is true of economies in general. Nations can make laws that force employers to retain unproductive workers (or strong labor unions can force factories to agree to such rules), but the whole process of paying workers who have no productive work to do, and thus paying people for no economic productivity, drains resources from useful economic production and hinders rather than helps nations move from poverty to greater prosperity.

One might think that rules that make it difficult to lay off or fire workers would protect laborers from difficult periods of unemployment. In fact, the opposite is the case. Rules against firing employees generally result in higher rates of structural unemployment in the long term. Landes says that in France, which guarantees workers long paid vacations and early retirement, employers are "slow to hire, because every hire is laden with associated costs and potential liabilities. The effect: a high unemployment rate that hits especially hard at the young."[36] France has a strong economy, but it is not as prosperous as it would be without such hindrances.

When workers are laid off or fired, do they just go without pay and drift into poverty? Ordinarily no—at least not in a free-market

---

[36] Landes, *Wealth and Poverty*, 470.

economy that is functioning effectively and that guarantees the freedoms we describe in this chapter. Some people who are fired find employment in other companies. Others start their own small businesses, perhaps going to work as painters or home repair handymen, or starting day-care centers for children or housecleaning services. Others go to school to obtain training in other growing industries.

To the extent that it is able, a government should provide some unemployment benefits for those who need help for a limited transition time until they can find new jobs. This costs a nation something, but it is far preferable to keeping employees on a business payroll when there is no work for them to do. The important thing is to keep the main goal in mind. In order to move from poverty toward greater prosperity, the nation must continually produce more goods and services of value. No nation will ever become productive by paying people to do nothing.

Once again, the question a nation must face is whether it believes that the free market or extensive government regulation of businesses leads to the most economic growth. If a nation truly wants to grow from poverty toward prosperity by producing more goods and services of value, then it will allow the free market to function. The free market will effectively direct workers to the places where they can be most productive for the economy and, in the long run, where they will be best rewarded for their work.

12. Freedom for employers to hire and promote employees based on merit

A business that has more skillful, reliable, and hard-working employees is more productive than one that has unskilled, untrustworthy, and lazy employees. In order to get better employees, a business must hire and promote based on merit (that is, competence and performance), not on family relationships, friendships, or mere seniority.[37]

Landes says that an ideally productive society would be one that "chose people for jobs by competence and relative merit," and that

---

[37] However, there may be instances when a familial relationship or friendship is the basis for prior knowledge of a person's competence or trustworthiness. But those are factors that may be included in merit.

"promoted and demoted on the basis of performance."[38] By contrast, David Maranz points out that often in Africa:

> Giving preference to the employment of kin over nonkin is a normal expression of family responsibility and solidarity. . . . In many African countries, perhaps in most, nepotism is also officially considered to be an evil and detrimental to the proper functioning of government and commerce, but in practice it has been difficult to eradicate. . . . This is especially true where relatives in high places are expected to provide for their own, and where not doing so is seen as a betrayal of the highly placed person's group. . . . The people involved see nepotism as being more ethical than failing to provide for the family.[39]

Maranz quotes another researcher on economic development as saying:

> Managers whose primary concern is the production of quality work tend to be isolated and unorganized. If they do not accede to the demands of people placed higher or people with higher-level patrons, they bring trouble on themselves in the course of doing what they see as a good job. . . . More often than not, merit is not merely ignored, it is penalized. People who seek the public welfare rather than the welfare of patrons and clients (both kin and friends) create enemies and stay impoverished, even when occupying very high government positions, because they eliminate the possibility of significantly augmenting their low official salary.[40]

The solution for countries that seek to grow economically is to establish policies that allow employers to hire and promote employees based on merit rather than on other factors.

13. Freedom to utilize energy resources

While destruction of the environment can prevent people from making use of natural resources (see previous chapter, 250–52), the same economic harm can come about when a government places excessive restrictions on the use of resources. Since Genesis 1:28 is God's com-

---

[38] Landes, *Wealth and Poverty*, 217.
[39] David Maranz, *African Friends and Money Matters* (Dallas: SIL International, 2001), 114–15.
[40] Ibid., 136, quoting W. Penn Hanwerker, "Fiscal Corruption and the Moral Economy of Resource Acquisition," in Barry L. Isaac, ed., *Research in Economic Anthropology* (Greenwich, CT: JAI Press, 1987), 332.

mand to human beings to "subdue" the earth and "have dominion" over its creatures, we need to be able to access the earth's resources in order to make them useful for mankind.

But recently, in more developed countries such as the United States, national and state governments have placed increasingly harsh restrictions on the use of some resources. For example, vast amounts of oil are available in the United States, but they cannot be tapped because of government laws that bar access to them (these include offshore oil reserves near many states, resources in vast areas of land owned by the government in the American West, and extensive additional resources in Alaska).

Just as environmental policies that are too lax allow for the careless destruction of the environment, so environmental policies that are too strict prohibit wise use of the environment, and these restrictions also hinder economic growth in a nation.

The freedom to utilize the earth's resources is particularly important in the case of energy resources, since energy is an important factor in nearly all production of goods and services. Energy resources enable human beings to do immensely greater amounts of work than they can do if they use only their own power or animal power. A man driving a diesel-powered tractor can plow dozens of acres in the time it would take a man guiding a horse to plow only part of one acre. A man driving a semitrailer or a locomotive can haul many thousands of times the weight of goods that can be hauled by a man with a wheelbarrow, a bicycle, or a horse-drawn wagon, and can travel hundreds of miles more safely and in far less time. Oil-based gasoline or diesel power enables all of these tasks.

Matt Ridley tells how all of this came about historically:

> The story of energy is simple. Once upon a time all work was done by people for themselves using their own muscles. Then there came a time when some people got other people to do the work for them, and the result was pyramids and leisure for a few, drudgery and exhaustion for the many. Then there was a gradual progression from one source of energy to another: human to animal to water to wind to fossil fuel. In each case, the amount of work one man could do for another was amplified by the animal or the machine. . . . The Euro-

pean early Middle Ages were the age of the ox. . . . With the invention of the horse collar, oxen then gave way to horses, which can plough at nearly twice the speed of an ox, thus doubling the productivity of a man and enabling each farmer either to feed more people or to spend more time consuming others' work. . . .

In turn oxen and horses were soon being replaced by inanimate power. . . . By 1300 there were sixty-eight watermills on a single mile of the Seine in Paris, and others floating on barges. . . .

The windmill appeared first in the twelfth century and spread rapidly throughout the Low Countries, where water power was not an option. . . . Gradually, erratically, more and more of the goods people made were made with fossil energy. . . . Fossil fuels cannot explain the start of the industrial revolution. But they do explain why it did not end. Once fossil fuels joined in, economic growth truly took off.[41]

Even on the household level, energy resources save vast amounts of human time and effort. A busy mother can load and start a washing machine, transfer the clothes to the dryer, and take them out in a total of perhaps five minutes of actual work time, whereas washing, scrubbing, rinsing, and hanging those clothes out to dry might take an hour or more by hand. An electric dishwasher saves quite a bit of time and effort each day. A gas furnace enables people to heat their homes without chopping wood or shoveling coal.

All of the time saved by these mechanical devices is then freed up for other uses. Does this extra time contribute to greater economic productivity in a country? Certainly it does, because a good portion of that extra time is used in other economically productive activities that could not be done without the energy-driven machines, or in leisure time, which also has value.

Energy sources such as water power, coal, oil, and natural gas (and wind and solar if they ever become economically competitive without subsidies) all make a nation economically more productive. The more energy that is available for use, the more productive a nation can become. Therefore, if a nation wants to move from poverty toward greater

---

[41] Matt Ridley, *The Rational Optimist: How Prosperity Evolves* (New York: HarperCollins, 2010), 214–16. Economist and neurologist William J. Bernstein devotes an entire chapter of his book *The Birth of Plenty* to the fascinating story of energy power, speed, and light, and their enormous impact on human activity and productivity; see Bernstein, *The Birth of Plenty: How the Prosperity of the Modern World Was Created* (New York: McGraw-Hill, 2004), 161–88.

prosperity by continually producing more goods and services of value, it must seek to maximize the energy resources that are available for people in the nation to use.[42]

By contrast, if the energy resources of a nation are unavailable because they are selfishly locked up in the hands of monopoly owners; if they are located on government-owned land and the government refuses to allow anyone to extract them; or if the government even prohibits people from extracting resources on their own property, then the economic productivity of the nation is hindered to the degree that the resources are hoarded, and the nation is poorer than it would be if people had freedom to purchase and utilize those resources in the free market.

We discussed this in chapter 1 (59–61), but it is worth repeating that God gave human beings stewardship of the earth and expects them to use its resources for their benefit. He told Adam and Eve to "subdue" the earth and to "have dominion" over its creatures (Gen. 1:28). The psalmist says, "You [God] have given him [man] dominion over the works of your hands; you have put all things under his feet" (Ps. 8:6). Therefore, we think it is right to use the energy resources that are found in the earth for our benefit, and to do so with thanksgiving to God. We are convinced that God has given us an immensely abundant earth, filled with rich storehouses of energy supplies of different types, and these energy resources, many of which can substitute for each other, are unlikely ever to be exhausted (see discussion 339–40).

These considerations apply not only to energy resources, of course, but to all the natural resources of the earth, including land, water, forest, mineral, and other resources. Therefore, our concerns in this section have application to more than energy resources. But at the present time, it is energy resources that face the most significant usage restrictions. And energy resources are singularly important for economic development.

Landes says, "All economic [industrial] revolutions have at their core an enhancement of the supply of energy, because this feeds and changes all aspects of human activity."[43]

---

[42] Perhaps the most thorough explanation of the modern economic and geopolitical implications of energy is now Daniel Yergin, *The Quest: Energy, Security and the Remaking of the Modern World* (New York: Penguin, 2011).

[43] Landes, *Wealth and Poverty*, 40.

Speaking specifically of Britain, Landes says that two of the fundamental changes that enabled the Industrial Revolution were (1) "the substitution of machines—rapid, regular, precise, tireless—for human skill and effort," and (2) "the substitution of inanimate for animate sources of power, in particular, the invention of engines for converting heat into work, thereby opening an almost unlimited supply of energy."[44]

If any nation wants to grow from poverty toward greater economic productivity and prosperity, it must allow the people of the nation the freedom to acquire and utilize vast amounts of energy resources.[45]

14. Freedom to change and modernize

If any nation is going to move from poverty toward greater prosperity by continually producing more goods and services of value, then some changes must be made. The nation simply cannot go on doing what it has been doing, or it will get the same results. It will remain trapped in poverty. Therefore, people who have new ideas about how to increase economic productivity must have the freedom to experiment with different methods and products. They must have the liberty to try to change old, poverty-producing ways and adopt new ways of work and production.

Landes says that an ideally productive and growing economy knows how "to create, adapt, and master new techniques on the technological frontier." It values "new as against old" and "change and risk as against safety."[46]

A cultural aversion to change was one of the reasons why China, in spite of its remarkable early history of significant inventions, languished in poverty for centuries. Landes writes, "The foreigner became

---

[44] Ibid., 186.

[45] Unfortunately, some wealthy countries are moving in exactly the opposite direction. When we see Germany deciding to shut down all of its nuclear reactors (a fantastic source of energy) (BBC, "Germany: Nuclear power plants to close by 2022," May 30, 2011, accessed October 16, 2012, http://www.bbc.co.uk/news/world-europe-13592208); when we see the United States refusing to allow its citizens access to vast oil reserves within the nation and offshore; when we see President Obama blocking the building of the Keystone Oil Pipeline; or when we see the U.S. Environmental Protection Agency (EPA) issue absurd restrictions on trace amounts of mercury emissions that will force the closure of a large number of coal-fired electrical plants in the United States (even though the EPA's own documents report that no discernible health benefits will come from the new regulations), then these nations have taken foolish steps that will hinder their future economic development and leave them less prosperous than they otherwise would have been. And they will be less able to contribute beneficially to the world's supply of economic goods and services.

[46] Landes, *Wealth and Poverty*, 217–18.

a focus of fear and hatred, the presumed source of difficulty." Mechanization of factories was equated with "oppression" and was resisted until well into the twentieth century, whereas it had taken hold in many European factories from 1770 onward. While European science and technology were marching ahead decade after decade, the Chinese "aversion to change" was remarked on by successive generations of visitors to China. A British visitor noted, "They think that everything is excellent and that proposals for improvement would be superfluous if not blameworthy."[47]

In many nations dominated by tribal religions today, there is resistance to change due to superstition and long-standing traditions. And in many Muslim nations, a fatalistic attitude causes people to have no hope that change can make anything better.

Regarding the painfully slow economic development of Latin America over the last two hundred years of political independence, Landes says that the "pattern of arrested development" was a reflection of the "tenacious resistance of old ways and vested interests." Progress was often hindered by "powerful, reactionary elites ill-suited and hostile to an industrial world."[48]

He also explains that in India, production methods could not shift from manual human labor to machinery because too many cultural traditions would have had to change. It "would have entailed a shift from hand skills nurtured from childhood, linked to caste identity and division of labor by sex and age." It seems that even habits of manual labor could not be changed. British engineers who built the railways in India assumed that earth and rock would be moved by manual labor, but they thought that the laborers could at least use wheelbarrows. "Not at all: the Indians were used to moving heavy burdens in a basket on their head and refused to change."[49]

15. Freedom to access useful knowledge (freedom of information)

If any nation is going to move out of poverty and grow toward greater prosperity, it must allow new knowledge to spread freely through-

[47] Ibid., 342, 345.
[48] Ibid., 492–93.
[49] Ibid., 229.

out the society. Imagine what would happen to any modern country today if its citizens did not have access to computers or did not have the skills to use them. Imagine if a country did not have cell phones or did not allow its population to use them. Without these tools, it would be impossible to continually produce more goods and services of value on a modern scale, and so it would be impossible to move toward greater prosperity.

Sadly, throughout history, many nations have not allowed such freedom of information. They failed to give their people access to useful knowledge of new inventions and technological developments, so they sometimes lagged behind developing nations for centuries.

Johannes Gutenberg invented movable-type printing in Germany in 1439 and published his famous Bible in 1452–1455. Suddenly, books no longer had to be copied slowly by hand, but could be quickly produced by the thousands, and knowledge of scientific and technological discoveries could explode throughout the world. In religion, this development laid the foundation for the rapid spread of the Protestant Reformation, beginning with Martin Luther's posting of his Ninety-five Theses in 1517. In science and technology, it meant that reports of discoveries could be printed and transmitted to anyone in the world who was able to read.

Unfortunately, some societies and cultures opposed the printing press and would not allow it in their countries. "Islam's greatest mistake . . . was the refusal of the printing press, which was seen as a potential instrument of sacrilege and heresy. Nothing did more to cut Muslims off from the mainstream of knowledge." This opposition to freedom of information hastened the steady decline of the Ottoman Empire.[50]

The same was true in India. Remarkably, the first printing press was not installed in India until early in the nineteenth century.[51]

While the Chinese had invented printing in the ninth century, they used mostly block printing rather than moveable type. In China, "much publication depended on government initiative, and the Confucian mandarinate discouraged dissent and new ideas."[52]

The same was true of knowledge of time, increasingly made pos-

---

[50] Ibid., 401–2; 52.
[51] Gucharan Das, *India Unbound* (New York: Alfred Knopf, 2001), 73.
[52] Landes, *Wealth and Poverty*, 51.

sible for everyone by the development of the mechanical clock. People previously had measured time with sundials, which were useless at night or on cloudy days. But sometime around 1275, mechanical clocks began to appear in both England and Italy (developed by unknown inventors). When they improved in reliability and accuracy, every city and town wanted a clock in their town squares. Suddenly, meetings could be planned, shops could open and close at predictable hours, and workers could start and end their shifts at agreed times. Productivity could be measured accurately, and people could seek new methods to increase the amounts of products that were made per unit of time.

But the Chinese did not see knowledge of time as something to be disseminated among the ordinary people. Neither did they see improvements in clocks as a priority. "By the time the Jesuit missionary Matteo Ricci brought European clocks to China in the late sixteenth century, they were so much superior to their Oriental counterparts that they were greeted with dismay."[53] Similarly, Muslims "were much taken with Western clocks and watches," but they did not use them to create "a public sense of time," because they did not want to establish public clocks and thereby diminish the authority of their public calls to prayer.[54]

The years following the invention of the printing press in 1439 were bad years to be cut off from the spread of knowledge in the rest of the world. Columbus discovered the New World in 1492, and many other voyages and discoveries followed. Vasco da Gama first sailed from Portugal to India and back in 1497–1499. Ferdinand Magellan led the first expedition to sail entirely around the world in 1519–1522 (though he died in the Philippines before his ships could return to Portugal).

The Englishman William Harvey published his evidence that blood circulates in the body (rather than remaining stationary and simply being cooled by the actions of the heart and lungs) in Frankfurt, Germany, in 1628. Sir Isaac Newton published his *Principia Mathematica*, with his universal laws of gravitation and three laws of motion, in England in 1687. During Newton's lifetime, he also published his groundbreaking discoveries of the nature of light and color, and of the use of

---

[53] Ferguson, *Civilization*, 41.
[54] Landes, *Wealth and Poverty*, 51.

calculus (also discovered by Gottfried Leibniz). One discovery led to another as knowledge spread like wildfire. It was not a good time to resist new technologies for the spread of information.

The Roman Catholic countries of Southern Europe sadly made costly mistakes in excluding many sources of knowledge during the Inquisition. Actually, the systematic exclusion of other religions was in place before the Reformation began in 1517, because from 1492 to 1506, both Spain and Portugal expelled all Jews, including those who had brought astronomical and mathematical knowledge that had enabled Portugal to become master of the seas. Then the Portuguese Inquisition began in the 1540s, and it soon drove both Jews and Protestants, and all their knowledge, out of the country. Landes describes the result: "[Those who left] took with them money, commercial know-how, connections, knowledge, and—even more serious—those immeasurable qualities of curiosity and dissent that are the leaven of thought. . . . By 1513, Portugal wanted for astronomers; by the 1520s, scientific leadership had gone." Portugal excluded the ideas of Harvey (on blood circulation), Copernicus and Galileo (on astronomy), and Newton—all of their "dangerous" ideas were "banned by the Jesuits as late as 1746."[55] Portuguese students were not allowed to study abroad, and there were strict controls on the import of books. As a result, "by 1600, even more by 1700, Portugal had become a backward, weak country."[56]

In Spain, the death penalty was established in 1558 for the crime of importing foreign books without permission. No students were allowed to study abroad, except in three "safe" Catholic cities in Italy. Landes concludes, "So Iberia and indeed Mediterranean Europe as a whole missed the train of the so-called scientific revolution." He notes that British historian Hugh Trevor-Roper has argued that "this reactionary, anti-Protestant backlash, more than Protestantism itself, sealed the fate of southern Europe for the next 300 years."[57]

Latin America suffered from the same mistakes. Spain exported its exclusion of knowledge to the New World, so that Protestants and Jews were systematically excluded. "Everywhere in the Spanish colonies . . .

---

[55] Ibid., 133–134.
[56] Ibid., 134–136.
[57] Ibid., 181, citing a 1961 paper given at an academic conference of historians.

the Inquisition pursued heresy. . . . All of this proved great for purity but bad for business, knowledge, and know-how."[58]

The remarkable economic growth of Europe during and after the Industrial Revolution was in large measure the result of "the growing *autonomy* of intellectual inquiry" and "the development of unity in disunity in the form of a common, implicitly adversarial method" for proving scientific conclusions.[59] That is, inventors and scientists argued in person and through scientific papers until they eventually reached a correct result. Landes cites a seventeenth-century writer, who observed, "One knows that magic and divining are not science because their practitioners do not argue with one another."[60]

When James Watt finally discovered how to make a reliable, economically efficient steam engine between 1763 and 1775, he made use of the knowledge of scientists and inventors who had worked to solve this problem during the previous 150 years. His steam engine became the workhorse that provided the power essential for the Industrial Revolution, but he built on "accumulated knowledge and ideas" that were available because of the free access to knowledge in British society.[61]

It was tragic for Japan, by contrast, that it banned all Christians from the nation in 1612, banned all foreign merchant vessels from all but two ports in 1616, and prohibited everyone from leaving the country at all in 1637.

In China, because the emperor had totalitarian control over all areas of life, the nation had no institutions for developing knowledge through use of facts, reasons, and arguments. "China lacked institutions for finding and learning—schools, academies, learned societies, challenges and competitions."[62] Confucianism carried an "easy disdain for scientific research," which it thought to be "superficial." So Chinese scientists and intellectuals "had no way of knowing when they were right."[63] A missionary who traveled in China from 1839 to 1851 wrote: "Unquestionably there can be found in no other country such a depth of disastrous poverty as in the Celestial Empire. Not a year passes in

---

[58] Ibid., 311. Roman Catholic leaders today generally agree that the Inquisition was a mistake.
[59] Ibid., 201.
[60] Ibid., 203.
[61] Ibid., 206.
[62] Ibid., 343.
[63] Ibid., 343–44.

which a terrific number of persons do not perish of famine in some part or other of China."[64]

It is not surprising that the freedom to disseminate and access new knowledge took hold most firmly in the Protestant countries of Northern Europe and North America. Following Luther, Protestantism emphasized "the priesthood of the believer," so that individual Christians were encouraged to read the Bible and think about and interpret it for themselves. No longer were people to be taught only by the priests and no longer was the Bible to be confined to the academic language of Latin.

This emphasis is consistent with the pattern of evangelism that was modeled by Jesus, who proclaimed his teaching openly in public places throughout his ministry and did not confine his discussions only to the highly-educated circles of the rabbis in Jerusalem. Similarly, after Jesus returned to heaven, his apostles proclaimed the gospel openly and engaged in public discussions and arguments day after day as they went from city to city throughout the Roman Empire (see Acts 2:14; 3:12; 5:21, 25, 42; 8:5–6; 9:28–29; 13:5, 14–16, 44; 14:1–3, 14; 17:2–3, 10–11, 22; 18:4–5, 19; 19:8–10; 21:40; 24:10, 25; 26:1; 28:23, 30–31).

The early church came to a crucial decision regarding Jewish ceremonial laws "after there had been *much debate*" (Acts 15:7). Paul wrote, "By *the open statement of the truth* we would commend ourselves to everyone's consciousness in the sight of God" (2 Cor. 4:2). And James wrote that "the wisdom from above" is "first pure, then peaceable, gentle, open to reason, full of mercy and good fruits, impartial and sincere" (James 3:17). Freedom of information and full access to new knowledge are characteristic of the Christian gospel, and they were appropriately characteristic of countries affected by the Protestant Reformation in Europe.

Today, if any country is going to grow from poverty toward greater prosperity, it must not make the same mistakes that many countries did previously. It must allow people open and easy access to knowledge, and the ability to innovate and publish new ideas without fear of penalty.

[64] Ibid., 346.

In one sense, developing countries are fortunate in today's world. Economic growth hinges on knowledge, know-how, and technology. Dissemination of that knowledge is a primary issue, and many developing countries are in the process of accomplishing this goal. Meanwhile, the cost of dissemination of knowledge is falling remarkably. Technology and know-how speak through trade, developed country partnerships, and the continued development of the Internet. Each country varies in education, attitudes, and the willingness to import technology and know-how, but because of far easier access to information today, developing countries can leap-frog over processes that once took decades or even centuries to develop, and have such knowledge instantly. Michael Spence explains:

> The high-speed growth in the postwar period in the developing world is enabled by knowledge transfer and the reduction in barriers and impediments to the flow of goods, services, and capital in a global economy. The speed is accounted for by the size of the knowledge differential and the rapid transfer of knowledge across borders.[65]

Access to useful knowledge played a significant role in China's recent economic growth. In the late 1970s, Chinese leader Deng Xiaoping began to forsake some of communism's key principles and allow some private enterprise in the agricultural sector. Incentives to produce improved dramatically, and China was off and running toward three decades of economic growth. But the Chinese had to learn how a market economy worked. Tens of thousands of Chinese each year were trained in foreign schools, mostly in the United States. When these students returned to China, the economy began to benefit. The new knowledge and training, and the gearing up of communications through the Internet, soon turned China into a high-speed learning environment.

16. Freedom for all people to be educated

If a skilled workforce is important for helping a nation become more economically productive, then every person in the nation must have

---

[65] Michael Spence, *The Next Convergence: The Future of Economic Growth in a Multispeed World* (New York: Farrar, Straus, & Giroux, 2011), 62.

access to at least basic educational skills such as reading and mathematics. Only then does every person have the opportunity to make a positive contribution to the economic production of the country.

Since it is impossible to predict where children with great intelligence and creativity will arise, such education must be available to boys and girls alike, and to children from all racial and religious backgrounds. If it is not, the important contributions that some child from a minority group could have made are lost from the economy forever, and it cannot move as quickly from poverty toward greater prosperity. (We discussed the need for a nation to require universal education in chapter 7, 253–56.)

17. Freedom for women as well as men

If a nation truly wants to move from poverty toward greater prosperity, it must insure that all of the freedoms we have discussed up to this point in this chapter are available to women as well as to men.

The teachings of the Bible give honor and value to women as well as to men. The very first chapter of the Bible says that "God created man in his own image, *in the image of God* he created him; *male and female* he created them" (Gen. 1:27). Men and women share the most privileged status of all creatures in the universe, that of being made "in the image of God" (that means they are more like God than all other creatures and that they represent God on the earth).

In addition, the portrayal of the "ideal wife" in Proverbs 31 shows that she is someone who engages in various commercial activities in the public marketplace: "She considers a field and buys it; with the fruit of her hands she plants a vineyard. . . . She perceives that her merchandise is profitable . . . she makes linen garments and sells them; she delivers sashes to the merchant" (vv. 16, 18, 24; see also Gal. 3:28). This means that women should have the same opportunities as men to hold jobs, to be educated, to be trained for careers, to inherit, and to own property or businesses.

However, we must emphasize the important role of mothers in raising and nurturing children. We understand this to be a God-given responsibility, one that we hope many women will choose to pursue full time while they have children at home and are able to do so.

But even in earlier centuries and in agricultural societies, women often contributed to the work of the farm in various ways while they raised their children. In fact, women actually taught their children to work as well. Today, modern transportation and technology mean that many mothers have opportunities to work from their homes or to work part-time if they choose to do so.

Interestingly, even though nineteenth-century Japan was a very traditional society, with women having almost entire responsibility for caring for their households and for raising children, women still had an active role in "enforcing frugality, engaging in farming and industry, and building prosperity."[66] Starting in 1870, all girls as well as all boys were required to attend elementary schooling and become literate, and by 1910, 97.4 percent of eligible girls were attending school. Women had the same complete access as men to public places,[67] very unlike traditional Muslim societies.

To recap what we have specified above, economic freedom for women must include the freedom to start and own businesses; to own property; to inherit; to buy and sell, and to negotiate contracts; to travel and relocate anywhere in the country (as long as this is consistent with family responsibilities); to invent and profit from invention; and to have free access to useful knowledge and information.

Landes notes that the Muslim nations of the Middle East continue today to fail to develop economically apart from the influence of oil wealth. One reason is that "rates of illiteracy are scandalously high and much higher for women than for men." Muslim society "accords women an inferior place." He adds:

> The economic implications of gender discrimination are most serious. To deny women is to deprive a country of labor and talent, but—even worse—*to undermine the drive to achievement of boys and men.* . . . In general, the best clue to a nation's growth and development potential is the status and role of women. This is the greatest handicap of Muslim Middle Eastern societies today, the flaw that most drives them from modernity.[68]

---

[66] Landes, *Wealth and Poverty*, 418.
[67] Ibid., 418–19.
[68] Ibid., 410–14, emphasis added.

18. Freedom for people of all races and all national, religious, and ethnic origins

What we said in the previous section about the importance of allowing women to contribute fully and truly to the workforce also applies to people of various racial, national, religious, and ethnic backgrounds. In fact, freedom for women and freedom for people of all kinds of backgrounds are simply two specific aspects of allowing the free market to function properly and to most effectively allocate economic resources to their most productive uses.

The Bible strongly affirms the equality of all people as creatures made in the image of God and the moral wrong of discrimination based on racial, national, or ethnic distinctions. The historical narrative in Genesis starts with the creation of Adam and Eve, the parents of the entire human race. The apostle Paul taught that God "made *from one man* every nation of mankind to live on all the face of the earth" (Acts 17:26). If we all are descended from these two parents, then on what basis can we discriminate against any other human beings?

Paul also wrote that there should be no racial discrimination, because in Christ "there is neither Jew nor Greek, there is neither slave nor free, there is no male and female, for you are all one in Christ Jesus" (Gal. 3:28). The picture of the future revealed in the book of Revelation shows "a great multitude that no one could number, from every nation, from all tribes and peoples and languages, standing before the throne" of God and worshiping (Rev. 7:9).

Linda Gorman points out how a genuinely free market counters discrimination: "Many people believe that only government intervention prevents rampant discrimination in the private sector. Economic theory predicts the opposite: market mechanisms impose inescapable penalties on profits whenever for-profit entrepreneurs discriminate against individuals on any basis other than productivity."[69]

Non-discrimination was another trait by which Britain profited greatly when unwanted people fled from other countries and brought developed economic skills with them. Weavers came with skills from the southern Netherlands, and farmers brought more productive ag-

---

[69] Linda Gorman, "Discrimination," in Henderson, *The Concise Encyclopedia of Economics*, 116.

ricultural methods. Jews from Spain and other areas where they were persecuted came with vast knowledge and experience in financial matters. The Protestant Huguenots came from France, bringing great skills as merchants, craftsmen, traders, and managers of financial matters.[70]

Ferguson tells how Spanish and British colonial settlers in North and South America differed in this respect:

> Our story begins with two ships. On one, landing in northern Ecuador in 1532, were fewer than 200 Spaniards accompanying the man who already claimed the title "Governor of Peru". Their ambition was to conquer the Inca Empire for the King of Spain and to secure a large share of its reputed wealth of precious metal for themselves.
>
> The other ship, the *Carolina*, reached the New World 138 years later, in 1670, at an island off the coast of what today is South Carolina. Among those on board were servants whose modest ambition was to find a better life than the grinding poverty they had left behind in England.
>
> The two ships symbolized this tale of two Americas. On one, conquistadors; on the other indentured servants. One group dreamt of instant plunder—of mountains of Mayan gold, there for the taking. The others knew that they had years of toil ahead of them, but also that they would be rewarded with one of the world's most attractive assets—prime North American land—plus a share in the process of law-making. Real estate plus representation: that was the North American dream.[71]

The United States allowed vast numbers of people to immigrate in the mid- to late 1800s and early 1900s. During some years in this period, more than one million immigrants entered America. When the population of the United States went from 10 million to 94 million people between 1821 and 1914, 32 million of them were immigrants, and many of them in the later years were children, grandchildren, and great-grandchildren of immigrants who had come earlier in that period.[72] Many of the immigrants to the United States were literate, some were highly productive farmers, and many were trained craftsman.

By contrast, the Roman Catholic countries of Latin America excluded Northern Europeans and most North Americans, and thereby

---

[70] Landes, *Wealth and Poverty*, 223.
[71] Ferguson, *Civilization*, 98–99.
[72] Landes, *Wealth and Poverty*, 321.

excluded many of the talented workers they needed for economic development.[73] As recently as 1900, in Italy, Spain, and Portugal, "the religious persecutions of old—the massacres, hunts, expulsions, forced conversions, and self-imposed intellectual closure—proved to be a kind of original sin. Their effects would not wear off until the twentieth century . . . and not always even then."[74]

The Balkan countries of Eastern Europe allowed people from other nations, but, because of a kind of ethnic and national prejudice, there was wide resentment toward the Greeks, Jews, Armenians, and Germans who came to these nations, worked hard, and became wealthy. When the Balkan nations became independent, "the natives did their best to drive out the strangers, that is, to expel the most active elements in the economy. . . . The Balkans remain poor today. In the absence of metics [foreign workers] they war on one another and blame their misery on exploitation by richer economies in Western Europe."[75]

Algeria is another example. When it gained independence from France in 1962, more than a million Europeans were living among more than 10 million native Algerians. After independence, even the Europeans who wanted to stay "were sped on their way by insults, threats, violence, seizures back of properties seized in the first place." But they had formed much of the backbone of the Algerian economy:

> The successful ones owned the best land, grew the wine and wheat that were the great exports, handled the shipping, managed the banks, made the economy go. . . . The loss of these human resources was a crushing blow. Over the years, the Algerian economy slowed, and even oil and gas could not stem the tide.[76]

Landes, writing in 1999, says that "in the last few years, the country has faltered and festered. Almost three quarters of the young men from seventeen to twenty-three years of age are unemployed." The industrial infrastructure has deteriorated, and Algeria "can no longer feed itself. So it imports increasing quantities of foods."[77]

---

[73] Ibid., 317, 324, 329.
[74] Ibid., 250. (But see note 58 above.)
[75] Ibid., 252.
[76] Ibid., 440–41.
[77] Ibid., 507–9.

Freedom for people from all races and from all national, religious, and ethnic origins is crucial for any country's economic development.

19. Freedom to move upward in social and economic status

Multiple opportunities for individual economic success must be available in a society. In an ideally productive society, according to Landes, people "would rise and fall as they made something or nothing of themselves. . . . It would not be a society of equal shares, because talents are not equal; but it would tend to a more even distribution of income than is found with privilege and favor. It would have a relatively large middle class."[78]

During key years in their economic development, Britain had a large and relatively prosperous middle class, and the United States was a society of many small landowners and relatively well-paid workers. The American people's sense of equality "bred self-esteem, ambition, a readiness to enter and compete in the marketplace, a spirit of individualism and contentiousness."[79]

By contrast, there was little social or economic mobility in a number of other nations. The barrier to mobility in German lands was "the division of society into status groups . . . of reserved vocation and privilege . . . lords . . . serfs and tenants . . . soldiers . . . merchants . . . journeymen [for the industrial crafts]." Similar social and economic stratification occurred among groups in India and Japan.[80] Once a person was a part of one group, his social and economic status were determined, and it was difficult if not impossible to break free and move to another group.

Economic growth is stifled by structures and traditions that prevent social and economic mobility. Benjamin Friedman explains:

> Stagnant economies do not breed support for economic mobility or for openness of opportunity. In short, they discriminate. Getting ahead is almost always linked to either getting in politics, with access to the national treasury, or by taking what others have. When growth prospects are absent, anyone with even the slightest evidence of wealth or capital accumulation is viewed suspiciously. Positive mea-

---

[78] Ibid., 218.
[79] Ibid., 221 (on Britain), and 297 (on the United States).
[80] Ibid., 239.

sures to promote economic mobility are absent and discrimination based on birth is the norm. Issues like openness and tolerance are in the first instance a matter of making good the basic principle of equal opportunity, which in turn holds out the prospect of real economic and social mobility.[81]

Countries also can stifle economic growth by allowing wealth to be concentrated in the hands of a few specially privileged and powerful families while the vast majority of people are trapped in poverty. In Russia and in other Slavic countries, "serfdom persisted in its worst form" long after the Industrial Revolution in Northern Europe. "So much wealth" was held "in the hands of a spendthrift nobility," but the poor peasants had so little they could not even provide adequate demand for the purchase of ordinary consumer goods if such goods had been produced.[82] Russia under the czars had "a privileged, self-indulgent aristocracy contemptuously resisting modernization."[83]

Many newly independent countries in Latin America had similar problems, with a very few wealthy people at the top and masses trapped in poverty: "At the top, a small group of rascals, well taught by their earlier colonial masters, looted freely. Below, the masses squatted and scraped."[84] Landes sums up what happens in these situations, to the detriment of both rich and poor:

> Where society is divided between a privileged few landowners and a large mass of poor, dependent, perhaps un-free laborers—in effect, between a school for laziness (or self-indulgence) over against a slough of despond—what the incentive [sic] to change and improve? At the top, a lofty indifference; below, the resignation of despair.[85]

In every case where vast wealth is held in the hands of a privileged few and everyone else is trapped in poverty, the free market is not allowed to operate. Certain wealthy people are above the law. Crimes can be committed and contracts broken without fear of punishment.

---

[81] Benjamin Friedman, *The Moral Consequences of Economic Growth* (New York: First Vintage Books, 2005), 86, 95.
[82] Landes, *Wealth and Poverty*, 251.
[83] Ibid., 268.
[84] Ibid., 313.
[85] Ibid., 296.

Monopolies are tolerated or even enforced by government. Obtaining a license to run a business or obtaining documented ownership of property is so difficult that it is essentially impossible for ordinary people.

These are not the failures of the free market, but the failures of a government to protect the free market and allow everyone to compete fairly in it. Where a government allows the free market to operate, ordinary human ingenuity and ambition provide more and more competition and diversity in the marketplace. More and more people find that they can rapidly advance to higher levels of income and status in society simply by hard work and skill in what they do. The free market, if it is truly allowed to function, provides such social and economic freedom to move upward in generation after generation.

Economic mobility in the United States is still a significant part of its strong economy today: "Eighty percent of America's millionaires are first-generation rich," Thomas Stanley and William Danko reported several years ago.[86] Moreover, most of them did not inherit their wealth, because fewer than 20 percent of millionaires inherited 10 percent or more of their wealth, and fewer than 25 percent of them ever received a gift of $10,000 or more from parents or other relatives.[87]

Many of "the poor" do not, for the most part, remain poor generation after generation, or even year after year, but many advance to higher economic levels. Neither do "the rich" necessarily stay rich year after year and generation after generation.

Many people who are poor one year actually start becoming wealthier in the next year.[88] If we divide the U.S. population into five groups, with 20 percent of the people in each group (five quintiles), and study what happened to each group from 1975 to 1991 (sixteen years), we find that 98 percent of those in the lowest income group moved to a higher group! In the next-lowest income group, 78 percent moved to a higher income group, while 58 percent of those in the third group moved to a higher group. On the other hand, 31 percent of those in the top income group moved to a lower group, as did 24 percent of those in the second-highest group (see Figure 3 following page 192).

Such patterns have also been seen in more recent studies. A study

---

[86] Thomas Stanley and William Danko, *The Millionaire Next Door* (New York: Pocket Books, 1996), 3.
[87] Ibid., 16.
[88] The following four paragraphs are taken from Grudem, *Politics*, 302–304.

on income mobility for 1996–2005 found that for those in the lowest income brackets, median pre-tax income rose 77.2 percent, compared with 67.8 percent for the previous period.[89] Another study by the Department of the Treasury found that roughly half of the taxpayers who began in the bottom quintile in 1996 had moved to a higher tax bracket by 2005. The study also found that among those with the very highest incomes in 1996—the top 1/100 of 1 percent—only 25 percent remained in this group in 2005. In addition, their median real income dropped during this period as well.[90] Income mobility often works both ways: up and down.

One example of such movement would be a poor medical school student who is barely supporting herself, but who then graduates and moves from "low income" status to "moderate/high income" status in one year, and soon after that to "high income" status. A similar thing happens, in general, to poor college students who earn a small amount at part-time jobs in college, but then graduate and begin climbing their career ladders. It also happens to poor immigrant families who initially are learning the language and looking for business opportunities, at which they soon begin to succeed.[91] This shift from "low income" to "high income" also happens to "low income" entrepreneurs who take very low salaries and live primarily off savings for two or three years while starting businesses; they show up as "the poor" in national income distribution charts, but when their businesses do well, they quickly join the ranks of middle- or upper-middle-income earners. So when people talk about "the poor" and "the rich," we must remember that there are different people in the groups over time.

In other words, various measures show that there has been tremendous income mobility over time in the United States (although this has diminished somewhat in recent years with a relatively stagnant economy and persistent high unemployment). This kind of free economic mobility is crucial for nations that want to move from poverty toward greater prosperity.

---

[89] "Income Mobility in the United States: New Evidence from Income Tax Data," *National Tax Journal* 62, no. 2 (June 2009): 315.
[90] "Income Mobility in the United States: 1996–2005," a report of the U.S. Department of the Treasury (Nov. 13, 2007), 2.
[91] For numerous examples, see Stanley and Danko, *The Millionaire Next Door*, especially 16–25.

20. Freedom to become wealthy by legal means

If a country is going to grow from poverty toward increasing prosperity, it must protect the freedom for anyone in the society not only to move to a higher income level, but to accumulate and retain even large amounts of wealth, so long as they do so by legal means and activities. This is the opposite of the situation that we mentioned in the previous section, in which the wealth of a nation is concentrated in the hands of a few privileged families and no one else has the opportunity to become wealthy. Instead, we are speaking of a society that promotes opportunity for anyone who works hard and has skill to increase his economic status as much as he is able.

Once again, government leaders must keep in mind the one thing that will lift their nation from poverty toward increasing prosperity: continually producing more goods and services of value. If that is going to happen, every person in the nation must somehow be motivated to contribute what he or she can to the increase in productive economic activity.

What most effectively motivates people to make their best contributions toward a more productive economy? They are best motivated by the hope of earning more and bettering their positions in life, as well as those of their families. Nothing else provides the needed motivation—not appeals to patriotism, not challenges to love their fellow man, not calls to do more to help the poor, not envy of the rich, and certainly not forced labor in systems of slavery or totalitarianism. Nothing motivates a person nearly as well as his self-interest; that is, the hope of earning more money and bettering his own condition.

But if people are going to be motivated by the hope of earning more money, they must be able to see *actual evidence* that this is possible. They must be able to look around and see examples of people who started out poor and then became rich or at least moderately well-off. People must be able to see that a measure of financial success is possible with good work habits, honesty, thrift, and perseverance.[92]

If people know that they live in a country where no one is able to improve his family's economic condition, such as a communist coun-

---

[92] Stanley and Danko, *The Millionaire Next Door*, is filled with such examples, as well as numerous studies of the surprisingly frugal and unassuming lifestyles of most American millionaires.

try, where wages are set by the government, then no one tries. Likewise, if people live in a country where powerful government officials and a few wealthy families have kept all the wealth for themselves for generations, and where the poor really have no opportunity to work hard and succeed economically, then again they do not try.

A tragic example of economic and cultural systems that trap people in poverty by preventing anyone from getting ahead is seen in much of sub-Saharan Africa. Maranz, an expert on Africa, explains:

> It is a general rule that people expect that money and commodities will be used or spent as soon as they are available. If the possessor does not have immediate need to spend or use a resource, relatives and friends certainly do. To have resources and not use them is hoarding, which is considered to be unsocial.[93]

To be fair, we must note that Maranz sympathetically views the reason for such customs: guaranteeing that everyone will survive, especially during severe circumstances of drought or famine. He writes at the beginning of his book:

> What is the one most fundamental **economic** consideration in the majority of African societies? I believe the answer is approximately this: the distribution of economic resources so that all persons may have their minimum needs met, or at least that they may survive. This distribution is the African social security system. . . . Do Africans achieve the main goal of their economic system? Yes, they achieve it amazingly well. . . . [Even in bleak economies with 50% unemployment] people continue to eat, are clothed and housed, and they survive. Those who have even meager means share with kin and close friends. There are no riots. People live their lives with, it seems to me, at least as much contentment as Westerners do in their home countries. Of course, they all hope for better days, but in the meantime, they make the most of their situations.[94]

So we are not saying that these customs have served no good purpose at all. But we are saying that today they are a significant hindrance to economic growth, because they prevent anyone from getting ahead

---

[93] Maranz, *African Friends*, 16.
[94] Ibid., 4, emphasis in original.

economically. In fact, Maranz himself says that the result of these customs is a continual "leveling" of society so that no one is able to get ahead of others:

> The unwritten rules governing the loaning and sharing of money and goods, and the extreme social pressure on individuals to conform to these rules or face sanctions, serve as leveling mechanisms to keep people from getting ahead of others. . . . Extreme social pressure is exerted on those who have resources to share them with those members of society who have less. The effect is to prevent anyone from getting ahead and basically acts as a brake on economic development.[95]

What is the result of believing the lie that economic equality is more important than economic growth (progressive subduing of the earth, Gen. 1:28), property ownership ("you shall not steal," "you shall not covet"), or getting a just reward for one's labor? It is entrapment in poverty.

The need for people to see examples of others who have gone from poverty to wealth means that it is very destructive for a society to continually vilify "the rich," to portray them as evil, and to promote envy and hatred toward them. (The idea that wealth comes from the exploitation of others rather than from creating new value is a Marxist idea, not a Christian viewpoint.) Such class-warfare rhetoric tends to discourage poorer people from trying to succeed in business and become wealthy through hard work and perseverance (for who wants to be hated by everyone else?). If a society focuses on envy or hatred of the rich, it significantly hinders its economic productivity.

Every time a nation moves from poverty toward increasing prosperity, some people will do better economically than others. People have different gifts and skills, different levels of ambition, different work habits, and different levels of intelligence in various areas. Many people will become moderately prosperous because they do quite a good job of providing useful products of value for the economy. The government—and the customs of the society—must allow them to keep the fruits of their labor, because this is what motivates them to continue to make valuable contributions to the economy. In fact, in

---

[95] Ibid., 150.

free societies, most of the people who become moderately wealthy have quite "ordinary" occupations.

Then there will be a very few people who become spectacularly successful. Often they are people who invent new products or new ways to mass-produce products. In the history of the United States, these have been the people who figured out how to build an assembly line to mass-produce automobiles for ordinary families (Henry Ford), how to build a vast network of railroads (Cornelius Vanderbilt), or how to build huge steel mills (Andrew Carnegie, founder of U.S. Steel). They included those who developed home computers and a new generation of cell phones (Steve Jobs, founder of Apple), a computer operating system that is used in every country of the world (Bill Gates, founder of Microsoft), and an Internet marketing firm that delivers thousands of products quickly to any home (Jeff Bezos, founder of Amazon.com).

The important point for the United States' economic development is not that each of these men made millions of dollars. It is that each of these business leaders contributed a vast amount of economic productivity to his nation and, in many cases, to the entire world. These people and others like them enabled the United States to continually produce more products and services of value beyond anything that could be imagined from the efforts of one person. They succeeded, and the economy of their country grew significantly as a result of their efforts.

This kind of thing happens only in a nation that allows people unlimited opportunities to earn money with the hope of keeping large amounts of it. The people who can earn such millions of dollars are very rare, but they provide immense economic productivity for the society as a whole.

Frederick Catherwood rightly says, "The teaching of the Bible would appear to be that it is not the amount of a man's wealth which matters; what matters is the method by which he acquires it, how he uses it and his attitude of mind toward it.[96]

If a nation allows the freedom for anyone to accumulate much wealth in this way, it encourages multitudes of people to try. Some fail, many do moderately well, and only a very few become truly wealthy. But the millions who do moderately well form the backbone of a

---

[96] H. F. R. Catherwood, *The Christian in Industrial Society* (London: Tyndale Press, 1964), 9.

healthy economy, and those who become extremely wealthy provide significant benefit to that economy.

If the opportunity to work hard, succeed, and become wealthy is removed by government policies (such as extremely high rates of taxation on "the rich," or arbitrary and biased trials and imprisonments of high-profile wealthy people, as in Russia or China), then hardly anyone will try to become wealthy by building a productive business, and this will keep the entire nation from much of the economic growth that it could have experienced.

Therefore, if a nation is going to grow from poverty toward increasing prosperity, it must not confiscate wealth through punitive taxes on the rich, through high inheritance taxes, through unjust court decisions against the rich, or through social ostracism or moral condemnations of prosperity.

But what if people live in a country where nearly all the rich people have gained their wealth *through immoral means*, such as drug dealing, theft, or political corruption? In such cases, the society somehow needs to find enough strength to punish those criminals for the evil things they have done—not punishing them for the wealth itself, but for the wrongful means they used to gain that wealth. Then it needs to open up and protect genuine opportunities for anyone to become rich by legal, morally right means. If the only rich people in a nation are known to have become wealthy through bribery, theft, or corruption, then no honest people will believe there is any hope for them to increase their own wealth.

Pastors and other spiritual leaders in a nation have an important role here. They need to speak against the rich who have used lying, cheating, stealing, or the promotion of immorality to become wealthy. They also need to speak against wrongful government penalization or social ostracism of the rich. But if their sermons contain habitual criticisms even of the rich who have earned their money in morally good and legally correct ways, they will harm the economic growth of their nation by discouraging people from ever seeking to work hard and do very well economically.

The Bible does not say it is wrong for someone to say, "Today or tomorrow we will go into such and such a town and spend a year there and trade *and make a profit*," but rather that it is wrong to say this proudly without acknowledging that this can happen only "if the Lord wills" (see James 4:13, 15). The book of James does have some harsh words of condemnation for rich people (see 5:1–6), but these are people who have unjustly laid up excessive luxuries for themselves (vv. 2–3), have wrongly held back wages (v. 4), and who "live on the earth in luxury and self-indulgence" and have even wrongfully condemned and murdered righteous people (vv. 5–6). James is not referring to all rich people but to selfish, greedy, dishonest, unjust, self-indulgent rich people who have no care for others and do not act righteously.

In addition, there is this Old Testament warning: "Do not wear yourself out to become rich; be wise enough to restrain yourself" (Prov. 23:4, NET).[97]

This is related to a New Testament passage that warns against *desiring* to be rich:

> But *those who desire to be rich* fall into temptation, into a snare, into many senseless and harmful desires that plunge people into ruin and destruction. For the love of money is a root of all kinds of evils. It is through this craving that some have wandered away from the faith and pierced themselves with many pangs. (1 Tim. 6: 9–10)

Here we must distinguish between, on the one hand, the "desire to be rich" and the "love of money" that Paul is talking about, and, on the other hand, a desire to work hard, do well, and better one's economic situation, which the Bible never condemns.

There are always many people whose goal is not wealth but doing well at their jobs or businesses and earning a decent living, and who are continually promoted at work or else invent products that sell remarkably well, and suddenly discover that they are becoming wealthy beyond anything they expected or even sought. In a free-market economy, that happens fairly often.

In addition, there are always many people in a society who know nothing about the Bible's teachings and think there is nothing at all

---

[97] The ESV translation gives a similar sense: "Do not toil to acquire wealth; be discerning enough to desist," as long as it is understood that "toil" represents the Hebrew word *yaga'*, which means "toil, grow, or be weary," and implies working hard to the point of great weariness.

wrong with wanting to be rich. They, in fact, make it their goal to become wealthy. But one of the amazing aspects of a free-market system is that it often uses the immense energies these people devote to becoming rich for the economic good of the society as a whole. In order to gain more profit, these people work to create valuable new goods and services that bring great benefit to the society.

If a society does not allow people the freedom to become wealthy by legal means, then it loses many of the benefits that these people would have brought to the economy. They do not work nearly as hard or produce nearly as much, or else they move to other countries, where they can use their skills to become wealthy, and the other countries get the benefits of their economic productivity.

21. Freedom of religion

This freedom was implied in sections 15 and 18 above (and see also chapter 7, 258), but we state it explicitly here. Religious bigotry and intolerance in the past have led to the exclusion of valuable skills and knowledge in many countries, and significantly hindered economic development. In order to prevent such losses of knowledge and skill, it is important that a nation establish and protect freedom for every religious viewpoint.

Several Muslim nations today continue to exercise extreme exclusion of other religions, and they suffer negative economic consequences as a result. Communist nations such as North Korea and the former Soviet Union have excluded religion generally and have thus experienced the economic loss that comes from excluding people of various religious convictions from productive participation in the economy.

C. Conclusion

If the leaders of a nation make up their minds to protect the twenty-one freedoms outlined in this chapter, these freedoms will release the tremendous economic productivity of the people in the nation, and it will begin to produce more and more goods and services of value. As it does this, it will begin to make large strides in its journey from poverty toward ever-increasing prosperity.

9

THE VALUES OF
THE SYSTEM

Cultural Beliefs That Will
Encourage Economic Growth

How can any nation hope to make the economic and political changes that we outlined in the previous chapters?

The most effective way to do this, and the only way that will bring long-term change to a nation, is to persuade people to change any cultural beliefs and traditions that are hindering economic development. If these beliefs and traditions can be replaced with new ones that promote economic growth, the nation will change.

These cultural values are therefore the most strategic matters that we discuss in this book, because they will ultimately determine all the other factors. The cultural values of a nation determine what kind of economic system it adopts, what kinds of laws and policies the government enacts, whether corruption is tolerated, whether freedoms are protected, and what kinds of goals individuals set for their personal lives. It is important, therefore, to understand exactly what kinds of cultural values lead a nation to support the kinds of economic and governmental systems we described in earlier chapters.

Daron Acemoglu and James A. Robinson, in their frequently insightful book *Why Nations Fail*, dismiss the idea that cultural values have much influence on the economic development of a nation. They write:

> Is the culture hypothesis useful for understanding world inequality? Yes and no. Yes, in the sense that social norms, which are related to culture, matter and can be hard to change, and they also sometimes support institutional differences, this book's explanation for world inequality. But mostly no, because those aspects of culture often emphasized—religion, national ethics, African or Latin values—are just not important for understanding how we got here and why the inequalities of the world persist. Other aspects, such as the extent to which people trust each other or are able to cooperate, are important but they are mostly an outcome of institutions, not an independent cause.[1]

Our response to Acemoglu and Robinson is to say, first, that we agree that economic and political institutions have a massive impact on the economic development of a nation. That is why we devoted chapters 3, 4, 5, and 6 to discussing the kind of economic system that is needed, and chapters 7 and 8 to the kind of governmental system that is needed for an economically productive society. In fact, the economic and political institutions that Acemoglu and Robinson recommend as "inclusive" have many of the characteristics that we recommended in these chapters.[2]

However, our second response is that Acemoglu and Robinson wrongfully minimize or even dismiss the role of cultural values both in enabling nations to adopt the wealth-creating inclusive institutions that they recommend and in helping people who live under those institutions to function in more economically productive ways. It is not a one-way street. Yes, institutions modify cultural values, but cultural values also create and modify institutions.

This shortcoming in the analysis of Acemoglu and Robinson is

---

[1] Daron Acemoglu and James A. Robinson, *Why Nations Fail: The Origins of Power, Prosperity and Poverty* (New York: Crown Publishers, 2012), 57.

[2] See their description of inclusive institutions on pages 73–83. Inclusive *economic* institutions "allow and encourage participation by the great mass of people in economic activities that make the best use of their talent and skills," and also have "secure private property, an unbiased system of law" and other features permitting free exchange and ease of entry into business and careers (74–75). They say that inclusive *political* institutions have enough centralized power to govern effectively and also "distribute power broadly in society and subject it to constraints" (80–81).

evident when they try to explain why certain countries adopted the inclusive institutions that they recommend while other countries did not. In proposing a solution for poor nations, they write: "The solution to the economic and political failure of nations today is to transform their extractive institutions toward inclusive ones. . . . This is not easy."[3]

They then say that the transformation of institutions in a nation requires "the presence of broad coalitions leading the fight against the existing regime," but they fail to explain what will motivate these broad coalitions to form or to act. In another place, they say that nations that have successfully established inclusive institutions "succeeded in empowering a fairly broad cross-section of society," but they do not say how this happened. In fact, they say, "The honest answer of course is that there is no recipe for building such institutions."[4]

When they actually analyze how nations succeeded at previous points in history in establishing inclusive institutions, their explanation seems to come down to mere luck, or what they sometimes call "contingency" (which we take as another word for inexplicable luck). At other times, they say that changes happened because of what they call "institutional drift," but they add that it is impossible to predict whether an institution will drift one way or another. They write (all emphases added):

> Two otherwise similar societies will also slowly drift apart institutionally. . . . *Institutional drift* has no predetermined path.[5]

> [In the Glorious Revolution of 1688 in England, which led to inclusive institutions,] the entire path leading up to this political revolution was at the mercy of *contingent* events.[6]

> In India, *institutional drift* worked differently and led to the development of a uniquely rigid hereditary caste system that limited the functioning of markets and the allocation of labor across occupations.[7]

---

[3] Acemoglu and Robinson, *Why Nations Fail*, 402.
[4] Ibid., 458, 460.
[5] Ibid., 108–9.
[6] Ibid., 110.
[7] Ibid., 118. Acemoglu and Robinson fail to mention any religious beliefs or cultural values from Hinduism that might have led to this caste system.

Fortunate turns of *contingency* [were partially responsible for strengthening inclusive institutions in England].[8]

[France, Japan, the United States, and Australia] pulled ahead of the rest. . . . Many challenges to inclusive institutions were overcome, sometimes because of the dynamics of the virtuous circle [that is, inclusive institutions perpetuating inclusive institutions], sometimes thanks to the *contingent* path of history.[9]

Still none of this [that is, history prior to 1688 in England] made a truly pluralistic regime inevitable, and its emergence was in part a consequence of the *contingent* path of history. . . . The path of major institutional change was, as usual, no less *contingent* than the outcome of other political conflicts. . . . In this instance, therefore, *contingency* and a broad coalition were deciding factors underpinning the emergence of pluralism and inclusive institutions.[10]

[In England's Glorious Revolution of 1688] *luck* was on the side of Parliament against James II.[11]

Things could have turned out very differently in Botswana, especially if it hadn't been so *fortunate* as to have leaders such as Seretse Khama, or Quett Masire.[12]

No less important, the *contingent* path of history worked in Botswana's favor. It was particularly *lucky* because Seretse Khama and Quett Masire were not Siaka Stevens [dictator in Sierra Leone] and Robert Mugabe [dictator in Zimbabwe].[13]

In addition some *luck* is key, because history always unfolds in a *contingent* way.[14]

There was no historical necessity that Peru end up so much poorer than Western Europe or the United States. . . . The turning point was the way in which this area was colonized and how this contrasted

---

[8] Ibid., 122.
[9] Ibid., 123.
[10] Ibid., 211–12.
[11] Ibid., 403.
[12] Ibid., 410–11.
[13] Ibid., 413.
[14] Ibid., 427.

with the colonization of North America. This resulted not from a historically predetermined process but as the *contingent* outcome of several pivotal institutional developments during critical junctures.[15]

Naturally, the predictive power of a theory where both small differences and *contingency* play key roles will be limited.[16]

Whether such a process will . . . open the door to further empowerment, and ultimately to durable political reform [in China] will depend . . . on the history of economic and political institutions, on many small differences that matter and on the very *contingent* path of history.[17]

One of the most important historical events that Acemoglu and Robinson discuss is the Glorious Revolution in England in 1688, when Protestant leaders in Parliament invited William of Orange to invade England and become king. When William arrived with a Dutch army of fifteen thousand men, King James II did not even offer resistance. In the ensuing events, William (who became King William III of England) agreed with Parliament on many changes:

The Glorious Revolution limited the power of the king and the executive, and relocated to Parliament the power to determine economic institutions. At the same time it opened up the political system to a broad cross section of society. . . . The Glorious Revolution was the foundation for creating a pluralistic society. . . . It created the world's first set of inclusive political institutions.[18]

But Acemoglu and Robinson fail to even mention that William of Orange had been educated in Holland under Protestant teaching since childhood, especially in Calvinistic Reformed theology.[19]

The same failure to mention strong Protestant training in the background of a significant leader occurs in Acemoglu and Robinson's discussion of Botswana. They report that most of the continent of

---

[15] Ibid., 432–33. Acemoglu and Robinson fail to even mention the possibility that differing cultural values derived from differences between Roman Catholic Spain (which colonized Peru) and Protestant Britain (which colonized the United States) had anything to do with the "contingent outcome" of these historical events.

[16] Ibid., 434.

[17] Ibid., 462. This is the last sentence of the book.

[18] Ibid., 102.

[19] See Acemoglu and Robinson, 190, where no mention of William's Protestant Calvinistic training is found. The changes instituted in the Glorious Revolution are detailed on pages 102–5 and 191–97.

Africa "has experienced a long vicious circle of the persistence and re-creation of extractive political and economic institutions," but then they say, "Botswana is the exception." They attribute this primarily to Seretse Khama, who became king of Botswana at a decisive time. They say, "Khama was an extraordinary man, uninterested in personal wealth and dedicated to the building of his country."[20]

Khama made a crucial decision affecting Botswana's history when diamonds were discovered:

> The first big diamond discovery was under Ngwato land, Seretse Khama's traditional homeland. Before the discovery was announced, Khama instigated a change in the law so that all subsoil mineral rights were vested in the nation, not the tribe. This ensured that diamond wealth would not create great inequities in Botswana.[21]

The result of such enlightened leadership is that Botswana became "one of the fastest-growing countries in the world. Today Botswana has the highest per capita income in sub-Saharan Africa."[22]

But Acemoglu and Robinson fail to mention Khama's strong educational background in Protestant Christian schools. Do they think that such training in biblical moral values had no role whatsoever in the formation of the moral character of such a remarkable leader?

Historian Susan Williams writes that Khama "had attended the premier schools for Africans in South Africa: Adams College, a mission school near Durban; the missionary-run Lovedale College in Alice, in the Eastern Cape; and Tiger Kloof in Vryburg, which was . . . run by the London Missionary Society."[23]

In an article published in the United States in 1951, Khama wrote:

> I have every intention of going back to my country with my wife by my side. For like the Ruth of the Bible, we often find our strength and our comfort in this passage of Scripture: "Entreat me not to leave Thee or return from following after Thee, for whither Thou goest I will go and where Thou lodgest I will lodge. Thy people shall be my people and Thy God my God."[24]

---

[20] Ibid., 116–17.
[21] Ibid., 412.
[22] Ibid., 409.
[23] Susan Williams, *Colour Bar: The Triumph of Seretse Khama and His Nation* (London: Penguin, 2006), 4.
[24] Seretse Khama, "Why I Gave Up My Throne for Love," *Ebony* 6, no. 8 (June 1951): 43.

In fact, Khama's Christian heritage can be traced back to his grand-father, Khama III, who was king of Bechuanaland (now Botswana) from 1875 to 1923. Early in his life, Khama III became a Christian and decided to promote the Christian faith by helping the establishment of many churches and schools throughout the country, especially by the London Missionary Society. Dickson Mungazi writes:

> [Khama III] adopted Christianity as the basis for new life for his peo-ple. . . . For many years, the education of Africans was totally in the hands of the missionaries. Both Africans and missionaries felt that they both had one thing in common: a desire to initiate change that was designed to accelerate the rate of African advancement.[25]

But as they do in the case of William of Orange, Acemoglu and Rob-inson fail to mention the Christian background in Khama's training.

Finally, Acemoglu and Robinson, in their attempt to show *that inclusive institutions* are the single reason why nations succeed eco-nomically, fail to mention, or mention only in passing, many of the factors that we name in this book as important for economic develop-ment. These include a stable currency, low taxes, a free-market sys-tem (though that might be the implication of what they call inclusive economic institutions), separation of powers in government, a fair court system, absence of bribery, protection of patents and copyrights, protection against foreign invasion, avoidance of wars of conquest, protection against destruction of the environment, freedom to use resources, universal education, stable families, and freedom to acquire wealth and become rich by legal means. They also fail to discuss the economic importance of values such as belief in God; accountability to God; belief that God approves of productivity and that it is morally right; moral constraints against stealing, lying, and discrimination; the belief that time is valuable and that change is possible; as well as many other beliefs that we mention in the remainder of this chapter.

Changing deeply held cultural beliefs is never easy. In fact, it is the most difficult of all the solutions we discuss in this book. Values that are embedded in a nation's history, traditions, customs, music, litera-

---

[25] Dickson Mungazi, *We Shall Not Fail: Values in the National Leadership of Seretse Khama, Nelson Mandela, and Julius Nyerere* (Trenton, NJ: Africa World Press, 2005), 46–47; see also 36–37.

ture, patterns of language, religious institutions, beliefs, educational systems, and parenting habits represent hundreds, if not thousands, of years of enculturation.

However, that does not mean that beliefs and values can never be changed. In fact, Lawrence E. Harrison of Tufts University summarizes the hopeful conclusions of about sixty scholars involved in the Culture Matters Research Project in the book *The Central Liberal Truth: How Politics Can Change a Culture and Save It from Itself*. Harrison provides extensive summaries of effective ways that leaders within nations have brought about cultural changes in several nations, changes that not only helped improve the material prosperity of those nations, but also their quality of life.

Harrison recognizes that some of his more specific recommendations are controversial, but he believes that "a majority of the world's people surely would agree with the following assertions" (derived from the 1948 United Nations Universal Declaration of Human Rights):

1. Life is better than death.
2. Health is better than sickness.
3. Liberty is better than slavery.
4. Prosperity is better than poverty.
5. Education is better than ignorance.
6. Justice is better than injustice.[26]

While changing cultural values is difficult, it is the place where religious organizations—especially, from our perspective, Christian churches and organizations that emphasize Christian teaching—can have a great influence for good on a nation. In fact, Christian teaching has often transformed cultures in very positive ways in the past.

Pastors especially can contribute by teaching Christian cultural values in ways that promote better moral standards within a nation and also contribute to helping a nation's economy.[27] (See further comments about pastors at 32, 161, 186, 305, 366–67.)

---

[26] Lawrence E. Harrison, *The Central Liberal Truth: How Politics Can Change a Culture and Save It from Itself* (Oxford: Oxford University Press, 2006), 9.

[27] Darrow L. Miller and Stan Guthrie, *Discipling Nations: The Power of Truth to Transform Cultures* (Seattle: YWAM, 1998), 246, summarize the differences between animism, theism, and secularism regarding cultural values that have economic implications. One entire chapter (243–56) explains how those differences affect one's view of productive work in society, and, in a larger sense, the entire book

The history of economic development also indicates the importance of culture. At the conclusion of his massive study of economic development in various nations of the world, David S. Landes concludes, "If we learn anything from the history of economic development, it is that culture makes all the difference."[28]

To take one example among many, Landes notes the lack of economic development (except for oil wealth) in Middle Eastern nations. He says that the reason for this lack of development lies "with the culture, which (1) does not generate an informed and capable workforce; (2) continues to mistrust or reject new techniques and ideas that come from the enemy West (Christendom); (3) does not respect such knowledge as members do manage to achieve, whether by study abroad or by good fortune at home."[29]

In this chapter, we discuss cultural beliefs in thirteen broad categories. Each category contains cultural beliefs that contribute positively to economic development. If these beliefs are rejected, economic development will be hindered to some degree.

Some of the sections in this chapter return to themes mentioned earlier in the book. For example, in chapters 3, 4, and 8, we mentioned the economic importance of private ownership of property. But in this chapter, we emphasize the need for a society to *believe* that private ownership of property is morally right, and therefore we discuss the Bible's teachings about private property. The material on private property in this chapter is intended to inform the cultural value of respecting private ownership of property, and that cultural value is the necessary ingredient for establishing and maintaining a system that protects private property in a nation.

Similarly, in this chapter we discuss the *belief* that the purpose of government is to serve the nation and bring benefit to the people as a whole. If that belief is deeply held, it provides the strongest protection against government corruption, which occurs when people use

---

discusses ways in which cultural values derived from the Bible lead to economic activity that produces bounty and prosperity (see their discussion of the "development ethic" on 169–77 and the definition on 287).

[28] David S. Landes, *The Wealth and Poverty of Nations: Why Some Are So Rich and Some So Poor* (New York: W. W. Norton, 1999), 516.

[29] Ibid., 410.

their government positions for personal gain rather than for the good of the nation as a whole.

This chapter does not list all the values that are important for a society. We do not list generosity, hospitality, and kindness, for example, but the Bible surely counts these as important. And many poor countries excel in these values more than some wealthy Western societies. In this chapter, however, our purpose is to discuss those cultural values that are most directly related to the specific steps toward economic prosperity that we have discussed in the previous chapters. This chapter therefore outlines the deeply held values that will enable a country to adopt and maintain the solutions discussed to this point in this book.

A. Beliefs about religious matters

1. The society believes that there is a God who holds all people accountable for their actions

[handwritten marginalia: ? when poverty > moral compass 80% christian ?]

When a national culture includes a widespread belief that there is a God who holds all people accountable for their actions, it tends to produce individuals who act with honesty, care for others, keep their promises, work diligently, and care about the quality of their work.

On the other hand, if the culture holds the idea that there is no God, and therefore no ultimate moral accountability (as, for example, in communist nations), there is more dishonesty, more selfishness, and a greater tendency toward untrustworthiness, unreliability regarding commitments, and carelessness in work. Robbery and bribery are more common, as is considerable corruption in government, the legal system, the universities, businesses, the press, and even the churches.

The Bible specifies that all people will one day be accountable to the God who created the world. The apostle Paul told a gathering of pagan Greek philosophers in Athens that God "has fixed a day on which *he will judge the world in righteousness* by a man whom he has appointed; and of this he has given assurance to all by raising him from the dead" (Acts 17:31). Similarly, the apostle Peter wrote to many churches in Asia Minor about the unbelievers who were treating them with hostility: "They are surprised when you do not join them in the same flood of debauchery, and they malign you; but *they will give account* to him who is ready to judge the living and the dead" (1 Peter 4:4–5).

Paul noted that when a society becomes more corrupt, with increasing alienation from God, the people seem to overflow with evil conduct (see Rom. 3:10–17). The culmination of his description of such a society is that "there is *no fear of God* before their eyes" (Rom. 3:18). Rampant evil is the result of lack of belief in God and accountability to him.

Belief in God is a cultural value in which many African and Latin American societies are stronger than many wealthy Western societies.

2. The society believes that God approves of several character traits related to work and productivity

In 1904–05, German sociologist Max Weber published an influential essay that later became a book called *The Protestant Ethic and the Spirit of Capitalism*.[30] Weber argued that certain character traits that were inculcated by Protestantism were responsible for the remarkable economic development of Northern European nations and the United States.

More recently, Landes has concluded that, in spite of much scholarly criticism of Weber, he was essentially correct. At one point in his book *The Wealth and Poverty of Nations: Why Some Are So Rich and Some So Poor*, Landes says, with respect to the idea that culture makes all the difference in economic development, "Here Max Weber was right on."[31]

In Landes's words, "The heart of the matter lay indeed in the making of a new kind of man—rational, ordered, diligent, productive. These virtues, while not new, were hardly commonplace. Protestantism generalized them among its adherents."[32]

Landes mentions two special characteristics of Protestants:

> The first was stress on instruction and literacy, for girls as well as boys. This was a by-product of Bible reading. Good Protestants were expected to read the holy scriptures for themselves. . . . The second was importance accorded to time. . . . In that place and time (northern Europe, sixteenth to eighteenth centuries), religion encouraged the appearance in numbers of a personality type that had been exceptional

---

[30] Published in English as Max Weber, *The Protestant Ethic and the Spirit of Capitalism*, trans. Talcott Parsons (1930; repr., Los Angeles: Roxbury, 1996).
[31] Landes, *Wealth and Poverty*, 516. See also the perceptive analysis of Weber's theory by H. F. R. Catherwood, *The Christian in Industrial Society* (London: Tyndale Press, 1964), 114–26.
[32] Ibid., 177.

and adventitious before; and . . . this type created a new economy (a new mode of production) that we know as (industrial) capitalism.[33]

Landes also says, "Weber's point is that Protestantism produced a new kind of businessman, a different kind of person, one who aimed to live and work a certain way. It was the *way* that mattered, and riches were at best a by-product."[34]

Many of the aspects of this "Protestant" approach to work and productivity will be explained in the pages that follow. But at this point, we can mention several factors. It includes pursuing one's job as a calling from God; being able to read; and being honest and diligent at work, because one is working "as for the Lord and not for men" (Col. 3:23). In addition, workers should be thrifty in time and money (which they have as a stewardship entrusted to them from God). They should see the creation and production of goods from the earth as a calling from God (according to Gen. 1:28), and something they can do joyfully and with thanksgiving. They should not be superstitious but realize that God made an orderly world that is subject to rational investigation. They should think that new inventions of products from the earth are to be received as wonderful blessings from God.

It should not be surprising that a belief that God approves such things, once it spreads throughout a society, leads to greater economic growth in a nation. It is not surprising, therefore, that Harrison has compiled a remarkable table of various nations categorized according to the dominant religious backgrounds that influenced their cultures in the past. It shows that countries with primarily Protestant backgrounds influencing their cultural values score the highest in terms of per capita gross domestic product (GDP).

Religious background to culture of nations	Per capita GDP
Protestant	$29,784
Jewish	$19,320
Roman Catholic	$9,358
Orthodox	$7,045

[33] Ibid., 178.
[34] Ibid., 175.

Confucian	$6,691
Buddhist	$4,813
Islamic	$3,142
Hindu	$2,390[35]

At this point, we also need to make clear that when we talk about belief in God and certain moral standards, we are definitely not affirming the "health-and-wealth gospel." That is a teaching in some Christian circles that if you have enough faith, God will reward you with material prosperity. Steve Corbett and Brian Fikkert rightly criticize this view:

> At its core, the health and wealth gospel teaches that God rewards increasing levels of faith with greater amounts of wealth. When stated this way, the health and wealth gospel is easy to reject on a host of biblical grounds. Take the case of Job, for example. He had enormous faith and lived a godly life, but he went from riches to poverty *because* he was righteous and God wanted to prove this to Satan. . . .
>
> The poor could be poor due to injustices committed against them. . . . [During a visit to the massive Kibera slum of Nairobi, Kenya,] I was . . . amazed to see people . . . who were simultaneously so spiritually strong and so devastatingly poor. Right down there in the bowels of hell was this Kenyan church, filled with spiritual giants who were struggling just to eat every day. This shocked me. At some level I had implicitly assumed that my economic superiority goes hand in hand with my spiritual superiority. This is none other than the lie of the health and wealth gospel: spiritual maturity leads to financial prosperity.[36]

What we are saying throughout this book is that obedience to biblical teachings in the conduct of government and economic systems in a nation leads to increasing prosperity, and that belief in biblical values also contributes to prosperity in the lives of individuals and nations. But poverty is the result of many factors. Individual poor people may be spiritually mature and still materially poor because of injustices committed against them, because of personal tragedies or misfortunes,

---

[35] Harrison, *The Central Liberal Truth*, 88–89.
[36] Steve Corbett and Brian Fikkert, *When Helping Hurts: How to Alleviate Poverty Without Hurting the Poor—and Yourself* (Chicago: Moody, 2009), 69–70.

or because of the destructive systems, laws, and policies in the nation in which they live.

B. Beliefs about moral standards

3. The society values truthfulness

Most business transactions depend on trust. A businessperson has to trust that a supplier will deliver a product on the date that he specified, and that the product will have the agreed quality and specifications. The supplier has to trust that the buyer will pay for the product when he promised to do so. When buyers and sellers are in the habit of telling the truth and keeping their word, business transactions run smoothly and the economy functions efficiently. When a business is building a highly complex product (such as an airplane or automobile), there can be hundreds or even thousands of suppliers and workers on which the company depends in order to make a quality product in a timely manner.

But if a culture tolerates lying and breaking one's word, then the entire economic system begins to break down. Products are not delivered on time. Needed parts come in the wrong sizes or do not meet quality standards. Invoices and accounting reports are falsified so that companies no longer have an accurate picture of their inventories or costs of goods. Additional time-wasting procedures have to be built in to check and doublecheck the accuracy of every report. Economic productivity begins a rapid, downward spiral. Therefore, it is not surprising that William Easterly reports that cultures with high levels of trust have higher per capita incomes, and cultures with lower levels of trust have significantly lower per capita incomes.[37] (We mentioned in chapter 6 that a free-market system tends to foster a climate of truthfulness more than economic systems that are not as free; see 191–93.)

The Bible opposes such a breakdown in culture by upholding a high standard of truthfulness in speech. It says, "You shall not bear false witness against your neighbor" (Ex. 20:16), and, "Do not lie to one another" (Col. 3:9). A society that honors these commands will value and expect truthfulness.

---

[37] William Easterly, *The White Man's Burden: Why the West's Efforts to Aid the Rest Have Done So Much Ill and So Little Good* (New York: Penguin, 2006), 79–81.

On the other hand, if a society abandons these standards, it will be increasingly filled with lying, deceit, and slander. Little shame will be attached to lying and getting away with it. In some cultures, those who can lie successfully and cheat others are honored rather than despised. Such cultural values cause disrespect for truth in a society, and become a significant hindrance to economic development.

David Maranz points out many ways in which the requirements of truthfulness and honesty in speech are commonly disregarded in many African societies:

> Africans find security in ambiguous arrangements, plans, and speech. . . . The following are areas where ambiguity is often seen . . . allowing for the renegotiation of agreements in the light of changed facts, or a hoped for basis for claiming a better agreement. . . . Not keeping accurate or precise financial records. . . . Arriving or starting times for meetings or gatherings being indefinitely later than the announced times.[38]

Maranz also says that if people are paid before a job is completed, they often fail to complete the job, which Westerners see as failing to keep one's word:

> A contract or a bill paid in full before the service is completed is money lost, with few exceptions. A Westerner engaged a man to trim some trees in his yard. After they had settled on a price, the tree trimmer was paid in full. The Westerner never saw the man again. A similar experience happened with a tiling contractor.[39]

Maranz gives another example:

> You make an agreement with a painter on painting your house. He will paint the house for a set amount with the cost of the paint and other materials being separate. He begins to paint, with an advance on the contract price, but then stops. Days go by and he does not show up. . . . You query him why the job is not finished. He then informs you there was a mistake. The price you gave him was too low and he cannot continue unless you increase the amount you will pay.[40]

---

[38] David Maranz, *African Friends and Money Matters* (Dallas: SIL International, 2001), 88.
[39] Ibid., 177.
[40] Ibid., 185.

In describing an ideal economically productive society, Landes explains what it means to value honesty: "This ideal society would also be honest. Such honesty would be enforced by law, but ideally, the law would not be needed. People would believe that honesty is right (also that it pays) and would live and act accordingly."[41]

4. The society respects private ownership of property

We have already discussed the crucial importance of private property for economic development (see 114–16 and 141–54). Here we wish to emphasize that honoring and respecting the ownership of private property must be a cultural value that is reinforced from generation to generation.

This is a value clearly taught in the Bible. Not only does the Bible command, "You shall not *steal*" (Ex. 20:15), but it also prohibits even the *desire* to steal, for it says, "You shall not *covet* your neighbor's house; you shall not *covet* your neighbor's wife, or his male servant, or his female servant, or his ox, or his donkey, or anything that is your neighbor's" (Ex. 20:17).

One must not steal from anyone, rich or poor. In ancient Israel, there were detailed laws about penalties to be imposed if someone stole an ox or a sheep (see Ex. 22:1), ruined a neighbor's crops (Ex. 22:5), or started a fire that destroyed someone else's stored grain (Ex. 22:6; see also Deut. 22:1–4).

Maranz reports several ways in which property is not respected and stealing is an acceptable form of behavior in many parts of African culture. For example:

> Precision is to be avoided in accounting as it shows the lack of a generous spirit. Precision and rigor in keeping accounts show a lack of generosity. It is nontrusting. It is not what a friend does. Moreover, it is foreign, threatening, and indicates a lack of understanding of the needs of ordinary people.[42]

Another example is failure to repay loans. Maranz says:

---

[41] Landes, *Wealth and Poverty*, 218.
[42] Maranz, *African Friends*, 38.

Even banks often go bankrupt because individuals and governments do not repay their loans, which are in effect uncollectable. . . . Practically no one repays a loan voluntarily, even if a promissory note or other document has been signed. I think there is also an underlying concept that a bank is there to provide and loan money—its coffers are full of money, it has far more money than I do, and therefore is it not a little absurd to think of me giving money to a bank? A bank, and people of means, are there to be givers, not receivers.[43]

The Bible's perspective is different: "The wicked borrows but does not pay back" (Ps. 37:21).

Maranz notes that even when money is stolen, and people know who stole it, there is often a reluctance to hold the culprit responsible:

A church was in need of benches. A Westerner made a donation, but was told sometime later that the money had disappeared, the church treasury having been cleaned out by the church treasurer. Church elders also informed the donor that the treasurer had just bought a new radio-cassette player. The donor suggested they sell the cassette player and put the proceeds back in the church treasury. The elders exclaimed, "You wouldn't take a radio-cassette player away from a poor man, would you?"[44]

Such cultural acceptance of failure to respect private ownership of property has negative economic consequences. It tends to destroy incentives to work harder and earn more, because what a person earns or buys might suddenly be taken away from him by someone who thinks he "needs" it more. It also tends to prevent anyone from lending money to others—there is no certainty of getting repaid. In addition, it discourages employment because an employer cannot trust an employee to deal honestly with any funds that are entrusted to him. Therefore, the employer has to perform many routine transactions and errands himself when his time could be better spent in more productive activities.

---

[43] Ibid., 152. But also note the comments by Maranz that we cited in an earlier section, to the effect that the primary economic consideration in many African societies is that all persons might have their minimum needs met (see 302).
[44] Ibid., 111.

5. The society honors other moral values

Although truthfulness and not stealing are the two most crucial moral standards with respect to economic productivity, other moral values taught in the Bible also have an important role. Our main examples will be taken from the Ten Commandments in Exodus 20:1–17.

The Bible teaches that children should honor their parents, for it says in the Ten Commandments, "Honor your father and your mother" (Ex. 20:12), and Paul writes, "Children, obey your parents in the Lord, for this is right" (Eph. 6:1). This is economically significant because respectful and obedient children will likely be more successful in school, will develop generally better work habits, and will be more productive throughout their lives. This value also affects future generations, because a stable family structure will be conducive to passing down the values of a culture from one generation to the next. In addition, respect for one's parents generally will produce respect for governments, laws, teachers, and employers, all benefiting economic productivity.

Honoring one's parents is a cultural value in which many African, Asian, and Latin American societies are stronger than many wealthy Western societies.

The Bible also says, "You shall not murder" (Ex. 20:13). Murder is, of course, terribly destructive, for it takes away the productive contribution that the victim could have made to the economy and to other people. In addition, a high murder rate in a society forces people to spend their valuable time and resources protecting themselves against harm. They will be less likely to take risks in business and less confident that they will be able to enjoy the fruits of their labor, even if their businesses succeed. In societies where murder is rampant, entrepreneurs might think that more success makes them more likely to become victims. All of this is detrimental to an economy.

What about laws concerning abortion? The command, "You shall not murder," when understood in connection with other passages in the Bible (see Gen. 25:22–23; Ex. 21:22–25; Pss. 51:5; 139:13; Luke 1:41–44), indicates that the life of an unborn (or pre-born) child should not be taken in an abortion.[45] From an economic standpoint, an abortion

---

[45] For further information on the biblical teaching about abortion as it relates to laws in a nation, see Wayne Grudem, *Politics—According to the Bible* (Grand Rapids: Zondervan, 2010), 157–78.

takes away the economic productivity that the unborn child could have contributed to the nation when he or she grew to adulthood. A high abortion rate can lead to a significant decline in a nation's population, so that eventually there will not be enough younger workers to support the older, retired people, creating a huge strain on the economy. Western Europe, Japan, Russia, and China will all pay a high price for producing too few children in the last few generations.

Another moral standard found in the Ten Commandments is, "You shall not commit adultery" (Ex. 20:14). From an economic standpoint, a society that honors faithfulness in marriage and disapproves of sexual intimacy outside of marriage tends to have more stable marriages and families. Stable marriages, in turn, generally lead to higher educational and economic achievement for children when they grow up.[46] Stable marriages also generally lead to higher economic productivity and stability for the individuals in those marriages.[47] And sexual faithfulness protects against AIDS and other sexually transmitted diseases.

Honoring sexual purity and faithfulness in marriage is a cultural value in which some poor countries would assess themselves to be stronger than many wealthy Western societies because of the prevalent approval of sexual immorality in the dominant media, entertainment, and educational cultures in many wealthy societies.

The last of the Ten Commandments is, "You shall not covet" (Ex. 20:17). In a society that is filled with envy and coveting, people will spend much of their emotional energy seeking ways to take things

---

[46] See Mary Parke, "Are Married Parents Really Better for Children?" *Center for Law and Social Policy* (May 2003): 1–7, accessed March 17, 2013, http://www.clasp.org/admin/site/publications_archive/files/0128.pdf; Robert I. Lerman, "Marriage and the Economic Well-Being of Families with Children: A Review of the Literature," a report for the U.S. Department of Health and Human Services http://www.urban.org/publications/410541.html; Robert I. Lerman, "How Do Marriage, Cohabitation, and Single Parenthood Affect the Material Hardships of Families With Children?" a report for the U.S. Department of Health and Human Services, http://www.urban.org/publications/410539.html; Robert I. Lerman, "Married and Unmarried Parenthood and Economic Well-Being: A Dynamic Analysis of a Recent Cohort," a report for the U.S. Department of Health and Human Services, http://www.urban.org/publications/410540.html; W. Bradford Wilcox, *Why Marriage Matters: Twenty-One Conclusions from the Social Sciences* (New York: Institute for American Values, 2002); Judith S. Wallerstein and Sandra Blakeslee, *Second Chances: Men, Women, & Children a Decade After Divorce* (New York: Ticknor & Fields [Houghton Mifflin], 1989), 148–49; 156–57.

[47] See Linda J. Waite and Maggie Gallagher, *The Case for Marriage: Why Married People Are Happier, Healthier, and Better Off Financially* (New York: Doubleday, 2000), cited in Jeffrey H. Larson, "The Verdict on Cohabitation vs. Marriage," *Marriage and Families*, January 2001, http://marriageandfamilies.byu.edu/issues/2001/January/cohabitation.aspx. See also the extensive data on the economic benefits of stable marriages cited in Grudem, *Politics*, 224–26.

from other people or resenting what other people have. This is not economically productive. By contrast, in a society that is less covetous, people will spend more of their energies seeking personal economic advancement, with little regard for what other people have. This results in greater economic productivity, because people's efforts are directed toward improving their own situations rather than destroying the situations of others.

In addition to these moral values taken directly from the Ten Commandments, we mentioned earlier that free markets tend to promote what Harrison calls the "lesser virtues" (see 201–202). These values also should be honored by every society. They have economic value, for as Harrison says: "A job well-done, tidiness, courtesy and punctuality are lubricants of both the economic and politico-social systems. The lesser virtues can translate into hard economic data: punctuality is practiced in all the top 15 countries on the World Economic Forum's competitiveness rankings."[48] By contrast, he quotes *The Economist* as saying, "Punctuality is not a Latin American comparative advantage," and notes one estimate that "tardiness costs Ecuador upwards of $700 million per year—more than 4 percent of GDP."[49]

Maranz writes that he has often observed in African cultures "a spirit of just getting by," which clashes with the importance of courtesy and a job well done:

> The spirit of just getting by is quite pervasive. It is in evidence with masons, carpenters, electricians, and other tradesmen who do not come to work with even the basic tools they need to do a job properly. . . . It is largely an attitude of mind. . . . The roadways will often be almost so blocked that two vehicles cannot pass. . . . When a vehicle breaks down, it is often repaired right in the middle of the road or street where it stopped, with other vehicles passing with difficulty. Sometimes traffic is backed up for blocks. No attempt is made even to push the vehicle out of the middle of the street. Repairs on vehicles are minimally done, just enough to get by for a short time rather than make a repair that will last indefinitely. Even educated people typically do not pay attention to punctuation and proper spelling, even when they have had years of university study.

---

[48] Harrison, *Central Liberal Truth*, 42.
[49] Ibid.

Souvenirs in many tourist markets are poorly made, revealing a lack of pride in fine craftsmanship. . . . Although the examples may be quite insignificant in themselves, they reveal characteristics of the cultures that are deep-seated and significant. . . . Perhaps experience has taught individuals and society that the future is so unsure that the best strategy in life is to seize the advantages of the moment, with little regard for the future. Whatever the reasons may be, society as a whole is the loser.[50]

Any economy that seeks to grow from poverty toward greater prosperity will regularly honor the moral values of respect for parents and other authorities; protection of and respect for human life; respect for sexual purity and faithfulness; disapproval of coveting; and honoring of the "lesser virtues" of pride in a job well-done, tidiness, courtesy, and punctuality. *Idk about that.*

C. Beliefs about human nature

6. The society believes that there are both good and evil in every human heart

The belief that there are both a tendency to do good and a tendency to do evil in every person's heart undergirds a sense of moral responsibility and individual accountability in a society.

If a society believes that each person has tendencies to both good and evil, then it will see it as the person's responsibility to *decide* to do good and *decide not* to do evil. This means that people who decide to be honest, work hard, and be productive should be rewarded. But people who decide to do harmful and evil things to others should be punished for the harm they do.

By contrast, if a culture believes that each person is basically good, it will regard the bad choices he makes as the fault of outside factors that have hindered him. Less accountability and individual responsibility will inevitably be the outcome of this belief.

The Bible clearly teaches that there is a tendency to sin or evil in every person's heart, for it says, "All have sinned and fall short of the glory of God" (Rom. 3:23).

---

[50] Maranz, *African Friends*, 183–84.

But it also recognizes that even people who do not have the written law of God (that is, the Bible) are still able "by nature" to "do what the law requires," and when this happens "they show that the work of the law is written on their hearts, while their conscience also bears witness" (Rom. 2:14–15). In theological terms, this is called "common grace," which is the undeserved favor that God gives to every human being whether one believes in him or not. Every person has a conscience and a moral sense of right and wrong. This moral sense may not be perfect, but people still will often "do what the law requires," and their actions will often conform at least outwardly to the moral law of God. Because of this common grace, and the knowledge of right and wrong that people possess, Paul says that "the whole world" will be "held accountable to God" (Rom. 3:19).

7. The society believes that individuals are responsible for their own actions

This cultural belief follows from the previous one. If people have the ability to make good or evil choices, then those who make good choices should be rewarded through the ordinary ways in which a society functions. Those who produce good products and bring benefit to others should receive some benefit from their work. By contrast, people who make poor choices and do very little that is of value to others should not be rewarded in the same way (though they should certainly be cared for so that they do not lack essential food, clothing, shelter, and opportunities for additional job training).

In addition, a belief in individual responsibility and accountability means that people who make foolish business investments or produce products of poor quality and low value should be allowed to fail economically, because they should bear the legitimate consequences of their poor work.

In contrast to a society that values individual responsibility and accountability, a society trapped in poverty will often think that those who succeed are simply lucky, that those who fail economically are victims of bad luck or fate, and that those who do serious wrongs are victims of a bad system. Moral accountability is minimized.

8. The society highly values individual freedom

While governments should have laws against crime in order to prevent people from harming one another (see discussion above, 134–35), they also should provide significant protection of human freedoms, as we explained in chapter 8. When people are allowed to live in substantial freedom, the economy gets a big boost. As people try countless ways to make useful goods and serve customers, their earned success benefits everyone.

But if human freedoms are going to be effectively protected in a society, then the culture must love individual freedom and place a high value on it.

The opposite of love for freedom is a societal longing for security and for government to regulate and control all of life. The governments of countries under strict Islamic law tend to control nearly every aspect of people's lives. This hinders individual freedom and therefore reduces economic prosperity. Communist countries such as North Korea and Cuba, and to some extent China (and certainly the former Soviet Union), legislate minute control over people's education, jobs, income levels, housing, and many other details of their lives. These nations suffer economically as a result. (China's economic growth began only when it set aside some communist policies and instituted some free-market reforms.)

The Bible frequently portrays the evils of "slavery" or government control of all of life. In fact, the Ten Commandments begin with God's reminder to the people of Israel, "I am the LORD your God, who brought you out of the land of Egypt, *out of the house of slavery*" (Ex. 20:2). The Year of Jubilee was an occasion when the people of Israel would "*proclaim liberty* throughout the land to all its inhabitants" (Lev. 25:10). Jesus announced that he had come to "*proclaim liberty* to the captives . . . to set at *liberty* those who are oppressed (Luke 4:18).

The ability to live in liberty, to make free choices and be responsible for them, is an essential component of genuine humanity as God intended it. It is important that cultures value and protect human liberty, and that they teach its value to younger generations. President Ronald Reagan said:

Freedom is never more than one generation away from extinction. We didn't pass it on to our children in their bloodstream. It must be fought for, protected, and handed on for them to do the same, or one day we will spend our sunset years telling our children and our children's children what it once was like in the United States when men were free.[51]

9. The society opposes discrimination against people on the basis of race, gender, or religion

As we explained in chapter 8, it is important for an economically productive society to guarantee the freedom for all citizens to be educated; freedom for women as well as men to work and own businesses and property; and freedom for people from all racial, national, religious, and ethnic backgrounds to participate fully in the economy and have all the rights the society affords. Too often nations have discriminated on the basis of race, gender, or religion, typically producing harmful consequences for economic development.

However, if non-discrimination is actually going to work in a nation, it is important that it be upheld not only by laws, but also by the cultural beliefs of the people. At this point, the Bible's teachings on the equality of all people before God are important. The Bible shows that all human beings are descended from Adam and Eve, our first parents, as indicated in Genesis 1–2. Therefore, every human being shares in the exalted status of being "in the image of God" (see Gen. 1:26–27; 5:1; 9:6; James 3:9). That means that no one should be thought to be superior or inferior to others because of his or her racial background, gender, or religion.

D. Beliefs about the family

We discussed in chapter 7 the importance of laws that give protections and economic incentives to stable family structures, promoting the idea of marriage as a union of one man and one woman, giving incentives for couples to stay married and bear children, and encouraging, as far as possible, that children are raised in homes with both a father

---

[51] Ronald Reagan, "Encroaching Control," speech to Chamber of Commerce in Phoenix, AZ, on March 30, 1961 (copy of original typed manuscript of speech obtained from Ronald Reagan Library, Simi Valley, CA).

and a mother present (see pages 256–57). All of these factors contribute positively to economic development within a nation. In this section, we want to call attention to the cultural values that must be adopted in order to support such policies.

10. The society honors marriage between one man and one woman

We gave reasons in a previous chapter to show that there are significant economic benefits for a society that encourages marriage between one man and one woman, particularly the educational and behavioral advantages to the children raised in such families (see 256–57).

The biblical teaching on marriage encourages this important value. From the very beginning, when God created Adam and Eve, he told them that together they should bear children: "Be fruitful and multiply and fill the earth and subdue it" (Gen. 1:28).

But were Adam and Eve actually a married couple? Yes, because the early chapters of Genesis call them "the man and his wife" (Gen. 2:25). In fact, that same chapter of Genesis views the relationship between Adam and Eve as the pattern for all marriages to follow on the earth, because immediately after God brings Eve to Adam, the biblical narrator says, "Therefore a man shall leave his father and his mother and hold fast to his wife, and they shall become one flesh" (Gen 2:24). This verse pictures a pattern in which a man departs from the household of which he has been a part and establishes a new household. Jesus quoted this passage when he taught about marriage in general in Matthew 19:3–6.

In addition, it is clear from the Bible that sexual faithfulness to one's partner is an essential component of marriage, for adultery is regularly viewed as a sin. The command, "You shall not commit adultery" (Ex. 20:14), is found in the Ten Commandments, and it is reaffirmed several times in the New Testament (see Matt. 19:18; Rom. 2:22; 13:9; James 2:11).[52]

Promotion of sexual faithfulness will also help to counteract the widespread incidence of AIDS and other sexually transmitted diseases,

---

[52] For further discussion of the Bible's teaching about marriage and sexual morality, see Grudem, *Politics*, 213–27.

which are so harmful in many poor countries, especially in Africa (see discussion on 241–42).

11. The society values permanency of marriage and has a low divorce rate

We explained in chapter 7 how rampant divorce and a high number of single-parent households are economically harmful to a society. Children in single-parent families are more likely to grow up with lower educational and economic achievement than their parents (see 256). For many poor countries, marriage is already a strength. They have much lower divorce rates than many wealthy countries, and their cultures place a high value on permanency in marriage. We encourage those societies to retain this emphasis and not to follow the mistaken views of wealthy countries in this regard.

The Bible's teachings encourage parents to think of marriage as a lifelong relationship, and to think of divorce as a step to be taken only in the most extreme circumstances (such as sexual immorality by one of the spouses or desertion that cannot be reconciled). Jesus said, "What therefore God has joined together, let not man separate" (Matt. 19:6; see also v. 9).[53]

Rather than allowing easy divorces, therefore, a society that seeks to move from poverty to increasing prosperity should promote the permanency of marriage as a valued and honored tradition in the culture.

In addition, the society should value children (see Ps. 127:3; Mal. 2:15; 1 Tim. 5:14). Children are important for the continued productivity of a nation. If a nation does not have at least enough children to replace the current generation, the population will eventually decline and the small number of younger workers will be inadequate to support the increasing number of older, retired people. A nation hinders its economic growth and eventually declines economically if it fails to have enough children. Japan is already discovering this, as are several European nations (such as Italy). China's "one child per family" policy also fails to recognize this truth.

Promoting permanence in marriage is a cultural value in which

---

[53] For further discussion of the biblical teaching on divorce, see Grudem, *Politics*, 219–20.

some poor countries are stronger than many wealthy Western societies, with their rampant divorce rates.

E. Beliefs about the earth

12. The society believes that human beings are more important than all other creatures on the earth

Jesus was clear in his teaching about the importance of human beings in comparison to animals. He said, "Of how much *more value* is a man than a sheep!" (Matt. 12:12). He also said, "Look at the birds of the air. . . . Are you not of *more value* than they?" (Matt. 6:26). And he said, "You are of *more value* than many sparrows" (Matt. 10:31).

These statements do not mean that human beings should be cruel to animals or destroy them in a reckless and wanton way. The Bible also says, "Whoever is righteous has regard for the life of his beast" (Prov. 12:10). But they do mean that we should not allow important and economically beneficial development projects to be hindered or stopped simply because they might disrupt the homes of some turtles, snails, or fish, as often happens in the United States and other developed countries.[54]

The correct approach is to weigh the costs and benefits of a development project. If it will help human beings but harm some part of nature, some value must be assigned to both the benefit and the cost, and then a decision can be made. Often a market-based approach is helpful, asking both those who want to preserve an untouched area and those who want to develop it how much they are willing to pay for their preference to be enacted. It is not a proper approach to simply say we should *never* interfere with some animal or plant. God deems us to be much more valuable than they are, and has given us "dominion" (Gen. 1:26; Ps. 8:6) over all the earth, both to preserve it and to use its resources wisely.

By contrast, if a culture believes that the earth is more important than human beings, or that all living beings are equally as important as human beings, then economic development will be hindered and poverty perpetuated. This happened, for example, in India in past

---

[54]See examples in Grudem, *Politics*, 326–29.

years, when huge portions of the grain production each year were destroyed because of Hindu beliefs that prohibited the killing of rats that destroyed the stored grain.[55] Another significant hindrance to productivity is the belief in some Native American religions that man is the servant of the earth rather than its master.

13. The society believes that the earth is here for the use and benefit of human beings

The Bible shows that God put human beings on the earth with the intention that they would develop it and make its resources useful. At the very beginning of creation, God told Adam and Eve, "Be fruitful and multiply and fill the earth *and subdue it and have dominion . . .* over every living thing that moves on the earth" (Gen. 1:28). He also told them how they were to care for the garden of Eden in particular; they were "to work it and keep it" (Gen. 2:15).

This responsibility to "subdue" the earth and "have dominion" over it implies that God expected Adam and Eve, and their descendants, to explore and develop the earth's resources in such a way that they would bring benefit to themselves and other human beings.[56] (The Hebrew word *kabash* means "to subdue, dominate, bring into servitude or bondage," and it is used later, for example, in connection with the subduing the land of Canaan so that it would serve and provide for the people of Israel; cf. Num. 32:22, 29; Josh. 18:1).

The responsibility to develop the earth and enjoy its resources continued after Adam and Eve's sin, for even then God told them, "You shall eat the plants of the field" (Gen. 3:18). This was further confirmed when God told Noah after the flood, "Every moving thing that lives shall be food for you" (Gen. 9:3).

Likewise, many years later, David wrote in Psalm 8:

What is man that you are mindful of him . . . ?
You have given him dominion over the works of your hands;
    you have put all things under his feet,

---

[55] In 1976, *Time* magazine could still report, "India's rats are believed to eat or destroy almost half the grain consumed in India—100 million tons. . . . Hence the need for more snakes [who kill the rats]. Curiously, both animals are considered sacred—and thus inviolable in some regions" ("War on Rats," *Time* [May 31, 1976]: 15).

[56] The next six paragraphs are taken from Grudem, *Politics*, 325–26.

all sheep and oxen,
     and also the beasts of the field,
the birds of the heavens, and the fish of the sea,
     whatever passes along the paths of the seas. (Ps. 8:4–8)

In the New Testament, Paul implies that eating meat (a form of subduing the animal kingdom) is morally right, and no one should pass judgment on another person for doing so (see Rom. 14:2–3; 1 Cor. 8:7–13; 1 Tim. 4:4; also Mark 7:19, which says that Jesus "declared all foods clean").

Once again, we must emphasize that these commands to subdue the earth and have dominion over it do not mean that we should use the earth in a wasteful or destructive way, or intentionally treat animals with cruelty. Rather, "whoever is righteous has regard for the life of his beast" (Prov. 12:10). God also told the people of Israel to take care to protect fruit trees during a time of war (see Deut. 20:19–20). In addition, the command, "You shall love your neighbor as yourself" (Matt. 22:39), implies a responsibility to think of the needs of other human beings, even those who will come in future generations. Therefore, we should use the resources of the earth wisely, as good stewards, not wastefully or abusively. But we should do this eagerly, with the knowledge that the earth has been created by God for our benefit. The earth's purpose is to serve the well-being of the human race.

This cultural belief is crucial for economic development. Landes notes that in the Industrial Revolution, one of the key factors was "the Judeo-Christian subordination of nature to man." He writes:

> This is a sharp departure from widespread animistic beliefs and practices that saw something of the divine in every tree and stream. . . . Ecologists today might think these animistic beliefs preferable to what replaced them, but no one was listening to pagan nature worshippers in Christian Europe.[57]

14. The society believes that economic development is a good thing and shows the excellence of the earth

Sometimes a culture promotes beliefs that oppose economic development, such as the "spiritual"-sounding idea that making more products

---

[57] Landes, *Wealth and Poverty*, 58–59.

from the earth is mere "materialism" or wrongfully promotes "greed." Sometimes people think economic development is wrong because they hold animistic religious ideas and are afraid to disrupt the religious spirits that they believe are inhabiting the earth, the soil, plants, and animals. A similar fear is expressed by modern environmentalists, who argue that development projects might upset the ecological balance in a region or might use up an important natural resource.

But an economically productive culture that is moving from poverty toward greater prosperity will have a different view. It will believe that wise development of the earth's resources for human benefit is a good thing and that it demonstrates the excellence of the earth and all its resources.

This second view is certainly the perspective of the Bible. Of course, the Bible affirms that "the earth is the LORD's and the fullness thereof" (Ps. 24:1), but it also says that he has given it to us as stewards and he expects us to develop its resources: "Be fruitful and multiply and fill the earth and *subdue* it and *have dominion*" (Gen. 1:28). Also, "The heavens are the LORD's heavens, but the earth he has given to the children of man" (Ps. 115:16).

Therefore, what Paul says about various kinds of foods (which come from the earth) can also be applied to other products made from the earth: "For *everything* created by God is good, and nothing is to be rejected if it is received with thanksgiving, for it is made holy by the word of God and prayer" (1 Tim. 4:4–5).

This means that a productive culture, one that is following biblical values, will welcome with joy the development of new products (such as computers and cell phones), better crops, new materials for making durable clothing, or higher-quality homes and other buildings. A growing economy will not hinder and criticize but will encourage the development of these and many thousands of other products from the earth.

In general, when a culture believes that economic development is a good thing, the people in that culture will view economic development with joy and with moral approval. This value, then, will provide the society with a tremendous incentive for economic growth and for moving from poverty toward increasing prosperity.

15. The society believes that the earth's resources will never be exhausted

If a culture worries that the earth soon will run out of productive land to grow food or of other resources, such as trees, water, or oil and natural gas, then it will become paralyzed by a fear of developing these things, and this fear will hinder its economic development.

In fact, it is highly unlikely that any resources will be used up in the foreseeable future (as one of us has argued elsewhere with reference to extensive studies of the earth's resources).[58] One reason for this conclusion is that we keep discovering huge new reserves of resources and inventing more creative ways to access them (such as the phenomenal rise in the known quantities of U.S. oil and natural gas available for development in the last fifty years).[59]

Another reason resources are unlikely to be used up is that human ingenuity gives us the ability to develop substitutes if any particular resource becomes more scarce. For instance, in countries where fresh water supplies are limited, desalination of seawater has become more and more economical, and is being much more widely used. Although desalination is still somewhat more expensive than using fresh water, the cost is not prohibitive. To take another example, when the price of oil increases, it becomes more economical to substitute natural gas, nuclear power, or other sources of energy.

The remarkable discoveries of new sources and massive supplies of energy are not surprising in light of the Bible's teachings, which remind us that when God created the earth he saw that "it was very good" (Gen. 1:31). He wanted human beings to develop its resources and make them useful (see Gen. 1:28). The New Testament says that God "richly provides us with everything to enjoy" (1 Tim. 6:17). *hope*

Given the earth's abundance, and the remarkable human ingenuity that develops substitutes whenever a resource becomes scarce, it is not

---

[58] See Grudem, *Politics*, 320–86.
[59] See E. Calvin Beisner, *Where Garden Meets Wilderness: Evangelical Entry into the Environmental Debate* (Grand Rapids: Eerdmans and Acton Institute, 1997), 63–64. See also Julian Simon, *The Ultimate Resource 2* (Princeton: Princeton University Press, 1996), esp. chapter 11, "When Will We Run Out of Oil? Never!" 162–81; Julian Simon, ed., *The State of Humanity* (Oxford, UK, and Cambridge, MA: Blackwell, 1995), 280–293; Bjorn Lomborg, *The Skeptical Environmentalist* (Cambridge: Cambridge University Press, 2001), 118–36. These books also provide helpful overviews of the state of natural resources more generally in the earth.

wrong to think that the earth's resources, for all practical purposes, will never be exhausted.

16. The society believes that the earth is orderly and subject to rational investigation

If a society believes that the earth is controlled by invisible spirits or that events are subject to unpredictable and uncontrollable fate, it will have little incentive for investigation of the earth and development of new products from its resources.

But if a society believes that the earth is orderly and predictable, and therefore subject to rational investigation, this will provide a positive incentive for some people to work at large-scale inventions and for millions of others to "tinker" with small improvements in the way products are made and processed. Such a culture of inventiveness will lead to increasing economic development as a country moves from poverty to prosperity.[60]

This is consistent with a Christian worldview, which is illustrated in Psalm 111:2: "Great are the works of the LORD, studied by all who delight in them." This verse (which was inscribed in Latin over the archway to the main scientific laboratory at Cambridge University in England for many years) indicates a belief that God is pleased when human beings study and investigate the earth's resources, learn from them, and therefore develop them in ways that are useful for mankind.

Landes says that the Industrial Revolution began first in Britain and then spread to much of Northern Europe because of a widespread agreement on how intellectual knowledge would progress: (1) intellectual inquiry would be "autonomous" (free from both superstition and church dogma); (2) it would take shape in a recognized "adversarial method" by which discoveries could be proved and understood; and (3) people would support the "routinization" of methods of research and the spread of knowledge.[61]

---

[60] Miller and Guthrie, *Discipling Nations*, 95–119, have a very helpful discussion of the Christian view that God is rational and therefore he wants us to investigate the world with the use of our rational minds. Miller and Guthrie contrast this idea with non-Christian views that do not lead to a similar emphasis on developing and creating useful products from the earth.
[61] See Landes, *Wealth and Poverty*, 201–6.

Landes notes, by contrast, that in the Islamic world, medical knowledge, for example, fell farther and farther behind what was happening in Northern Europe. This was because scientists in Muslim countries were unwilling to read and learn from European scientific research, but continued reading the same Muslim scientific books over and over again.[62]

17. The society believes that the earth is a place of opportunity

If a society believes that developing the earth's resources is morally right and in fact is approved by God (as evidenced by Gen. 1:28; Ps. 8:6–9; 24:1), then people will think of the world as a place of opportunity, where hard work and inventiveness will lead to further discoveries of beneficial uses of the earth's resources.

By contrast, in some primitive societies, the world is viewed primarily as a place of danger. People are unwilling to take risks because something bad might happen. In these places, economic development is viewed with fear and even moral condemnation, because change is more likely to bring harmful results than helpful ones.

F. Beliefs about time and change

18. The society believes that time is linear, and therefore there is hope for improvement in the lives of human beings and nations

Hope is an important factor in a culture's progress from poverty toward prosperity. If a culture views time as linear (that is, that history moves forward in a sort of "line" so that progress can be made), it has hope for improvement. A linear view of time bolsters hope that individual lives, as well as entire nations and their economies, can be made better.

On the other hand, if a culture believes that time is circular and repetitive (so that the same things happen again and again, year after year, with no progress), then it tends to think that there is no hope for life in general or for the nation to improve. The things that happened in the past will merely occur again.[63]

---

[62] See ibid., 203, 550n10.

[63] Miller and Guthrie, *Discipling Nations*, 272–79, have a very helpful discussion of a Christian view of time in contrast to animist and secular views of time.

The entire structure of the Bible argues for a linear approach to history. The Bible starts with a beginning at creation (in the book of Genesis) and moves forward to a conclusion that predicts a final judgment and a glorious future (in the book of Revelation).

Jesus also implied a linear view of time in which God's purposes progress toward a goal and his influence on the earth increases. For example, he told a parable of a mustard seed that grew to become a large tree:

> He put another parable before them, saying, "The kingdom of heaven is like a grain of mustard seed that a man took and sowed in his field. It is the smallest of all seeds, but when it has grown it is larger than all the garden plants and becomes a tree, so that the birds of the air come and make nests in its branches." (Matt. 13:31–32)

The apostle Paul also taught that history is moving forward toward a culmination in a final judgment. He told the pagan Greek philosophers in Athens that God "has fixed a day on which he will judge the world in righteousness by a man whom he has appointed" (Acts 17:31).

Landes says that the linear view of time was one of the crucial factors that led to a joy in discovering new and better ways of doing things, and a widespread cultivation of invention. He summarizes the European view of time as follows:

> [One reason for the European joy in invention and discovery was] the Judeo-Christian sense of linear time. Other societies thought of time as cyclical, returning to earlier stages and starting over again. Linear time is progressive or regressive, moving on to better things or declining from some earlier, happier state. For Europeans in our period, the progressive view prevailed.[64]

19. The society believes that time is a valuable resource and should be used wisely

This cultural belief is related to the previous one. If history moves forward and circumstances become better or worse, then people naturally sense a responsibility to use their time in a positive way, hoping

---

[64] Landes, *Wealth and Poverty*, 59.

to make their circumstances better. This is consistent with the teaching of the New Testament: "Look carefully then how you walk, not as unwise but as wise, *making the best use of the time*, because the days are evil" (Eph. 5:15–16).

By contrast, unproductive societies that remain in poverty often view time not as something valuable but as something to be endured, or as something to be used for seeking immediate pleasure and comfort.

Landes says that Protestant Northern Europe placed a much higher value on the use of time than other parts of the world. The use of clocks and watches "was far more advanced in Britain and Holland then in Catholic countries."[65] This led these countries to be more productive.

The high value given to time and to saving time was most evident in Britain:

> The British were in the eighteenth century the world's leading producers and consumers of time keepers, in the country as in the city. . . . The coaching services reflected this temporal sensibility: schedules to the minute, widely advertised; closely calculated arrival times and transfers; drivers checked by sealed clocks; speed over comfort; lots of dead horses.[66]

20. The society manifests a widespread desire to improve on life—to do better, to innovate, and to become more productive

This desire to improve and to do things better than they have been done before is reflected to some degree in the New Testament. Paul writes, "Whoever sows sparingly will also reap sparingly, and whoever sows bountifully will also reap bountifully" (2 Cor. 9:6). Certainly the basic command to "subdue" the earth (Gen. 1:28) implies a desire to learn more and more about it, to innovate, to invent, and to improve the products that are being made. As we noted above, Landes sees this desire to invent and improve as a major factor in the Industrial Revolution in Northern Europe.

By contrast, a cultural desire to improve on life was, for the most part, lacking in a country such as India, which never developed

---

[65] Ibid., 178.
[66] Ibid., 224.

economically as Northern Europe did. "No one seems to have had a passionate interest in simplifying and easing tasks. Both worker and employer saw hard labor as the worker's lot—and as appropriate."[67]

21. The society is open to change, and the people therefore work to solve problems and make things better

This cultural value is related to the previous three. If time is linear and there is hope for improvement in life; if time is a valuable resource and should be used wisely; and if people have a desire to improve, then there will be a natural openness to change and hope that problems can be solved so that life can be improved. In a culture with this belief, people will be eager to work to make things better and will take risks to solve problems because they have hope that human effort can change the history of a family, a factory, a city, or even a nation.

By contrast, a society that has a fear of change or new ideas, and simply clings to traditions or cultural habits that may be harmful or may hinder productivity, will find economic progress hard to achieve. People in such a society will not work for change as much as they simply complain about circumstances but avoid taking risks. This is because they have little hope for good results and experience frequent despair about life. Such beliefs are more common in tribal societies that are resistant to changing their traditions or in Muslim nations where a fatalistic attitude toward life has taken hold.

In Britain, Landes says, the Industrial Revolution depended on three types of innovation that resulted from people being open to change and working for improvement in the way things were done: (1) the substitution of machines for human skill and effort; (2) the substitution of inanimate sources of power (especially coal) for human and animal power; and (3) the use of new and abundant raw materials in manufacturing.[68] The rapid growth of the cotton industry, the primary force that drove the Industrial Revolution in Britain, was a result of constant learning and teaching of new processes for manufacturing.[69]

In more general terms, Landes says that an ideally productive so-

---

[67] Ibid., 227.
[68] Ibid., 186.
[69] Ibid., 207.

ciety "would value new as against old . . . change and risk as against safety."[70] This vision was embraced in Europe and even more so in the United States, where the innovations brought about by new machines and the development of routine processes in factories were even more pronounced than in Europe.[71]

By contrast, for centuries, while European and American science and technology were marching forward, China remained resistant to any change. Landes quotes various visitors to China as saying that the Chinese "are more fond of the most defective piece of antiquity than of the most perfect of the modern" (see similar quotations in an earlier section, 284–85). Visitors also reported that "any man of genius is paralyzed immediately by the thought that his efforts will win him punishments rather than rewards."[72] Therefore, China "slipped into technological and scientific torpor."[73]

G. Beliefs about work and economic productivity

22. The society honors productive work

A positive view of productive work is an essential value if a society wants to make progress from poverty toward greater prosperity. It is important for people to think of an "ideal" life as one of joyful productivity that benefits both themselves and others. A productive culture values and honors people who continue to work as long as they are willing and able to do so, because as long as people are working they are adding productivity to society. Rather than accepting the false idea that the number of jobs in a society is fixed, the society will believe that the potential for creating new jobs is unlimited due to human creativity and inventiveness in finding new ways to make useful products and services for other people (see discussion, 173–74). These values will be taught to children and represented in the way a society encourages and rewards people in the workplace.

By contrast, in a society that is stuck in poverty, people will view work as a necessary evil, as a decree of fate (as in some Muslim societies), or even as the "just punishment" that is due them for wrongful

---

[70] Ibid., 218.
[71] Ibid., 303.
[72] Ibid., 342.
[73] Ibid., 342

deeds done in previous lives (as in much of Hinduism). In a poor society that is not increasing its productivity, people will think of the "ideal" life as one of ease, in which a person simply enjoys himself and his friends, and never has to work at a productive job. In such a society, people will wrongly believe that the number of jobs in the economy is fixed, which means that still-productive workers will be encouraged to retire early so that "others can have their jobs."

The Bible places a high value on productive work. The book of Proverbs says, "A slack hand causes poverty, but the hand of the diligent makes rich" (Prov. 10:4). Likewise, Paul told the Thessalonian Christians "to work with your hands, as we instructed you . . . and be dependent on no one" (1 Thess. 4:11–12). They were even to "keep away from any brother who is walking in idleness" (2 Thess. 3:6), and were to imitate Paul's example of working "night and day" (v. 8). He even said, "If anyone is not willing to work, let him not eat" (v. 10).

Economic history shows the importance of a society's view of work. We mentioned earlier that Landes emphasizes "the Judeo-Christian respect for manual labor" as another key to the success of the Industrial Revolution in Northern Europe. The emphasis on hard work in the "Protestant Ethic" led to a society in which people were expected to be "rational, ordered, diligent, productive" in their ordinary work.[74]

Historians have argued that Protestant societies were not alone in developing a higher appreciation for work and productivity.[75] It should not surprise us that some other cultures also valued these virtues, since by common grace people generally have a God-given inner sense that it is right to be productive and to attempt to better one's own condition.

For example, while Japan did not have a Protestant Ethic, "its businessmen adopted a similar work ethic," especially because of a Buddhist idea that "through work we are able to obtain Buddhahood [salvation]."[76] Landes also mentions the "work values" and "sense of purpose" that were found in the cultures of South Korea and Taiwan. These were part of the reason for the remarkable economic growth of these countries beginning around 1950.[77]

---

[74] Ibid., 175–77.
[75] See Dierdre McCloskey, *Bourgeois Dignity* (Chicago: University of Chicago Press, 2010).
[76] Landes, *Wealth and Poverty*, 363, quoting a 1982 study by Shichihei Yamamoto; see also 383, 391.
[77] Ibid., 437.

In a country that honors productive work, the quality of work will also matter. A productive society will naturally give higher honor to work of higher quality. One of the reasons for the astounding economic development of Japan was that the Japanese became world leaders in making the highest quality automobiles, photographic equipment, robotics, and other electronic products. The factories in Japan instituted "the world's most effective quality controls,"[78] thus giving high value to the highest quality of work.

Good work habits also matter. They will be inculcated and reinforced by the society. Workers will take pride in being diligent, thrifty, honest, punctual, courteous, faithful in their performance of work, respectful toward authority, cheerful, and proud of their high quality of work.

There are several good historical examples. One of the reasons for the remarkable economic recovery of Germany after World War II was "the energy and work habits of the defeated Germans," who rebuilt their economy on "work, education, determination."[79]

Similarly, the four "Asian tigers" of Southeast Asia that have made such remarkable economic growth in recent years (Taiwan, South Korea, Singapore, and Hong Kong) had as their primary asset "a work ethic that yields high product for low wages."[80] Furthermore, the Chinese who have immigrated into these countries and others in Southeast Asia (such as Malaysia, Thailand, and Indonesia) "cherish a work ethic that would make a Weberian Calvinist envious," and they provide significant economic energy to all of these economies.[81]

It is not surprising that the Bible commends workers who have good work habits rather than poor ones: Paul writes:

> Bondservants, obey in everything those who are your earthly masters, not by way of eye-service, as people-pleasers, but with sincerity of heart, fearing the Lord. Whatever you do, work heartily, as for the Lord and not for men, knowing that from the Lord you will receive the inheritance as your reward. You are serving the Lord Christ. For

---

[78] Ibid., 472; see also 485.
[79] Ibid., 471.
[80] Ibid., 475.
[81] Ibid., 477.

the wrongdoer will be paid back for the wrong he has done, and there is no partiality. (Col. 3:22–25; see also Eph. 6:5–8)

Paul also wants employees "to be well-pleasing, not argumentative, not pilfering, but showing all good faith, so that in everything they may adorn the doctrine of God our Savior" (Titus 2:9–10).

On the other hand, in a country that is trapped in poverty, honor will be given to people who can "game the system" and be paid even while being lazy, wasteful, dishonest, unfaithful to commitments, frequently late, disrespectful, arrogant, discontented, and careless in their work.

23. The society honors economically productive people, companies, inventions, and careers

A society uses various means to honor certain people, companies, inventions, and careers. For example, the "hero stories" that children are told can hold up one kind of person or another, or one kind of career or another, as either good examples to imitate or bad examples to avoid. Movies and television shows in a culture do the same thing, and so does popular music. The moral instruction that children are given in schools and churches provides another way of honoring various people and careers. Teachers in schools can have a huge impact on the kinds of people and careers that students think to be honorable, and the kinds of literature and historical studies that children read in schools also have a significant impact. In addition, the speeches given by governmental leaders and political campaigners have an effect on the kinds of careers and people that are honored in the society.

If a country is going to move from poverty toward greater prosperity, its culture should honor economically productive people who create economic development for different segments of the economy. It should honor entrepreneurs who build small or large companies that provide jobs for many people and produce valuable goods or services for the people in the society. It should honor inventors and innovators, and the things they create. Finally, the culture should honor careers that produce goods and services with economic value.

By contrast, a society that is trapped in poverty will place little or no value on people and careers that create and produce goods and services. Through movies, music, literature, political speeches, and instruction in schools and churches, the society will honor those who get something for nothing, whether through luck, through getting paid without working very hard, by making a lot of money while producing little of value, or by depending on government handouts. It might even honor, through its literature, films, and television programming, those who live by theft and extortion. Such a society will view economically productive people with disdain, guilt, shame, or envy.

On a broader scale, when people in such a society speak of their hope for economic progress in the nation, they will focus mostly on getting grants from the government or aid from other nations. The hope for progress also may be focused on attempts to redistribute income from the rich to the poor in a society rather than on opportunities for the poor to earn money and become wealthy themselves.

Several passages in the Bible give honor to those who are economically productive. Jesus's parable of the talents, for example, honors the servant whose five talents made five talents more and the servant whose two talents made two talents more (see Matt. 25:20–22).

In the Old Testament, God's promises of blessings to the people of Israel, if they were obedient, included abundant agricultural productivity (see Deut. 28:1–14). In Proverbs 31, the ideal wife is portrayed as one whose merchandise is "profitable" (Prov. 31:18). By contrast, the disreputable "sluggard" in Proverbs is one who is lazy and produces very little of value (6:9; 13:4; 20:4).

Once again, in accordance with this biblical pattern, economic history points to the influence of the Protestant Ethic in Northern Europe, one part of which was the honor given to those who were economically productive and successful in the business world.[82]

By contrast, cultural values in India placed a high premium on perpetuating the old tradition of hard manual labor for most of the lower castes. As a result, no one placed much value on innovations that would have made labor easier or would have introduced machines to replace human and animal effort.[83]

---

[82] See ibid., 175–78; see also, on Britain, 234–35.
[83] See ibid., 225–30. However, many Hindus also think it a meritous good deed to help a suffering person.

One reason for the amazing increase in productivity in the United States was a willingness to value change and innovation, as well as standardization of methods of manufacturing and specifications of the goods produced, so that an entire society focused much of its effort on improving methods of production and encouraging continued innovation and change to better and better machines.[84]

A productive society that honors economically productive people, companies, and careers will not focus on the question, "How much more does person A have than person B?" (for such a question produces envy and resentment). Rather, it will focus on the questions, "How much has person A contributed to the economic well-being of society?" and, "Has person A earned his money by legal means?" The emphasis in a productive society will be on productivity, not equality.

24. The society's business owners and workers view their companies primarily as means of providing customers with things of value, for which they will then be paid according to that value

If productivity is going to increase in a society, and if individual businesses are going to succeed over the long run, then business owners and workers have to provide products that customers genuinely believe to be valuable for them. Price, quality, and service must be the ongoing areas of focus. This can happen only when owners and workers alike are constantly focusing on delivering products of genuine value to their customers.

This, of course, is the attitude that results if people genuinely internalize the "Golden Rule" that Jesus taught: "So whatever you wish that others would do to you, do also to them, for this is the Law and the Prophets" (Matt. 7:12). This is also the attitude that results from obedience to Jesus's commandment, "You shall love your neighbor as yourself" (Matt. 22:39).

By contrast, a society that is trapped in poverty will reveal a very different attitude among business owners and employees. The owners will view their businesses primarily as means of getting money from people, by whatever method possible, even if it means selling cheap, defective, and inferior products. Workers will see their primary goal

---

[84] See ibid., 297–305.

as getting paid rather than producing work that brings genuine value to their companies and customers. This short-sighted "selfishness" will hinder economic productivity.

25. The society places a high value on saving in contrast to spending

One of the significant factors in the Protestant Ethic that contributed so much to economic development in Britain, Northern Europe, and the United States was an emphasis on thrift and frugality, coupled with a teaching that one should not spend money excessively on oneself. A belief in thrift and frugality will lead to higher rates of giving as well as to higher rates of saving.[85]

But does the Bible teach that it is right for people to save a reasonable amount of money for the future? This idea can be supported by the teaching that people are to work so as to support themselves and not depend on others to support them (see 1 Thess. 4:11–12; 2 Thess. 3:6–12). But if most everyone will grow old to the point where they are physically unable to work and support themselves, then it is wise for them to lay up some savings for that future time, so that they do not become dependent on their families and others in old age.

H. Beliefs about buying and selling

26. The society believes that mutual gains come from voluntary exchanges, and therefore a business deal is "good" if it brings benefits to both buyer and seller

If a society is going to grow from poverty toward greater productivity and prosperity, then it is important that people understand the amazing creation of value that occurs as a result of voluntary buying and selling in the marketplace. The society must realize that buying and selling are normally not situations of exploitation of one person by another, but rather win-win transactions in which both buyer and seller end up better off than they were before.

The sale of a loaf of bread is a simple example. If it costs the baker $3 in materials to make a loaf of bread, and he sells it to me for $4,

---

[85] See ibid., 175.

we both think we are better off after the sale. I think I am better off because I wanted the loaf of bread more than I wanted my $4. Otherwise, I would not have traded the money for the bread. But the baker thinks he is better off because he wanted my $4 more than he wanted that loaf of bread (which would grow stale by the next day). Otherwise, he would not have traded the bread for the money. I am better off and he is better off.

This is the wonder of voluntary exchanges in a free market. A society that understands this simple concept will have a positive view of business transactions, and people will enjoy doing business with one another because both parties end up better off. Buyers and sellers will be happy not only for the value that they *derive* from a transaction, but also for the fact that they *give* some value, that the business transaction is a "good deal" to the other person as well. Another benefit of this cultural attitude is that companies will value long-term business relationships with their customers.

Similarly, this win-win perspective will apply to employer and employee relationships. Employers will recognize that their businesses are better off after employees have done a good day's work. They can be happy for this. But employees will also recognize that they are better off after getting paid for a day's work, because they will have more money than they had before. Most employers and employees, then, can think of their relationship as a win-win relationship.

We believe the Bible supports such a win-win viewpoint. Buyers and sellers, and employers and employees, can all think of themselves as fulfilling the Golden Rule through their business relationships. Business transactions can be thought of as one way of loving one's neighbor as oneself.[86]

By contrast, if a society does not have this kind of attitude, then suspicion and mistrust will proliferate. The society will believe that businesses generally "win" and customers and employees generally "lose" in voluntary exchanges in the marketplace. Also, people will quibble endlessly before making business agreements, because they suspect that business deals generally have a "winner" and a "loser"

---

[86] See a discussion of this viewpoint in Wayne Grudem, *Business for the Glory of God* (Wheaton: Crossway, 2003).

rather than two winners. In such a society, companies will place a low value on developing long-term business relationships or long-term employee relationships, and customers and employees will simply look for every opportunity to defraud businesses or to get paid without doing high-quality work that is worthy of the pay they are receiving.

One of the reasons why China stagnated economically for several centuries was that beginning in the 1430s, a form of Confucianism came to dominance: "Mandarins who scorned and distrusted commerce."[87] As it was then, so it is today: an attitude of hostility toward business tends to hinder economic productivity and keep a nation trapped in poverty.

I. Beliefs about knowledge and education

27. The society values knowledge from any source and makes it widely available

In productive societies, useful knowledge that comes from people of any national, religious, or ethnic group is held to be valuable and is widely disseminated through a society. For example, in Northern Europe during the Industrial Revolution, knowledge about new machinery and sources of power (such as the steam engine) spread rapidly from one nation to another. But the Roman Catholic countries of Southern Europe distrusted many of the discoveries coming from the "Protestant" countries, and so, during the Inquisition, they prohibited the importation of books that were not first approved by Roman Catholic Church authorities. Similarly, Muslim countries fell far behind other countries in technological and scientific development because they would not accept or even allow into their countries the new discoveries that were made by the "Christian" nations or by Jewish experts in various fields.

The Bible places a high value on acquiring knowledge: "The fear of the LORD is the beginning of knowledge; fools despise wisdom and instruction" (Prov. 1:7). A little later in Proverbs, we read that Wisdom says, "Take my *instruction* instead of silver, and *knowledge* rather than choice gold" (8:10).

---

[87] Landes, *Wealth and Poverty*, 95.

Jesus teaches that the Devil disregards the truth: he "has nothing to do with the truth, because there is no truth in him" (John 8:44).

In an ideal economically productive society, knowledge will be important. The society will know how "to operate, manage, and build the instruments of production," and also how "to create, adapt, and master new techniques on the technological frontier." In addition, the society will be "able to impart this knowledge and know-how to the young."[88] (We discussed the value of compulsory universal education of children in chapter 7, 253–56.)

By contrast, sadly, Middle Eastern Islamic societies have a cultural attitude toward knowledge and education that continues to hinder economic development. The culture "continues to mistrust or reject new techniques and ideas that come from the enemy West (Christendom)."[89]

28. The society values a highly trained workforce

This cultural value follows from the previous one. As an economy grows toward greater prosperity, the higher-value products often will be technologically complex ones, such as medical and scientific equipment, electronic devices, complex transportation systems, computer programs, and financial services. For such industries, knowledge eventually will become the key to even greater economic development.

Landes traces various ways in which the growth of technical and scientific knowledge brought wave after wave of economic development to Britain and then to other European countries, such as Germany, which imitated and then in some areas surpassed Britain in knowledge.[90] Highly trained and skilled craftsmen and technological workers proved increasingly valuable in industrial production.

By contrast, the nations in South America did not attract or keep highly trained and skilled workers in sufficient numbers during the eighteenth to twentieth centuries. For example, Argentina had an abundance of productive land and good climate, but it lacked skilled craftsmen, tools, and the ability to develop industrial production.[91] And because of the dominance of the Roman Catholic Church in Latin

---

[88] Ibid., 217.
[89] Ibid., 410–11.
[90] See ibid., 276–85.
[91] Ibid., 315–16.

American countries, for many years most Northern Europeans and North Americans (mainly Protestants and some Jews) were excluded, and their knowledge and skills were excluded, too.[92]

29. The society assumes that there must be a rational basis for knowledge and recognized channels for spreading and testing knowledge

If a society is going to escape from poverty and grow toward prosperity, it must overcome old superstitions, folklore, and mythology about the natural world. It must adopt a widely accepted method for reaching conclusions about nature.

In the Industrial Revolution in Britain and the rest of Northern Europe, an important factor was the widespread acceptance of the scientific method, which gained knowledge by purposeful experiments that could be repeated by others and thereby verified or disproved. Discoveries about nature were widely reported in established journals, and new theories could be disputed and tested again and again.[93]

Acceptance of such a rational, verifiable process for knowing about the world is important in poor nations today if they are going to overcome traditional methods of agriculture, for instance, or adapt new tools and machinery in factories. But many nations resist this rational basis for knowledge.

For example, Haiti retains a widespread belief in voodoo as the controlling force in nature and as a way to get people and objects to do things.[94] Likewise, in previous centuries, many Islamic nations routinely rejected reports of discoveries in science or technology that came from outside the Islamic world, and they even prohibited or destroyed books that came from other sources, thus guaranteeing that they would stagnate economically and remain largely trapped in poverty.[95]

China faced similar obstacles. Although the Chinese were responsible for a long list of inventions that should have contributed to centuries of economic development, China had no established means of

---

[92] Ibid., 317. Latin American countries today admit people from all religious backgrounds.
[93] Ibid., 200–10.
[94] Harrison, *Central Liberal Truth*, 29–31.
[95] See Landes, *Wealth and Poverty*, 54.

testing and transmitting new knowledge to other areas of the country and to successive generations. The problem was a government that was totalitarian, monopolizing knowledge simply for the purpose of maintaining its hold on power. As a result, no one had any incentive to develop and promote new methods of manufacturing or new machines. The government controlled everything and prevented ordinary people from advancing economically in any significant way.[96]

Similarly, one reason why India failed for so long to advance economically was the lack of an agreed-upon rational basis for knowledge and for disseminating and testing reports of discoveries and information. In India in the eighteenth century, "There had been no marked progress in scientific knowledge for many centuries, and the intellectual apparatus for a diffusion and systematic recording of the inherited skills was seriously defective."[97]

J. Beliefs about humility and the value of learning from others

30. The society demonstrates a humble willingness to learn from other people, other nations, and members of other religions

One of the tragedies of the history of economic development is that many nations, for one reason or another, systematically excluded knowledge that they could have learned from other nations that had made new discoveries.

For example, as we explained earlier, Spain and Portugal, during the period of the Inquisition, made a great mistake—they excluded knowledge they could have learned from nations that were not Roman Catholic, and especially from Protestant and Jewish inventors and scientists (see 286–90).

China made a similar mistake. In 1551, the country made it a crime for anyone in China to go to sea on a multimasted ship, thus closing the nation to the possibility of learning from the remarkable discoveries and advances in manufacturing that were about to take place in Europe. This closure of the nation, sadly, "set them, complacent and stubborn, against the lessons and novelties that European travelers

---

[96] See ibid., 55–57.
[97] Ibid., 229, quoting K. N. Chaudhuri, *The Trading World of Asia and the English East India Company 1660–1760* (Cambridge: Cambridge University Press, 1978), 273–74.

would soon be bringing." Though Europeans were traveling to China, for centuries there were "no Chinese vessels in the harbors of Europe. . . . The first such vessel . . . visited London for the Great Exhibition of 1851." When the Chinese eventually did travel, "they went to show themselves, not to see and learn; to bestow their presence, not to stay. . . . They were what they were and did not have to change."[98] Northern Europe far outdistanced China in economic growth because, "unlike China, Europe was a learner" and was eager to adopt knowledge from any country in which it could be found.[99]

Fortunately for China, such prior attitudes changed in the late twentieth century, and today China is eagerly adopting (regretfully, even stealing!) ideas and technology from other nations.

Japan offers perhaps the most remarkable example of significant economic development because of a willingness to learn from other nations. When Europeans initially came to Japan in the mid-sixteenth century, they "got a much warmer greeting than they had received in China," and "when the Japanese encountered the Europeans, they went about learning their ways."[100] Unfortunately, in 1612, the Japanese Emperor Tokugawa Ieyasu banned the Christian religion, and hundreds of thousands were put to death. Soon, Japan closed itself to outside influence, and this significantly hindered its economic development.[101] Economic growth was stalled until the Meiji Restoration in 1867–1868.

After World War II, Japan once again began to prosper by humbly learning from and then imitating the best manufacturing processes from European and American examples. The Japanese learned how to make automobiles better than the Americans, and learned how to make better high-tech products, such as cameras and precision machinery and instruments. They learned these things by sending representatives "to visit western lands and humbly learn by watching and asking, photographing and tape-recording."[102] Soon they were doing nearly everything better than those they were imitating.

---

[98] Landes, *Wealth and Poverty*, 96. See also 335–49.
[99] Ibid., 348.
[100] Ibid., 351–53.
[101] Ibid., 355–56.
[102] Ibid., 472.

K. Beliefs about government

31. The society believes that the purpose of government is to serve the nation and bring benefit to the people as a whole

This cultural belief is immensely important. What a culture believes about the purpose of government affects everything else we say in this book about the laws and policies that a government should enact, because it determines whether government officials make decisions for the good of the nation or for their own personal benefit.

If the cultural values in a society encourage people to think that government work and government power are rightfully used to enrich oneself and to give privileges and income to one's family and friends, then the decisions of the government will not be for the good of the nation but for the good of the rulers. The Bible warns about this in several places, as we explained in chapter 7 (see 223–29).

The Bible also gives some examples of good rulers who served not primarily for their own benefit but for the benefit of the people. Moses was such an example, for in the middle of a conflict with Dathan and Abiram, Moses said to God, "I have not taken one donkey from them, and I have not harmed one of them" (Num. 16:15). Similarly, Samuel, at the end of his term as judge over Israel, proclaimed that he was innocent of using his office for personal gain (1 Sam. 12:3–4).

If a society gives widespread assent to the values found in these biblical passages, then it will also be in agreement with Romans 13:4, which says that the governmental authority "is God's servant *for your good*." When a society truly believes this, then serving in government will be an honor, even if it comes with some personal sacrifice.

The importance of this belief cannot be overemphasized. The cultural value that the purpose of government is to serve and bring benefit to the people as a whole will likely serve as the single greatest deterrent against corruption in government.

Where this belief is established, people will be convinced that government power and jobs are primarily ways to serve the country and to do good for the society as a whole. Then they will truly seek policies that promote the economic growth of the nation.

But where officials believe that government jobs are merely a means to enrich themselves and their family and friends, the nation will tend to tolerate high levels of corruption and bribery. This belief will also lead, in many cases, to a kind of "crony capitalism" or an "oligarchic capitalism" in which a small number of very wealthy families are intertwined in close friendships with highly placed government officials, and the government officials will continue to enact policies and distort laws so that their wealthy friends benefit. Then, of course, the wealthy friends will also funnel money back to the highly placed government officials. In such a case, there is little hope for genuine economic growth in the nation as a whole, and almost no hope that the vast majority of people, who are trapped in poverty, will ever make any economic progress. All this goes back to a culture's beliefs about the purpose of government and government jobs.

32. The society believes that government should punish evil and promote good

We explained above that it is the responsibility of government to punish crime and to protect people from the greedy and powerful who would wrongly take advantage of them (see 239–41). In other words, government is to do what Peter says: "To punish those who do evil and to praise those who do good" (1 Peter 2:14).

This cultural value is important so that government officials do not begin showing favoritism to evildoers who happen to be their friends or who might give them bribes.

L. Beliefs about the nation itself

33. The society values patriotism and reinforces a shared sense of national identity and purpose

One of the benefits that gave Britain a great economic advantage in the Industrial Revolution was that it was "a self-conscious self-aware unit characterized by common identity and loyalty and by equality of civil status."[103] The nation as a whole had a "collective synergy" in which "the whole is more than the sum of the parts."[104]

Japan, similarly, had a strong sense of patriotism that began to contribute positively to economic development in the late 1800s.

---

[103] Ibid., 219.
[104] Ibid.

Widespread general education instilled in children a respect for (even adoration of) the emperor, and this served to establish a strong national identity. In addition, universal military service "nurtured nationalist pride."[105] A sense of patriotism encouraged every Japanese citizen to exercise personal discipline in daily life and to "fully discharge one's responsibility on the job."[106]

Such a sense of patriotism seems to us to be consistent with biblical values. Because any nation can have rulers who are evil, a Christian view of government should never endorse a kind of "blind patriotism," according to which a citizen must never criticize a country or its leaders. In fact, a genuine patriotism, which always seeks to promote the good of the nation, promotes honest criticism of the government and its leaders when they do things contrary to biblical moral standards.[107] It also drives criticism of the cultural traditions and values of a nation when they run contrary to biblical values.

But is patriotism actually a virtue at all? The Bible supports a genuine kind of patriotism in which citizens love, support, and defend their own country.

a. Biblical reasons for patriotism

Biblical support for the idea of patriotism begins with a recognition that God has established nations on the earth. Speaking in Athens, Paul said that God "made from one man every *nation* of mankind to live on all the face of the earth, having determined allotted periods and the boundaries of their dwelling place" (Acts 17:26).

One example of this establishment of nations is found in God's promise to make the descendants of Abram (later Abraham) into a distinct nation: "And I will make of you a great *nation*, and I will bless you and make your name great, so that you will be a blessing" (Gen. 12:2). Later, God says to Abraham, "In your offspring shall *all the nations* of the earth be blessed" (Gen. 22:18).

The ancient origin of many nations on earth is recorded in the Table of Nations descended from Noah in Genesis 10, which concludes,

---

[105] Ibid., 376.
[106] Ibid., 383.
[107] This paragraph and the remainder of this section on patriotism (000–000) are adapted from Grudem, *Politics*, 109–12.

"These are the clans of the sons of Noah, according to their genealogies, *in their nations*, and from these the nations spread abroad on the earth after the flood" (v. 32). In the ongoing progress of history, Job says that God "*makes nations great*, and he destroys them; he enlarges nations, and leads them away" (Job 12:23).

The meaning of the word *nation* as it is used in the Bible is not different in any substantial way from the meaning we attach to it today—a group of people, living under one government, that is sovereign and independent in its relationship to other nations. The existence of many independent nations on the earth, then, should be considered a blessing from God.

One benefit of the existence of nations is that they divide and disperse government power throughout the earth. In this way, they prevent the rule of any one worldwide dictator, which would be more horrible than any single evil government, both because it would affect everyone on earth and because there would be no other nation that could challenge it. History has shown repeatedly that rulers with unchecked and unlimited power become more and more corrupt.

The Bible also teaches Christians to obey and honor the leaders of the nations in which they live. Peter tells Christians to "honor the emperor" (1 Peter 2:17), and he also says, "Be subject for the Lord's sake to every human institution, whether it be to the emperor as supreme, or to governors" (vv. 13–14).

Paul likewise encourages not only obedience but also honor and appreciation for civil rulers: "Let every person be subject to the governing authorities" (Rom. 13:1). He also says that the ruler is "God's servant for your good" (v. 4). He concludes this section by implying that Christians should not only pay taxes but also give respect and honor, at least in some measure, to rulers in civil government: "Pay to all what is owed to them: taxes to whom taxes are owed, revenue to whom revenue is owed, *respect to whom respect is owed, honor to whom honor is owed*" (v. 7).

These commands follow a pattern found in the Old Testament as well, as the following verses indicate:

My son, fear the LORD and the king, and do not join with those who do otherwise. (Prov. 24:21)

> Even in your thoughts, do not curse the king, nor in your bedroom curse the rich. (Eccl. 10:20)

> Thus says the LORD of hosts, the God of Israel, to all the exiles whom I have sent into exile from Jerusalem to Babylon. . . . Seek the welfare of the city where I have sent you into exile, and pray to the LORD on its behalf, for in its welfare you will find your welfare. (Jer. 29:4–7)

God's establishment of individual nations, the benefits that come to the world from the existence of nations, and the biblical commands that imply that people should give appreciation and support to the government leaders where they live all tend to support the idea of patriotism in a nation.

b. Aspects of patriotism

With these factors in mind, we would define genuine patriotism more fully as including the following factors:

(1) *A sense of belonging to a larger community of people.* This sense provides one aspect of a person's sense of identity and obligation to others.

(2) *Gratitude for the benefits that a nation provides.* These might include the protection of life, liberty, and property, the existence of laws to deter wrongdoing and encourage good, the establishment of a monetary system and economic markets, and the establishment of a common language or languages.

(3) *A shared sense of pride in the achievements of other individuals to whom one "belongs" as a fellow citizen of the same nation.* This might include pride in athletic, scientific, economic, artistic, philanthropic, or other endeavors.

(4) *A sense of pride for the good things that a nation has done.* This sense is developed by a proper understanding of the nation's history and a sense of belonging to a group of people that includes previous generations within that nation.

(5) *A sense of security with respect to the future.* This sense develops because of an expectation that the larger group—that is, everyone in the nation—is working for the good of the nation and therefore will defend each person in the nation from attacks by violent evildoers, whether from within or outside its borders.

(6) *A sense of obligation to serve the nation and do good for it in various ways.* These ways might include defending it from military attack or from unfair criticism by others, protecting the existence and character of the nation for future generations, and improving the nation in various ways where possible, even through helpful criticism of things that are done wrong within the nation.

(7) *A sense of obligation to live by and to transmit to newcomers and succeeding generations a shared sense of moral values and standards that are widely valued by those within the nation.*[108] Such a sense of obligation to shared moral standards is more likely to happen within a nation than within the world as a whole, because a person can act as a moral agent and be evaluated by others within the context of an entire nation, but very seldom does anyone have enough prominence to act with respect to the entire world. Also, while values and standards can readily spread to most of the citizens of one nation (especially where most speak a common language), the world is so large and diverse that it is difficult to find many moral values and standards that are shared throughout all nations, or any awareness in one nation of what values are held in other nations. If such moral values and national ideals are to be preserved and transmitted within a nation, it is usually necessary for the citizens to share a common sense of the origins of the nation and its history.

By contrast, the opposite of patriotism is an attitude of dislike or even scorn or hatred for one's nation, accompanied by continual criticism of it. Rather than sharing in gratitude for the benefits provided by the country and pride in the good things it has done, those opposed to patriotism will repeatedly emphasize negative aspects of the country's actions, no matter how ancient or how minor compared with the whole of its history. They will not be proud of the nation or its history, and they will not be very willing to sacrifice for it, to serve it, or to protect and defend it. Such anti-patriotic attitudes will continually erode the ability of the nation to function effectively and will eventually tend to undermine the very existence of the nation itself. In such cases, a healthy but limited criticism of the wrongs of a na-

---

[108] Christians, of course, will be able to affirm only those values that are consistent with a biblical worldview.

tion becomes exaggerated to the point where reality is distorted and a person becomes basically opposed to the good of the nation in general.

To take a modern example, a patriotic citizen of Iran in 2013 might well say, "I love my country and its great traditions, ideals, and history, but I'm deeply saddened by the oppressive and evil nature of the current totalitarian government." A patriotic citizen of North Korea might say something similar. A patriotic citizen of Iraq under the regime of Saddam Hussein might have said similar things as well.

To take another example, a patriotic citizen of Germany might say, "I love my nation and I'm proud of its great historical achievements in science, literature, music, and many other areas of human thought, though I am deeply grieved by the evils perpetrated under the leadership of Adolf Hitler, and I am glad that we were finally liberated from his oppressive rule."

These examples illustrate that even citizens of countries with evil rulers can retain a genuine patriotism that is combined with sober and truthful criticism of current or past leaders. But such patriotism still includes the valuable components mentioned above, such as a sense of belonging to a particular nation, gratitude for the benefits it gives, shared pride in its achievements, a sense of security, a sense of obligation to serve and protect it (and hopefully to change any evil leadership), and a sense of obligation to follow and transmit shared values and ideals that represent the best of the country's history.

If such things can be true of even nations with bad governments, then certainly patriotism can be a value inculcated in all the other nations of the world as well. In this sense, a Christian view of government encourages and supports genuine patriotism within a nation.

M. Beliefs about economic, relational, and spiritual values

34. The society counts family, friends, and joy in life as more important than material wealth

Because this book has focused on solving the problem of poverty in poor nations, its emphasis has been on economic issues and growth in material prosperity. But we must also emphasize that financial well-being is never presented as the ultimate goal in life, according to the Bible. Other things are more important, especially relationships with family members, friends, and other people, and one's relationship with God (see the next section).

In the Ten Commandments, the fifth commandment says, "Honor your father and your mother" (Ex. 20:12). Here God establishes and protects the importance of maintaining strong relationships that include honor and respect within a family. Other Bible passages give instructions on how to maintain a healthy marriage and how parents should care for and discipline their children (see Eph. 5:22–6:4; Col. 3:18–21).

In addition, Jesus said that the second greatest commandment is, "You shall love your neighbor as yourself" (Matt. 22:39). Therefore, relationships with other people, and particularly relationships with one's family, are of great importance to God.

This means that a society that genuinely seeks to follow biblical principles will not place material prosperity as the highest goal. While seeking to grow in economic productivity, an ideal economically productive society will continually keep in mind the higher value of positive, healthy interpersonal relationships with others. Without such relationships, what benefit is there in amassing more and more personal wealth? "He who loves money will not be satisfied with money, nor he who loves wealth with his income; this also is vanity" (Eccl. 5:10).

On the other hand, if a society makes material prosperity its ultimate good, then greed and selfishness, bitterness and frustration will increasingly characterize that society. Family relationships and friendships will be destroyed in the quest for ever more material prosperity. But this relentless quest for wealth can never satisfy, for it will leave a person with no one with whom to enjoy his prosperity.

At this point, we must honestly say that in many poor countries today, this cultural value is already held strongly, more strongly than in some highly individualistic Western societies. People in many poor nations count relationships with family members and friends as extremely important. Our hope is not that they will abandon this value, but that they will maintain it while they also take the other steps described in this book in order to move toward greater economic prosperity.

This is not impossible. There are many thousands of individuals in wealthy countries who are notable exceptions to Western patterns of excessive individualism and whose strong family lives testify to the fact that it is possible even for wealthier people with highly productive jobs to give significant attention to one's family and friends.

35. The society counts spiritual well-being and a relationship with God as more important than material wealth

While we do not believe that any government should attempt to compel its citizens to follow any particular religion, and while we strongly support the idea of freedom of religion within every nation, we realize that the beliefs and values that are common in a society often have a spiritual component to them. In some societies, sincere religious beliefs can be widely mocked and scorned, and routinely devalued. But in other societies, there is a generally acknowledged respect and appreciation for sincere religious beliefs and practices. To be truly wealthy, a nation needs more than material prosperity. It also needs to be spiritually wealthy, to have a widespread cultural belief that each person's spiritual health and relationship with God are far more important than economic prosperity.

This value leads us once again to emphasize the crucial role that we think wise pastors can play in helping to move any nation from poverty toward greater prosperity.[109] Pastors can teach the values in this chapter (in fact, in this entire book) in a way that encourages a balanced emphasis on economic productivity along with relational and spiritual growth. And pastors can do this using the Bible as an authority that is more persuasive than any arguments from economists. It might be that the pastors in poor nations will not make the national headlines but will gradually transform the values held by their people, and these values will effectively lead the nation to adopt better laws and economic policies.[110] In that way, we hope that pastors and other Christian leaders will play a very significant role in moving their countries from poverty toward ever greater material *and* spiritual prosperity.

---

[109] By speaking of "pastors," we do not mean to imply that only Christian leaders can effectively promote the cultural values that we describe in this last chapter. We would encourage religious leaders from Judaism, Buddhism, Hinduism, Islam, and other religions also to promote belief in honesty, hard work, economic productivity, respect for property, education, humility, and other productive values. But because we are evangelical Christians, we believe that the Bible provides an entire worldview that most fully and consistently promotes these values, and we are writing primarily to Christians who share that viewpoint.

[110] See the additional comments about pastors at 32, 161, 186, 305, 316.

N. Conclusion

Our conclusion to this book brings us back to what we said at the beginning. We recognize that material prosperity is a secondary issue, though it is still very important. More important than prosperity, however, is a person's relationship with God.

We encourage every reader of this book to remember Jesus's warning: "No servant can serve two masters, for either he will hate the one and love the other, or he will be devoted to the one and despise the other. You cannot serve God and money" (Luke 16:13).

Therefore, we close by encouraging rich and poor alike to make their own personal relationship with God the first priority of their lives. We hope that the pursuit of greater material prosperity will not come at the cost of alienation from God. Our hope is rather that every reader will come to a deeply satisfying and rewarding relationship with God through Jesus Christ, so that each person who reads this book will be able to say to God:

> Whom have I in heaven but you?
>   And there is nothing on earth that I desire besides you.
> My flesh and my heart may fail,
>   but God is the strength of my heart and my portion forever.
>   (Ps. 73:25–26)

APPENDIX

A Composite List of Factors That Will
Enable a Nation to Overcome Poverty

A. The Nation's Economic System (details in chapter 4)

1. The nation has a free-market economy. (131–221)
2. The nation has widespread private ownership of property. (141–54)
3. The nation has an easy and quick process for people to gain documented, legally binding ownership of property. (149–54)
4. The nation maintains a stable currency. (155–58)
5. The nation has relatively low tax rates. (158–62)
6. The nation is annually improving its score on an international index of economic freedom. (162)

B. The Nation's Government (details in chapter 7)

1. Every person in the nation is equally accountable to the laws (including wealthy and powerful people). (225–26)
2. The nation's courts show no favoritism or bias, but enforce justice impartially. (227)
3. Bribery and corruption are rare in government offices, and they are quickly punished when discovered. (227–29)
4. The nation's government has adequate power to maintain governmental stability and to prevent crime. (229–30)
5. There are adequate limits on the powers of the nation's government so that personal freedoms are protected. (230–33)
6. The powers of the government are clearly separated between national, regional, and local levels, and between different branches at each level. (234–36)
7. The government is accountable to the people through regular, fair, open elections, and through freedom of the press and free access to information about government activities. (236–39)

8. The government adequately protects citizens against crime. (239–41)

9. The government adequately protects citizens against epidemics of disease. (241–42)

10. The nation's legal system adequately protects people and businesses against violations of contracts. (242–43)

11. The nation's legal system adequately protects people and businesses against violations of patents and copyrights. (243–46)

12. The government effectively protects the nation against foreign invasion. (246–48)

13. The government avoids useless wars of conquest against other nations. (248–50)

14. The nation's laws protect the country against destruction of its environment. (250–52)

15. The nation requires universal education of children up to a level where people are able to earn a living and contribute positively to society. (253–56)

16. The nation's laws protect and give some economic incentives to stable family structures. (256–57)

17. The nation's laws protect freedom of religion for all religious groups and give some benefits to religions generally. (258)

C. The Nation's Freedoms (details in chapter 8)

1. Everyone in the nation has freedom to own property. (263)

2. Everyone in the nation has freedom to buy and sell goods and services, so that there are no protected monopolies. (263–64)

3. Everyone in the nation has freedom to travel and transport goods anywhere within the nation. (264–67)

4. Everyone in the nation has freedom to relocate anywhere within the nation. (267)

5. Everyone in the nation has freedom to trade with other countries without dealing with restrictive quotas or tariffs. (267–269)

6. Everyone in the nation has freedom to start and register a business quickly and inexpensively. (269–271)

7. Everyone in the nation has freedom from expensive and burdensome government regulations. (271–72)

8. Everyone in the nation has freedom from demands for bribes. (272–75)

9. Everyone in the nation has freedom to work in whatever job he or she chooses. (275–77)

10. Every worker in the nation has freedom to be rewarded for his or her work at a level that motivates good job performance. (277–78)

11. Every employer has freedom to hire and fire employees based on job performance and changing business cycles. (278–79)

12. Every employer in the nation has freedom to hire and promote employees based on merit, regardless of family connections or personal relationships. (279–80)

13. Everyone in the nation has freedom to use the earth's resources wisely, and particularly to utilize any type of energy resource. (280–84)

14. Everyone in the nation has freedom to change and adopt newer, more effective means of work and production. (284–85)

15. Everyone in the nation has freedom to access useful knowledge, inventions, and technological developments. (285–91)

16. Everyone in the nation has freedom to be educated. (291–92)

17. Every woman in the nation has the same educational, economic, and political freedoms as men. (292–93)

18. Everyone in the nation, from every national, religious, racial, and ethnic origin, has the same educational, economic, and political freedoms as those from other backgrounds. (294–97)

19. Everyone in the nation has freedom to move upward in social and economic status. (297–300)

20. Everyone in the nation has freedom to become wealthy by legal means. (301–7)

21. Everyone in the nation has freedom to practice any religion. (307)

D. The Nation's Values (details in chapter 9)

1. The society in general believes that there is a God who will hold all people accountable for their actions. (318–19)

2. The society in general believes that God approves of several character traits related to work and productivity. (319–22)

3. The society in general values truthfulness. (322–24)

4. The society in general respects private ownership of property. (324–26)

5. The society in general gives honor to several other moral values. (326–29)

6. The society in general believes that there are both good and evil in every human heart. (329–30)

7. The society in general believes that individuals are responsible for their actions. (330–31)

8. The society in general highly values individual freedom. (331–32)
9. The society in general opposes discrimination against people on the basis of race, gender, or religion. (332)
10. The society in general honors marriage between one man and one woman. (333–34)
11. The society in general values permanency of marriage and has a low divorce rate. (334–35)
12. The society in general believes that human beings are more important than all other creatures on the earth. (335–36)
13. The society in general believes that the earth is here for the use and benefit of human beings. (336–37)
14. The society in general believes that economic development is a good thing and shows the excellence of the earth. (337–38)
15. The society in general believes that the earth's resources will never be exhausted. (339–40)
16. The society in general believes that the earth is orderly and subject to rational investigation. (340–41)
17. The society in general believes that the earth is a place of opportunity. (341)
18. The society in general believes that time is linear and therefore there is hope for improvement in the lives of human beings and nations. (341–42)
19. The society in general believes that time is a valuable resource and should be used wisely. (342–43)
20. The society in general manifests a widespread desire to improve on life, to do better, to innovate, and to become more productive. (343–44)
21. The society in general is open to change, and people therefore work to solve problems and make things better. (344–45)
22. The society in general gives honor to productive work. (345–48)
23. The society in general gives honor to economically productive people, companies, inventions, and careers. (348–50)
24. The society's business owners and workers in general view their companies primarily as means of providing customers with things of value, for which they will then be paid according to that value. (350–51)
25. The society in general places a high value on savings in contrast to spending. (351)
26. The society in general believes that mutual gains come from voluntary exchanges, and therefore a business deal is "good" if it brings benefits to both buyer and seller. (351–53)

27. The society in general values knowledge from any source and makes it widely available. (353–54)
28. The society in general values a highly trained workforce. (354–55)
29. The society in general assumes that there must be a rational basis for knowledge and recognized channels for spreading and testing knowledge. (355–56)
30. The society in general demonstrates a humble willingness to learn from other people, other nations, and members of other religions. (356–57)
31. The society in general believes that the purpose of government is to serve the nation and bring benefit to the people as a whole. (358–59)
32. The society in general believes that government should punish evil and promote good. (359)
33. The society in general values patriotism and reinforces a shared sense of national identity and purpose. (359–64)
34. The society in general counts family, friends, and joy in life as more important than material wealth. (364–66)
35. The society in general counts spiritual well-being and a relationship with God as more important than material wealth. (366–67)

BIBLIOGRAPHY

Acemoglu, Daron, and James A. Robinson. *Why Nations Fail: The Origins of Power, Prosperity and Poverty*. New York: Crown Publishers, 2012.

Aikman, David. *The Beijing Factor: How Christianity Is Transforming China and Changing the Global Balance of Power*. Oxford: Monarch, 2003.

Anderson, Terry. "The Right to Own Property on Reservations." *PERC Reports* 30, no. 2 (Summer/Fall 2012).

Aristotle. *Politics*. Translated by H. Rackham. Loeb Classical Library. Cambridge, MA: Harvard University Press, 1932.

Asmus, Barry. *The Best Is Yet to Come*. Phoenix: Ameripress, 2001.

Asmus, Barry, and Donald B. Billings. *Crossroads: The Great American Experiment: The Rise, Decline, and Restoration of Freedom and the Market Economy*. Lanham, MD: University Press of America, 1984.

Asmus, Barry, and Wayne Grudem. "Property Rights Inherent in the Eighth Commandment Are Essential for Human Flourishing." In *Business Ethics Today: Stealing*, edited by Philip J. Clements, 119–36. Philadelphia: Center for Christian Business Ethics Today, 2011.

Axelrod, Robert. *The Evolution of Cooperation*. New York: Basic Books, 1984.

Banerjee, Abhijit Vinayak et al. *Making Aid Work*. Cambridge, MA: The MIT Press, 2007.

Bastiat, Frédéric. *Economic Harmonies*. Irvington, NY: Foundation for Economic Education, 1997.

Bauer, P. T. *Equality, the Third World, and Economic Delusion*. Cambridge, MA: Harvard University Press, 1981.

Baumol, William J., Robert E. Litan, and Carl J. Schramm. *Good Capitalism, Bad Capitalism, and the Economics of Growth and Prosperity*. New Haven, CT: Yale University Press, 2007.

BBC News. "Germany: Nuclear power plants to close by 2022." May 30, 2011. http://www.bbc.co.uk/news/world-europe-13592208.

———. "Indonesia's Muhammad Nazaruddin Guilty of Corruption." April 20, 2012. http://www.bbc.co.uk/news/world-asia-17781379.

Beisner, E. Calvin. *Prosperity and Poverty.* Westchester, IL: Crossway, 1988.

———. "Stewardship in a Free Market." In *Morality and the Marketplace*, edited by Michael Bauman. Hillsdale, MI: Hillsdale College Press, 1994.

———. *Where Garden Meets Wilderness: Evangelical Entry into the Environmental Debate*. Grand Rapids: Eerdmans and Acton Institute, 1997.

Berlinski, Claire. *There Is No Alternative: Why Margaret Thatcher Matters*. New York: Basic Books, 2008.

Berman, Harold. *Law and Revolution: The Formation of the Western Legal Tradition*. Cambridge, MA: Harvard University Press, 1983.

Bernstein, William J. *The Birth of Plenty: How the Prosperity of the Modern World Was Created*. New York: McGraw-Hill, 2004.

Billington, James H. *Fire in the Minds of Men*. New York: Basic Books, 1980.

Blomberg, Craig. *Neither Poverty Nor Riches*. Grand Rapids: Eerdmans, 1999.

Bloom, Josh. "Should Patents on Pharmaceuticals Be Extended to Encourage Innovation? Yes: Innovation Demands It." *The Wall Street Journal*, January 23, 2012. http://online.wsj.com/article/SB10001424052970204542404577156993191655000.html.

Boudreaux, Donald J. "Comparative Advantage." In *The Concise Encyclopedia of Economics*, edited by David R. Henderson. Indianapolis: Liberty Fund, 2008.

Brooks, Arthur C. *The Battle: How the Fight between Free Enterprise and Big Government Will Shape America's Future*. New York: Basic Books, 2010.

Carson, Clarence B. "The Founding of the American Republic: 6. The Mercantile Impasse." *The Freeman* 22, no. 1 (January 1972).

Catherwood, H. F. R. *The Christian in Industrial Society*. London: Tyndale Press, 1964.

Central Intelligence Agency. *CIA World Factbook*. https://www.cia.gov/library/publications/the-world-factbook/rankorder/2004rank.html.

Chaudhuri, K. N. *The Trading World of Asia and the English East India Company 1660–1760*. Cambridge, UK: Cambridge University Press, 1978.

Claar, Victor. *Fair Trade? Its Prospects as a Poverty Solution*. Grand Rapids: Poverty Cure, 2012.

Clark, J. R., and Dwight R. Lee. "Markets and Morality." *Cato Journal* 31, no. 2 (Winter 2011).

Coleson, Edward. "Capitalism and Morality." In *The Morality of Capitalism*, edited by Mark W. Hendrickson. Irvington, NY: Foundation for Economic Education, 1996.

Collier, Paul. *The Bottom Billion: Why the Poorest Countries Are Failing and What Can Be Done About It.* Oxford: Oxford University Press, 2007.

Corbett, Steve, and Brian Fikkert. *When Helping Hurts: How to Alleviate Poverty Without Hurting the Poor—and Yourself.* Chicago: Moody, 2009.

Courtois, Stéphane, and Mark Kramer. *The Black Book of Communism: Crimes, Terror, Repression.* Cambridge, MA: Harvard University Press, 1999.

Cox, W. Michael, and Richard Alm. "Creative Destruction." In *The Concise Encyclopedia of Economics*, edited by David R. Henderson. Indianapolis: Liberty Fund, 2008.

Das, Gucharan. *India Unbound.* New York: Alfred Knopf, 2001.

Denny, Charlotte. "Suharto, Marcos and Mobutu head corruption table with $50bn scams." *The Guardian* (UK), March 26, 2004. http://www.guardian.co.uk/world/2004/mar/26/indonesia.philippines.

De Soto, Hernando. *The Mystery of Capital: Why Capitalism Triumphs in the West and Fails Everywhere Else.* New York: Basic Books, 2000.

Diamond, Jared. *Guns, Germs, and Steel: The Fates of Human Societies.* New York: W. W. Norton, 1999.

Dillard, Dudley, *Economic Development of the North Atlantic Community: Historical Introduction to Modern Economics.* Englewood Cliffs, NJ: Prentice-Hall, 1967.

Drescher, Seymore, and Stanley L. Engerman. *A Historical Guide to World Slavery.* Oxford: Oxford University Press, 1998.

D'Souza, Dinesh. *What's So Great About America.* New York: Penguin, 2002.

Easterly, William. *The Elusive Quest for Growth: Economists' Adventures and Misadventures in the Tropics.* Cambridge, MA: The MIT Press, 2001.

———. *The White Man's Burden: Why the West's Efforts to Aid the Rest Have Done So Much Ill and So Little Good.* New York: Penguin, 2006.

Evans, M. Stanton. *The Theme Is Freedom: Religion, Politics, and the American Tradition.* Washington: Regnery, 1994.

Ferguson, Niall. *Civilization: The West and the Rest.* New York: Penguin, 2011.

Forbes, Steve, and Elizabeth Ames. *How Capitalism Will Save Us: Why Free People and Free Markets Are the Best Answer in Today's Economy.* New York: Crown Business, 2009.

Friedman, Benjamin. *The Moral Consequences of Economic Growth*. New York: First Vintage Books, 2005.

Friedman, Milton. *Capitalism and Freedom: A Leading Economist's View on the Proper Role of Competitive Capitalism*. Chicago: University of Chicago Press, 1962.

———. "Created Equal." *Free to Choose* video lecture series, Part 5. www.freeto choose.tv.

———. "The Hong Kong Experiment." *Hoover Digest* 3, July 30, 1998. http://www .hoover.org/publications/hoover-digest/article/7696.

Friedman, Milton, and Rose Friedman. *Free to Choose: A Personal Statement*. New York: Harcourt Brace Jovanovich, 1980.

"From Hero to Knave." *The Economist*, August 25–31, 2012. http://www .economist.com/node/21560872.

Gilder, George. *Wealth and Poverty*. New York: Basic Books, 1981.

Gorman, Linda. "Discrimination." In *The Concise Encyclopedia of Economics*, edited by David R. Henderson. Indianapolis: Liberty Fund, 2008.

Gresham, Perry E. "Think Twice Before You Disparage Capitalism." *The Freeman* 27, no. 3 (March 1977). http://www.thefreemanonline.org/features/think -twice-before-you-disparage-capitalism/.

Griffiths, Brian. *The Creation of Wealth*. London: Hodder and Stoughton, 1984.

Grudem, Wayne. *Business for the Glory of God*. Wheaton: Crossway, 2003.

———, general editor. *ESV Study Bible*. Wheaton: Crossway, 2009.

———. *Politics—According to the Bible*. Grand Rapids: Zondervan, 2010.

Guest, Robert. *The Shackled Continent: Africa's Past, Present, and Future*. London: Macmillan, 2004.

Gwartney, James, and Richard L. Stroup. *Economics: Private and Public Choice*. New York: Harcourt Brace Jovanovich, 1987.

Gwartney, James, Robert Lawson, and Joshua Hall. *Economic Freedom of the World: 2012 Annual Report*. Vancouver, BC: Fraser Institute, 2012.

Haber, Stephen, Douglass C. North, and Barry R. Weingast. "The Poverty Trap." *Hoover Digest* 4 (October 30, 2002).

Hanwerker, W. Penn. "Fiscal Corruption and the Moral Economy of Resource Acquisition." In *Research in Economic Anthropology*, edited by Barry L. Isaac. Greenwich, CT: JAI Press, 1987.

Hardin, Garrett. "The Tragedy of the Commons." *Science* 162, no. 3859 (1968).

Harrison, Lawrence E. *The Central Liberal Truth: How Politics Can Change a Culture and Save It from Itself*. Oxford: Oxford University Press, 2006.

Hayek, Friedrich A. *The Road to Serfdom*. Chicago: University of Chicago Press, 1944. Reprint, Washington: Heritage Foundation, 1994.

———. "The Use of Knowledge in Society." *American Economic Review* 35, no. 4 (September 1945).

Heckscher, Eli. *Mercantilism*. 2 vols. New York: Macmillan, 1955.

HELP (Helping to Enhance the Livelihood of People Around the Globe) Commission. Report on Foreign Assistance Reform (December 7, 2007), 24. http://www.americanprogress.org/wp-content/uploads/issues/2007/12/pdf/beyond_assistence .pdf.

Henderson, David R. "Rent Seeking." In *The Concise Encyclopedia of Economics*, edited by David R. Henderson. Indianapolis: Liberty Fund, 2008.

Hessen, Robert. "Capitalism." In *The Concise Encyclopedia of Economics*, edited by David R. Henderson. Indianapolis: Liberty Fund, 2008.

Hill, Austin, and Scott Rae. *The Virtues of Capitalism: A Moral Case for Free Markets*. Chicago: Northfield, 2010.

Hill, P. J. "Environmental Problems under Socialism." *Cato Journal* 12, no. 2 (Fall 1992).

———. "Markets and Morality." In *The Morality of Capitalism*, edited by Mark W. Hendrickson. Irvington, NY: Foundation for Economic Education, 1996.

iPolitics. "Ex-Indonesia bank official found guilty of bribery." September 27, 2012. http://www.ipolitics.ca/2012/09/27/ex-indonesia-bank-official-found-guilty-of-bribery/.

Kaidantzis, Janet Beales. "Property Rights for 'Sesame Street.'" In *The Concise Encyclopedia of Economics*, edited by David R. Henderson. Indianapolis: Liberty Fund, 2008.

Keynes, John Maynard. *Economic Consequences of the Peace*. New York: Harcourt, Brace, and Howe, 1920.

Khama, Seretse. "Why I Gave Up My Throne for Love." *Ebony* 6, no. 8 (June 1951).

Kidd, Thomas. *God of Liberty: A Religious History of the American Revolution*. New York: Basic Books, 2010.

Kirzner, Israel. *Competition and Entrepreneurship*. Chicago: University of Chicago Press, 1973.

Laffer, Arthur. "The Laffer Curve: Past, Present, and Future." *The Heritage Foundation Backgrounder*, no. 176 (June 1, 2004).

LaHaye, Laura. "Mercantilism." In *The Concise Encyclopedia of Economics*, edited by David R. Henderson. Indianapolis: Liberty Fund, 2008.

Landes, David S. *The Wealth and Poverty of Nations: Why Some Are So Rich and Some So Poor*. New York: W. W. Norton, 1999.

Larson, Jeffrey H. "The Verdict on Cohabitation vs. Marriage." *Marriage and Families*, January 2001. http://marriageandfamilies.byu.edu/issues/2001/January/cohabitation.aspx.

Lerman, Robert I. "How Do Marriage, Cohabitation, and Single Parenthood Affect the Material Hardships of Families with Children?" July 1, 2002. http://www.urban.org/publications/410539.html.

———. "Marriage and the Economic Well-Being of Families with Children: A Review of the Literature." July 1, 2002. http://www.urban.org/publications/410541.html.

———. "Married and Unmarried Parenthood and Economic Well-Being: A Dynamic Analysis of a Recent Cohort." July 1, 2002. http://www.urban.org/publications/41054 0.html.

Locke, John. *The Second Treatise of Civil Government*. In *Locke, Berkeley, Hume. Great Books of the Western World, Vol. 35*, edited by Robert Maynard Hutchins and Mortimer J. Adler. London: Oxford University Press, 1952.

Lomborg, Bjorn. *The Skeptical Environmentalist*. Cambridge, UK: Cambridge University Press, 2001.

Makarewicz, Joseph C., and Paul Bertram. "Evidence for the Restoration of the Lake Erie Ecosystem." *BioScience* 41 (January 1991). http://www.epa.gov/greatlakes/monitoring/publications/articles/restore_lake_erie.pdf.

Mankiw, N. Gregory. *Principles of Economics*. Orlando, FL: Dryden Press, 1998.

Maranz, David. *African Friends and Money Matters*. Dallas: SIL International, 2001.

Marx, Karl. *Critique of the Gotha Program*. Rockville, MD: Wildside Press, 2008.

———. *Das Capital*. Washington: Regnery, 2000.

Marx, Karl, and Friedrich Engels. *Communist Manifesto*. 1848; reprinted, New York: Monthly Review Press, 1968.

———. *The Marx-Engels Reader*. Edited by Robert C. Tucker. New York: Norton, 1972.

Mauldin, John, and Jonathan Tepper. *Endgame: The End of the Debt Supercycle and How It Changes Everything*. Hoboken, NJ: John Wiley & Sons, 2011.

McCloskey, Dierdre. *Bourgeois Dignity*. Chicago: University of Chicago Press, 2010.

Meltzer, Milton. *Slavery: A World History*. Cambridge, MA: Da Capo Press, 1993.

Middelmann, Udo. *Christianity Versus Fatalistic Religions in the War Against Poverty*. Colorado Springs: Paternoster, 2007.

Miller, Darrow L., and Stan Guthrie. *Discipling Nations: The Power of Truth to Transform Cultures*. Seattle: YWAM, 1998.

Miller, Terry, Kim R. Holmes, and Edwin Feulner, editors. *2012 Index of Economic Freedom*. Washington: Heritage Foundation/New York: *The Wall Street Journal*, 2012.

Milton, Giles. *White Gold: The Extraordinary Story of Thomas Pellow and Islam's One Million White Slaves*. New York: Farrar, Straus & Giroux, 2004.

Moore, Stephen. *Who's the Fairest of Them All?* New York: Encounter Books, 2012.

Moore, Stephen, and Julian Simon. *It's Getting Better All the Time: Greatest Trends of the Last 100 Years*. Washington: Cato Institute, 2000.

Moyo, Dambisa. *Dead Aid: Why Aid Is Not Working and How There Is a Better Way for Africa*. New York: Farrar, Straus & Giroux, 2009.

Mungazi, Dickson. *We Shall Not Fail: Values in the National Leadership of Seretse Khama, Nelson Mandela, and Julius Nyerere*. Trenton, NJ: Africa World Press, 2005.

Murray, Charles A. *In Pursuit of Happiness and Good Government*. New York: Simon and Schuster, 1989.

National Tax Journal. "Income Mobility in the United States: New Evidence from Income Tax Data." 62, no. 2 (June 2009).

Norberg, Johan. *In Defense of Global Capitalism*. Washington: Cato Institute, 2003.

North, Douglass C., and Robert Paul Thomas. *The Rise of the Western World: A New Economic History*. Cambridge, UK: Cambridge University Press, 1976.

Novak, Michael. *The Spirit of Democratic Capitalism*. New York: Simon and Schuster, 1982.

Oheson, James R. "An Audacious Promise: The Moral Case for Capitalism." *Manhattan Institute* no. 12 (May 2012).

Parke, Mary. "Are Married Parents Really Better for Children?" *Center for Law and Social Policy*, May 2003. http://www.clasp.org/admin/site/publications_archive/files/0128.pdf.

Peron, James. "The Sorry Record of Foreign Aid in Africa." *The Freeman* 51, no. 8 (August 2001). http://www.thefreemanonline.org/features/the-sorry-record-of-foreign-aid-in-africa/.

Powell, Jim. *The Triumph of Liberty*. New York: Free Press, 2000.

Prager, Dennis. *Still the Best Hope*. New York: HarperCollins, 2012.

Prahalad, C. K. *The Fortune at the Bottom of the Pyramid*. Upper Saddle River, NJ: Wharton, 2005.

Rabushka, Alvin. "Taxation, Economic Growth, and Liberty." *Cato Journal* 7, no. 1 (Spring/Summer 1987).

Rahn, Richard W. "Price Controls Can Be Lethal." *Washington Times*, October 28, 2003. http://www.washingtontimes.com/news/2003/oct/28/20031028 -083515-6228r/?page=all.

Read, Leonard. *I, Pencil: My Family Tree as Told to Leonard E. Read*. Irvington, NY: Foundation for Economic Education, 2006.

Reagan, Ronald. "Encroaching Control" speech given to Chamber of Commerce, Phoenix, Arizona, March 30, 1961.

Rector, Robert. "Marriage: America's Greatest Weapon Against Child Poverty." *Heritage Foundation Special Report*, September 5, 2012. http://www.heritage .org/research/reports/2012/09/marriage-americas-greatest-weapon-against -child-poverty#_ftn1.

Regnerus, Mark. "How different are the adult children of parents who have same-sex relationships? Findings from the New Family Structures Study." *Social Science Research* 41 (2012). http://www.sciencedirect.com/science /article/pii/S0049089X12000610.

Richards, Jay W. *Money, Greed, and God: Why Capitalism Is the Solution and Not the Problem*. New York: HarperOne, 2009.

Ridley, Matt. *The Rational Optimist: How Prosperity Evolves*. New York: HarperCollins, 2010.

"The Romney Hood Fairy Tale." *The Wall Street Journal*, August 8, 2012, Review and Outlook section.

Rothbard, Murray N. "Free Market." In *The Concise Encyclopedia of Economics*, edited by David R. Henderson. Indianapolis: Liberty Fund, 2008.

———. "Mercantilism: A Lesson for Our Times." *The Freeman* 13, no. 11 (November 1963). https://mises.org/daily/4304.

Sachs, Jeffrey. *The End of Poverty*. New York: Penguin, 2005.

Sawyer, John E. "Entrepreneurial Error and Economic Growth." *Explorations in Entrepreneurial History* 4 (May 1952).

Schluter, Michael, and John Ashcroft. *Jubilee Manifesto: A Framework, Agenda & Strategy for Christian Social Reform*. Leicester, UK: Inter-Varsity, 2005.

Schmidt, Alvin. *How Christianity Changed the World*. Grand Rapids: Zondervan, 2004.

Schumpeter, Joseph A. *Capitalism, Socialism, and Democracy*. Taylor & Francis e-Library, 2003.

Sharansky, Natan. *The Case for Democracy*. New York: Public Affairs, 2004.

Shenfield, Arthur. "Capitalism Under the Tests of Ethics." *Imprimis* 10, no. 12 (December 1981).

Sider, Ron. *Rich Christians in an Age of Hunger*. Nashville: Thomas Nelson, 2005.

Simon, Julian, editor. *The State of Humanity*. Oxford, UK/Cambridge, MA: Blackwell, 1995.

———. *The Ultimate Resource* 2. Princeton, NJ: Princeton University Press, 1996.

Singh, Manmohan. Speech given at Oxford University, July 8, 2005, on acceptance of an honorary degree. Transcript published in *The Hindu*. http://www .hindu.com/nic/0046/pmspeech.htm.

Sirico, Robert. *Defending the Free Market: The Moral Case for a Free Economy*. Washington: Regnery, 2012.

Smith, Adam. *An Inquiry into the Nature and Causes of the Wealth of Nations*. Edited by Edwin Cannan. 1776; reprinted New York: Modern Library, 1994.

Sowell, Thomas. *Knowledge and Decisions*. New York: Basic Books, 1980.

Spence, Michael. *The Next Convergence: The Future of Economic Growth in a Multispeed World*. New York: Farrar, Straus & Giroux, 2011.

Stanley, Thomas, and William Danko. *The Millionaire Next Door*. New York: Pocket Books, 1996.

Stern, Sheldon M. "The Atlantic Slave Trade—The Full Story." *Academic Questions* (Summer 2005).

Suddath, Claire. "It's Illegal for Monks to Sell Caskets in Louisiana." *Bloomberg Businessweek*, June 1, 2012. http://www.businessweek.com/articles/2012-06 -01/its-illegal-for-monks-to-sell-caskets-in-louisiana.

Taurel, Sidney. "Hands Off My Industry." *The Wall Street Journal*, November 3, 2003.

Time. "America's Sewage System and the Price of Optimism." August 1, 1969. http://www.time.com/time/magazine/article/0,9171,901182,00.html.

Time. "War on Rats." May 31, 1976. http://www.time.com/time/magazine/article /0,9171,947662,00.html.

United Nations. *UNAIDS Report on the Global AIDS Epidemic 2010*, 180–207. http://www.unaids.org/globalreport/Global_report.htm.

U.S. Department of the Treasury. "Income Mobility in the United States: 1996– 2005," November 13, 2007. http://www.treasury.gov/resource-center/tax -policy/Documents/incomemobilitystudy03-08revise.pdf.

Viner, Jacob. *Studies in the Theory of International Trade*. New York: Harper and Brothers, 1937.

Von Mises, Ludwig. *Human Action: A Treatise on Economics*. Chicago: Henry Regnery, 1966.

Waite, Linda J., and Maggie Gallagher. *The Case for Marriage: Why Married People Are Happier, Healthier, and Better Off Financially*. New York: Doubleday, 2000.

Wallerstein, Judith S., and Sandra Blakeslee. *Second Chances: Men, Women, and Children a Decade After Divorce*. New York: Ticknor & Fields, 1989.

Weber, Max. *The Protestant Ethic and the Spirit of Colonialism*. Translated by Talcott Parsons. 1930. Reprinted, Los Angeles: Roxbury, 1996.

Wilcox, W. Bradford. *Why Marriage Matters: Twenty-One Conclusions from the Social Sciences*. New York: Institute for American Values, 2002.

Williams, Susan. *Colour Bar: The Triumph of Seretse Khama and His Nation*. London: Penguin, 2006.

World Health Organization. "Weekly epidemiological record" (August 2012): 289. http://www.who.int/wer/2012/wer8731_32.pdf.

Wriston, Walter B. *Risk and Other Four-Letter Words*. New York: Harper and Row, 1986.

Yergin, Daniel. *The Quest: Energy, Security and the Remaking of the Modern World*. New York: Penguin, 2011.

Zupan, Mark A. "The Virtues of Free Markets." *Cato Journal* 31, no. 2 (Spring/Summer 2011).

GENERAL INDEX

SCRIPTURE INDEX